The
Good Holiday
Cottage Guide

The
Good Holiday
Cottage Guide

Edited by
Bryn Frank

In search of perfection...

'Firstly, we'll send for brochures. The internet's fine, but cramming mums and dads and grandads into the office to look at the computer, or leaning over our shoulders at the laptop, doesn't work. We'll browse through our favourite brochures, marking what appeals, then get back-up detail on the web from the individual places on our short-list. Between us we have a list of maybe 20 'essentials', which varies a bit from year to year, such as being fairly near the sea but not right by it, having an open fire except at the height of summer, five foot beds or bigger, absolute peace and quiet, baths and not just showers, and more. We always spend some time on the phone with owners and/or agents, checking all sorts of details.

'We're very fussy, but several owners have told us they prefer that. It saves misunderstandings later. We're a big group and we're not silly: we know high standards and good facilities cost money. We're happy to pay big weekly rents which, shared among a number of people, never seem excessive, to get exactly what we want.'

Notes from a phone conversation with a regular reader of The Good Holiday Cottage Guide.

Going the extra mile...

Before the self catering holiday business became as streamlined as the advertising industry we used to get occasional friendly calls asking for advice from the depths of 'the Shires' on these lines: 'I am a retired bank manager/army officer/solicitor/head teacher, and my wife and I have decided in our retirement to buy half a dozen holiday cottages. We thought we'd spend a bit of money smartening them up and then get somebody to keep an eye on them, bring in some cleaners on a Saturday and basically run them for us while we go travelling. We thought it sounded fun'.

No – that's not how it works! Running a self catering business is all about going the extra mile, adding value, being around (or at least arranging to have a caretaker around and able to deal with emergencies). Because there is now an excess of properties over demand, owners and agents are having to work harder than ever, though demand is uneven: there are never enough properties in holiday hot-spots during the main summer holidays and the school half-terms – depending on how popular the location – and for Christmas and/or New Year.

And owners seem to need to look over their shoulders all the time to keep up with trends. Computerised 'virtual tours' for example have never really taken off (one up-market owner told us: 'With virtual tours, holidaymakers miss out on The Wow Factor', and we miss seeing their faces), hot tubs may not last, woodburners and open fires seem to be here to stay, wi-fi access is increasingly queried.

Readers sometimes ask 'How do owners/agents get to be in this guide?' Most come via reader recommendations, occasionally from regional tourist boards. Others contact us directly. Regular readers might spot cottages they have not seen for years: it could be that a cottage or group of cottages have been on a long let or have been marketed through an 'exclusive' agency, or that there has been a change of ownership: we may have dropped the cottages when they were under the previous ownership.

All the properties featured are visited, including those picked out within agency profiles, but occasionally a highly recommended cottage is only visited after publication.

The help of the following in preparing this guide is gratefully acknowledged:
Leyla Ali, Richard Bamforth, Carole Frank, John Harrison, Jan James, Stephen Joyce,
Nicky Phillips, Paul Phillips, Debbie Richardson, John Ruler and Gillian Thomas.

Printed by Stephen Austin & Sons Ltd, Caxton Hill, Hertford SG13 7LU.
Telephone 01992 584955.

Distributed by Portfolio Ltd, Suite 3 & 4, Great West House, Great West Road,
Brentford, Middx TW8 9DF. Telephone 020 8326 5620; fax 020 8326 5621.

Front cover

Top: Thatched Cottage, Lewdon (Helpful Holidays: Pages 191–193)
Bottom left: Castello la Rocca (Interhome: Page 254)
Bottom right: Compton Pool cottages (Page 194)

Back cover

Top left: Gardens at Docklow Manor (Page 214)
Top right: Cottage at Owlpen Manor (Page 212)
Bottom: Maison Pastorale (Quality Villas: Pages 246–247)

**Please note: an asterisk against a company name in the main text
within the guide indicates that it is an agency.**

**Please note: the properties at Vere Lodge, featured on Pages 48–50,
are no longer available for holiday letting. But they are available for
long lets.**

When times are tight...

A number of the owners we feature take pride in paring their prices down to the minimum, and are happy furthermore to have their properties singled out as 'inexpensive'. (Some owners hate it: one, in the Cotswolds, said: 'How dare you suggest we're "bargain basement"?') Here is a short list of those who have asked to be included – not a comprehensive but, we hope, a useful selection:

Bones Cottage, Page 56

Jockey Cottage, Page 33

Jenny's Cottage, Page 46

Carpenter's Cottages No 6, Page 57

Stubbs Cottages, Page 60

Sarah's Cottage, Page 75

Long Byres, Page 121

Hockadays, Page 178

Chapel Cottages, Page 159

Cider Room Cottage, Page 190

Hidden Europe magazine: a real find...

The best thing we've come across in our travels this year is not a holiday cottage but a magazine. It could be of great interest to self caterers, among other travellers, mainly to mainland Europe, but it has some occasional features about little-known corners of the UK. Published in Berlin and available mainly on subscription (though individual copies are available), *hidden europe* is a rare gem. It is not hidebound by advertising. Written, edited and published by Nicky Gardner and Susanne Kries, it is unique in our experience, and a real labour of love. We can't improve on Nicky Gardner's own thumbnail sketch about herself: 'An inveterate traveller who always opts for the routes less travelled! Devoted to the rural and the off-beat with a passion for Europe's minority cultures. Loves spots no sane tourist would ever venture. Takes her time and savours slow travel.'

In this day of false-economy package tours that don't really give satisfaction, *hidden europe* reminds us what travel, as comfortable or as rough as you like, is all about. Admittedly, we ourselves are sold on 'Old Europe', and that is what this exceptional publication is mainly about.

See Page 267 for further details.

'Green and pleasant land?'...

In Cornwall (it seems) the grass is greener. We hear that cottage owners in Scotland are becoming more 'environmentally aware' than most, but it's several in the West Country that we know more about.

Bosinver, Cornwall – See Page 155. Says owner Pat Smith: 'Fresh air, clean coasts, unpolluted countryside. In Cornwall we work hard to look after the environment for our own and others' enjoyment. At Bosinver visitors are firmly encouraged to recycle and compost during their stay. Cottages are fitted with low energy bulbs, cleaning materials are low phosphate and we actively encourage bike hire, walking and the use of public transport. We are as green as our lovely rural setting.'

Pollaughan, Cornwall – See Page 173. 'Pollaughan Cottages, on the stunning Roseland Peninsula, in Cornwall, were the first to be awarded at Gold Level in the Green Tourism Business scheme. We like to think Pollaughan is a good example of combining a sustainable ethos with cottages that are both high quality and a real home from home. Recycling, local purchasing, energy and water conservation, encouraging visitors to explore the beautiful coastline by boat and foot and the wildlife on site, are all part of our outlook'.

Compton Pool, Devon – See Page 194. 'Hot on the heels of achieving Five Stars for all the cottages and the Gold Award for the best tourism website in the South West, Compton Pool Farm have achieved yet another top honour. That is, the Gold Award for Green Tourism, for our review of energy use, waste management and care for the local environment. A new environmental policy has increased awareness of the owners, staff and guests to the sensitivity of this area of outstanding natural beauty. It has always been a key objective for the farm to be a fully sustainable business.'

Tremaine Green, Cornwall – See Page 151. Writes Bryn Frank: 'Also festooned with awards, and a long-standing member of the cottage-guide 'family', Tremaine Green is widely known for its serious attention to environmental issues. In 2007 they won, not for the first time, the 'Best Conservation Garden' in the Caradon In Bloom scheme and the Green Acorn Award for sustainable tourism from the South East Cornwall Tourism Association.'

A possible source of information for people, including owners, who want to know more about all this is the Green Tourism Business Scheme. This organisation says 'We are the largest and most successful environmental accreditation body of tourism-related businesses in Europe, and have over 500 members in the UK.
www.green-business.co.uk

Escape with
EUROPCAR

Wherever you plan to escape, get there in safety, comfort and style with Europcar. Whether you need a bit more room or a bit more vroom Europcar will have a car to suit. All our cars are under six months old, fully maintained, and come with 24/7 breakdown recovery. With the UK's largest rental fleet of 60,000 vehicles, plus a nationwide network of over 250 locations, Europcar combines quality and convenience with great rates.

Planning an escape to the coast or country? Why not save wear and tear on your own car and rent instead? Rent a car with room for all the family, the luggage and that all-important bucket and spade. No need for back-seat drivers: you can share the driving by renting from Europcar. If it's a chic city break why not head off in a nippy hatchback – ideal for a weekend in one of our cultural towns or cities.

Whatever your plans, once you're there, enjoy the freedom to explore at your own pace and to your own itinerary – that's what self-catering holidays are all about!

Alternatively, if you fancy a bit of luxury then indulge in a driving experience from Europcar Prestige. Whether it's a Porsche, Mercedes or a Land Rover, Europcar Prestige has a car for even the most discerning driver.

Renting is easy with Europcar. Simply book with one click at www.europcar.co.uk. Alternatively call our dedicated reservation line on 0870 607 5000 or visit your local branch.

'Do as you would be done by...'

Some advice for self caterers

Don't be afraid of the open fire or woodburner: we hear from some owners that even in cold weather some tenants ignore them because they have never seen one before. Don't be embarrassed to ask for instructions.

Don't, if you are wanting absolute peace and quiet, overlook nearby airports, and check on flight paths.

Do check out as you approach your holiday destination where local shops are, especially if they stay open late: so useful for last-minute items on your first evening.

Do pack a couple of 60 watt light bulbs. The more chic the cottage, the greater the risk that reading lights only contain the dreaded 40 watt bulb that are inadequate for reading by. But be careful not to burn lampshades.

Do ask where the trip-switch is, in case a fuse blows: we once spent a long winter evening in the dark in Bourton-on-the-Water not knowing where the trip switch was. (It was discreetly hidden in the cellar.)

Do the garden if you feel like it. Many a green-fingered grandad prefers to potter and dead-head even in somebody else's garden to going out and about every day.

Do start a hare running in the visitors' book. Write local restaurant reviews, describe bird-watching and wildlife watching. Anything other than, 'We had a lovely time'. We once enjoyed reading about a family of spiders in the garden shed written over several weeks by different groups of children.

Don't be ashamed to have a good lie-in when you fancy it. It is something one can never really do in an hotel.

Don't arrive before 3pm unless you want to embarrass the cleaner or, even worse, surprise the dowager duchess who owns the cottages on her hands and knees in the kitchen.

Do take a few favourite ornaments and, especially, books; these work wonders if you don't easily feel at home in strange houses. A pair of favourite bookends is a handy thing to pack.

Do take hot water bottles, and maybe even a portable heater. Remember the old adage: 'my house is cosy, yours is warm-*enough*, his is freezing'.

Don't forget that a lot of excellent rural properties are still accessible by rail and that most owners will meet you at a convenient station.

Contents

Colour section: Pages 161-172.

11

THE COTTAGE COLLECTION

This fine collection of British properties has really made an impact in the last couple of years. You can check the availability of all the cottages on-line or speak to the Call Centre to book one without spending time contacting owners who may be full.

Impressively, Cottage Collection's Chairman Robert Dossor has doubled the choice in his portfolio in just three years, and created for the discerning holidaymaker a tempting choice of coastal or rural retreats where seclusion and privacy can easily be dovetailed with activities such as walking, climbing, horse-riding, fishing, golf or watersports, as well as visits to nearby attractions.

'Romantics' will be spoilt for choice, with everything from a coastal Cornish cottage to a delightful Derbyshire Peak District retreat. Or they can even wake up in a castle in Wales.

Cottage accommodation that offers that great luxury of today, 'peace and quiet', can be pinpointed in every Area of Outstanding Natural Beauty around Great Britain and families, as well as other large parties, can be readily accommodated in a number of places.

With 'Pets Welcome' signs at most locations, and those with disabled facilities also in the portfolio, we suggest you visit the impressive, inter-active website.

Spending time on The Cottage Collection's website brings one in touch with special offers, particularly off-peak promotions, which might include, for example, gourmet meals or cream teas on arrival.

www.the-cottage-collection.co.uk

Bed and breakfast/hotel accommodation

We often receive requests from readers wanting somewhere to stay en route to distant cottages and for friends and family to base themselves for a night or two while visiting people staying in a holiday property. They are sometimes able to book in as 'extra people', but – as standards have improved and zed-beds are not so popular – not usually. So here below is some information (mostly in the owners' words) about self catering places linked with hotels and 'b&b'...

Alderton Hall, Suffolk.
(Suffolk Coastal Cottages)
Having spent all too many nights in poky bed and breakfast places (writes Stephen Joyce) we are always alert to staying in a spacious 'hall'. At Alderton Hall in Suffolk, a medieval Grade II listed country house with good access to the coast, and where Suffolk Cottage Holidays is based, there is a fascinating Tudor dining room and three lovingly restored, newly refurbished and extremely comfortable double bedrooms, all ensuite, which make up the house's south wing.
Contact: Lizzie Hammond, Suffolk Cottage Holidays Ltd.
Telephone 01394 412306, fax 412309.
www.suffolkcottageholidays.com

Gladwins Farm, Suffolk. See Page 34.
'Home-from-home farmhouse B&B in a typical Suffolk farmhouse; en-suite rooms, direct dial telephone, lounge area. From £65 per night B&B for 2. Amid Suffolk's rolling 'Constable Country', with great views. Heated indoor pool, sauna, hot tub, tennis court. **'Visit Britain' Four Stars**.
Contact: Robert and Pauline Dossor, Gladwins Farm, Harpers Hill, Nayland, Suffolk CO6 4NU. Telephone 01206 262261. Fax 263001.
Email: GladwinsFarm@aol.com www.gladwinsfarm.co.uk

High House Farm, Suffolk. See Page 39.
'Beautifully restored 15th century farmhouse on family run arable farm. Featuring exposed beams and inglenook fireplaces, spacious and comfortable accommodation. Explore the heart of rural Suffolk, local vineyards, Easton Park Farm, Framlingham and Orford Castles, Minsmere, Snape Maltings, Woodland Trust and the Heritage Coast. B&B from £22. Reductions for children.'
Contact: Mrs Sarah Kindred, High House Farm, Cransford, Woodbridge, Suffolk IP13 9PD. Telephone 01728 663461. Fax 663409.
Email: b&b@highhousefarm.co.uk www.highhousefarm.co.uk

13

Bylaugh Hall, Norfolk. See Page 51.
'Relax into the splendour of Bylaugh Hall Norfolk, amid beautiful countryside, and convenient for Norwich and the north Norfolk coast. Lovingly restored, this historic country house welcomes you to a comfortable stay. Ensuite bedrooms and luxury suites combine modern comfort with the elegance of the past. There's a restaurant, bar and spa for guests, with magnificent reception rooms also available for functions.
Telephone 01362 688121.
Email: info@bylaugh.com
www.bylaugh.com

Cote Bank Farm, Derbyshire. See Page 82.
'Wake to birdsong, stunning views and the smell of freshly baked bread. The same care and attention given to guests in Cote Bank Cottages is lavished on them in our farmhouse. Two doubles, one twin, all en-suite, TV, tea/coffee trays. B&B from £33. Open March to November.'
Contact: Pamela Broadhurst, Cote Bank Farm, Buxworth, High Peak, Derbyshire SK23 7NP.
Telephone/fax 01663 750566.
Email: cotebank@btinternet.com
www.cotebank.co.uk

Holmhead Farm and Guest House, Northumberland. See Page 83.
'This 19th century former farmhouse (AA/'**Visit Britain' Four Stars**) is within the Hadrian's Wall World Heritage Site, with panoramic views over part of the Northumbria National Park. Stay at Holmhead and experience delicious food and comfortable ensuite bedrooms. No smoking; tourist information; sightseeing planning – especially Hadrian's Wall.' Tariff from £35.
Contact: Brian and Pauline Staff, Holmhead, Hadrian's Wall. Greenhead CA8 7HY. Telephone 016977 47402.
www.holmhead.com

Machrie Hotel and golf links, Isle of Islay. See Page 116.
'The "Machrie" lies close to its 15 self-catering cottages. Along with
11 twin rooms and five double rooms, it has two bars, a dining room, a
function room and a private dining room. The food is predominantly local,
with Islay beef, lamb and shellfish a speciality. Bar meals are served both
at lunchtime and in the evening.'
Contact: Machrie Hotel, Port Ellen, Isle of Islay, Argyll PA42 7AN.
Telephone 01496 302310. Fax 302404.
Email: machrie@machrie.com
www.machrie.com

Bailey Mill, Roxburghshire. See Page 131.
'Friendly farm holiday complex offering bed and breakfast from £25 per
person, per night or self catering courtyard apartments (short breaks
available). This is an ideal location for walking, cycling or horse-riding
through the beautiful Scottish/Cumbria border country. Guests are
welcome to relax in our jacuzzi, sauna etc before enjoying
a drink and/or meal in our cosy bar.'
Contact: Bailey Mill, Newcastleton, Roxburghshire TD9 0TR.
Telephone: 01697 748617.
Email: pam@baileymill.fsnet.co.uk
www.holidaycottagescumbria.co.uk

Land Ends Country Lodge, Cumbria. See Page 118.
'Enjoy a real country experience at Land Ends. Our converted farmhouse
and barn are in 25 acres with lakes, pretty courtyard, fishpond. We have
ducks, moorhens, red squirrels, wonderful birdlife. All rooms en-suite.
'Visit Britain' **Three Diamonds.** From £30. Doubles, twins and singles.'
Contact: Barbara Holmes, Land Ends Country Lodge,
Watermillock, near Ullswater, Cumbria CA11 0NB.
Telephone: 017684 86438.
Email: infolandends@btinternet.com
www.landends.co.uk

Trevorrick Farm, Cornwall. See Page 178.

'In our family home there are two double rooms and one twin, all with en suite bathroom with bath and shower-over, TV, tea and coffee making facilities. There is a separate lounge for guests with colour television and video/DVD. Guests have the use of the swimming pool during opening hours from Easter to October and the games room. There are two local pubs and a beautiful 45 minute walk into Padstow, along footpaths and the Camel Trail.'

Contact: Melanie Benwell, Trevorrick Farm Cottages, St Issey, Wadebridge, Cornwall PL27 7QH.

Telephone/fax 01841 540574.

Email: info@trevorrick.co.uk   www.trevorrick.co.uk

Delphi Lodge, Co Galway. See Page 234.

'You don't have to be a salmon fisherman to enjoy the exquisite and peaceful surroundings at this well known but never overrun place (never overrun because accommodation is limited). In addition to the authentically restored, cosy cottages, there are twelve guest rooms. The place is organised in house-party style, so there is no room service, and guests generally eat communally in candlelight around a fine, huge dining table. It's a bonus for lone travellers or people from overseas wanting to make new friends.'

Contact: Peter Mantle, Delphi Lodge, Leenane, Co Galway.

Telephone 00 353 95 42222. Fax 42296.

Email: stay@delphilodge.ie   www.delphilodge.ie

The editors of *The Good Holiday Cottage Guide* welcome personal calls and emails from readers about properties in the British Isles or abroad, and about things to see and do in the area that is of interest. Every property featured in this guide has been seen by at least one inspector, sometimes two or three of them, but there may be specific questions readers want to ask that are not covered in individual write-ups or round-up agency features. We are always very pleased to link people up with properties that may suit them, and there is no charge...

Telephone 01438 869489.

email: info@goodcottageguide.com

Recommended Cottage Holidays*

There's always room for a good national cottage-letting agency: 'good' meaning efficient and user-friendly, with a wide and varied portfolio.

This is a good one. Fairly new but meteorically successful, Recommended Cottage Holidays has grown beyond its original boundaries and gone countrywide, though – and people like this – keeping its Yorkshire roots.

Just outside Beverley is a fine collection of six newly renovated cottages with the added bonus of stabling and grazing. Situated in the Wolds and surrounded by open countryside, the location of these cottages is just right for wanting to be well placed for both the coast and the moors. Each cottage is well equipped and pets are welcome . Together the properties **sleep 36** and are rated 4*. Ref M109/110/111/112/113/114.

In rural Shropshire, handy for sought-after Ludlow, a series of barn conversions has created accommodation that can **sleep 22** – a great opportunity for families or groups of friends. Grouped around a prettily landscaped, south-facing courtyard, each cottage has its own character. Here too there's (coarse) fishing in the grounds. There are four properties available, **sleeping respectively 6, 6, 4 and 6**: Refs T65/66/67/68. 4*.

Near Westbury, Wiltshire, a good point from which to visit, say, Longleat, Bath and Stonehenge, there's a very comfortable, spacious, detached family house **sleeping 10**. Equipped to high standards, it features four bedrooms and a modern fitted kitchen with French doors leading out on to a rear patio: a charming spot for guests to enjoy a leisurely barbecue. A super place with, not surprisingly, 5*. Ref B31.

Just outside Beverley, these are newly renovated, and well located for touring.

There are five inviting barn conversions on the coast near famous Hartland Point.

In reliably pretty rural Devon there are five delightful barn conversions at Hartland, near Bideford. Only a mile and a half from the coast, and easy to get to, they are grouped around a courtyard and have a children's play paddock along with use of a sauna and hot tub for the adults. They make a memorable base for a holiday at any time of the year and are rated 4*. Ref R222/223/224/225/226: taken together they **sleep 19 people**.

Details and an excellent brochure from Recommended Cottage Holidays, Eastgate House, Pickering, North Yorkshire YO18 7DW. Telephone 01751 475547; fax 475559. (* These are Recommended Cottages' own gradings, based on **'Visit Britain'** criteria.)

www.recommended-cottages.co.uk

email: sales@recommended-cottages.co.uk

Dales Holiday Cottages*

We know from our correspondence that Dales Holiday Cottages have introduced many south-of-England based readers to the best of England's North Country – with detours into some of Scotland's most scenic corners. Wild moors, hidden valleys, tree-lined rivers, ancient market towns, villages that seem hardly to have changed for 300 years, little-used roads snaking up into the hills: all this is 'Dales' territory.

We know much of Yorkshire, Derbyshire, Cumbria, Northumberland and Scotland, but this agency is full of topographical surprises. Among so very many gems are *The Bothy*, near Nenthead, which is in turn near Alston – a hilltop delight that's just inside Cumbria but close to the most beautiful part of underrated County Durham and to the 'best-kept-secret' that's the South Tyne Valley. Within an outstandingly attractive detached stone barn that embraces three properties, *The Bothy* **sleeps just 2** in a king-sized bed, and among many good things has a jacuzzi and fine rural views. Ref 4313.

Deep among the Yorkshire Dales, in the sort of location we love (along a quiet lane in a village), *The Bull Barn* – another skilful conversion –

Beckhouse (not featured) is a classic, substantial Yorkshire beauty. Ref 3179.

Viewfield, in Scotland, is a classic in its way, but 'cottagey'. Not featured. Ref 3677.

sleeps 6 in great contemporary style. There's a woodburning stove and, indicative of the attention to detail and comfort, underfloor heating. Also, for example, there's a TV in each of the three bedrooms. This is a delightful corner of Yorkshire, just two miles from Malham Tarn. Ref 4329.

There are yet more barn conversions, again exquisitely located, this time in a Derbyshire village. Dating from about 1750 in Kniveton, near Ashbourne, *The Creamery* is one of three, thoughtfully and charmingly furnished, with lots of attention to detail. It **sleeps 2**. Ref 4164.

Over the border, among so many appealing Scottish properties, newly built, detached *Magnelia House* – **sleeping 8** – has great views and the advantage of being situated within the owner's spacious grounds. We know this part of Scotland well, and yet again the location is terrific. The 'capital of the Highlands', Inverness, is just 15 minutes away, as are glorious routes to the north west. Ref 4293.

The Dales Holiday Cottage website is attractive and very user-friendly, but happily is enhanced by a busy and attractive brochure. Copies of this and other details from Dales Holiday Cottages, Carleton Business Park, Carleton New Road, Skipton, North Yorkshire BD23 2AA. Telephone 01756 790919; fax 797012.

www.dales-holiday-cottages.com
email: info@dales-holiday-cottages.com

Interhome* (Great Britain)

Probably best known and admired for its quite extraordinary variety of self catering accommodation in mainland Europe and elsewhere in the world, Interhome has a notable UK portfolio too.

Just at random, within a terrace of cottages with a fine view of Cardigan Bay, two-storeyed *Ty Cerrig Cottage* stands in a quiet location above New Quay and just a mile or so from the beach. There's shared use of a lawned area for sunning yourself, a garden with garden furniture and a barbecue, with shops and a restaurant also about a mile away: just a nice distance on foot on a sunny day. **Sleeps 6;** one dog welcome. Ref GB6170/102.1.

Even if we don't know the properties, we often know the locations. We've noticed a keen eye on the part of the Interhome people for pinpointing nice places. In Morebath, for example, about ten miles from from Tiverton, in Devon, and on the edge of the Exmoor National Park, a quietly situated terraced house, *Beech Cottage*, **sleeping 4**, makes a good West Country base that's 'not a million miles from London'. Ref GB5400/100.1.

Beech Cottage is happily located on the edge of the Exmoor National Park (which is probably our own favourite).

An apartment in Kingston-on-Thames is very nicely situated in its own right and handy for the train to central London.

Of course, one of the strengths of this impressive organisation is its range of properties in or within easy access of major cities. One example is a comfortable, modern two-room first floor apartment in a new three-storeyed apartment house in Kingston-on-Thames, just about ten miles from London. In a central, quiet position, about 300 yards from the Thames, on a side street, it is not 'suburban', but enjoys all the facilities of what is effectively a lively (and historic) market town in its own right. Trains from Kingston to London Waterloo take approximately 35 minutes. **Sleeps 4**. Ref G1037/520.1.

But these amount to nothing more than a snapshot of what's available. Interhome has an extraordinary reputation for competitively priced accommodation and for efficiency – we hear from readers who use the company regularly, and say things like 'We are Interhome people'.

Telephone 020 8780 6633, fax 020 8780 6631, or see the Great Britain pages of the Interhome website: **www.interhome.co.uk**

(on line booking possible; short breaks and bookings of flexible duration available)

See also Pages 254 and 259.

Hoseasons Country Cottages*

There's an impressive range of holiday properties on offer from this famous agency. Just for starters: thatched cottages, one-time barns, pubs, chapels, farmhouses, manor houses, converted watermills, schools, stables and coach houses!

Hoseasons have always been based in East Anglia, so it's not surprising that they offer a particularly good choice there. One of these is *Envirobarns*, which offer a unique and very special holiday experience. Four barns have been converted with environmental issues in mind. They **sleep from 2 to 5**. Refs E4312, E4313, E4314 & E4315.

Readers also appreciate thatched cottages, such as pretty 18th century *Greengrove Cottage*, in Edington, Wiltshire. In a peaceful village, it makes a relaxing base from which to explore the many attractions of an often overlooked region. **Sleeps 3**. Ref E2483.

Located at the bottom of the National Trust's Grabbist Hill, in the Exmoor National Park, *Ellicombe Cottages* are Grade II listed, in the grounds of 16th century Ellicombe Manor. There are many facilities to be enjoyed, such as the shared outdoor heated swimming pool* and the acre of sub tropical gardens. The gardens are a special feature of Ellicombe Manor, filled with mature palm trees, named exotic plants and shrubs and quiet corners with seating. Here, too, visitors may discover the 'secret garden'. Ellicombe Cottages are well placed for beach trips (within five miles) and countryside walks. **Sleeps 2 to 6** plus cot. Refs E2224, E2225, E2226, E2227.

Greengrove Cottage is a delight, in a village that's a great base for touring.

The Ellicombe Cottages enjoy, among other facilities, a super shared pool.

In Wales, *Globe House* is a Grade II listed building (**sleeping 10**) in the Pembrokeshire National Park. Just a short walk from a sandy beach, it's ideally placed for exploring the coastal path and for bird-watching, as the cliffs are home to seabirds such as cormorants and fulmers. Ref W7142.

If you fancy some monster spotting, one of the *Loch Ness Cottages* or *Ness-Side Cottages*, four miles from Drumnadrochit, would be ideal as they have a glorious panoramic view across the famous loch. Three cottages **sleep 2** in king-size four-posters and two **sleep 4**. Ref S4104, S4249, S4105, S4077 and S4351.

Details from Hoseasons Holidays, Lowestoft, Suffolk, NR32 2LW. Telephone: 0870 534 2342. Fax 0870 902 2090.

* The pool is open from April 26th to September 27th (10am – 4pm).

www.hoseasons.co.uk

Sykes Cottages*

This highly regarded independent agency, based in Chester, has an impressive portfolio of over 1000 properties throughout the UK, including the South West, Northumberland, Yorkshire, Scotland, Wales and the Heart of England. In 2007, the company undertook an exciting expansion by launching their range of quality properties in Ireland.

Sykes Cottages was started over 25 years ago by the mother of owner and managing director Clive Sykes. Each cottage is inspected and carries either its local tourist board grading or the agency's own rating. On the

St Mary's Mission Room, at Ebberston, North Yorkshire, sleeps eleven.

The Old Farmhouse, near Ross-on-Wye, is close to famous Symonds Yat. Sleeps six.

agency's informative and easy-to-use website (www.sykescottages.co.uk) you can search availability, view full property details (including photos) and see what previous holidaymakers thought of each property. You can also use the site's property reservation and online payment options.

For those who love messing about in boats, *Lake Cottage* (2172, **sleeping 6**) is ideal. Set on the very banks of Coniston Water in the Lake District, the cottage boasts a full length veranda to enjoy the lake views, as well as a woodburning stove and free use of the owner's boats, with a private launching facility for those who prefer to bring their own dinghy.

A conversion with character, *The Old Mill* (2068, **sleeping 6**) is in a picturesque hamlet on the outskirts of Belford in Northumberland. With en-suite bedrooms, original mill machinery in the kitchen and a woodburning stove, The Old Mill is ideal for exploring. If you fancy a swimming pool, consider *Peak View* (2262, **sleeping 8**), four miles from Ladybower Reservoir in the Peak District National Park. With breathtaking views, original stone and oak floors and exposed beams, the character of this conversion has been preserved. Guests have use of the owner's heated swimming pool, and the paddock with resident ponies and pot-bellied pigs! When booked with *Copse View* (2263), these properties **can accommodate 16**.

Those keen to sample Sykes's new portfolio in Ireland might like *Teachers Cottage* (2195, **sleeping 4**). Located on Whiddy Island, off the coast of Bantry in West Cork, the cottage offers simple, light and airy accommodation, with an open fire and spectacular views over Bantry Bay. There is a small pebble beach at the bottom of the garden.

Details from Sykes Cottages, Lime Tree House, Hoole Lane, Chester CH2 3EG. Telephone 01244 356896. Fax 321442.

www.sykescottages.co.uk
email: info@sykescottages.co.uk

Stately Holiday Homes*

We have rarely come across a portfolio of holiday properties so perfectly 'up our readers' street' as those handled by Stately Holiday Homes. As readers might have noticed, we're keen both on holiday houses of comfort and character and 'the stately homes of England' (as well as Wales, Scotland and Ireland). Courtesy of this splendid organisation and their impressive contacts the two elements come together delightfully.

Notable locations include, for example, Haddon Hall, in Derbyshire. Three miles from 'the big house', *Rock Cottage* – **sleeping up to 5** – is a

Essex is full of surprises: you can stay within the grounds of Castle Hedingham.

A classic rural scene, at Glanusk Park. Three super cottages are available.

fine, clean-cut, greystone house with a most attractive interior: it's interesting to note that so many of these estate properties are understated and easy on the eye, both inside and out. In a peaceful location (another big bonus), the house has **Four Stars** from **'Visit Britain'**.

Coniston Water is one of our own favourites among Cumbria's 'Lakes', and two properties converted by the owners of Nibthwaite Grange, in the hamlet of Nibthwaite, near the southern tip of the lake, make most enviable homes-from-home from which to enjoy this very special corner of England. *Peat House* and *Nibthwaite Studio* respectively **sleep up to 4** and **up to 2,** the former being a two storeyed stone cottage, the latter also on two floors, but primarily a spacious living/dining room with a double bed. The wife of the owner of Nibthwaite was brought up at Holker Hall, and a nice touch here is that holiday tenants have complimentary admission there.

The 4500 acre Houghton Estate in Norfolk has been the home of the Marquesses of Cholmondeley since 1797. (The Queen, at Sandringham, is a next-door neighbour.) There are three cottages on offer: *The Water House* has a super walled garden, *Bunker's Hill* is especially cosy in all weathers, with central heating as well as log fires, and *The South Lodge* is as neat and pretty a traditional roadside lodge (but very quiet) as we have ever seen on our travels. *See also Page 45.* We saw these recently, and loved them. We also visited *Snape Castle*, in North Yorkshire, and admired a warm and sympathetic conversion of a part of the main castle building. *See also Page 74.*

There are several Stately Holiday Homes properties in Scotland, Ireland and Wales. *Glanusk Park*, in the Brecon Beacons National Park, is very popular. Three traditional, stone-built cottages have stunning views over the estate and the Black Mountains. Each is single storeyed, fitting most harmoniously into its beautiful surroundings. *Library Cottage*, for example, has an especially impressive outlook, *Garden Cottage* has a memorable walled garden, and *The Kennels,* which is very quiet and peaceful, has a small stream running close. Garden ideally **sleeps 2** in a twin, but a single room is also available. The other two **sleep 4** in a twin and a double. All three have an open fire.

Among so many other good things, outstanding even in this exalted company, *Mead Cottage*, in the grounds of one of the most elegant, sumptuously comfortable manor-house hotels in Britain, is eye-poppingly 'last word'. It's in Castle Combe, one of this country's most photogenic, most

Mead Cottage, in Castle Combe, is at the heart of a classic 'picture-book' village.

Belle Isle: a super base for exploring beautiful, underrated Northern Ireland.

unspoiled villages. There is for example a charming and unusual divided 'double-living room' in which on one 'more formal' side there's a Scandinavian wood stove. The delightful small dining room used to be an ice house – but have no anxiety on that score: it has underfloor heating. **Sleeps 4** in great comfort.

Much less exalted than Castle Combe, but actually one of (much underrated) rural Essex's 'best kept secrets', the village of Castle Hedingham is dominated by the mainly 12th century castle. Within the castle grounds – accessed via a private gravel drive – *Garden Cottage* is a red brick, red tiled two-storeyed beauty **sleeping up to 5**. There's also *East-* and *West Lodge*, **sleeping 2/4 and 6/8** respectively.

A bonus here is that complimentary tickets are included for cottage guests to the popular jousting and 'medieval' events held at the castle.

Not yet seen by us but high on our schedule for 2008 is *Gilar Farmhouse*, close to the edge of the Snowdonia National Park. This is a real one-off, a remarkable survivor (**WTB Five Stars**) from the past, full of original features: it dates back partly to about 1660 and has, among so many memorable features, a seven-foot-wide four poster bed.

In Ireland *Belle Isle Castle*, Co. Fermanagh, is perfect for larger groups. **Sleeping up to 14**, with seven bathrooms, the mansion stands in a 470-acre estate consisting of eight separate islands.

For the company's brochure, telephone 01638 674749; fax 663995.

www.statelyholidayhomes.co.uk
email: admin@shhl.co.uk

National Trust Cottages

A 'cottage guide' reader from Suffolk who told us she'd never previously stayed in a National Trust property had a few days in the summer of 2007 in *89 Church Lawn*, right by the entrance to Stourhead, in Wiltshire (Ref 003017). We liked her comment about this glorious rarity: 'It's true that the perfect weather helped, but it was unforgettable. It was a birthday-week treat for my mum, who's a keen gardener'.

When holidaying in a National Trust property it's a bonus to know that the rent you pay helps preserve Britain's heritage of great estates and glorious countryside. Over 350 properties are available, scattered across England, Wales and Northern Ireland. Furthermore, as you'd expect, the choice encompasses many unique buildings.

Each is helpfully graded with an Acorn rating that ranges from One up to

The Birdcage, in Port Isaac, Cornwall is quite something. Sleeps 2 (small) people! *Mill Cottage is on the Blickling Estate, in Norfolk. Pretty as a picture, sleeping 6.*

Five. This covers the environment (the location, setting and exterior of the building) and the interior (style of decoration, furnishings and fittings, allowing for any normal wear and tear). Readers of this guide who two years ago were first-time visitors to the Isle of Wight stayed in Knowles Farm Cottage (3-Acorns). **Sleeping 3**, it stands close to the lighthouse at St Catherine's Point there's no foghorn! and as you'd imagine there are fantastic views. Ref 001005. And a visitor from Germany who joined English friends staying in Darnbrook Cottage, (3-Acorns, **sleeping 3**) on Malham Moor, in North Yorkshire, enthused about the views and the open fire, among much else. Ref 020020.

The two apartments (both **sleeping 3**) in the 400-year old Fountains Hall at Ripon in Yorkshire are 4-Acorns. Proctor, on the third floor, is furnished and decorated in the style of Charles Rennie Mackintosh; Vyner, on the second floor, follows the style of Edwin Lutyens. Ref 020016/7. Nearby, in the Studley Royal Deer Park, a 5-Acorn property, Choristers' House (**sleeping 10**) is available. Its has three double bedrooms and two twins. Ref 020022.

One in the 'quirky' category that intrigues us is Doyden Castle (**sleeping 3**), which stands on the cliff-edge mid-way between Polzeath and Port Isaac in North Cornwall. Graded 4 Acorns, it's actually a small two-storey castellated folly rather than a real castle. With views of Lundy Bay, it was built in about 1830 by a local bon viveur for nights of feasting, drinking and gambling. Guests can drive to it via a cliff-edge track to unload, but cars have to be parked five minutes' walk away. Ref 011030.

Anyone who dreams of a romantic stay in a secluded thatched cottage would be enchanted by *Wood Cottage* (2 Acorns) at Durgan, beside the Helford estuary in south Cornwall. Originally an apple store, this tiny timber-built bungalow (**sleeping 2**) now has a cosy open-plan kitchen/dining/sitting room and double bedroom. The National Trust's Glendurgan Garden and Trelissick Garden are both nearby. Ref 011026.

Holidaymakers staying in *East Cottage*, near Dover, on the famous White Cliffs, have an incomparable view of shipping passing to and fro in the Channel with (on clear days) the French coast. At the foot of the South Foreland lighthouse, it's a former keeper's cottage (3 Acorns), which **sleeps 4** in two bedrooms – a double and a single. The lighthouse itself, no longer operational, is open to visitors on a limited basis. Ref 021003.

Close to another popular coast, *Mustard Pot Cottage* (**sleeping 4**) is on the Felbrigg Estate in Norfolk, about three miles inland from Cromer. In

Mortuary Cottage, near Barnstaple, is a really cosy hideaway for just two people.

Also for two is The Old Coastguard Station, in Yorkshire. Sea views assured!

its own fenced garden at the end of a woodland track, it's a simple two-storey octagonal building (3 Acorns) with ground-floor extensions containing kitchen, bathroom, twin bedroom and a conservatory. What makes it special is the original part, with sitting-room (open fire) on the ground floor and, above it, up narrow winding stairs, a double bedroom. Ref 010019. Three other cottages and two apartments (**sleeping 2 to 5**) are also available on the estate, whose grand 17th-century house and grounds are open to the public on most days. Ref 010015/6, 010026, 010034/5.

For a really 'rustic' holiday amid wonderful scenery, *High Hallgarth* is a 17th-century stone cottage (**sleeping 7**) in a remote location overlooking Little Langdale Tarn, in the Lake District. As it has no bathroom and the toilet is an earth closet in an outbuilding, it is the sort of place children will find really exciting and remember all their lives. Ref 009002.

Murlough Gate Lodge, at Keel Point in County Down, Northern Ireland, is a charming stone cottage built in 1870 beside Dundrum Inner Bay, on the edge of the Murlough National Nature Reserve. It enjoys glorious views of the Mountains of Mourne, which provide some of the best hill-walking in Ireland. **Sleeping 4**, it has 4 Acorns. Ref 019014.

There is a user-friendly website where you can see all the cottages inside and out, check availability and book: **www.nationaltrustcottages.co.uk**

Or call 0844 800 2020 for a brochure or 0844 800 2070 to book.

A voluntary contribution of £3 towards production, postage and packing of the brochure will be requested.

The Vivat Trust

Established in 1981, Vivat is devoted to rescuing and restoring neglected and dilapidated listed historic buildings and then letting them out for luxury self-catering holidays. Without wanting to seem sentimental, it's the sort of organisation that makes us a bit 'proud to be British'.

The geographical spread of its 22 properties, scattered from Dorset to Fife, could be the making of a voyage of discovery for holidaymakers with an interest in history and architecture.

We recently visited the two at Thistlewood, about 15 miles north-west of Penrith, so well-placed for exploring the northern part of the Lake District. They stand on one side of a cobbled courtyard surrounded by former farm buildings beside a small river.

Thistlewood Tower (**sleeping 5**) is a Grade-1 listed building with a defensive tower dating back to 1332 and well-stocked garden. It now offers elegantly-furnished accommodation on three floors. The top one, in the tower, reached by a narrow stone staircase, houses a romantic master bedroom with vaulted ceiling, wall paintings, four-poster bed and en-suite bathroom.

Alongside it, *Thistlewood Byre* (**sleeping 2**) is a former cowshed that was built in the early 19th century. Surprisingly spacious and light inside, it too is rather luxurious, with top-quality furniture, including an antique brass bedstead, and modern kitchen and bathroom. Its small garden contains ancient herbs and roses, and as we walked around (in the autumn of 2007) we picked up all sorts of intriguing scents.

Thistlewood Tower and Byre, full of interest, are handy for the northern lakes.

The Summer House, in Shropshire (not featured) is all that remains of a great house.

As at all the Trust's properties, arriving guests are greeted by a welcome hamper made up as far as possible from locally sourced produce, plus a bottle of wine.

Near Maidstone in Kent, the 14th-century *Nettlestead Place Gatehouse* **sleeps 2** in a four-poster bed. Or for family or group holidays, the elegant 1703 Queen Anne house of *Glenhurst* at Bewdley, in Worcestershire, **sleeps 10** people.

Despite Vivat's serious purpose and very high standards, there is nothing austere about these or any of its properties. They feel like lived-in homes, not museums, and for added comfort most have open fires or woodburners.

For a highly informative glossy brochure, contact The Vivat Trust, 70 Cowcross Street, London EC1M 6EJ. Telephone 0845 0900194. Fax 0845 0900174.

www.vivat.org.uk   email: enquiries@vivat.org.uk

England and Wales:
'Large Holiday Houses in England and Wales'

Large streams from little fountains flow, great oaks from little acorns grow: what better example of this than the success of Large Holiday Houses (LHH)?

Formed in 1993 by people making their own large house available for holiday lets, this amazing organisation has gone from strength to strength, firstly by helping other large holiday home owners find lets for their castles and mansions in Scotland, subsequently by inviting cottage owners in Scotland to join the portfolio. Then, following on from the phenomenal success of both those ventures (See Pages 100 and 101) by launching LHH England and Wales in 2008.

Plas Newydd, at Rhoshirwaun, on the beautiful Lleyn Peninsula in North Wales, is a Welsh farmhouse dating back to the 18th century. **Sleeping 10 'plus 4'**, it is in a secluded position and retains many original features. There is an outdoor heated swimming pool, as well as a natural stream flowing through the one-acre garden. This is a comparatively little known part of North Wales, though much to be recommended. (We'd say that one not-to-be-missed point en route is Portmeirion.)

There are three properties **sleeping 4** available in an idyllic position on the hillside overlooking the beautiful sea cove at Robin Hoods Bay in Yorkshire, an ancient seaside hamlet, nestled precariously between fossil laden cliffs and steeped in tales of smuggling and contraband. Within easy reach of sandy beaches and the Norfolk Broads, *Honeysuckle Cottage*, formerly a terrace of three, **sleeps 10 'plus 5'**.

LHH has quickly gained a strong foothold in the West Country, with 18 properties available, all very easily accessible to beautiful sandy beaches, and most of which are in or close to the much-loved, pleasantly old-fashoned resort of Bude, with just a couple in Devon.

Located close to Hartland Quay, in a designated Area of Outstanding Natural Beauty, *The Old Roundhouse* is a stunning barn conversion with magnificent, uninterrupted countryside views. And the village of Hartland is a charmer. Luckily it's in easy walking distance, as there are three pubs! Standards here are exceptionally high, and there's wheelchair access. **Sleeps 10**.

Bush Meadows, just north of Bude, was hand-built by the owner using Cornish stone. The conservatory, delightfully, looks over a five-acre meadow where you might spot herons, buzzards, kingfishers and rabbits. **Sleeps 12**. *Kingfishers Apartment* is a new and superior first floor apartment overlooking Bude Canal and the eclectic wildlife on the River Neet Nature Reserve opposite. **Sleeps 6** in great comfort.

For full details of these and other properties, together with excellent colour photos, go to:

www.LHHEngland.com.
email:LHH@LHHEngland.com

The National Trust for Scotland
Holiday Accommodation Programme

We've met self catering enthusiasts who've 'discovered Scotland' via the NTS holiday cottage programme. It's a great thing to do, even if it offers a slightly rarified side of the country!

Among other properties we're hoping to see a particular rarity on the Isle of Skye. This is *Beaton's Croft*, a traditional croft house, internally reconstructed for the sake of comfort but with the original ambience retained. **Sleeping 2** (with – of course! – a peat fire) it is at Bornesketaig, and has fabulous views across to the Outer Hebrides.

Consider fabulously situated *Mar Lodge*, on Royal Deeside. We know the place and if we had to choose one great estate – there are over 77000 acres of it – that encapsulates the romance and beauty of mainland Scotland, this might be it. All five of the elegant apartments are graded **Four Stars** by '**Visit Britain**', and three of them have the advantage of access via the impressive main entrance. One of them, *Bynack* is notably roomy, and **can sleep up to 15** (though it is available to smaller groups).

Most recently, during a journey through the east of Scotland, we saw the first floor apartment (**sleeping 4**) at *St Andrew's House*, built in the 17th century as an overflow for courtiers attending royal visitors to the Falkland Palace next door. It is in the heart of attractive little Falkland.

And between Perth and St Andrews, we found two attractive little bungalows (**sleeping 4 and 5**) in the extensive grounds of the *Hill of Tarvit* mansion, built in 1904. A spacious, elegantly furnished apartment (**sleeping 4**) with views over farmland is also available on the second floor.

We also visited Culzean Castle (pronounced 'Cullane'), a magnificent building on the Ayrshire coast, and were impressed by the spacious, high-ceilinged *Brewhouse Flat*, in the west wing, and by *Royal Artillery Cottage*, that forms part of the courtyard next to the castle. Each **sleeps 4**.

One of the 'attractive little bungalows' in the grounds of the Hill of Tarvit mansion.

This is Steading Cottage, in the grounds of (and facing) Craigievar Castle.

One can also stay in the most attractive detached cottages in the grounds of picturesque Craigievar Castle. Both **sleeping 4**, *Kennels Cottage* and *Steading Cottage* are only about a hundred yards from the fabulous castle. For a copy of the irresistible brochure contact Holidays Department, The National Trust for Scotland, Wemyss House, 28 Charlotte Square, Edinburgh EH2 4ET. Telephone 0131 243 9331. Fax 0131 243 9594.

www.nts.org.uk email: holidays@nts.org.uk

'Lakesbreaks'

Lakesbreaks, the website of the Cumbria and Lakeland Self Caterers' Association (www.lakesbreaks.co.uk), carries an impressive selection of cottages, lodges and apartments across Cumbria and the Lake District. The properties featured are of at least Three Star (Visit Britain) quality, with many rated more highly: all are maintained to the highest standards. They are all independently owned and managed by members of the Association, like-minded people willing to share their expertise and experience.

At the click of a mouse, you can find full details, search for availability and prices, and book the accommodation of your choice.

There are properties from Carlisle, standing proudly on the English and Scottish borders, in the north, to Broughton-in-Furness, with its Georgian market square and obelisk, erected to mark the jubilee of George III in 1810, in the south; from Cockermouth, an attractive market town on the junction of the Rivers Cocker and Derwent and the birthplace of William Wordsworth, in the west, to Alston, England's highest market town, in the east. And, of course, there are many in the heart of the Lake District National Park.

Searching the website will show you many romantic hideaways for just 2, but you'll also find places for larger groups. We've spotted at least one with fabulous views, though to be honest that's no great tribute to our powers of observation, as good views are commonplace!

There really is 'something to suit every taste': panoramic views; beautiful fell and valley walks right from the door; ideal bases for walking, touring, climbing; open fires; four posters and canopied beds; characterful old stone and beams; converted 17th and 18th century buildings; nooks and crannies; and many of these within Areas of Outstanding Natural Beauty.

Many holidaymakers in the Lakes are looking for simplicity and 'peace and quiet', but in line with trends elsewhere, a number of CALSCA members offer last-word luxury – even pampering...

Check online for current special offers, particularly off-peak promotions.

Stop Press

Throcking, near Buntingford
Southfields Cottages

Charming, unpretentious, each sleeps five.

Well located for people who want to be within half an hour's drive of Cambridge and within reach – best by train, via Stevenage – of London, these are only occasionally available for holiday letting. On a working (but not noisy or smelly) farm, well away from the main road, each of the semi-detached but private and self-contained pair enjoys good views and is pleasant and unpretentious. Among the details that impressed us were bright, cottagey bedrooms (plain white walls in most cases), some traditional knick-knacks, a sitting-out area at the rear. There is central heating, linen is provided and, although electric fires are installed, you can have usually have an open fire too. Not suitable for dogs. TVs.

Details from Mrs I Murchie 07913 480095.

Stoke Tye, near Dedham
Louie's Cottage   map 1/2

A classic thatched cottage: rural Essex is one of southern England's surprises...

'Constable Country', a rural survivor in the face of relentless development on and around the Suffolk-Essex border, contains within its low hills and exceptionally fertile farmland some delightful surprises. The tiny hamlet that surrounds this classic thatched and 'pargetted' cottage is one such delight. The house itself is used by the owners for their own holidays and weekends, and is suitably 'lived in', containing family antiques, charming knick-knacks, chintzy covered armchairs, a rocking chair and, for example, an upholstered window seat: very much our sort of place.

We noticed an open fire, a separate study, a standard lamp, lots and lots of books – not just in one room but in several. There are two twin bedrooms with fitted carpets, and even a Victorian rocking horse! **Sleeps 4**.

TV. Dogs welcome. No linen provided. Central heating throughout.

Details from 01438 869489.

Stop Press

Edwardstone, near Lavenham
Grove Cottages

During the last few years we've watched this charming, skilfully, lovingly converted group of 300-year-old cottages become established as one of the finest of its kind in East Anglia.

It's just two hours' drive from London (and therefore great for short breaks): but as you meander along West Suffolk's sleepy country lanes you might feel you are 200 miles from any big city. The location is ideal for walking, cycling (free bikes), exploring the beautiful River Stour on canoes (for hire), horse-riding, golfing, touring and 'pubbing'.

We have admired and noted so many good things. Such as charming 'ragged' walls, an original bread oven in *The Bakery*, original brick walls, wooden floors, beams. Plus personal touches such as fresh flowers, locally hand-made soaps, fridges stocked for you with the makings of a full English breakfast, a communal fridge-freezer.

Don's Barn, is a sympathetic conversion **for a couple only** – a five feet wide bed: excellent – of a property that dates from the early 1700s. There's period furniture and a big log fire. **'Visit Britain' Four Stars**.

If you can drag yourself away from all this you will not want to miss picture postcard Kersey and a remarkable throwback to the medieval age, preserved-in-aspic Lavenham. Bury St Edmunds and Cambridge are an easy meander (avoiding main roads) and Norwich is not a lot further.

With a great commitment both to the history of the properties and to 21st century comfort, these are very special.

All the (very pretty and cottagey) main bedrooms have five-foot beds, and four of the five cottages have an open fire.

Sleep from 2 to 6. TV, stereo, CD player, selection of music and books. Spacious power showers, no baths. Finest cotton linen and towels provided. Pets welcome. Non-smokers or very considerate smokers preferred. **'Visit Britain' Four Stars**. Cost: about £193 to £853. Details and a brochure from Mark Scott, The Grove Cottages, Priory Green, Edwardstone, Suffolk CO10 5PP. Telephone 01787 211115. Fax 211220 or 211511.

www.grove-cottages.co.uk   email: mark@grove-cottages.co.uk

Stop Press

Goodrich, near Ross-on-Wye
Mainoaks Farm

We can hardly think of a more agreeable place from which to explore the Welsh borders and 'deepest Herefordshire', and it was a pleasure recently rather than a duty to revisit these superbly well situated cottages. 'Superbly well' means close to the shores of the River Wye, which is quite rare for a holiday house and much sought-after.

Turning off a B-road, we followed a farm lane and arrived at this quiet enclave of well converted stone built farm cottages. Each has its own character, ranging from 'bijou' to 'farmhousey and rambling'. Arriving by chance as a team of cleaners was busy preparing the cottages for incoming guests, we took time to look at all the cottages, noting for example the fine views from some windows, exposed beams, a nice spiral staircase.

They vary usefully in size – *Cider Mill*, for example, **sleeps up to 7**. We noted a number of appealing features: a woodburning stove in *Peregrine*, **sleeping 6**, which we also thought had 'a nice family atmosphere' and which was *converted* in 1659! It has a cruck beam in the bedrooms; Cider Mill's big, convivial dining table; the four poster bed in *Huntsham* (**sleeps 4**); the upstairs sitting room in *The Malthouse* (an 'upside-down' house, so designed as to make the most of the view).

Ross-on-Wye and Monmouth are about ten minutes' drive, and

A marvellous and unusual location, and very sympathetic conversion work.

Rather 'rustic' and comfortable rooms that reflect the very stylish exteriors.

Cheltenham Spa and the cathedral cities of Hereford, Worcester and Gloucester are easily accessible. The farm has a mile of frontage to the River Wye, and salmon and course fishing beats can be booked locally.

TVs, DVDs, radios/CD players and microwaves in each. Linen and towels included. Dogs by arrangement. Short breaks available. '**Visit Britain' Three/Four Stars**. Open all year. Cost: about £230 to £790.

Details from Patricia Unwin, Hill House, Chase End, Bromesberrow, Ledbury, Herefordshire HR8 1SE. Telephone 01531 650448.

www.mainoaks.co.uk email: info@mainoaks.co.uk

East Anglia, East Midlands and The Shires

Perhaps the secret of East Anglia's abiding popularity with a kind of holidaymaker is that it combines fabulous sandy beaches with 'bucket-and-spade' family resorts, and shingly beaches and stiff winds with nice-day-out attractions such as steam trains and boat trips on Suffolk's rivers. Suffolk especially enjoys quick and easy access from London. From Scotland, it takes about four hours, from the Midlands perhaps two. Among so many good things to see in Norfolk is the North Norfolk steam railway (with - most impressively - links to regional rail services). Cottage roofs are thatched with Norfolk reed that lasts up to about 80 years, churches the size of cathedrals dominate the skyline, meandering rivers are the haunt of wildfowl. Even if you are holidaying near the coast, visit Norwich: the cathedral, the castle, the open-air market. Even if you are staying in a self catering cottage, you can hire a boat on the Broads by the hour or by the day. To the west lie the prosperous farms of Leicestershire and Northamptonshire, underrated counties of golden limestone villages and elegant churches. To the north are the Lincolnshire Wolds and the haunting, flat fenland, and well into Lincolnshire are some of the finest sandy beaches in England, where without exaggeration you can be virtually alone during a sunny Bank Holiday.

Dalham Vale, near Newmarket
Jockey Cottage (map 1/1)

Right at the heart of a village close to the Suffolk/Cambridgeshire border, a few easy furlongs from horsey Newmarket, this most attractive and 'traditional' thatched cottage is well placed for exploring the best of rural Suffolk, a good part of Norfolk, Cambridge, Ely and the low key but fascinating Fen Country. Handy for a good village pub, it is one of those places that makes a really pleasant

Many years in this guide, lots of praise.

base to return to after touring (we have heard this from a number of overseas readers). Standing well back from the quiet road through this pleasant off-the-beaten-track conservation village, it has been tastefully and considerately restored and furnished. For example, there is a skilful blend of country furniture and top-notch contemporary soft furnishings, plus a new kitchen and a dishwasher. It has a woodburning stove in an inglenook fireplace, and **sleeps 4**. Remote control television. You'll find a welcome pack, a payphone and a garden.

Pets are possible by arrangement. Linen and towels are included. Cost: about £260 to £360. Weekend breaks are available from about £130. Further details from Richard Williams, Scorrier House, Redruth, Cornwall TR16 5AU. Telephone 01209 820264.   **email: rwill10442@aol.com**

Dedham Vale, near Nayland
Gladwins Farm Cottages

Over 20 years in this guide, with nothing but glowing praise from readers: an impressive record. Gladwins is easily accessible – less than two hours' drive from London, about three from Birmingham – but still deeply rural.

This extraordinarily well situated group of cottages, in which guests are well placed for exploring east and west Suffolk and, say, the Norfolk border and Norwich, has high standards and excellent facilities, and we have seen for ourselves the warm welcome from the owners, the far-reaching country views, the fine indoor pool, the sheep and the pigs!

All but three properties face on to a courtyard. *Chelsworth Cottage*, **sleeping 8**, is very private and has spectacular views over the Vale of Dedham, an Area of Outstanding Natural Beauty. It has a four-poster bed, TV and ensuites in *all* bedrooms, a log burner, central heating and stereo. And it even has its own hot tub! A real bonus is that it has a specially adapted ground floor twin room for disabled people. *Wiston Cottage,* **sleeping 6**, has three en-suite rooms, all with their own TV, its own garden and the same impressive views. Pets are welcome here.

Hadleigh **sleeps 4/5** and is attached to the owners' home; *Constable* **sleeps 6**, *Gainsborough* and *Dedham* both **sleep 4**, *Lavenham* **sleeps 4 'plus 1'**, *Melford* **sleeps 2** in a four poster 'for that special occasion' and also has its own hot tub. *Kersey* **sleeps 2 plus 1**. All could be described as 'little showhouses' with their cosy, comfortable interiors, woodburners, modern pine, good fitted carpets and local pictures. (There's another hot tub adjacent to the pool buildings for all the other cottages to share.)

There is access to 22 acres, an air-conditioned pool and sauna building, an adventure playground, an all-weather tennis court and a trout lake.

Excellent facilities and an outstanding situation in Constable Country'...

Interiors have been sympathetically done: this (appropriately!) is 'Chelsworth'...

Pets welcome, except in Lavenham and Hadleigh. Small-screen TVs with Freeview/video/DVD players. Wifi internet access. Cost: £275 to £1900. **Sleep 2 to 8**. Open all year; short breaks. Chelsworth and Wiston are suitable for accompanied disabled visitors. On-line availability can be checked via the website.

Further details from Pauline and Robert Dossor, Gladwins Farm, Harpers Hill, Nayland, Suffolk CO6 4NU. Telephone Nayland 01206 262261, fax 263001. Bed and breakfast is also available.

www.gladwinsfarm.co.uk   email: GladwinsFarm@aol.com

Brundish, near Framlingham
Potash Barns

One reader who stayed here during 2007 wrote to say: 'We'll be back, mainly because of the children. They just loved the animals, and we had quite a job getting them to leave the property at all.' From the time we first saw 'Potash' we knew the Hebridean sheep, the ducks and the goats and the hens would go down well.

Another reader, who joined family and friends for a couple of days here, spoke glowingly of the accommodation. She knew the coast but not the deeply rural interior of Suffolk.

Of the three cottages, all of which we have visited, *Cart Lodge* is free-standing and just a step away from the other two, *Old Oak* and *Goat Willow*. These two are linked via a large central hall with sofas and a fire-place: ideal when renting both cottages.

Each cottage has a different layout, incorporating two bedrooms, a comfortable living room, and a well-equipped kitchen. The decor is both stylish and rustic, with solid wooden beams, elm or terracotta floors, and high quality fittings. The solid wood kitchens all have large fridges, dish-washers, ranges and porcelain sinks.

We admired the magnificent flower arrangements in each cottage, and the fresh, top quality organic veg and groceries that owner Rob supplies win accolades too. He can also arrange for a meal to be waiting in the oven. Each cottage has an outdoor eating area with BBQ, and there's a separate games room with table tennis, table football and a variety of games.

The cottages each **sleep 4 or 5** plus two on double sofa beds in each living room. The master bedroom at Old Oak has a huge glass skylight, enabling you to lie in bed and gaze at the stars. Cart Lodge is laid out on one floor, and has a walk in shower as well as a bath – useful for less mobile guests. Each has TV, video, DVD, washer and dryer, bath and power shower, a CD player, books and games, a woodburner and central heating. All three cottages are **'Visit Britain' Four Stars**. Children have their own play area with swings and trampoline. Most pets can be accom-modated in Cart Lodge. Cost : about £250 to £665.

Details from Rob Spendlove, Potash Farm, The Street, Brundish, Suffolk, IP13 8BL. Telephone 07747 038386. Fax 01379 384819.

www.potashbarns.co.uk   email: enquiries@potashbarns.co.uk

We were wowed by the rural location, the animals, the easy-going comfort...

Colleagues still enthuse about a stay they arranged for a group of friends.

Woodbridge, Orford and around
Mrs Jane Good (Holidays) Ltd *

We would rate this family run, long established agency as one of the finest, most user-friendly and reliable in the country. And if you believe that first impressions count, you'll appreciate the exquisitely situated offices: right by the yachting marina and The Quay that are a major draw in what is one of the most attractive market towns in England.

It's a fitting base for an agency with (in many cases) exceptionally well situated properties that deals exclusively with rural and coastal Suffolk. Readers will know how highly we rate it: it is well organised and features a notable number of classically pretty and highly photogenic cottages.

Lavender Cottage, sleeping 4 (but spaciously) offers a rare chance to be at the very heart of delightful Woodbridge.

Hacheston is a charmer, and this beauty, called Lodge Cottage, has been done out to a high standard. Sleeps five 'plus 1'.

Appropriately, Mrs Jane Good (Holidays) Ltd have a number of properties close to the water in Woodbridge itself.

Among several holiday homes on the agency's books in the town is *No 12 St John's Terrace*. Near the centre of town, with a neat garden, it has been lovingly restored. Close to the fine parish church (one bedroom overlooks it), it **sleeps 4** and is just three minutes' walk from the town centre. Another well presented (and Grade II listed) terraced cottage in Woodbridge – **sleeping 3** – is *Treetops*. Both have private parking.

A few miles west of Woodbridge, in a very peaceful location on the owners' farm on the outskirts of Witnesham, *The Old Stable* is an absolutely pristine, quite superb, loving recreation of a traditional cottage, **sleeping 4 'plus 2'**, plus a dog. With underfloor heating and a number of original features retained, it is a gem, likely to be much appreciated by people with a sense of history.

We're increasingly fond of Orford. Despite being a fashionable place for second home owners it remains an unspoilt historic gem, seldom crowded. And we especially like it in autumn and winter. Happily the agency has a number of properties here. These include, very well located on the market place, *The Old Post Office*, expensively and tastefully renovated, **sleeping up to 8.** Another gem in Orford is *Oxo Cottage*, also **sleeping 8**, which has masses of period charm and also the bonus of inglenooks and a big garden. Both of these allow a dog.

Quite near Orford is *Forresters Cottage*, as might be imagined, on the edge of woodland: step out of the cottage and there are some memorable walks and cycling routes to enjoy. **Sleeping 4**, it has an open fire and pleasant rural views. A nice touch: (a first for us) the owners also have a beach hut at Felixstowe, which visitors can hire at £25 per day.

And just a few minutes' drive from Orford, close to the Snape Maltings, *No 8 Blyth Cottages* is a spacious semi-detached modern property handily opposite the village shop and **sleeping 5/6**. A dog is allowed. (Like several properties promoted by this agency, there is wireless broadband.)

Low Farm is on the outskirts of the pleasant village of Waldringfield beside open fields but is still within walking distance of river and pub. Here five properties have recently been converted from redundant single storey farm buildings to provide accommodation **for about 20 people** and have **Four 'Visit Britain' Stars**.

On the outskirts of Pettistree, Grove Stables is an excellent conversion, with a tennis court for hire. Sleeps four.

Shingle Street is a fascinating place, and Windy Ridge, sleeping six, offers a chance to get seriously 'away from it all'.

At Otley, about six miles from Woodbridge, *The Coach House* is a recently refurbished, self-contained cottage adjacent to the owners' delightful house and provides spacious accommodation **for 2**. A dog is allowed.

Between the villages of Brandeston and Cretingham, about five miles from historic Framlingham, is *The Potash*, a detached, mainly 16th century, thatched house. There is a large garden and views over fields and the upper reaches of the River Deben. The spacious sitting room has an open fire and a grand piano! **Sleeps 8** in two doubles and two twins.

Just two miles north of Aldeburgh lies Thorpeness, a charming seaside place, created as a holiday resort by the Victorians. *Westdene* is a handsome half timbered house **sleeping up to 8**. It is accessed via a little-used unmade track, and has an open fire. Also in Thorpeness are two substantial houses that will suit birdwatchers. *Bittern* and *Crossing Cottage* respectively **sleep 10 and 8**. Bittern is a handsome family house with a private jetty, is adjacent to the golf club and has a full size snooker table; there is easy access from both properties to an RSPB's bird reserve, and in fact *Crossing Cottage*, **sleeping 8**, is within it. All these allow one well-behaved dog.

We like the agency's handy A5 brochure detailing all the 70 or so properties on their books, and the fact that each cottage gets from five stars for 'excellent' to one for 'basic'.

For a copy of the brochure (always a good read) contact Penny at Mrs Jane Good (Holidays) Ltd, Little Bass, Ferry Quay, Woodbridge, Suffolk IP12 1BW. Telephone/fax: 01394 382770. Fax 07092 863089.

www.mrsjanegoodltd.co.uk   email: theoffice@mrsjanegoodltd.co.uk

Dunwich/Badingham
'The Cottage'/The Mill

At Badingham, close to the small castle-town of Framlingham, *The Mill* (Ref BQW) is a substantial house, worth seeking out for itself but, as a bonus, also just half an hour's drive from the coast. **Sleeping 8,** it has a woodburner and a spacious sitting room. By 'the coast', we are thinking mainly of one of our all-time favourite Suffolk places, which is Dunwich. There you'll find *The Cottage* (Ref

The Mill is a very special property, a memorable family base from which to enjoy the whole of magical Suffolk.

BEV), just 200 yards from a low cliff-top path above an uncrowded shingle beach. **Sleeping 6,** this pretty and very comfortable 19th-century cottage enjoys an idyllic location within half a mile of Dunwich village and its excellent inn, as well as the famous fish and chip shop close to the beach. Within its own peaceful and sunny lawned garden and four acres of private, open ground and woodland, the property benefits greatly from a private tennis court on site. It is surrounded by more woodland at the end of a leafy lane.

Details from English Country Cottages, Stoney Bank Road, Earby, Barnoldswick BB94 0AA. For bookings and brochures: 0845 268 0942.

www.english-country-cottages.co.uk

Bruisyard, near Framlingham map 1/9
Margaret's Cottage

On a silent sunny summer afternoon we turned off a little used country lane to a peaceful hideaway that has been created from the coach house, stables and outbuildings of nearby Cransford Hall. We loved the combination of tall, shady trees and manicured gardens, and much admired the Edwardian walled garden that originally belonged to 'the big house'. Effectively one wing of the owners' substantial house, Margaret's Cottage is a real charmer. We loved the light, bright, spacious

There's a shared swimming pool and a games room with snooker. A fine base from which to enjoy mid- and coastal Suffolk.

lemon-coloured main bedroom, the deep terracotta armchairs and the green sofa in the spacious sitting room, the well equipped solid oak kitchen, the wood-stove that guarantees a cosy autumn or winter break. There's an exceptional shared games room, with the joy of a full size snooker table, and access to a shared open-air heated pool. **Sleeps 4** in a double and a twin. Cost: about £350 to £650. Not suitable for pets; no smokers. Linen and towels included. Details from Mr and Mrs Roberts, The Clock House, Bruisyard, Saxmundham, Suffolk IP17 2EA. Telephone 01728 663512, fax 663301.

www.theclockhousebruisyard.co.uk email: cherianroberts@yahoo.co.uk

Westleton, near Aldeburgh
Middle Cottage

This absolute charmer, exuding 'tender loving care', is on the edge of one of our favourite Suffolk villages, almost exactly half-way between Southwold and Aldeburgh, and just two-and-a-half miles from the sea. Away from through-traffic, it feels very welcoming, with lots of colourful personal touches and a charming, south-facing conservatory/kitchen/dining-room that can be

Neat and pretty to look at, a delight inside. A rarity in a nicely preserved village.

sunny and warm even in winter. This struck us as a delightful spot for those cosy 'where shall we go today?' discussions and it leads in turn to a most interesting, unusual and rather private garden arrangement! Built in 1840, the cottage has been painstakingly renovated and retains many of the original features, including the crooked fireplace beam and latched cottage doors, carefully preserved. The interior is well thought out, elegant and stylish. The cottage **sleeps three** in two bedrooms and has full central heating and a woodburning stove.

Details from Richard Webster. Telephone: 01865 558596.

email: richardwebster@ntlworld.com
website: www.suffolkcottage.net

Cransford, near Framlingham
Wood Lodge map 1/8

A long-time favourite of ours, this is a 'cottage guide' classic, tucked away and quiet. We remember detouring from the charming and historic town of Framlingham for a recent revisit, and meeting cottage guide readers sunning themselves in the big lawned garden. We like the deep armchairs, the big wood stove guaranteed to create a warm and cosy atmosphere, off which the central heating runs, its masses of space, its character, its

A readers' favourite for many years, this is spacious, quiet, cosy and unpretentious.

history (it dates from about 1800), and its attractive pictures. It even boasts a complete Encyclopedia Britannica 'of a certain age'! The kitchen is well equipped, and includes a dishwasher, the dining room is inviting, bedrooms are spacious. **Sleeps 8 plus cot. 'Visit Britain' Three Stars**. TV and DVD/video, stereo and CD player. Dogs by arrangement. Free logs. Cost: £250 to £700. Linen and towels for hire. 'B & B' available. Details from Tim and Sarah Kindred, High House Farm, Cransford, near Woodbridge, Suffolk IP13 9PD. Telephone 01728 663461. Fax 663409.

www.highhousefarm.co.uk email:Woodlodge@highhousefarm.co.uk

Southwold and beyond
Suffolk Secrets*

We've been pleased to observe the gradual extension of the admirable Norfolk Country Cottages (see Page 43) into Suffolk – over 140 properties now – and have spent some time looking at properties in and near Southwold that come under the umbrella of that part of their Suffolk operation known as 'Suffolk Secrets'.

Firstly, just inland from the daytime hustle and bustle of Southwold (at Reydon) we admired an absolutely pristine modern house – many of our readers choose these in preference to 'olde worlde' properties. Finished to a very high standard, and under the same discriminating ownership, *Cherry Trees* – **sleeping 6** – is a very quietly situated jewel, with a superb standard of finish both inside and out. It has off-road parking and for example (just the sort of detail we would have expected) king sized beds in the main bedroom.

Almost close enough to the sea to try angling for fish, *Shrimp Cottage* is a pretty, pastel and white coloured 'bijou' delight, an absolute classic seaside cottage, complete with seasidey knick knacks and charming pictures. (We love one particular detail in the agency description: 'there's a sea view from the sitting room – even when you're seated'.) **Sleeps up to 4 'plus 1'** in two doubles and a small single – two rooms on the second floor via very steep, narrow stairs.

From a rear window of another property we were delighted to find ourselves gazing at one of the most famous views in Suffolk: Southwold across the marshes, hardly changed for a hundred years or more, an attractive skyline against a background of scudding clouds in a pale blue sky. *Blackshore Corner*, **sleeping 6** in three bedrooms and **'Visit Britain' Four Stars,** is a remarkable house, very close to the beach and next door to a pub of character. (On a summer day it's a bustling scene, but calmer and more beautiful 'after hours'.) The spacious sitting room is on the first floor to make the most of the *front* view of river and sea.

Details from Suffolk Secrets, The Old Water Tower, The Common, Southwold, Suffolk IP18 6TB. Telephone 01502 722717.

www.suffolk-secrets.co.uk

email: holidays@suffolk-secrets.co.uk

Thorpeness is a desirable, rather low-key seaside place about two miles to the north of Aldeburgh. This is No 2, The Dunes.

Westleton is one of our favourite Suffolk villages. (Among other good things there's a super bookshop.) This is Garden House.

Wortham, near Diss
Ivy House Farm

Very well placed for exploring much of the best of Suffolk and of Norfolk, these properties are pleasantly situated on the edge of the 2004 'Suffolk Village of the Year' (very close to the Norfolk border). Well back from a quiet road, there are three cottages in a row, a detached cottage and, across the yard, a historic Suffolk 'long

A much-liked set-up, on the rural edge of a Suffolk village by the Norfolk border.

house'. The fine detached modern cottage, built to high specifications, is designated as the owners' retirement home. **Sleeps 6.** The three places opposite have mainly open plan living areas and comfortable bedrooms. Each **sleeps 4.** The 'long house' is packed with character: we've long admired a cosy kitchen, an inglenook log fire in one sitting room, a superb dining room, spacious bedrooms (the 'master bedroom' is triple-aspect), good views from all bedrooms. **Sleeps up to 10.** The leisure centre has pool and table-tennis tables and a full-sized snooker table, and there's an excellent indoor swimming pool. Dogs welcome. Fuel, linen and towels included. TVs, videos, CD players. Cost: £260 to £1720. Details: Paul and Jacky Bradley, Ivy House Farm, Wortham, Diss, Norfolk IP22 1RD. Telephone/fax 01379 898395.

email: prjsbrad@aol.com
www.ivyhousefarmcottages.co.uk

Stanhoe, near Burnham Market map 1/19
Little Barwick

The location is superb. Just six miles from the coast, this attractive period home (Ref 18648) is one of those rare properties that are suitable for large-family holidays all year round. Surrounded by its own large lawned garden, with open views across unspoilt countryside, it is very comfortable and full of charm and character. For example, there are open fires, wood flooring, original

A super house, in a great location near Burnham Market, that sleeps fourteen.

panelled walls, and an impressive large stained glass window. The house **sleeps up to 14** in seven bedrooms. There are memorable beaches at Brancaster, Holkham and Wells-next-the-Sea, and it's only ten minutes to Burnham Market: one of the finest large villages in North Norfolk. Coastal path and RSPB salt marshes offer excellent walking and bird watching, and there are seal watching trips.

Details from Country Holidays, Spring Mill, Barnoldswick, Lancashire BB94 0AA. Bookings/brochures: 0845 268 0945.

Live search and book: www.country-holidays.co.uk

Norfolk, countywide
The Great Escape Holiday Company*

Virtually a household name in Norfolk, 'The Great Escape Holiday Company' is much loved by self-caterers who have an eye for properties of special character and style. They also seem to like the fact that most cottages and houses are used occasionally by the owners themselves.

We looked most recently at a couple of properties in Docking, where The Great Escape is is based. **Sleeping 6** in a king-sized double, a double and a twin, the former bakery that is *Oldholme* is, intriguingly, on three floors. At the very heart of this underrated village (opposite the village shop, in fact), it has a long and enclosed garden, mostly laid to grass. In the garden, quite close to the house, is a separate garden room with wet room and WC. This has a sofa bed that can be used by teenagers and this room can also accommodate a further Z-bed. The property is very suitable for two families holidaying together, especially with teenagers wishing to have their own space.

Also in Docking, *The Cowshed*, **sleeping 7,** bears absolutely no resemblance to its former incarnation! We thought it was a spacious delight, done to a very high standard. Among too many good things to mention in full we noticed a large terrace for *alfresco* dining, complete with ample outside furniture and barbecue, a very large sitting room with wood burning stove, 42-inch Plasma TV, DVD, mini-hifi centre. The kitchen is superb. There are four fine bedrooms. The generously sized master bedroom, for example, has an ensuite shower room and a dressing room that has been made into a self contained additional single room (with another pull out bed).

In Old Hunstanton, the 'posh end' of this much-loved seaside town, *The Seaside House* is a charmer. You would hardly believe it was once a council house! With a light and bright interior, and an emphasis on 'seaside colours', it is very modern but retains an open fire. There's a charming, lovingly tended garden partly shaded by apple trees, and sea views from some rooms. There's sufficient parking for three vehicles.

Properties of great character in North Norfolk, with some impressive interiors.

A Great Escape 'home from home': pretty as a picture, both inside and out.

Details/brochures from Marian Rose-Cartwright, The Great Escape Holiday Company, The Granary, Docking, Norfolk PE31 8LY. Telephone 01485 518717. Fax 518937.

www.thegreatescapeholiday.com

email: bookings@thegreatescapeholiday.com

Norfolk and beyond
Norfolk Country Cottages*

With about 340 properties covering the whole of Norfolk and North Suffolk, this hugely successful letting agency is based just off the well-preserved market place of the attractive small town of Reepham (visitors are welcome in the office). They can also be found at their newly opened office in The Old Crab Shop at Holt.

We have visited a number of pin-drop-quiet cottages in deeply rural inland corners of the county and some cosy and convenient cottages (and more modern houses) in the much sought after family resorts of the north coast.

Among inland villages we especially remember Aldborough. It was 'well

Woodmill Lodge is at Southrepps, near Mundesley. Sleeping 'five plus two', it's in an especially peaceful rural locaton.

Green Side Cottage is in one of our favourite villages, Thornham. Sleeping 4, it's just a short walk from the sea.

worth the detour', because we saw the delightful *Virginia Cottage*, right on the big village green: a picture book snapshot of 'olde England'. **Sleeping 5**, it's pristine and modern inside, but altogether inviting (the original very steep stairs remain!). We noticed among other good things stylish real-wood flooring, a wood burner and a king-sized bed.

In Reepham itself, just a few yards from where this enterprising agency is based, single-storeyed *Church View No 3* is an unexpectedly bright and light little hideaway **just for 2** owned by the antique dealers who live (and have their shop) next door. But it too is modern, not ancient, in style. A pleasant base, we thought, for the noticeable number of self caterers who like a small town or 'large village' base.

And then to an absolutely top notch recent conversion close to but completely separate from the owners' house. This is *The Old Forge* at Frettenham, near Coltishall. Done to the highest specification, it has **Five Stars** from **'Visit Britain'** (we'd have thought Ten!), combining a good degree of 'cottageness' with an impressive range of mod cons. There's a very comfortable beamed sitting room, with a deep sofa and armchairs, and a really charming big kitchen/diner. **Sleeps 8.**

Details/brochure available from Norfolk Country Cottages, Carlton House, Market Place, Reepham, Norfolk NR10 4JJ. Telephone 01603 871872. Fax 870304.

You can check property details and availability online at:
www.norfolkcottages.co.uk
email: info@norfolkcottages.co.uk

Castle Acre, near King's Lynn
Heron Cottage

Castle Acre is a little gem: very much 'in Norfolk' but in the south of the county, and easy to get to. The famous coast is only about 45 minutes' drive, Sandringham say 25. On recent autumn day we met the new owners here. They have transformed an already pleasant cottage, just a few feet from a fine 13th century 'bailey gate' at the heart of the historic village into a delight, *A recent upgrading of a fairly modern house in a historic location.* with for example cool cream walls, pleasant 'seagrass' matting, a top-flight kitchen-diner, a bigger than average bed in the main bedroom, a top of the range shower (there's no bath), an open fire in the sitting room that runs the central heating, plus storage radiators. There is (such a luxury in this sort of location) a lock-up garage, plus a small garden yard.

Sleeps 4 in a double and a twin. Not suitable for dogs. Linen included but not towels. Cost: about £190 to £350. Available all year; short breaks possible. Further details available from Marian Sanders: telephone (in France) 00 33 546040166.

email: marianatmoreau@hotmail.com

Castle Acre, near King's Lynn
Peddars Cottage map 1/22

In the autumn of 2006 we revisited this cosy, rather 'traditional' cottage, used occasionally (as many readers like) by the owners themselves. Fitting well into its historic surroundings (see our photo!) the house has had an ongoing makeover that includes a refurbished and much admired honey-coloured bathroom and shower and redecorated bedrooms, with new soft furnishings. The cosy interior incorporates an

Castle Acre is just off the beaten track, and this too makes a delightful base...

open fire, repro oak furniture, a traditional 'cottage suite', old local prints, a modern fitted pine kitchen. There are attractive table and standard lamps and lots of books. There are carpets virtually throughout. TV. One pet possible. Garage. Linen and towels included. **Sleeps 6** in a double, a twin and an adult-sized two-bunk-bedroom. Cost: £300 to £350. Details: Mrs Angela Swindell, St Saviour's Rectory, St Saviour, Jersey, Channel Isles JE2 7NP. Telephone 01534 736679. Fax 727480.

www.castleacre.org also **www.castleacre.org.uk**
email: angelaswindell@googlemail.com

Burnham Thorpe
The Corner Pightle

A classic Norfolk country cottage situated – better yet – in a famous village.

Among the many peaceful, unspoilt villages of rural Norfolk Burnham Thorpe – birthplace of Lord Nelson – could well be our personal favourite. It's very close to Burnham Market, but half-hidden away. We recently visited this traditional, cosy, rather rambling house in pristine flint set off prettily in white and with one of those pantiled roofs that add so much to the charm of the region, about 20 minutes' drive from, say, Hunstanton and just about three miles from the famous sands at Holkham. **Sleeping up to 6** in four bedrooms, overlooking the village green towards a pub named after Lord Nelson, it has so many good things going for it, such as a safely enclosed south-west facing garden, a wood-burning stove, a downstairs bedroom for convenience, a number of original beams. As with the Hunstanton properties in the same ownership (see Page 58) it is sympathetically lit, comfortably furnished and full of tender loving care. Linen and towels included. Not suitable for dogs. Cost: about £350 to £750.

Details from Nicky and Angus Runciman, 8 Luard Rd, Cambridge CB2 2PJ. Telephone 01223 246382.

www.sunnyhunny.com   email: angusrunciman@hotmail.com

Houghton Hall, near Sandringham
The Water House, South Lodge, Bunkers Hill

Bunker's Hill is just one of the delightful holiday cottages on the Houghton estate.

Houghton Hall (**map 1/27**) stands in many-acred splendour about seven miles from Royal Sandringham and about fifteen from the north coast at Holkham, Brancaster and Burnham. With two holiday cottages, one as pretty a gatehouse as you'll ever find, only recently available, this is a peaceful holiday base. Most of the time cottage guests will feel they have the vast estate, the woods and the herds of deer to themselves: delightful. The cottages themselves are real charmers. While 'bijou', recently available *South Lodge,* **sleeping 4**, is a gem, we'd find it hard to decide – for peace and quiet and a memorable escape from everyday cares – between *Bunker's Hill* and *The Water House.* These respectively **sleep 4** and **5**. Among many memorable features we appreciated comfortable 'cottagey' interiors, a sense of colour – we love the painted wooden furniture – the 'country antiques', the well chosen lamps and pictures, the rugs – all combined with a feel for history.

See the Stately Holiday Homes feature on **Pages 22-23.**

Brancaster
Sussex Farm Holiday Cottages

Many years in this guide, the five cottages at Sussex Farm are ideally located. One reader who stayed recently thinks so. She wrote: 'We love the way you can have a day on the coast, perhaps on a sandy beach, and then leave all the crowds behind to escape to your own quiet little hideaway among the trees'. There's the detached *Park Drive*, *The Pheasantry* and *One Hundred Acre*,

Both deep in the country and near the sea.

and the semi-detached *Apple Tree* and *Beech Tree*, **sleeping 10, 8, 7, 8 and 8** respectively. They are spacious and full of character. Two are suitable for people of limited mobility. We have always found the cottages clean and tidy, with original features that add to the charm, with good carpets, microwave ovens, radio cassette players, washing machines, TVs and videos. All have dishwashers and large freezers. All have central heating *and* open fires (logs included). Linen and towels included. Dogs (one per property) welcome. Cost: about £450 to £1200. Short breaks welcome. Details/brochure from Jane Thompson, The Hall, Brancaster, Norfolk PE31 8AF. Telephone and fax: 01485 210000.

www.tbfholidayhomes.co.uk email: info@tbfholidayhomes.co.uk

Blakeney
Jenny's Cottage map 1/28

This cottage is a rare (and inexpensive) jewel at the heart of not-to-be-missed Blakeney. It is one of the most loved places on the North Norfolk coast, notable for the beauty of the tidal shore, the walks to Blakeney Point, the birdlife, boat trips to see the seals. Comfortable holiday cottages are hard to come by here, but happily this is a small-scale, Grade II listed, flint and tiled gem (dating from 1839), with a pretty courtyard garden that in summer overflows with hollyhocks. In the heart of the village, near a welcoming pub and a well stocked shop, it is

A rare chance to stay in the centre of famous Blakeney.

ideal for a couple with a small child (a double and small single). It's full of charm and comfort: a wood burner in an inglenook fireplace, well arranged lighting. Though space is limited, the main bedroom, via steep and narrow stairs, is quite a good size, and there is even a bath (we approve) in which serious walkers can ease their aching bones. We thought this would make a good and inexpensive base for a winter holiday. Well behaved dogs are welcome. Linen and towels can be hired. TV. Non smokers only. Cost: about £200 to £350. Further details from Simon Flint, Sherwood, Sandy Lane, South Wootton, King's Lynn, Norfolk PE30 3NX. Telephone 01553 672208.
email: Simon@flint2.fsnet.co.uk

Brancaster Staithe
Vista Cottage/Carpenter's Cottage

We have had so many enthusiastic reader reports about these two well cared for cottages, memorably situated right on the North Norfolk coast. They glow with 'tender loving care'. Each has **'Visit Britain' Three Stars**: we'd have thought Four.

In both *Vista* and *Carpenter's* you can almost reach out and touch one of the most beautiful coastlines in Britain. To be exact, you can walk down the cottage gardens right on to the salty marshes and join the coastal footpath, or make your way somewhat more directly towards the water.

From the back windows of both the properties in the ownership of the Smith family, muddy inlets dotted with yachts and fishing boats snake as prettily as in any sailor's favourite picture out towards the North Sea. Bring your binoculars!

Being on the A149 Cromer to Hunstanton coast road (mostly local or day time traffic) they are not remote or irritatingly difficult to find after a long

Vista has a big garden, unforgettable views out to sea and (it's not always the case with coastal properties) immediate access to the water. It's also very cosy...

Carpenter's (also with some marvellous views) is a pretty 'upside down' cottage for 2.

journey. There is a patio with a gas barbecue, and two good pubs nearby.

In Vista Cottage, **sleeping 6**, we met a family who were enjoying spending time in a 'family-friendly' kitchen/diner with original stone flags and excellent fittings, such as washing machine and dishwasher. There is a very cosy sitting room with open fire. On the first floor, via a steep staircase, there is a double, a twin and a bunk bedded room (adult sized). The house is well carpeted and there is plenty of heating.

Next door is Carpenter's Cottage, set back from the road by a small, safely enclosed courtyard. In the owners' family for over a hundred years, it is a delightful 'upside down' house with a sitting room/kitchen/diner on the first floor and a very cosy, 'compact' double bedded room on the ground floor. The original fireplace has been restored: a lovely focal point on an autumn or spring evening, and there is a well planned window seat from which to enjoy those fabulous views. **Sleeps 2**.

Dogs are welcome in both. Linen and towels are included. Cost: approximately £240 to £750. (Pro-rata off season short breaks are available, for a minimum of three nights.) TVs.

Details from Mrs G J Smith, Dale View, Main Road, Brancaster Staithe, King's Lynn, Norfolk PE31 8BY. Telephone/fax 01485 210497.

South Raynham, near Fakenham
Idyllic Cottages@Vere Lodge

This is a lovely place. We've stayed here from time to time, and it is always a joy: the absolute peace and quiet, the beautifully kept gardens (especially the manicured, sweeping lawns) the pristine tennis court, the 'Secret Garden', the indoor swimming pool, and more.

Most recently, we stayed in *Thyme Cottage*, **sleeping 6**, which stands right by the front entrance (but there's hardly any traffic on the little lane by which one approaches Vere Lodge). This most welcoming west-facing cottage is especially memorable for the fabulous sunsets seen from the upstairs sitting room. It adjoins *Dahlia*, which has the advantage of an upstairs en-suite bathroom, and which also **sleeps 6**. Both have their own sitting-out patios.

During another recent visit we stayed in *Pump Cottage*, a private-seeming and plushly comfortable **Four Star** delight **just for 2**. Though it has no garden, it looks on to lawns. It has a most cosy sitting room and a charming, rather 'feminine' double bedroom.

Family members staying at the same time with two small children greatly enjoyed *Honeysuckle Cottage*. Their main reason for liking it was not hard to discover: they were literally a 30-second patter of tiny wet feet from the doors of the pool!

There is a magic to this place which even the detailed and colourful

Vere Lodge is a place for all seasons.   *Rose Cottage is handsome and relaxing.*

brochure fails to capture. Children relish the eight acres of freedom, the company of new friends, the daily feeding-round of the many tame animals and birds. Parents can relax, knowing their young ones are safe and happy.

An impressive leisure centre is the icing on the Vere Lodge cake. There's a large, very warm covered pool (36 feet by 18), with a shallow end with steps for children, and a slide.

There's a sauna, solarium, games room with table tennis and pool table, and a centrally heated lounge looking on to the pool. Doors open on to two grass and paved sun patios, so that on hot summer days this effectively becomes an open air pool.

There's also a small shop, a launderette and a range of home-cooked frozen foods. If you *are* considering a break between, say, October and March, you'll find the pool as warm then (80° plus) as in high summer, and all the other facilities are available.

We have always appreciated the 'little touches' – good pictures, stylish flower arrangements, pretty ornaments – which help to set Vere Lodge out of the ordinary. Not surprisingly, Vere Lodge enjoys a high tourist board grading.

Secret Garden and *The Robin's Nest* are two spacious single-storey cottages built on what was once the kitchen garden to Vere Lodge. We thought them delightful, noting especially masses of space and privacy, deep sofas, good carpets, a combination of character and comfort. Both are extremely quiet and secluded with about half an acre each of garden, mainly lawn, surrounded by high flint walls. They **sleep 6** in three bedrooms – one double, two twins – and have an impressive lounge with an open fire. They are approached via Church Lane, a narrow and barely-used lane which forms the southern boundary to Vere Lodge and leads only to the tiny church and former rectory. On the other side of the lane lie the leisure centre and the seven acre grounds.

The other properties are more part of the Vere Lodge 'family'. *Apple Cottage* is a spacious and entirely self-contained ground-floor apartment, plush and comfortable, which faces on to a large landscaped courtyard. Suitable for retired couples, young couples with a baby, or the elderly or partially disabled. **Sleeps 3**.

The Dolls House is a small, simple 'budget' cottage, the ground floor of which was once a part of a gun room. Complete with huge doll, it looks out over lawns to the horseshoe of beeches and flowering cherries beyond. It is warm, comfortable and compact. **Sleeps 4**.

Apple, suitable for the partially disabled.   *Children and animals are welcome here.*

Dove Cottage is furnished to a standard not generally found in a holiday cottage. It has panoramic views of the grounds, woods, and surrounding countryside from the upstairs living room which opens on to its own completely private roof-terrace. We very much like the cool, soft, grey blue ambiance, and the open fireplace. **Sleeps 2 plus 2**.

Garden Wing is undoubtedly the most popular of all the cottages: ground-floor throughout, it is especially suitable for the disabled or indeed people of limited mobility. The large and elegant sitting-room looks out over the croquet lawn to woodland beyond. **Sleeps 4**.

Lavender Cottage, large and west facing, once housed coaches and a harness room. It is a long raised-level cottage, outside which is a large terrace screened by a hedge, with a flight of steps up to the front door. It **sleeps 6**.

It's furnished in log-cabin style, but to standards such as original log-cabins never enjoyed with, for example, carpets on polished wood floors. **Sleeps 6**. *Possum's*, once a full-size billiard-room, is a spacious and unusual apartment called after Miss 'Possum' Smith, who cared for the Bowlby children for over thirty years. Tall Georgian windows face on to formal yew-hedges and flower borders flood-lit by night. **Sleeps 3**. *Pump Cottage* was purpose-built and 'incorporates the lessons learned from 25 years' experience of self-catering'. All the accommodation is on the ground floor and is suitable for the elderly or partially disabled. Open fire-place here too. **Sleeps 2**. *Rose Cottage*, the largest of all the cottages, is south-facing and therefore very sunny, with its own private walled garden. It is bright and airy, with deep, comfy armchairs and sofa, an open fire and a downstairs shower and loo. **Sleeps 7**. *Rowan* and *Honeysuckle* are an identical pair of 19th century cottages. An unusual feature is the central fireplace, raised for the protection of young children, with a log-burning fire facing into the lounge and behind it an electric fire to warm the dining room. Both are furnished in 'country-style', with a raised south-facing terrace in front of each.

Among the many things they do so well at Vere Lodge are short breaks in autumn, winter, spring or early summer. To enhance that 'baby it's cold outside' mood, several cottages have open fires. Better yet, prices even in these very comfortable properties for a three-day break – starting or finishing on any day of the week – can be as low as £18 per night per person (6 persons), which includes the use of the leisure centre.

Vere Lodge is something of an animal sanctuary, too, delightful for young

Lavender Cottage once housed coaches.   *The most popular cottage is Garden Wing.*

children. At feeding time (9.00 am daily) there are freshly-laid eggs to be gathered, often from under an indignant hen. In the centre paddock, tame and gentle miniature Angora goats stand on their hind legs against the fence awaiting their turn, while Mingo the donkey, and Toby the docile pony, await theirs.

Children will also love the Enchanted Wood. We certainly do, but we won't spoil the surprise!

Dogs are welcome, and remote-control videos, televisions and clock radios are standard throughout. Details and a copy of an impressive full colour brochure from Vere Lodge, South Raynham, near Fakenham, Norfolk NR21 7HE. Telephone 01328 838261. Fax 838300.

www.verelodge.co.uk

email: major@verelodge.co.uk

Bylaugh, near East Dereham
Bylaugh Hall Holiday Homes

Readers of our guide have enthused about these. Deep in rural Norfolk, Bylaugh lies amid unspoiled farmland where the restoration of a fine country house goes hand in hand with the creation to a superb standard of substantial self-catering properties. Large groups can stay, yet smaller parties have privacy. To appreciate the range and quality of accommodation, look on the website

A fabulous base from which to explore deeply rural inland Norfolk...

for *The Coachman's Lodge, The Brewery, The Stables, The Smithy, The Courtyard Mews, The Front Mews* and, separate from the others, *The Manor,* a superb modern house that **sleeps up to 17,** *Old Heath House* (**sleeps 17**) and *The Oaks* cottages. Individual houses taken together can accommodate groups of up to 80. Note the splendid main hall and Orangery for a super wedding, party or conference venue. Adjoining the main hall and Orangery, the new Wintergarden restaurant is perfect for those who wish to take a night off self catering!

Details from Bylaugh Hall, Bylaugh Park, East Dereham, Norfolk NR20 4RL.Telephone 01362 688121. Fax 08701623993.

www.littlebigben.com or www.bylaugh.com email: info@bylaugh.com

---

Tunstead, near Wroxham   Colour section, Page 1
Old Farm Cottages map 1/34

Via quiet, ever more rural country lanes, it was a pleasure recently to revisit these beautifully converted and painstakingly run former barns. They make a fairly central point in rural Norfolk from which to explore the Broads – Wroxham, for example, is close – the exquisite North Norfolk coast, the more family-orientated east, the city of Norwich itself, and even

Peaceful Norfolk is all around, but the coast and the Broads are handy...

more beyond. A number of readers have commented on how much they enjoy the covered indoor pool at the end of a day's touring. This excellent pool is set off nicely by a fitness room, a spa, a solarium and a games room. Each of the six properties has its own enclosed patio and barbecue. There's a high degree of privacy in these spacious, pristinely cared-for conversions, but children also have the chance to make new friends. **Sleep 2 to 6**. Linen included. Dogs welcome in most. Cost: from (short breaks) £266 to (full weeks) £390 to £920. **'Visit Britain' Four Stars**.

For details, telephone 01692 536612.

www.oldfarmcottages.com   email: mail@oldfarmcottages.fsnet.co.uk

Hunstanton, Brancaster and beyond
Norfolk Holiday Homes*

So many of our readers have come to know and love Norfolk by booking properties through Norfolk Holiday Homes. In the 26 years in which we've featured the agency we've had nothing but glowing reports, *and have never once had any kind of complaint.* We've stayed in several properties, and never seen a dud. This would be admirable in a private cottage set-up – in an agency of any size it is remarkable.

Norfolk Holiday Homes specialises in the north west corner of the county: fine sandy beaches, tranquil villages, lonely church towers, the traditional seaside resort of Hunstanton, excellent bird watching and much more.

There are several properties in Old Hunstanton, which has all the advantages of a slightly old fashioned seaside atmosphere with easy access not only to a glorious sandy beach of its own but also to the bright lights of the lively 'family resort' of Hunstanton-proper, with its new pier.

Spindrift, for example, is literally a minute's walk from the beach, and also pubs, restaurants and shops. There is a pretty, enclosed courtyard garden as a bonus, and the property **sleeps 5 'plus 1'**.

Sandbanks is a superb, large, detached family residence (**sleeping 8**, on the outskirts of the town in a very desirable area, yet within easy reach of the cliff tops and the beach). There are rural views from the front and distant sea views from the rear first floor rooms.

Ashdale House is an exceptionally comfortable detached house tucked away in quiet surroundings, but still close to the beach, golf course and other holiday amenities. The garden is fully enclosed and there is ample parking. Furnished to a very high standard throughout, the property offers spacious accommodation **for 7 people**.

Within a newly refurbished, large three-storeyed Victorian terraced house proudly overlooking the Esplanade Gardens with magnificent, panoramic views across the Wash, *Serenity* is an apartment offering spacious ground

Close to beaches and an RSPB nature reserve, Sybil Cottage – built in 1908 – is a super house for families, sleeping eight.

The Old Coastguard Lookout is an extraordinary place: you'll have to get your booking in early! It sleeps three.

floor accommodation all on one level. It has gas central heating throughout, and is fully carpeted. **Sleeping 2 'plus 2'**, with the option of a further is furnished to a very comfortable, modern standard and has retained some of its Victorian character and charm.

Finally, but still only scratching the surface, *The Old Coastguard Lookout,* overlooking the clifftops near the lighthouse, has been thoughtfully restored since it was built in 1906 as a Marconi Wireless Station. It has associations with both World Wars, was once a maritime museum and spent its 'last years' as the Coastguard Lookout. It has unique accommodation on three storeys, and enjoys superb, uninterrupted panoramic views of the Wash and the coast. There is immediate access to the wide sandy beaches that make this one of the most popular resorts in the east of England, but you are well away from the brasher part of the town, with its fish and chip shops and amusement arcades. **Sleeps 3**.

Just off the village centre of Holme (extensive sandy beaches, with the RSPB nature reserve just down the road) *Sybil Cottage*, **sleeping 8**, is a lovely, semi-detached carrstone cottage built in 1908, with an acre of well-cared-for woodland gardens to the rear. An enchanted fairyland awaits visitors beyond the children's play area, with a covered pond, fairy lights and small woodland walk.

And just off the village green at Thornham is *Linzel Cottage*, a superb, 17th century cottage that has been tastefully restored to a high standard to reveal its original beauty and charm. **Sleeps 6** (See also Page 58).

It's worth remembering that even a cottage that on the map appears to be well inland is probably just a few minutes' drive from the coast. Some coast! The wide sandy beaches, typically set off by pine trees, are remarkable, but especially so because they're quiet even at the height of the season.

There is lots going to appeal to the whole family: children will especially like the entertainments at Thursford, the North Norfolk steam-railway, and the narrow gauge railway that puffs through idyllic, unspoiled pastureland between Wells-next-the-Sea and Walsingham.

Dogs are welcome in over half the properties on the agency's books, and several cottages have open fires, which can be the makings of an autumn or winter break. Also, a range of short breaks and special discounts may be available. All properties are inspected and graded by **'Visit Britain'**, and a number have ground floor accommodation suitable for disabled people.

Ashdale House, in Old Hunstanton, is exceptionally comfortable. It is close to the beach and the golf course.

Interior of Sandbanks, on the outskirts of Hunstanton. There are rural views and sea views, and - usefully - it sleeps eight.

An exceptionally good brochure, fully illustrated in colour, is available from Sandra Hohol, Norfolk Holiday Homes, 62 Westgate, Hunstanton, Norfolk PE36 5EL. Telephone 01485 534267/fax 535230.

www.norfolkholidayhomes-birds.co.uk

email: shohol@birdsnorfolkholidayhomes.co.uk

Horning (Norfolk Broads)
Little River View

Of all the bustling villages that are a focal point
for visitors to the Norfolk Broads (it's not all
lonely creeks and wildfowl-haunted marshes),
our own favourite is Horning. And at its very
heart, opposite a 100 year old pub of character
and handy for a range of village shops, stands a
pretty, charming cottage that – always a good
sign – is occasionally used by the owners themselves. We noted two comfy, deep sofas in the
very cosy sitting room, a 'proper' bath in the
(downstairs) bathroom, a spacious double and
twin bedroom on the first floor, an inviting
kitchen/diner. This is one of those places in
which the owners' concern for their guests'

*As neat and pretty a cottage
as we've seen in East Anglia.*

comfort is apparent, with, for example, books, games, information folders,
etc. Note too that landlubbers may hire a day boat nearby to get a flavour of
life on the Broads. This is a rarity in such a sought-after location! **Sleeps 4.**
TV/video/DVD. River views. Not suitable for pets. Cost: about £219 to
£539. Short breaks. Linen, towels and gas/electricity included. No smoking.
Details from Victoria Free. Telephone 07801 288822 or 07759 125919.

www.littleriverview.co.uk   email: info@littleriverview.co.uk

---

Horning map 1/35
Riverside Rentals

Any thatched cottage in Norfolk will be
sought-after by self-caterers. Put it right
by the water in the Norfolk Broads, and
people will go into raptures. *Box End*
(**sleeps 6 'plus 2'**) and *Willow Fen*
(**sleeps 6 'plus 2'**) are two thatched
beauties (Box End is pretty enough to
feature on our cover!) within a quartet

Sit and watch the boats go by...

of properties in the same ownership; the
other two are *Willow Lodge* (**sleeps 8 'plus 2'**) and *Little Wiluna*, which is a
smaller property within the grounds of Wiluna, a fine, imposing riverside
property. Add to all their considerable charms the fact that the three principal properties have substantial river frontages, moorings – day boats can
easily be hired locally – and gardens, and that they all have light, bright airy
rooms, and you have places 'worth the detour'. Also, pets are welcome by
arrangement in the three biggest properties, and each has bath *and* shower.

Linen is included. TV and DVD. Cost: about £215 to £1450. Details from
Grebe Island Leisure, Wiluna, Ferry Cott Lane, Horning, Norfolk NR12
8PP. Telephone/fax 01438 869489.

email: info@goodcottageguide.com

Clippesby (Norfolk Broads National Park)
Clippesby Holiday Cottages

With country views and a wheelchair ramp to the sun deck (**sleep 6**), there are three excellent *Pinelodges* in a woodland setting. We also like the quiet bungalows that overlook fields (two **sleep 4**, two **sleep 6**), and have admired two larger cottages (each **sleeps 8**) along with the two-storeyed *Clocktower Apartments* (**sleeping 4**) with first-floor sundecks looking on to gardens.

In the country but not far from the sea...

There's a heated open air pool, grass tennis courts, a family bar/restaurant serving evening meals, play areas, a small shop and coffee shop and an 18-hole mini-golf course. TVs, central heating and bed-linen; some have open fires too. (Tucked away among trees in a different landscaped area is a **'Visit Britain' Five Star** Holiday Park, with the David Bellamy Gold Award for Conservation.) Cottages etc are **'Visit Britain' Four Stars**. Cost: from £235 to £949, including bed-linen, electricity and heating. Brochure from the Lindsay family, Clippesby Hall, Clippesby, Norfolk NR29 3BL. Telephone 01493 367800; fax 367809.

www.clippesby.com or **www.discoverthebroads.com**
email: holidays@clippesby.com

Stanhoe, near Burnham Market   map 1/31
Post Office Cottage

From Docking, they said, look out for the cottage on the left just after the duck pond. Some duck pond! It's huge, a real eye-opener. But so is Post Office Cottage (Ref CSL) – a real gem in fact. It was originally three cottages, which always makes for an interesting interior. End-on to the road, therefore nice and quiet, with a garden and enclosed parking, we thought it a family house of great

An increasingly rare example of a 'traditional cottage', and super inside.

character. We liked the original paintings, the very comfortable sitting room, with open fire, that looks out on to the garden, and the charming kitchen-diner, with woodburner – not 'last word', but all the more attractive for that. Very usefully, there's a double room (zip-link six-foot wide bed: excellent), at ground floor level plus a bunk bedded room. Upstairs there are two very cosy double bedrooms, one of which charmingly has its own staircase from the ground floor, and a twin. **Sleeps 8 'plus 2'** in total.

Details from English Country Cottages, Stoney Bank Road, Earby, Barnoldswick BB94 0AA. For bookings and brochures, telephone 0845 268 0942.

www.english-country-cottages.co.uk

Norfolk Coast
Sowerbys Holiday Cottages*

Readers have consistently spoken well of this medium-sized agency of about 90 properties, based in sought-after Burnham Market. One in particular praised *Fern Cottage*, a real gem in that village that **sleeps 5**. Places that have caught our eye include *Coastguards' Cottage* in Thornham (**sleeps 10**). It's in an idyllic position on the village green *and* overlooks the marshes and the sea! At Holme-next-the-Sea we thought *Hope Cottage*,

We absolutely fell for Coastguards! It's in an enviable spot, and most inviting.

sleeping 2, and also near the water, an exquisite recent conversion. It's at the end of a tiny lane but is still within the village. In so-chic Burnham Market itself we were much impressed by brand new *Orchard House*, **sleeping 10**, in a leafy enclave on the edge of the village, and, just off the main street but very quiet, a superb 'hideaway' used from time to time by the owners themselves (which our readers like) called *Aviaries Barn*, **sleeping 2**. Further details from Sowerby's Holiday Cottages, Market Place, Burnham Market, Norfolk PE31 8HD. Telephone 01328 730880, fax 730522.

www.sowerbysholidaycottages.co.uk
email info@sowerbysholidaycottages.co.uk

Wiveton, near Blakeney
Bones Cottage map 1/38

Tucked well away but very handy for the fabulous North Norfolk coast, this little cottage sleeps **just 2 people**. In a blissfully quiet and peaceful setting, it is only about ten minutes' very pleasant walk from the hauntingly beautiful saltmarshes at Cley and twenty minutes from the quay at exquisite Blakeney. There is also a good pub just a short walk away. The owners' home (bed and

Private, inexpensive, close to one of the best parts of the coast.

breakfast also available) is adjacent, but the cottage feels very private. There is a neat, rather cosy kitchen/diner, a shower-room and, in short, a charming atmosphere. Among other details we liked the big window that seems to light up the whole cottage. It looks on to the front garden and gets the sun all day long. Note too that the cottage has its own driveway. Altogether, we thought *Bones* would make an excellent base from which to enjoy the coast, and it is notably inexpensive. Bed-linen is provided.

Small TV. Not suitable for dogs. Cost: about £230 to £300. Further details from Mrs Stocks, Bones Cottage, Hall Lane, Wiveton, Holt, Norfolk NR25 7TG. Telephone 01263 740840.

www.bonescottage.co.uk

Holt
No 6 Carpenters Cottages

In this guide for 26 years, with never a complaint! Conveniently situated, this most attractive flint and pantiled terraced cottage lies close to the centre of Holt, a small Georgian town of character. There are good pubs and restaurants, two department stores, antique shops and two fishmongers – good for local crabs! Best

A cosy, very convenient town house that is only twenty minutes from the exceptional North Norfolk coast.

of all is the easy access to the coast (delightful Blakeney is only about ten minutes away) and to such attractions as Felbrigg, Blickling and Holkham Hall. There's a well-equipped kitchen and a bright sitting/dining room, informal, comfortable and altogether inviting, opening on to a secluded walled garden area. The cottage is often used by the owners themselves, and its good standards reflect this fact. We spotted well chosen local pictures, books, including a number about Norfolk, board games and puzzles. The cottage **sleeps 3** in a good-sized twin room and a smallish single.

Cost: about £165 to £345. Small, well behaved dogs are welcome. Further details are available from Mrs Sally Beament, 36 Avranches Avenue, Crediton, Devon EX17 2HB. Telephone 01363 773789.

email: sallybeament@hotmail.com

East Rudham, near Fakenham map 1/41
18 The Green

We've stayed in many Norfolk holiday cottages, and enjoyed a few days in 2007 in this pristine, neat, clean and well equipped property. (We had friends staying near South Raynham, a 20 minute bike ride from the cottage.) The demand for Norfolk holiday cottages is highest when they are close to the coast, but East Rudham is only half an hour from, say, Wells-next-the

Clean and tidy, with everything 'just so'.

Sea or Hunstanton. It's also just 15 minutes' drive from pleasant Fakenham. Though it's close to the A148 King's Lynn to Cromer road the cottage is set well back from that across East Rudham's village green. Like many a Norfolk cottage No 18 and the adjacent No 17 (they're semi-detached) are very well kitted out. They have three smallish (double) bedrooms, a bathroom with bath and over-bath shower, and central heating. Two dogs per cottage are welcome, and there's ample parking.

Details from Norfolk Country Cottages, Carlton House, Market Place, Reepham, Norfolk NR10 4JJ. Telephone 01603 871872/fax 870304.

email: info@norfolkcottages.co.uk www.norfolkcottages.co.uk

Hunstanton
Northernhay/Highland House

Northernhay is one of our own all-time seaside favourites, a super family house in the 'traditional' resort of Hunstanton: amusement arcades, fish and chips, children running free on a super sandy beach. Parts of the town are quite chic, with good golf, cosy pubs and fine family houses that have easy access to the sands. A

Northernhay is one of the handsomest houses in what is known affectionately as 'Sunny Hunny' – see website details...

spacious and sunny Edwardian villa within a cliff-top conservation area, Northernhay has lots of original features, a conservatory and some bedrooms from which you can see the sea. Most usefully **sleeping 10** in four double bedrooms and a children's double-bunk room, it has a neat garden and secure parking for two cars. *Highland House*, with gardens front and back, is equally full of character and style. Also **sleeping 10** (in six bedrooms: two doubles, two twins and two singles) it combines a number of original features with modern comforts, such as a part-'island' kitchen with glass-fronted cupboard doors and two sumptuous family bathrooms. Linen and bath towels are included. Not suitable for pets. Cost: £375 to £875. Details from Nicky and Angus Runciman, 8 Luard Road, Cambridge CB2 2PJ. Telephone 01223 246382.

www.sunnyhunny.com email: angusrunciman@hotmail.com

Thornham, near Brancaster map 1/46
Linzel Cottage

A feather in the cap of the outstanding cottage letting agency Norfolk Holiday Homes, this is a delight. We have stayed here – an autumn break – and remember so many good things about it: the cosy double-aspect 'Smallbone' kitchen/diner, the small but charming dining room, the comfortable sitting room, with a woodburner. There are three

A warm and welcoming family cottage.

bedrooms: a double, a twin and pair of bunk beds. There's a small, enclosed sun-trap garden, a garage and plenty of parking outside the cottage in the lane. (Thornham gets a fair bit of through-traffic on the very scenic A149, but Linzel lies quietly up a little lane off that road.) The village-proper effectively starts about a hundred yards away, and via that one comes to the delightful old village green, from which there is footpath access to the marshes and, beyond, the sea. 'Visit Britain' **Four Stars**.

* We can recommend the nearby Orange Tree restaurant (a converted pub). Norfolk Holiday Homes, 62 Westgate, Hunstanton, Norfolk PE36 5EL. Telephone 01485 534267/fax 535230.

www.norfolkholidayhomes-birds.co.uk
email: shohol@birdsnorfolkholidayhomes.co.uk

Cambridgeshire/Lincolnshire/ Nottinghamshire

In our opinion these three counties represent one of eastern and middle England's best kept secrets. We're fond of Cambridgeshire (that exquisite 'city within a university', the vast skies above the Fens, the stark beauty of Ely cathedral), Lincolnshire (the endless sandy beaches, its own great cathedral at Lincoln, the usually deserted Wolds) and Nottinghamshire (deep, dark Sherwood forest, grand stately homes, memories of perhaps our finest novelist, D H Lawrence). Indeed, one of Lawrence's childhood homes is, against all the odds, available as a holiday home. In this corner of England, very soon after you leave main roads you are surrounded by quiet, rural, low key landscapes dotted with small market towns and sleepy villages. We think of Stamford, and marvellous Burghley House on its outskirts; of the genteel but not stuffy little town of Woodhall Spa, of climbing to the top of Boston Stump for marvellous panoramic views. On the coast, 'bracing' Skegness has a certain chic, and the RSPB reserve at nearby Gibraltar Point has an unforgettable atmosphere.

Denton, near Stilton (Cambridgeshire)
Orchard Cottage map 1/49

People who appreciate the classic picture-book country cottage will find this idyllic. Full of character and style (it's well out of earshot of any main roads, but easy to get to), it combines a powerful sense of the past with lots of comfort and warmth. It's like something from an idealised landscape painting by artists of 'the Norwich School'. In a historic part of 'the Shires' (peaceful stone villages, pubs with log fires,

Well away from main roads but actually quite accessible and not remote, this is one of our all-time favourite finds...

perhaps the ghostly echo of a hunting horn), Orchard is a rare example of a sympathetically converted 18th century cottage. In a half acre garden (with croquet), opposite a farm, with fields on three sides and farmland views, it is used from time to time by the owner herself, and is well planned, very comfortable and, in brief, a highly desirable holiday base. Much of the furniture is antique, and even the large bathroom has Victorian fittings; there is an open fireplace in the sitting room and a well appointed kitchen of character which leads into a conservatory. With a deep pond in the garden, this is unsuitable for small children. Dogs accepted by arrangement with the owner. **Sleeps 6**.

Linen and towels are included. Also a plentiful supply of wood and coal. Cost: about £450 to £950. Further details from Jenny Higgo, 22 Stocks Hill, Manton, Oakham, Rutland. Telephone 01572 737420.

www.higgo.com/orchard

email: orchard@higgo.com

Welton-le-Wold, near Louth
Stubbs Cottages

We've stayed in one of the Stubbs properties, namely *Foreman's Cottage*, and it has become a real favourite. **Sleeping 7**, it is located on a high lying part of the family farm, and has fine views. It's spacious and warm, and although it's not a traditional roses-round-the-door place, it's really 'nice to come home to'. All the Stubbs cottages, in this guide without a break for over 20 years, have a lasting reputation for being

Foreman's Cottage, deep in the Lincolnshire Wolds, is warm, comfy and surprisingly spacious. And as with all the Stubbs cottages, it is reasonably priced.

clean, nicely situated and *very reasonably priced*. They are located in the hilly, wooded Lincolnshire Wolds (where good self-catering accommodation is rather thin on the ground). Among other properties there is, in the nearby off-the-beaten-track village of Welton-le-Wold, *The Old Schoolhouse*, **sleeping 6** and dating from the 19th century. Dogs are welcome. Cost: (approximately) £250 to £395. A useful sketch map of Lincolnshire (so you don't miss the best beaches and resorts) is incorporated in the details, available from Margaret Stubbs, C V Stubbs and Sons, Manor Warren Farm, Welton-le-Wold, near Louth, Lincolnshire LN11 0QX. Telephone/fax 01507 604207.

Fulstow, near Louth
Bramble and Hawthorn

We revisited recently and appreciated, as we have for many years, the 'tender loving care' these charming single storeyed cottages exude. This part of Lincolnshire is a place of vast skies and near-empty roads, and there's easy access to the green and rolling Wolds. These (**map 1/58**) are

Deep in the country but handy for the sea.

just 20 minutes from the sea, and there's a water-sports centre a mile away. Both *Bramble* and *Hawthorn* overlook a paved, gravelled 'courtyard'. There are good-sized open plan sitting rooms with cosy coal-effect fires, spacious bathrooms, and well designed bedrooms (each has a double and twin, though Hawthorn can take 2 extra on a double sofa-bed, therefore **sleeping up to 6**). You'll find fresh flowers, a welcome tray and chilled wine. The 'Information Centre' stocks maps, books and guides, with a video library. Linen and towels included. Non smoking. Children over ten welcome. Not suitable for dogs. Cost: from about £160 for a three-night break to £370 per week, high season. Details: Cheryl and Paul Tinker, Waingrove Country Cottages, Fulstow, near Louth, Lincolnshire LN11 0XQ. Telephone: 01507 363704.

www.lincolnshirecottages.com   email: ptinker.tinkernet@virgin.net

Nassington, near Melton Mowbray
The Thatch

Don't underestimate the charms of 'the Shires'. This most attractive 18th century Grade II listed thatched cottage is situated in the pretty village of Nassington, perfectly situated for visiting Rutland Water: bird watching, fishing, watersports and cycling. Take a trip aboard the Rutland Belle Cruiser, visit Egleton Nature Reserve or Barnsdale Gardens. Historic towns and villages abound, such as Oundle, Stamford and Oakham, and country pubs serving real ale. The cottage **sleeps 4**, and among other notable

Lincolnshire, Leicestershire, Rutland and Nottinghamshire hide their light under a bushel! They contain tucked-away rural treaures, including some fine holiday houses...

features it has an enclosed garden with steps, patio and furniture. It's very 'beamy', and has for example steep, narrow stairs to the first floor, where there are two double bedrooms with low, sloping ceilings. Ref 17117

Details from Blakes Country Cottages, Spring Mill, Earby, Barnoldswick BB94 0AA. Brochures and bookings: 0845 268 0944.

Live search and book: www.blakes-cottages.co.uk

Langwith, near Mansfield   map 1/61
Blue Barn Cottage

This delightful family house on a mixed 450-acre farm near historic Sherwood Forest is a favourite of ours. (It has featured in this guide for many years.) It's close to the farmhouse at the end of a mile-long track from the village, yet very accessible, being only 15 minutes' drive from the M1 (junction 30). A cosy sitting room – all is very quiet here – with TV leads on to the dining room.

This quiet and spacious house is one of our personal long-term favourites...

Upstairs there is a double bedroom, a family room with a double and two singles, a twin room with cot and a small twin room, all opening off the landing. **'Visit Britain' Three Stars.** There is a large garden and barbecue. Cost: from a very reasonable £550, which includes all linen, towels, central heating and a 'welcome pack' of provisions. There is a big kitchen/breakfast room with Rayburn, electric cooker, microwave, fridge, freezer, and an extra downstairs toilet/shower. Not suitable for dogs. Further details, together with a colour leaflet, from June Ibbotson, Blue Barn Farm, Langwith, Nottinghamshire NG20 9JD. Telephone/fax 01623 742248.

email: bluebarnfarm@supanet.com
www.bluebarn_notts.co.uk

Yorkshire and The Peak District

It says a lot about the many charms of Yorkshire that of all the English counties, this is apparently the one whose inhabitants are most likely to holiday within their own county boundaries. The county's pride in its history and its landscapes is quite touching. There's ancient York itself, and comparatively unsung East Yorkshire, embracing such little known places as the quiet village of Lund and elegant Beverley. There are the renovated mills and industrial museums of West Yorkshire – whose rugged countryside has a charm of its own. And there are of course the better-known Yorkshire Dales and the North York Moors, as well as the North Yorkshire coast.

From the North York Moors, narrow roads lead to secret seaside resorts such as Robin Hood's Bay and Staithes. Nearby Whitby and Scarborough have their own character, but the real pleasure is seeking out little-known sandy coves and silent valleys among the dales and moors.

The best of Derbyshire and Staffordshire is contained within yet another National Park: the Peak District National Park is the longest-established in Britain, and attracts more visitors than any other, but on the whole this region's gritty but picturesque villages and great houses are little known among southerners.

York   map 3/69
York Lakeside Lodges

You'd think you were in the depths of the country rather than two miles from York.

It's great to be just two miles here from the historic heart of ancient York but seemingly in the country. It's a well planned, tranquil place, in which fourteen Scandinavian timber lodges stand (with lots of privacy) on the fringes of a large lake jumping with coarse fish. The fishing is one of the charms of the place: another is its location, with coaches going to the York centre every ten minutes, and a nearby 24-hour Tesco's. Four lodges are **'Visit Britain' Five Stars** (very private, with fine views): two with one bedroom, one with two bedrooms and one with three bedrooms; the others are **Four Stars**. Winner of a Yorkshire White Rose Award for tourism, and equipped to high standards, all are well insulated and double glazed: good for autumn and winter breaks. Options include one, two and three bedroom detached lodges, one bedroom semi-detached lodges, and one and three bedroom cottages at the rear of the owners' house. **Sleep 2 to 7**. Cost: £205 to £710 (and an admirable £98 for a two-night break in winter). Dogs welcome. Brochure from Mr Manasir, York Lakeside Lodges, Moor Lane, York YO24 2QU. Telephone 01904 702346. Fax 701631.

www.yorklakesidelodges.co.uk email: neil@yorklakesidelodges.co.uk

Sawdon, near Scarborough
Sawdon Country Cottages

We love driving via winding country lanes from, say, Pickering or Brompton towards the North York Moors. Without needing to be really remote, you are quickly away from bumper-to-bumper holiday traffic and in deepest rural North Yorkshire. One of our all-time favourite villages is Sawdon: comfortably hilly, a nice mixture of old cottages in varying

In a quiet village, this is lovely stuff, plus a shared garden with wide-ranging views.

styles, a sense of community, a good pub. Right at the centre of the village (but quiet) are four absolutely charming, very comfortable cottages: we noticed inviting deep sofas, lots of books, well chosen pictures. Two cottages (*Sheila's* and *Middle House*) back on to the village street, and face a pleasant courtyard; the other two (*The Owlery* and *Ivy*) are at right angles to the others, and also look out on to the courtyard. A nice arrangement.

'**Visit Britain' Four Stars. Sleep from 2 to 5.** Dogs are possible by arrangement. Cost: about £205 to £510. Short breaks. Details from Jenny Worsley, Kirkgate Lodge, Sawdon, near Scarborough, North Yorkshire YO13 9DU. Telephone 01723 859794. Fax 01723 859144.

www.sawdoncottages.co.uk email:jenny@sawdoncottages.co.uk

Brompton-by-Sawdon, nr Scarborough
Headon Farm Cottages

We get a buzz from following the no-through-road up to this group of cottages. Skilfully converted from 19th century farm buildings, Headon Farm Cottages (**map 3/76**) are handy for Scarborough and the Moors. *Byre* for example has a kitchen/diner and lounge/diner with plush sofa and chairs, from which open stairs lead up to a double and a twin bedroom with cot. *Barn* is similar, also with

Quiet but not remote, private without being out of touch with people: lovely!

patio doors to the courtyard from the kitchen. *Stables* has space, a beamed lounge, an open staircase off the hall leading to a light landing, a double overlooking the courtyard, a large beamed twin. *Farm House Cottages* have beamed lounge/diner/kitchen (open fire if desired), a double, a twin and a bathroom. All **sleep 4**, plus Z-bed on request in Byre and Stables. Well-behaved dogs welcome: two per cottage. Short breaks from £80. TV/video. Linen and towels provided. Cost: about £190 to £400. Details: Clive and Denise Proctor, Headon Farm Cottages, Wydale, Brompton-by-Sawdon, North Yorkshire YO13 9DG. Telephone 01723 859019.

www.headonholidaycottages.co.uk email: headonfarm@supanet.com

Wrelton, near Pickering
Beech Farm Cottages

We're not at all surprised that these cottages have been festooned with awards. Just for starters, the (then) English Tourism Council's prestigious 'England for Excellence' award and, *four times*, the Yorkshire Tourist Board's 'Self-Catering Holiday of the Year' award.

In a quiet village on the edge of the North York Moors, the cottages are ideally situated for the many attractions of North Yorkshire – moors, dales, forests, coastal walks, abbeys, castles, historic buildings, seaside resorts, steam railway across moors, historic York, market towns and small villages.

The cottages are in a peaceful and pretty courtyard opening on to fields. This is effectively a hamlet in its own right in which every house is a haven of comfort.

There is a good range of accommodation to choose from. The six larger cottages are rated **Five Stars** by **'Visit Britain'**, the highest quality rating possible. *Beech Royd* and *Tanglewood* both **sleep 4**. *Columbine* and *Bracken Brow* **sleep 6**. For larger groups *The Farmhouse* (a listed building) and *Shepherd's Lodge* both **sleep 10**. They are well equipped, including dishwashers, videos and digital TV. There are also two charming little detached **Four Star** cottages, *Fat Hen* and *Dove Tree*, that **sleep 2 or 3**.

There is an excellent indoor pool and sauna. Children love the play area, the animals (including two 'lovable' llamas) and the paddock. Included are

Effectively a hamlet in its own right, in which every house is a haven of comfort.

The accommodation is great, and the indoor swimming pool is a huge bonus.

electricity, gas (the cottages have gas central heating and double glazing and are cosy for winter), linen, towels, and the use of the swimming pool.

Guests can be certain of a warm welcome, and appreciate personal touches, such as fresh flowers and a home-made cake on arrival. We've met the owners, who take pride in ensuring everything is just right.

Open all year, with short breaks outside the school holidays. Details from Pat and Rooney Massara, Beech Farm, Wrelton, Pickering, North Yorkshire YO18 8PG. Telephone 01751 476612, fax 475032.

www.beechfarm.com
email: holiday@beechfarm.com

Glaisdale Head, near Whitby
Wheelhouse

What an exquisite location! We've seen some places in our time, but this one really stays in the memory. After our 'official' visit, we could hardly tear ourselves away. Within a small hamlet in the lee of Glaisdale Moor and Egton High Moor, this charming cottage has stunning views across the head of the valley and to the escarpments of the moors above. But it's not remote: Whitby is just 12 miles away, Pickering 15. Close by

This is a marvellously well situated cottage, with exceptionally kind and welcoming owners living next door...

is a station on the ultra-scenic railway line which runs to Whitby. Within the North York Moors National Park, the cottage has its spacious sitting room and kitchen upstairs (microwave and washing machine) to take advantage of those views. There is a multi-fuel stove in the sitting room. Downstairs are a double bedroom, a twin, a single and a lovely large bathroom. There is a terraced patio garden and parking for two cars. **Sleeps 5**. Small dogs are welcome by arrangement. Heating, linen and towels included. Cost: about £250 to £375. Special rates for couples. Details from Colin or Mary Douglass, The Wheelhouse, Glaisdale, Whitby YO21 2QA. Telephone 01947 897450.

Whitby/Sleights map 3/98
White Rose Holiday Cottages

Less than three miles from busy and thankfully unspoiled Whitby, Sleights is ideally situated for 'coast and country'. Within the village – one of those we most admire in this part of Yorkshire – 'White Rose' have three cottages in a courtyard known as Garbutts Yard; there are two bungalows and a smart dormer bungalow. In fact, these village properties are ideal for large-family or group bookings, and between them can take *up to 25 people*. Very conveniently, the owners

All three courtyard cottages are nicely maintained and very comfortable...the owners really do 'aim to please'.

themselves live in the village. All the properties are maintained to a high standard, and are **'Visit Britain' Three/Four Stars**. They **sleep from 2 to 10**. TVs, videos, DVDs. Linen and towels included. Cost: about £250 to £1250. Weekend breaks on application. Brochures from June and Ian Roberts, Greenacres, 5 Brook Park, Sleights, near Whitby YO21 1RT. Telephone 01947 810763. ('Please phone if possible: we like to deal with people personally')

www.whiterosecottages.co.uk email: enquiries@whiterosecottages.co.uk

Beadlam, nr Helmsley
Townend Cottage

During its (yes!) *23 years* in our guide, this charmer of a cottage has been consistently popular with readers. A wing of the owner's 18th century farmhouse, conveniently just off the main road that runs through the village, it stands on the edge of the North York Moors and is less than an hour from Scarborough and York. The cottage is comfortable and full of character, and with its Baxi open fire, notably cosy in winter or during those worthwhile autumn breaks. There are good beds, a fine kitchen and bathroom, and all is tastefully decorated and furnished, with double glazing, and gas fired central heating. Some internal stone walls are a feature, and there are oak beams to add character. We like the wide staircase and the big main bedroom.

A much-loved cottage from which to explore the North York Moors and beyond.

'Visit Britain' Four Stars. TV/Video/DVD/CD. **Sleeps 4**. Cost: about £210 to £385. Dogs and other pets are welcome. Details from Mrs Margaret Begg, Townend Farmhouse, Beadlam, Nawton, York YO62 7SY. Telephone 01439 770103.

www.visityorkshire.com   email: margaret.begg@ukgateway.net

'In Brief'...

Kirk Cottage, in Staithes, near Whitby (Ref 17016) is at the heart of that famous village, where good quality self catering cottages are at a premium. Grade II listed, it is memorably only 75 yards from the harbour, the beach and – which will inspire many a serious walker – the Cleveland Way. **Sleeps 3**. With steep steps up to the front door it is unsuitable for small children or people of limited mobility. There's an open fire.

Also right on the Cleveland Way in Staithes – not that it actually passes through the sitting room – *Cliff Cottage* (Ref 4635) is a charming former fisherman's property at the top of a cobbled street that climbs up from the harbour. It's just 100 yards from the beach and a pub, with views of the cottage garden and a secluded valley. (And there's great cliff-top walking almost from the front door.) Here too there's an open fire, and it's also unsuitable for small children or people of limited mobility. **Sleeps 4.**

Details from Blakes Country Cottages, Spring Mill, Earby, Barnoldswick BB94 0AA. Brochures and bookings: 0845 268 0944.

Live search and book: www.blakes-cottages.co.uk

Ebberston (near Scarborough)
Cliff House

We've had so many enthusiastic reader responses about these properties. Not surprising: they're among *the very best in Yorkshire*. The four acres of land, with the walled garden, an amazing pyramid-shaped treehouse, the secret wooded gardens and the trout pool, are a source of fascination. (Youngsters love the toddlers' play area and the animals.) There is a covered, heated pool with a jacuzzi, a hard tennis court and a big games room with table tennis, pool, and darts.

Cliff House stands conveniently on the A170 – though in several cottages you'd hardly know the road is there – and is only about ten miles inland from Scarborough, with the North York Moors on the doorstep.

Lilac **sleeps 4** in a downstairs twin with en-suite toilet and handbasin, and a first floor double room. There's a downstairs kitchen/diner with open fire, upstairs lounge with garden views, and bathroom. *Maple* with its own small courtyard, **sleeping 6** and suitable for people of limited mobility, has a downstairs en-suite twin, as well as two first floor bedrooms and bathroom. *Beech* (**sleeping 5**) has a downstairs twin room and bathroom, kitchen/diner and lounge with big picture windows enjoying excellent views, a single and a double room upstairs. *Pine* and *Willow* (**sleep 4**) are

A fine arrangement of houses, handy for the moors and the seaside.

There's a high standard of furnishing, comfort, and attention to detail.

'upside down' cottages with bathroom, toilet and two bedrooms on the ground floor; beamed lounge/diner/kitchen (with open fire) taking advantage of first floor views. *Holly* **sleeps 6** in a double and two twins, and is quietly situated near the gardens. Its lounge has an open fire and picture windows; there is a dishwasher. *Apple* (**sleeps 2**) is converted from the laundry and apple store of Cliff House and has a beamed lounge and kitchen/diner, with double bedroom – overlooking gardens and apple trees – and bathroom upstairs. *Pear* also **sleeps 2 (plus 1** in a pulldown bed) and we found it altogether individual and charming, light and interesting. A beamed kitchen/diner leads to the lounge and on into a beamed double bedroom with high sloping ceiling, overlooking the gardens.

'Visit Britain' Four Stars. TVs, videos and DVDs. Dishwashers in Holly, Beach, Maple and Lilac. Linen, towels, heating included. 'Sorry, no pets.' Cost: £250 to £1000. Brochure from Simon Morris, Cliff House, Ebberston, near Scarborough, North Yorkshire YO13 9PA. Tel 01723 859440. Fax 850005.

email: cliffhouseebberston@btinternet.com
www.cliffhouse-cottageholidays.co.uk

Scarborough/Scalby
Wrea Head Country Cottages

Only a short drive from Scarborough (you can see its ruined castle on the headland) and – better yet – at the end of a quiet lane, these cottages are exceptionally well placed for enjoying both seaside and countryside.

Skilfully converted farmhouses, they have proved a real favourite among readers of this guide for many years, *and we have never had a complaint*.

The mainly south-facing, well cared-for properties have been national winners of the then ETC's "England for Excellence" Award for Self-Catering Holiday of the Year. They were also *three time* winners of the 'White Rose Award' as the Yorkshire Tourist Board's Self-Catering Cottages of the Year.

There are nine in all, of differing sizes, with well-tended gardens. Most have sea views. On the edge of the North York Moors National Park, only an hour from York, this is an ideal location to explore villages and market towns, the Heritage Coast and neighbouring forest drives. There's a sauna and an indoor heated pool with a jacuzzi at one end. This sends small waves down the pool to the delight of young children, who also have their

Children love to stay here and to get to know the horses and the teddy bears!

The super swimming pool, the sauna and the jacuzzi add 'that extra something' here.

own Teddy Bears Cottage, a two-storey wooden playhouse complete with Father Bear, Mother Bear and Baby Bear upstairs in bed and its own fenced garden and picnic area. Older children will enjoy the unusually well-equipped adventure playground.

Hay Barn Cottage (**sleeps 8**) impressed us with its clever design whereby sitting room, dining room and kitchen are separate but linked. There are well-chosen fabrics throughout (bedrooms in particular with their pretty duvets, curtains and table lamps are charming). Kitchens are modern, mostly with dishwashers, and overhead beams add character. All have TVs and DVDs, gas central heating and **Four 'Visit Britain' Stars**. Ample parking, laundry room, library (DVDs, books and games); telephone and barbecues are available. No pets, no smoking. Open all year. Cost: from £275 to £1495 (includes indoor pool, gas and electricity, linen and towels). Good value special breaks during the off-season.

Further details from Tracy and Rob Lawty, Wrea Head House, Barmoor Lane, Scalby, Scarborough, North Yorkshire YO13 0PG. Telephone Scarborough 01723 375844.

www.wreahead.co.uk   email: rob@wreahead.co.uk

Robin Hood's Bay
Farsyde Farm Cottages

Just six miles from Whitby, and well
positioned in a memorable location
on Yorkshire's spectacular 'Heritage
Coast', these cottages are close to
the fine old fishing village of Robin
Hood's Bay. Delightfully, you can
walk to the village and beach in a
few minutes. The beach is partly
sand, with rock pools. *Mistal
Cottage*, where we've stayed, is out-

*There are marvellous views, and the
ambiance is appreciated by readers.*

standing, and deserves its **Four 'Visit Britain' Stars**. **Sleeping 4** (non-
smokers, please), it has a large living room with marvellous views. The
small indoor swimming pool (in a log cabin) is for the private use of
Mistal occupants, and Farsyde's fine horses are for guests to ride. The
four smaller, **Three Star** Mews cottages look over shared gardens
towards the moors. There's a skilful use of space. Gardens have patios,
and lawns with garden furniture. This is a farm with *real animals* (large
and small), including Paddington, the Newfoundland. Short breaks available October to May. Cost: about £185 to £630. Details/brochure from
Victor and Angela Green, Farsyde House, Robin Hood's Bay, Whitby,
North Yorkshire YO22 4UG. Telephone 01947 880249. Fax 880877.

www.farsydefarmcottages.co.uk email: farsydestud@talk21.com

Hawkswick, near Grassington　　map 3/93
Riverdale

With memorable dale and river
views from many rooms, and walks
right from the doorstep (gentle
strolls or bracing hikes), this
detached and spacious cottage is a
place of great character in a superb
location at the heart of the Yorkshire
Dales National Park. Riverdale (Ref
IGS) is beautifully furnished, and
has landscaped gardens that merge

*This is an exceptional property, a chance
to enjoy the Dales in style and comfort.*

with six-acre grounds that provide
total seclusion. Specifically, there are two sitting-rooms, *each* with a
wood-burning stove – that's a real luxury! – a dining-room, and a well-
equipped farmhouse kitchen with an Aga. There are two double bedrooms, one with a five foot bed and one with en-suite shower room, and
two twin-bedded rooms. There's a bathroom/wc with jacuzzi bath and
shower cubicle.

Details from English Country Cottages, Stoney Bank Road, Earby,
Barnoldswick BB94 0AA. For bookings and brochures: 0845 268 0942.

www.english-country-cottages.co.uk

Kettlewell
Fold Farm Cottages

The 'traditional' holiday cottage of nostalgic memory is increasingly rare – but here are several in one place! Kettlewell is one of the most sought-after villages in Yorkshire, and at its heart is a quartet of quiet, thick-stone-walled, warm and comfortable cottages next to the hospitable owners' farm. We've met

Right in the heart of the village, with the big advantage of private off-road parking.

several regulars, revelling in the well cared for interiors, the deep carpets, the good quality lined curtains, the books, the table lamps, the antique or 'country' furniture. Beds are excellent, and original features have been retained. The location is super for exploring the Yorkshire Dales National Park. **Sleep 2 to 4. 'Visit Britain' Four Stars.** TV. Linen/towels provided. Dishwashers in all but *Buttercup*.

Small dogs are welcome by arrangement, but one cottage is totally pet and smoking free, and smoking is discouraged in all the others. Private off-road parking. Cost: approximately £180 to £460. Details from Mrs B Lambert, Fold Farm, Kettlewell, near Skipton, North Yorkshire BD23 5RH. Telephone 01756 760886.

www.foldfarm.co.uk   email: info@foldfarm.co.uk

Burnt Yates (Nidderdale), near Harrogate
Dinmore Cottages map 3/74

Tucked away close to the owners' house at the end of a neatly maintained private lane, there are three cottages. We have stayed in the smallest, but even that is spacious and well-cared-for, with many excellent details such as wood burning stoves, tidy flower borders, attractive pictures and old prints, and Ordnance Survey maps. Plus quiet and privacy without isolation. Converted from 17th cen-

A delightful enclave of cottages, well away from the main road, handy for touring.

tury farm buildings in the landscaped grounds of the owners' fine country house, they are handy for exploring the whole of North Yorkshire and its historic towns, houses and gardens.

Sleep 2 to 5. 'Visit Britain' Four Stars. One is popular with disabled visitors. Linen included. TVs, videos, microwaves. Not suitable for dogs. Cost: about £250 to £600; short breaks from £175. Major credit cards accepted. Details from Alan Bottomley, Dinmore House, Burnt Yates, Harrogate, North Yorkshire HG3 3ET. Telephone/fax 01423 770860.

www.dinmore-cottages.co.uk
email: aib@dinmore-cottages.freeserve.co.uk

Reeth and Healaugh
Swaledale Cottages

Featured every year in this guide since it was first published in 1983, these cottages make a splendid base from which to explore the still miraculously unspoilt Yorkshire Dales. They are just a 20 minute drive from one of our favourite towns in the north of England – Richmond.

Two properties – *Thiernswood Cottage* and *The Bothy* – are within the wooded grounds of Thiernswood Hall, which is, delightfully, approached by a tree-lined drive a third of a mile long. With an open fire in the sitting room, Thiernswood Cottage is a really inviting place 'to come home to' after, say, walking in the Dales. It is deceptively spacious, with a well equipped kitchen, dining room and cosy sitting room with open fire, two charmingly co-ordinated bedrooms – one double, the other twin bedded, both with en-suite bathroom. **Sleeps 4**. Cost: about £252 to £499.

The Bothy is tucked away, and is **ideal for 2** – indeed, for honeymooners! It is a charming conversion of tack rooms above the old stone stable block of Thiernswood Hall, and, being out of sight of the big house, especially private. There are splendid rural views from the sitting room. Cost: £183 to £349.

Linen and towels are included in Thiernswood Cottage and The Bothy; with heating included in Thiernswood Cottage during the autumn and winter seasons.

In the village of Healaugh is a spacious four bedroomed listed cottage called *Swale View*. This has long been one of our personal Yorkshire favourites. Once the village inn, with many old features retained, it has an open fire in the sitting room, a new kitchen with barrelled dining area ceil-

Swale View used to be the village pub, and retains several original features, including – our favourite! – an open fire.

Thiernswood Cottage is 'deceptively spacious' and also has an open fire. It fits prettily into its wooded suroundings.

ing and also a formal dining room. The main bedroom has a four poster double bed and ensuite bathroom. **Sleeps 6**. Cost: about £309 to £650.

Short breaks in all cottages, £147 to £240. A dog is welcome in Swale View. All have gardens, off-road parking and great views. **'Visit Britain' Four Stars**. Details from Mrs J T Hughes, Thiernswood Hall, Healaugh, Richmond, North Yorkshire DL11 6UJ. Telephone 01748 884526.

www.swaledale-cottages.co.uk

email: thiernswood@talk21.com

Buckden, near Skipton
Dalegarth and The Ghyll Cottages

At the rear of *The Ghyll*, a very special trio of cottages indeed, is as pretty a bubbling beck – dropping down at a steep angle – as you'll see in the Yorkshire Dales. Because of the way the land lies and the situation of the cottages, this feels almost like a private enclave.

One of our longest-serving inspectors chose to spend a family holiday here. She was delighted by the place.

Featured by us *without a break since 1983*, both The Ghyll and the *Dalegarth* properties have **Four 'Visit Britain' Stars**, the latter Disabled Category 2. Better yet, we weren't surprised that owners Susan and David Lusted were recent runners-up in the Yorkshire Tourist Board's White Rose Award for 'Outstanding Customer Service'. This tribute came from a reader a couple of years ago: '(It is)...the best self catering we have

A neat cluster of purpose-built traditionally styled houses with superb facilities. The warm, covered pool, and the adjacent solarium, are irresistible, and the whole place is surrounded by the unspoilt beauty of Upper Wharfedale.

rented by far...a high standard of fittings and furnishings, extremely well maintained by the owner on site, for whom nothing is too much trouble...We are visiting in October for the sixth time...'

Lonely roads that go deep into wild country are pleasant enough for the tourist, but when such roads combine scenic beauty with ease of access it is twice as nice! The B6160, which runs from near Skipton, through Upper Wharfedale, to the heart of the Dales, is one of those roads.

A few yards off it, on the south side of the small village of Buckden, in what was once the kitchen garden of a great house nearby, *Dalegarth* consists of a neat cluster of eleven purpose built, traditionally styled stone houses grouped around a dog-leg cul-de-sac. They are modern, neat and tidy, and fit very attractively into the landscape.

During a recent visit we met regular visitors relaxing in their spacious sitting rooms (all are on the first floor) and enjoying woodland and hill views – this is fine walking and touring country. Serious walkers used to aching limbs should note that seven of the cottages (there are two types) have small sauna rooms.

The cottages, which are **ideal for 4 but can sleep 6** (each has two bedrooms, plus a bed-settee in lounge), have excellent bathrooms, state-of-the-art kitchens and large, comfortable lounges with TV/video/DVD players and natural stone fireplaces. They are classified as 'type A' and 'type B' and are identical except that 'type A' have a sauna in the bathroom.

You'll find a breakfast bar in the kitchen, patio-style windows leading out on to a balcony from the lounge and an en suite shower, toilet and vanity unit in the master bedroom.

Dalegarth has an impressive indoor swimming pool, plus a solarium and games/exercise room and an exceptionally attractive terrace to sit on after your swim and admire the scenery. Also, there is a full linen service, a well-equipped laundry room, and all the cottages have a freezer.

David and Susan Lusted live in one of the houses and keep these warmly carpeted, superbly-equipped properties clean and efficiently run.

The three *Ghyll Cottages* were designed specifically for those with mobility problems. Built in natural stone, set in secluded landscaped grounds to the rear of the village of Buckden, in a quiet, sunny location, they share the leisure amenities of Dalegarth, less than two hundred yards away.

Each of the cottages has a covered loggia leading to an entrance porch which opens into a large lounge/dining room, off which is a fully-fitted and extremely well-equipped kitchen, including microwave, dishwasher etc. A double bedroom, thoughtfully provided with versatile 'zip link' beds, a spacious ensuite bathroom with spa bath, walk-in shower, etc, completes the downstairs, with another double bedroom and bathroom upstairs (one cottage has two upstairs bedrooms). The south-facing lounges offer direct access to sunny patios and every property has remote control TV and audio centre, DVD player, video and video library, central heating and a full linen service. Main bedrooms have TV and radio. Wheelchair-bound people staying there have told us that The Ghyll has it 'just right' and could not be faulted for the facilities.

The Lusteds have a policy of welcoming inspection during changeover periods. No dogs at The Ghyll (except guide dogs) but a small dog at Dalegarth is possible by arrangement. All cottages are 'non-smoking'.

Cost: about £372 to £687. Special winter mini-breaks. Details and colour leaflet from Mr and Mrs D Lusted, 2 Dalegarth, Buckden, near Skipton, North Yorkshire BD23 5JU. Telephone/fax 01756 760877.

Disabled readers should note that some while ago The Ghyll Cottages were chosen as national winners by the Holiday Care Service, at the World Travel Exhibition in Earls Court, London.

www.dalegarth.co.uk
email: info@dalegarth.co.uk

The Ghyll represents a considerable investment that has really hit-the-spot...

It is marvellously well situated, with fabulous walking right from the door.

Sedbusk, Bainbridge, Hawes, West Burton
Clematis, Well, Shepherd's and Fell View Cottages

All of Anne Fawcett's old stone-built cottages are in picture-postcard locations. We've had so many compliments over the years, notably about spacious, Grade II-listed *Shepherd's Cottage*, about a mile from Hawes. Our readers have really taken to it. **Sleeping 6**, built in 1633, it's notable for its original mullioned windows and cosy farmhouse kitchen. There are three character bedrooms – two doubles and a twin. *Clematis*, perched on a bank in the sleepy ham-

Clematis has inspiring views, and is a house of great character and history.

let of Sedbusk, enjoys spectacular views. It has big rooms – notably the welcoming sitting room. **Sleeps up to 6**. In West Burton, 17th century *Well Cottage* **sleeps 4** (a twin and a double), with a pretty walled garden. Overlooking the green in attractive Bainbridge, *Fell View* **sleeps up to 5** in two doubles and a single. It has an open fire and an Aga. Each cottage is **'Visit Britain' Four Stars**. Linen/towels for hire. Central heating/electricity included. Dogs welcome. Cost: about £175 to £675. Details: Anne Fawcett, Mile House Farm, Hawes in Wensleydale, North Yorkshire DL8 3PT. Telephone/fax 01969 667481.

www.wensleydale.uk.com

email: milehousefarm@hotmail.com

Snape, near Bedale   map 3/105
The Undercroft (Snape Castle)

You'd hardly believe you're just 20 minutes' drive from the busy A1 as you approach the tranquil parkland which adjoins the village of Snape. The most imposing building by far is Grade I listed Snape Castle (*re*-built between 1420 and 1450!), whose most famous one-time resident, Catherine Parr, was to become Henry VIII's last wife. Providing a rare chance to stay (in 21st century com-fort!) surrounded by so much history,

Cleverly combining history and comfort.

The Undercroft is a beauty: spacious, thoughtfully lit, lovingly restored, warm (there's a wood stove, plus underfloor heating) and altogether invit-ing. We especially liked the deep sofas, the super, separate big shower and the neat stone stairway up to the small twin room, and noted that the good-sized downstairs double makes the property accessible to people with lim-ited mobility. **Sleeps 4**. No smoking, no pets.

For contact details, see the Stately Holiday Homes feature on Pages 22-23.

Stanbury, near Keighley
Sarah's Cottage

This was a real find for us: modestly priced, very comfortable, located in a most interesting and attractive part of West Yorkshire – a really worthwhile find on a bright, breezy day. It has easy access to invigorating country walks, and among much else the Keighley and Worth Valley (Steam) Railway, the Brontë Parsonage at Haworth. There is a well planned small garden, with a bird feeder that

Very modestly priced and lovingly cared-for by the owner – who lives next door.

attracts 'all sorts' and a garden seat from which to enjoy the view, an exceptionally comfortable deep-carpeted ambience, absolute cleanliness. We especially liked the table lamps, the main bedroom with its picture windows, the neat kitchen/diner. There is a small second bedroom with adult-sized bunks and an upstairs bathroom with a power-shower over the bath. There is also a garage. **'Visit Britain' Three Stars**: we'd say **Four**. One well behaved dog is possible. Television and video. Telephone and wi-fi. Linen and towels included. Cost: about £150 to £280. Further details from Brian Fuller, Emmanuel Farm, 101 Stanbury, Keighley, West Yorkshire BD22 0HA. Telephone 01535 643015.

email: brian.fuller2@btinternet.com

Haworth   map 3/108
Weavers Cottage

Weavers Cottage, part of a Grade II listed building dating from the 1780s, will appeal to steam railway fans, as it overlooks the Keighley and Worth Valley steam railway. Close to Haworth's main street, and therefore the Brontë Parsonage Museum, it's something of a historic rarity, and private and quiet to boot. (Haworth is one of the most visited places in West Yorkshire, but all the more enjoyable when day visitors have left.) Weavers also makes a good

This is a property of character, full of history, that will appeal to railway buffs.

base from which to retrace the Brontë Way, across the moors to Top Withins, or, as part of a wider canvas, to explore some of the Dales. There's an open fire, for which the basket of fuel is provided free, and gas-fired central heating. **Sleeps 4 'plus 1'.** Ref 17976.

Details from Country Holidays, Spring Mill, Earby, Barnoldswick, Lancashire BB94 0AA. For bookings, and brochures: 0845 268 0943.

Live search and book: www.country-holidays.co.uk

Derbyshire
Peak Cottages*

Readers have occasionally accused us of featuring mainly big houses, and one regular has as it happens stayed recently in two good-sized properties on the books of this very good agency, which has been highly instrumental in introducing hundreds of self caterers to the pleasures of 'the Peaks'.

One substantial property is *Harrow Cottage*, Great Longstone, near Bakewell. **Sleeping 6**, it's a typical, spacious barn conversion, with a number of original features and a woodburning stove. Next spring, in contrast, we'll look at the 'delightful' one-bedroom properties in rural surroundings at Biggin Grange (on the edge of Wolfescote Dale): *Cheese Press Cottage, The Old Farrowings* and *Courtyard Creamery*.

Riley Barns, near Eyam and Grindleford, will be available early in 2008 to provide welcoming accommodation in a peaceful high-lying location in the heart of the Peak District National Park, with excellent walking: for example, along the banks of the River Derwent down to Baslow and into the parkland at Chatsworth House. Further high-quality one bedroom conversions, *Hope Cottages*, are available on the very edge of this village, with a stream running nearby and views to Win Hill. Both properties are on one level (one at ground floor).

Barn Cottage, Bakewell (Ref PK666), sleeps just two. It's handy for Chatsworth.

Ivy Cottage at Aldwick (Ref PK337) is 300 years old. Sleeping four, it has lovely views.

There are over 220 cottages altogether, ranging from converted barns to spacious country houses. Beauties we know include *Reuben's Roost, Bremen's Barn, Hopes Hideaway* and *Purdy's Place*, which have top-quality accommodation. You can also enjoy rural tranquillity at *Butterton Barns* and *Taddington Barns*, which provide character accommodation in peaceful surroundings, both with the added advantage of a heated indoor swimming pool. Cost: about £140 to £2300.

At Hurdlow Grange, *Cruck'd Barn* and *Bats Belfry* are superior conversions of character, with cruck beams and king post trusses exposed and featured. These are ideal for groups: up to 44 people can be accommodated in three-, four- and seven-bedroomed properties within delightful rural surroundings.

Details/brochures: Colin MacQueen, Peak Cottages, Strawberry Lee Lane, Totley Bents, Sheffield S17 3BA. Tel 0114 262 0777. Fax 0114 262 0666. For information about on-line booking, a range of photos and details of the availability of the agency's 220 or so properties:

www. peakcottages.com   email: enquiries@peakcottages.com

Great Hucklow, near Castleton
The Hayloft

It's inexpensive, full of character, well situated. And getting there is half the fun. You'll drive through countryside criss-crossed by dry stone walls, then (usually) turn off the A623 towards an attractive stone-built farm. The first floor conversion provides comfortable accommodation (on one side, it overlooks the tidy farmyard and the valley beyond, on the other, higher and wilder country: every room has a good view). There is a good sized sitting room with open fire, well chosen rugs, a comfortable deep sofa, a grandfather clock and other antique pieces. The kitchen/diner is well appointed, the bathroom is spacious and warm,

At the end of a no-through-road, walkers will love this.

and there are two twin rooms. The owners' pretty and safely enclosed garden is freely available to guests.

TV. **Sleeps 4**. **Four 'Visit Britain' Stars**. Linen and towels. Dogs welcome. Cost: £260 to £350, less 10% for just 2. Friday to Friday bookings. Weekend breaks by arrangement. Details from Mrs M Darley, Stanley House Farm, Great Hucklow, Derbyshire SK17 8RL. Telephone 01298 871044.

email: margot.darley1@btinternet.com

Hartington   map 3/122
Hartington Cottages

The village of Hartington is one of the most sought-after in the Peak District: pubs, tea-shops, antique shops, excellent walking from the village centre. Also at its heart are three outstanding cottages. One, the inspiring *Knowl Cottage*, overlooks the village and is reckoned to be

Knowl Cottage – a Peak District gem...

between 500 and 700 years old. It has that magical combination – lots of original features (such as a part of the original cruck beams) and a powerful sense of history, plus masses of 21st century comfort. Combining both elements is an open fire in a handsome inglenook fireplace. Not surprisingly, the cottage (**sleeping 6**, with three ensuites) has **Five 'Visit Britain' Stars**. The other two cottages here, *Manifold* and *Dove*, side by side, are tucked away in a private little enclave just behind Knowl. Expensively converted from an old barn, they each have **Four Stars**. Dove **sleeps 2**, Manifold **2 'plus 1'**.

Details from Mrs Margaret Francis, 2 Clifton Road, Buxton SK17 6QL Telephone 01298 22287.

www.hartingtoncottages.co.uk
email: patrick@hartingtoncottages.co.uk

77

Cressbrook, near Bakewell
Cressbrook Hall Cottages

On a bright recent autumn day we travelled through dramatic and craggy scenery close to the very heart of the Peak District National Park to revisit Cressbrook Hall, half hidden away in glorious parkland. Here, *Hall Cottage* and *Garden Cottage* (each **sleeps 4 'plus 1'**, with the option of a reserve twin room) are private and self contained. We have always liked the cottages 200

We really like the comparatively little known location, a very good touring base.

yards away – especially the spectacular view of the Wye Valley enjoyed by *Lower Lodge, Rubicon Retreat* and the adjacent *Hidesaway*. **Sleeping 6**, this is suitable for wheelchairs. *Carriage Cottage* **sleeps 8/9**. Two bathrooms. Wheelchair-user-friendly. Well behaved dogs are welcome. Recently added are *High Spy* and *Top Spot*, adjacent, **sleeping 11** in five ensuite doubles and an ensuite single, all on the ground floor.

B and B available in The Hall. TVs. Linen included. Cost: £115 to £895. Details: Mrs Hull-Bailey, Cressbrook Hall, Cressbrook, near Buxton. Telephone 01298 871289; fax 871845. Freephone 0800 358 3003.

www.cressbrookhall.co.uk   email: stay@cressbrookhall.co.uk

Offcote, near Ashbourne
Offcote Grange Cottage Holidays   map 3/121

These are quite exceptional, with 'no expense spared'. Close to the edge of the Peak District National Park, each **sleeps up to 14** (plus two cots). And both have received the huge accolade of **Five Stars** from **'Visit Britain'**. *Hillside Croft* is a handsome stone-built Grade II listed country house in six acres. Dating from 1709, on three floors, it has two log burners, impressive ancient oak beams, a magnificent kitchen, dining room and sitting room,

Hillside Croft is an outstanding house.

and wide, shallow stairs that will suit the elderly and children. *Billy's Bothy* is a super brick-built conversion in peaceful pastureland. It has oak floors, underfloor heating in the ensuite bathrooms and brass and cast-iron beds, an exceptional farmhouse kitchen. There's a relaxation/sauna room – massage available – a small gym, and even a cinema room. Not suitable for pets, no smoking. Quality catering can be arranged. Cost: about £1200 to £1995. Details from Pat and Chris Walker, Offcote Grange, Offcote, Derbyshire DE6 1JQ. Telephone 01335 344795. Fax 348358. Mobile 0870 8899493.

www.offcotegrange.com
email: enquiries@offcotegrange.com

Biggin-by-Hartington
Cotterill Farm Holiday Cottages

This is a focal point of the Derbyshire Dales, the most impressive part of the Peak District. It's a pleasure to turn off a road, well away from traffic, towards these three skilful conversions. *Dale View* is an 'upside down' cottage to take advantage of the views (it has a shower, not a bath), This and *Liff's Cottage* each **sleeps 4** in a double and a twin. *The Dairy* is a **2-person** charmer, its one (double) bedroom in a gallery

Painstakingly cared-for cottages, in a lovely corner of the Derbyshire Dales.

overlooking a big living room. A wood-burner is a feature, and there is a spacious bathroom. (The views from the patio of The Dairy and also from the shared spacious gardens are amazing.) *The Milking Parlour*, a recent barn conversion, **sleeps 3**, and is on the ground floor, without steps. All are **'Visit Britain' Four Stars**. Linen, electricity and heating are included. Non-smoking. 'Sorry, no pets'. Cost: about £230 to £460, depending on which cottage and when. Details from Frances Skemp, Cotterill Farm, Biggin-by-Hartington, Buxton SK17 0DJ. Telephone 01298 84447.

www.cotterillfarm.co.uk   email: enquiries@cotterillfarm.co.uk

---

Bamford (Hope Valley, near Bakewell)
Shatton Hall Farm Cottages   map 3/128

It's over 20 years ago, since we first saw the Shatton Hall Farm properties. They struck us then, as now, as a haven of tranquillity. A mile from the main road, up a well surfaced lane, it is memorable for way-marked walks through woodland. *Orchard Cottage* and *The Hayloft*, skilful barn conversions, are next door to each other, have beamed living rooms furnished in old pine, and cosy coal-effect gas fires. *Paddock Cottage*, down the yard and with a wood burning stove,

In this guide for many years, and lots of very enthusiastic reports from readers...

is the perfect winter retreat, for a short break or longer. A well behaved dog is allowed there, as there is a fenced car park to this cottage. All the cottages **sleep 4** in two double bedrooms (one is a twin room) plus sofa-beds in Orchard and Hayloft. Recently renewed kitchens and bathrooms helped these thoughtfully planned cottages to achieve a **'Visit Britain' Four Star** rating. Cost: £290 to £490. Open all year. Details: Mrs Angela Kellie, Shatton Hall Farm, Bamford, Hope Valley S33 0BG. Telephone 01433 620635. Fax 620689.

www.peakfarmholidays.co.uk   email: ahk@peakfarmholidays.co.uk

79

Knockerdown (Carsington), near Ashbourne
Knockerdown Farm Cottages

We've featured this very family-friendly group of cottages for many years, with lots of praise from readers for the welcoming atmosphere and the facilities, as well as the flexible accommodation. We like the way for example that two units (*Bruns* and *Sabinhay*) interconnect to provide an extra-large property.

Families and smaller parties will both appreciate the new on-site Brackendale restaurant, open to the public, and the new Brackendale Spa, which offers among much else 'luxurious massage and facials'.

During one recent revisit to Knockerdown we stayed in *Farwell*, usefully **sleeping 6 'plus 2'** – the 2 in a comfortable and private ground floor bedroom. It is spacious, uncluttered, expensively fitted out: well recommended. And we've stayed in *Middleton*, a neat two storeyed cottage with a twin and a double bedroom and a good use of the available space.

Our main purpose was to visit nearby Chatsworth House and Haddon Hall, but we discovered what a useful touring base Knockerdown makes for other places, with the Dales on the doorstep. Carsington Water (all kinds of water sports, and cycle trails) is a few minutes away on foot.

We have stayed here ourselves, and appreciated the tidy, unfussy interiors...

...as well as the excellent swimming pool: it was very warm on a chilly autumn day.

Guests appreciate the excellent indoor, warm pool and leisure centre. It's a pleasant place to make new friends, but also quiet and private. There is an exceptional adventure playground, and three acres for children to romp in.

All the cottages, from one that **sleeps 2** to two that **sleep 10**, with fourteen others in between, **sleeping 4** plus cot **and 6** plus cot, are quite private. We noticed plain white walls, oak beams, pine fittings, good quality carpets, some exposed interior stone walls. Nearly all the cottages have an open plan arrangement of sitting room, dining room and kitchen. We applaud the 'instant heat' convector heater/storage radiators.

Videos (and DVDs in some cases), TVs. Video library. Linen and towels are included. No dogs. Cost (inc electricity): about £280 to £1940 weekly, with short breaks usually available (open all year) from about £187.

Details/brochure from Tina Lomas, Knockerdown Farm, near Ashbourne, Derbyshire DE6 1NQ. Telephone/fax 01629 540525.

www.derbyshireholidaycottages.co.uk
email: info@derbyshireholidaycottages.co.uk

Eyam/Hope
Dalehead Court

Here are excellent properties (in two separate locations) including, at Hope, a rather special small property available only for a couple of seasons. **Sleeping just 2** in a 'super king size' double that's convertible to twins, it has been done to **Five Star** specifications, and, usefully for people with limited mobility, is all on one level.

Derbyshire has great appeal, and all these superbly maintained cottages make a fine base.

Also at Hope are *Stables,* **sleeping 2**, and *Granary* and *The Lime Loft.* Each **sleeping 4**, they are by a tumbling river, with a good degree of spaciousness. Dogs are welcome in Granary and Stables.

A private courtyard in the heart of historic Eyam, with ample private parking, is the location of one of the two cottage-groups in the same ownership. All three at Eyam are finished expensively, with style. *Pinfold Barn,* **sleeping 6,** is an 'upside-down' house with an inviting first floor sitting room, three cosy bedrooms, a stunning 'undersea' bathroom, a separate shower and the main bedroom en-suite. *The Captain's House,* **sleeping '4 plus 1'**, is a Victorian beauty, with a big sitting room, surround-sound flat-screen TV (all have satellite TV) and a twin and a king-sized double bedroom. Attractive, stylish *Pinner Cottage* **sleeps 2**, also in a king-sized bed. **'Visit Britain' Four and Five Stars**. Dogs welcome in Pinner.

Cost: about £195 to £500. Linen and towels available (free for two-week stays); winter short breaks. Details from Mr and Mrs D Neary, Laneside Farm, Hope, Derbyshire S33 6RR. Telephone 01433 620214.

www.peakdistrictholidaycottages.com   email: laneside@lineone.net

---

'Who's in, who's out?'

Readers sometimes ask 'How are owners/agents chosen to be in *The Good Holiday Cottage Guide?*' The answer is that most people come via reader recommendations, and occasionally from regional tourist boards*. Others contact us directly, after which we arrange to see them at first hand.

Regular readers of the guide might spot cottages they have not seen for years: it could be that a cottage or group of cottages have been on a long let or have been marketed through an 'exclusive' agency that discourages owner-bookings, or that there has been a change of ownership: we may have dropped the cottages – perhaps if they were not up to scratch – when they were under the previous ownership.

An interesting observation: we are noticing an increase in the numbers of owners who no longer subscribe to the star grading scheme run by Visit Britain (we award it two words, as we find 'VisitBritain' prissy).

Chinley, near Buxton
Cherry Tree Cottage/The Old House

Twenty-six years in this guide, and never anything but wholehearted praise from readers both for owners Pam and Nic Broadhurst and their properties. It's a marvellous record.

Their two cottages are full of comfort and character, with great attention to detail. *Cherry Tree Cottage* **sleeps 6**. It overlooks the children's picturebook farmyard (little ones can feed the ducks and hens, and older ones are welcome to play more or less at will on the farm). We remember Cherry Tree's big dining room, and readers have written to say: 'The cottage was perfect – we felt at home and relaxed the moment we stepped through the door' and 'so sad to be leaving such great accommodation'.

There's an open fire (plus central heating throughout), fresh flowers, rugs, comfy armchairs and sofas, oak beams, antiques, lots of nooks and crannies, good paintings, excellent views, children's games and toys, comfortable bedrooms. The kitchen (with most attractive tiling) has a dishwasher and microwave. These are probably the best equipped farm-based cottages we know, with shaver points, electric blankets, rotary whisks, coffee filter machines, barbecues.

The more recent property is a historic and intriguing cottage dating from abut 1560, **sleeping 2** and appropriately called *The Old House*. You descend most cosily from a bedroom with a five foot double bed and inspiring views of the Blackbrook Valley, into a lower-level sitting room with antique oak furniture and inglenook fireplace with log burner.

Cherry Tree (on the right) quickly became a firm favourite among our readers, being extremely well equipped, cosy and comfortable.

The Old House is full of history, a most unusual property for just 2 people, who'll love (as we did) the antique oak and the inglenook fireplace with its log burner.

Situated as they are in the Peak District National Park (but only a mile from the village), the cottages make a fine base from which to explore the area. It is, by the way, easy to get here by train.

Both are **'Visit Britain' Four Stars**. Cost: about £230 to £630. Dogs are welcome. TVs/videos.

Further details from Mrs Broadhurst, Cote Bank Farm, Buxworth, via Whaley Bridge, High Peak, Derbyshire SK23 7NP. Telephone 01663 750566.

www.cotebank.co.uk   email: cotebank@btinternet.com

Northumberland and Durham

Drivers on the A1 in Northumberland who don't already know the coast must be intrigued by the glimpses they get of it, especially by the occasional distant sight of possibly the best beaches in England. This most northerly of all the English counties embraces a wide variety of countryside, much of it impressively 'wild and woolly' and some world-class castles: Alnwick, Warkworth, Lindisfarne, Dunstanburgh and Bamburgh. And if you venture into the Cheviot Hills, which beautifully straddle the English-Scottish border, you can be virtually alone except for curlews and skylarks even on an August Bank Holiday. Much further south, we are especially fond of the Tyne Valleys (North and South), and the Roman Wall country. We'd even say 'don't miss' the country between Haltwhistle and Alston. Especially little known are the beautiful windswept moors that characterise the three-way border between Northumberland and Durham and Northumberland and Cumbria. County Durham is in fact one of 'England's best kept secrets', not just for its deep, dark green river valleys, its stone villages set off so effectively by flowers, but its great castles (Barnard Castle is very impressive, as is the nearby Bowes Museum) and the historic city of Durham – a castle and a great, sombre cathedral. And one of the best family days out in the north of England is the Beamish Open Air Museum – full of nostalgia for mums and dads, full of things to amuse and educate children.

Greenhead (Hadrian's Wall)
Holmhead Cottage   map 3/136

Two summers ago we revisited this very well situated property. It's handy for the main Newcastle to Carlisle road but blissfully quiet, and you'll hardly find anywhere closer to the Roman Wall. Adjoining the owners' home-cum-guest house, the single-storeyed Holmhead Cottage has an open plan sitting room/kitchen/dining room, a twin and a double bedroom, all on the ground floor. There's central heating from the adjacent house (adjusted as required), electricity inclusive, hi-fi and CD player, wash-

Ideally placed for exploring 'the Wall', and very comfortable in its own right.

ing machine, dishwasher, microwave, TV, video. All linen and towels. Private walled garden. Shops, swimming, tennis, riding just three miles away; a pub, a bus stop and a cafe are just half a mile away in the village. Golf is just 500 yards away. Short breaks. Non-smokers only. Not suitable for dogs. Payphone. Note: the Roman Wall visitor centres are open all year: the cottage owner is an expert on the subject. Cost: about £220 to £420. Details from Pauline Staff, Holmhead Guest House, on Thirlwall Castle Farm, Hadrian's Wall, Greenhead-in-Northumberland, via Brampton CA8 7HY. Telephone/fax 016977 47402.

www.holmhead.com   email: via website

Ray Demesne, near Kirkwhelpington
Sweethope Crofts 1 and 2

Though we know Northumberland well, and have often travelled the surprisingly fast and well maintained roads – based in at least one case on an original Roman road – that link the River Tyne at Corbridge with the wild moorland and the forests that mark the nearness of the Scottish border, we'd never seen the lovely lough on Viscount Devonport's 'Ray Demesne' estate. Our excuse to go there, in the summer of 2006, was to see two very

An especially warm, inviting sitting room, and a delightful location...

appealing holiday houses, *1 and 2 Sweethope Crofts*. They were recommended to us by readers who'd stayed in other Stately Holiday Homes places featured by us in previous editions of this guide. Encouragingly, we arrived at the end of a delightful detour from Corbridge just as they were being spruced up for incoming guests.

The pair of traditional Northumbrian stone cottages at the very edge of Sweethope Lough each sleeps 4 in a double and a bunk-bedded room, with the huge advantage that they can linked to make a single property for a larger family or a group of friends. Among other good things they offer some of the finest lake fishing in the North of England: cottage guests are offered a very generous four free fishing sessions during say, one week's stay). Changeover is on a Friday. One dog is welcome in cottage No 2. Each has a washing machine and No 2 has a dishwasher too.

Details from Stately Holiday Homes: Page 22–23.

Four-legged friends

About 60% of the cottage owners featured in this guide accept dogs, which usually but not always means other pets too (a small number exclude cats, though usually on the grounds that kittens and expensive fabrics don't go well together: semi-comatose old moggies are less of a problem). Most owners charge between £10 and £20 per week per dog for the inevitable extra wear and tear on properties.

Please don't arrive with more dogs than you have permission to take, and do not sneak a dog into a cottage where it's not welcome.

Note too that, even when cottage owners say 'No dogs', dog lovers may still find themselves 'among friends': it could simply be that visiting town dogs don't take very well to cottages surrounded by farmland, perhaps with lots of sheep, or that the owners' dogs don't like strange animals.

Akeld, near Wooler
Akeld Manor and Cottages

On a quiet Saturday afternoon in 2006 we were much encouraged to see how inviting this exceptionally well cared for arrangement of cottages has remained over many years (we have featured it for fifteen years). All was being spruced up for the arrival of new holiday tenants.

One of our readers wrote to say she'd not expected to find a place quite so comfortable and with such extensive facilities on the edge of the 'wild and woolly' Cheviot Hills, with some of the finest and least-crowded beaches in Britain little more than half an hour's drive away.

The 'great comfort' involves interiors five-star hotels would be proud of, with deep carpets, subtle lighting that can add so much to the ambiance of holiday cottages, solid, handsome beds (five-feet wide in some cases), expensive fabrics, excellent insulation, last-word kitchens.

These are eight very sympathetic conversions of one-time farm buildings within 36 acres of the Northumbria National Park, and each one feels private and self contained. They range from a one bedroomed cottage **sleeping just 2, plus baby**, to four cottages that **sleep 4** and three that **sleep 6** (one of those actually **4 'plus 2'**). All have baths, and almost all have shower too. There's an indoor leisure centre, a warm and inviting pool, an antique full-sized snooker table (which might also have side-tracked us), a gym, solarium and games room.

Very sympathetic conversions, with sumptuously comfortable interiors...

...plus an up to the minute indoor leisure centre that is a huge attraction in itself.

To complement the excellent accommodation and leisure facilities, there is a tremendous selection of home made meals for guests who occasionally tire of self catering. Quality and prices are exceptional.

There is huge demand among readers of this guide for larger properties, and the splendid *Akeld Manor* can certainly oblige. For the main house of the original estate, **sleeping up to 15**, is a real showpiece. We have too little space to detail all its charms, but there is for example a games room with pool table, a five-foot four poster in one bedroom, a private walled garden, two open fires. Not suitable for pets. Resident on-site staff. Linen included but not towels. Cost: about £313 to £1175. Akeld Manor about £1232 to £2866 per week. Short breaks also available. Details from Pat and Sian Allan, Shoreston Hall, Shoreston, Seahouses, Northumberland NE68 7SX. Telephone 01665 721035. Fax 720951.

www.borderrose-holidays.co.uk email: allan.group@virgin.net.co.uk

Harehope Hall, near Alnwick
Cresswell Wing/Sawmill

Deep in rolling farmland, with views of the Cheviot Hills, Harehope Hall is an imposing mansion, and guests in *The Cresswell Wing* (it is on three floors) have a substantial part of it to themselves, so anyone who appreciates high ceilings, big windows and easy-going, traditional comfort will love it. We like the spacious drawing room with its deep sofas, the open fire

Pleasant accommodation, a fine estate...

(lit when we last called), the big bedrooms – including two atticky ones that would suit children – the 'country antiques'. **Sleeps 8** in two twins and two doubles. (Extra beds available, if needed, plus cot.) Central heating. Most recently available is *Riverview*, **sleeping 6**, adjacent to *Sawmill Cottage*, on a corner of the estate. **Sleeps 4**. These are splendid: better yet, they can be booked together by large groups. They are indeed next to a working sawmill. Linen/towels included. Dogs *and horses* welcome. Note: a speciality here are carriage driving/riding holidays, using the lanes of the estate (but bring your own horses/carriages!). TV. Cost: about £200 to £550. More details from Alison Wrangham, Harehope Hall, Harehope, near Alnwick, Northumberland NE66 2DP. Telephone 01668 217329.

email: john@wrangham.co.uk

Seahouses
Farne House map 3/142

On a bright and breezy day in much-loved Seahouses (a nice mixture of family resort and working fishing port) we visited these quite spectacularly located apartments. Five out of the seven overlook the harbour – always 'something going on' – with views out to sea, and even those that don't have those views reflect the

A spectacular location: comfortable too.

same high standards of comfort. In the same ownership as Akeld (see previous page) the style of the apartments is plush but rather understated, and definitely uncluttered. Fabrics, furnishings, beds and bedding and kitchens are to a high specification. There's a reliably warm indoor swimming pool and sauna (open 24 hours a day, all year round) with sun lounge. And although you are on the coast, there's easy access to much of the county: Bamburgh for example is a delightful three mile walk along the water's edge. Linen included but not towels. Cost: about £371 to £1031 per week. Short breaks available: you do not have to book a complete week.

Details from Pat and Sian Allan, Shoreston Hall, Shoreston, Seahouses, Northumberland NE68 7SX. Telephone 01665 721035. Fax 720951.

www.borderrose-holidays.co.uk email: allan.group@virgin.net.co.uk

Alnmouth, Bamburgh and around
Northumbria Coast and Country Properties*

We've featured this extremely well run cottage letting agency for over twenty years, and are especially pleased (we know it from reader reports) to have helped introduce so many people to the pleasures of self catering in this quite extraordinary corner of England.

Sandpiper, for example, is at the heart of the little known but most appealing seaside village of Low-Newton-by-the-Sea, close to a charming and unpretentious pub, and just yards from the water's edge. **Sleeping 6**, it is a listed 18th century, one-time fisherman's cottage of character, with a log-burning stove. Dogs are welcome.

At High-Newton-by-the-Sea, *Snook Point* is an extremely comfortable single-storeyed house with sea views. Among others by the coast, there are several properties in famous Bamburgh (best known for its castle and its beach), all of whose sitting room windows face the sea. There are cottages of character in Seahouses, Beadnell, Craster and Embleton, where readers have raved about the fabulous outlook from *Dunstanburgh View.*

This hugely respected agency covers one of the most scenically impressive corners of England, and is based in Alnmouth. We know three or four of the cottages in the village itself: all a delight! If you should book either of the two old 'smugglers' cottages' in Victoria Place (one is almost *on* the beach) or tucked away *Estuary View* (on three floors), you are in for a treat.

We like the atmosphere of old railways and especially old railway stations, and the agency has a real winner on its books. This is – yes – *The Old Station House*, at Low Akeld, near Wooler. It has been superbly preserved and restored and **sleeps 8/9**.

The brochure for the agency's 200-or-so properties carries a colour photo of each. As well as such highly rural but not remote cottages mentioned above, they include town properties in famous and handsome Alnwick and several in Warkworth (as with Alnwick, the town embraces one of northern England's most famous castles). Another example is the *Old Lifeboat Cottage*, **sleeping just 2**, right on the waterfront and shoreline of the River Tweed estuary at Berwick-upon-Tweed. An amazing location.

Details from Northumbria Coast and Country Cottages, Carpenters Court, Riverbank Road, Alnmouth, near Alnwick, Northumberland. Telephone Alnmouth 01665 830783/830902. Fax 830071.

www.northumbria-cottages.co.uk email: cottages@nccc.demon.co.uk

Glebe House, Bamburgh (not featured) is part of a handsome old vicarage. Sleeps 8.

Estuary View – and yes, the view from the house is as good as you'd hope!

Bamburgh, near Belford/Holy Island
Outchester and Ross Farm Cottages

These make a fine base from which to explore Northumberland's spectacular coast and castles. Stylish and comfortable, they have **Four 'Visit Britain' Stars** apiece. At *Outchester Manor* there are eight superb properties, recent winners in the 'Pride of Northumbria' awards. **Sleep from 2 to 6**. At Ross, there are cottages both in the peaceful hamlet and down the lane to the sea. Spacious *Sandpiper*

Everything is stylish and full of character.

and *Oystercatcher* have charming sitting rooms. Each **sleeps 4 to 6,** but can combine to **sleep 12**. Newly available next door is *Skylark*. Also **sleeps 4 to 6**. Along the sea lane, *West Coastguard Cottage* has a cosy, smallish sitting room, a separate dining room, great upstairs views. *East Coastguard Cottage* is similar (each **sleeps 2 to 4**). *Coastguard Lodge,* **sleeping 2 to 5**, is a gem: a neat garden, a fine sitting room, an expensive kitchen. Outchester cottages cost about £259 to £776, the Ross cottages about £300 to £776. Not suitable for pets, no smoking. Linen and towels are included. Details/brochure: from Mrs J B Sutherland, Ross Farm, Belford, Northumberland NE70 7EN. Telephone 01668 213336. Fax 219385.

www.rosscottages.co.uk   email: enquiry@rosscottages.co.uk

Rothbury   map 3/140
The Pele Tower

Quietly situated above Rothbury, though on account of trees out of sight of the town, this is a two-storeyed property of character, a 19th century extension to the original pele (fortified) tower, lovingly cared for by owners David and Anne Malia, who live in 'the big house' next door. Full of history *and* 21st century comfort,

This is a beauty, which we recently visited – always a pleasure!

the Grade II* listed, 14th century building is 'something special'. There are stone flags in the excellent modern kitchen, every labour saving device imaginable, video and digital satellite TV. CD/tape hi-fi, 'Play Station 2', a woodstove, extra TVs in bedrooms, teasmade, whirlpool bath and shower, mountain bikes and more. Unsurprisingly it has been shortlisted in the 'England for Excellence' awards and is a former 'Winner of the Lionheart Award: Most Popular Self Catering Accommodation'.

Sleeps 4 in a double room and a twin room. **'Visit Britain' Five Stars**. Unsuitable for pets or smokers. Cost: about £250 to £640. Details from David Malia, The Pele Tower, Whitton, Rothbury, Northumberland NE65 7RL. Telephone 01669 620410. Fax 621006.

www.thepeletower.com   email: info@thepeletower.com

Bowsden, near Bamburgh/Holy Island
The Old Smithy

We revisited two summers ago, rather enjoying the fact that the cottage is quite hard to find! Though it is indeed in a peaceful rural location, it's only five miles from the Northumberland coast (don't miss Holy Island). When we first called at the detached cottage conversion we met a couple happy to stay put: the wood-burner was warming the cottage, and they were comfortably ensconced in the kitchen/diner. Adjacent to that is a cosy sitting room (a former smithy) with a deep sofa/armchairs, attractive stripped pine, rugs, books, well chosen pictures, and other stylish things. This room

Warm and very well planned.

overlooks the south facing walled garden and the Cheviots. We liked the skilful conversion, with two bedrooms downstairs and one upstairs, the bathroom with shower, a loo on each floor, the central heating that's complemented by the woodburner. This is a traditional farm: natural calf rearing, summer-grass-fed lambs, free range chickens. **Sleeps 6**, plus cot. TV. Dogs welcome. Cost: £240 to £600. Details from John and Mary Barber, Brackenside, Bowsden, Berwick-on-Tweed, Northumberland TD15 2TQ. Telephone 01289 388293.

www.brackenside.co.uk   email: john.barber@virgin.net

Mindrum, near Cornhill-on-Tweed   map 3/150
Briar Cottage

Close enough to Scotland (though actually just inside Northumberland) to allow you to hear bagpipes and see haggis mating, this exudes TLC, amid very pleasant countryside. We've stayed, and remember such details as a log and coal fire lit ahead of our arrival. There are good-sized rooms: from the front window of one we watched cattle on the hills.

Consistently popular with our readers...

Used from time to time by the owners, and thus with all the essentials, the cottage has a twin and a double, a good sized bathroom with shower. Small front garden. There are large enclosed lawned gardens to the side and rear, with garden furniture. Private parking. The area is good for touring, with Scotland and the Cheviots so close, and the coast is just half an hour away. Dogs are welcome. TV/video/DVD. Linen, fuel, oil central heating, electricity included. Cost: £210 to £425.

Details from Northumbria Coast and Country Cottages, Carpenters Court, Riverbank Road, Alnmouth, Northumberland NE66 2RH. Telephone 01665 830783/830902. Fax 830071.

www.northumbria-cottages.co.uk   email: cottages@nccc.demon.co.uk

Beal, near Holy Island: Bee Hill House/West Lodge/ The Stables/The Coach House/Bee Cottage

The location of *Bee Cottage* (**sleeping 4**) is amazing: it has a memorable panoramic view from most rooms of Holy Island, accessible via the causeway at low tide. Close to newly available *Bee Hill House*, a detached beauty **sleeping 10 people**, which we'll see in 2008, it has a nicely lit sitting room with a log stove, a modern kitchen, a smart bathroom, a double and a twin. On a grander scale, *West Lodge, Stables* and *The Coach*

Everything here is aimed at the highest standards. See Colour section.

House (**sleeping respectively up to 8, 6 and 6 people**), are recent additions to the Nesbitts' 'family' of cottages. They are beauties: masses of space, grand sitting rooms, sumptuous bedrooms, super ultra-modern kitchens. You'll not get lost, as West Lodge, Stables and Coach House are in fairly close proximity to the A1. TVs. Dogs welcome. **'Visit Britain' Four/Five Stars**. Linen/towels provided. Cost: £270 to £1200. Details from Jackie Nesbitt, Springbank, Castle Terrace, Berwick-on-Tweed, Northumberland TD15 1NZ. Telephone 01289 303425. Fax 307902.

www.beehill.co.uk   email: info@beehill.co.uk

Belford, near Holy Island   map 3/156
Bluebell Farm Cottages

We recently revisited to see the considerable upgrading that has been carried out in this most appealing, quiet and competitively priced group of cottages. Tucked away off one of the roads leading out of the village of Belford, once a stage-coach stop between York and Edinburgh, they are five stone and pantiled farm-building conversions. Neatly within what is effectively a hamlet in its own right, and **sleeping from 2 to 6**,

We really liked these unpretentious cottages, and their convenient location.

each is *admirably spacious*, with big windows, lots of light and a good degree of privacy. We noted deep sofas and armchairs, patios with picnic-benches and access to barbecues, in the case of *Chillingham, Farne, Lindisfarne* and *St Abbs*, backing on to a little burn. (There is a caravan park in the same ownership, but out of sight of the cottages.)

TVs and DVD players. Bed-linen, gas central heating and electricity included. Towels for a small extra charge. Short breaks available. Pets by prior arrangement. Cost: about £210 to £530. Details from Phyl Carruthers, Bluebell Farm Cottages, Belford, Northumberland NE70 7QE. Telephone 01668 213362 or 0770 333 5430.

email: phyl.carruthers@virgin.net   www.bluebellfarmbelford.co.uk

Scotland

From our base in the south east of England we find we can't go long without a restorative dose of Scotland. We need a shot in the arm: nothing illicit, just the changing colours of the Cuillin Hills on Skye, absolute peace and quiet on half inhabited islands, an old-fashioned courtesy and integrity among most people one meets. Readers of this guide have described idyllic cottages from where they have explored lochs, glens and burns, mountains, forests and off-shore islands. The north-east of the country has one of the greatest collections of castles in the world, and you can follow a 'whisky trail' to some well-known distilleries. World-famous too are some of the golf courses, such as the Open Championship course at Carnoustie, and the course at St Andrews. For skiers, Glenshee and Aviemore are Scotland's main resorts, but we would say the mountains and hills are even more impressive in spring, summer and autumn. We are keen on the strange 'lunar landscapes' of the wild country to the north of Lochinver, on the Trossachs, and the rolling brown moors of the Border country that is thick with ancient castles and abbeys.

Duns map 4/154
Duns Castle Cottages

A reader from Reading who stayed here said 'It was magical!' And certainly, the idea of staying within or in the grounds of castles appeals greatly. Each property here has its own character, is very private but benefits greatly from the situation – either close to the grand Gothic-fantasy of a castle or on a slightly more distant corner of the estate. We remember the charming *Pavilion Lodge,* a 'folly' gatehouse, a cosy nest **for 2**, with a romantic turretted

A super base for exploring the Borders, interesting in itself, and only – for example – about an hour from Edinburgh.

bedroom reached via a winding stair, and an open fire (the only one that has an open fire, though some others have coal-effect gas fires). *St Mary's* is a rambling family house **sleeping 11** that may be joined to *Coach House* (**sleeps 3**) behind. *The White House*, **sleeping 6**, is private and comfy, *Azalea Cottage* is elegantly furnished and is located above the lake. *Carriage Mews*, **sleeping 5**, forms one wing of the attractive court-yard. Note: the seaside is only 20 minutes away, Edinburgh about an hour – an easy drive in both cases.

TVs. Linen included, towels available (extra charge). Cost: about £195 to £1180. Details from Natalie Scheff, Duns Castle, Duns, Berwickshire TD11 3NW. Telephone 01361 883211; fax 882015.

www.dunscastle.co.uk
email: info@dunscastle.co.uk

Gattonside, near Melrose
Drumblair

It was a reader who first told us of this 'outstandingly good' cottage, and we saw it for ourselves on a warm summer Saturday. It's a delight, with kind and considerate owners to boot. A detached bungalow in a quiet residential road in a village near Melrose, Drumblair has a pleasant, well tended garden and an absolutely pristine interior. Specifically, it **sleeps 4** in a bedroom (king size bed) with ensuite spa bathroom and

A convenient, beautifully cared-for base from which to explore the Scottish borders.

an ensuite (shower) twin room. There's double glazing and full gas central heating. The spacious sitting room/dining room has views of the Eildon Hills. The utility room houses a washing machine and tumble drier, and there's a store for bicycles or for drying outdoor gear.

Well behaved dogs by arrangement. Bedlinen, towels, gas, electricity included. **'Visit Britain' Four Stars**. Cost: about £295 to £425. Details from Mrs J Stevenson, Camberley, Abbotsford Road, Darnick, Melrose, Roxburghshire TD6 9AJ. Telephone 01896 823648.

www.drumblairontweed.co.uk
email: jacky.stevenson@drumblair.freeserve.co.uk

Short breaks

Readers often write or phone about short breaks, and sometimes ask why we don't list the properties that offer these. It's because about ninety per cent do. This can almost be taken for granted, depending on the time of year, and it is usually worth asking about a short break *even during the main holiday season*. Winter weekends especially can still be a bargain, but are more realistically priced than they used to be, when some owners were happy 'just to keep the places lived in'...

It's good to talk

We always recommend telephone discussions with an owner or agent about any properties that appeal, and the more detail you can give about particular concerns and requirements the better. It's possible to book direct from this guide, and readers often do so late in the season or at short notice. Elements essential to readers' holiday enjoyment and peace of mind should be double checked prior to making any commitment. This applies for example to the number of people a property comfortably sleeps, whether bedrooms are all upstairs, the types of bed ('firm', 'soft', etc), whether en suite, and whether bathrooms have bath or shower or both.

Straiton, near Maybole
Blairquhan

Two years ago, on a golden summer day, we turned off a country road to the beautiful Blairquhan estate, to revisit some of the most inviting Scottish cottages we know. They're easily accessible (about half an hour from Prestwick airport) and have been featured by us for over 20 years.

McDowall is one of several charmers on this lovely estate. Note that the upstairs twin room has views of the gardens. Note also: there's a downstairs double bedroom.

Cuninghame is a fairly recent conversion, with masses of character. Stay here and you'll experience the fabulous walled garden!

We know all seven properties. *Cuninghame*, converted in 1995 from the original potting shed and bothy and situated on the wall of the glorious walled garden which was a riot of colour when we visited, has a living/dining room/kitchen with woodburner, French windows and a huge arch-to-floor window; downstairs are two twin bedrooms and bathroom; upstairs a further twin room and a spacious playroom. *McDowall*, also a former bothy and on the garden wall, has a kitchen/living room with sofa bed and a double bedroom downstairs; upstairs is a twin room overlooking the gardens. *Kennedy Cottage* forms one side of a courtyard which is part of Blairquhan Castle and has stone carvings dating to 1575. *McIntyre, Farrer* and *Wauchope* are apartments in the former coachman's house and stables; we especially liked the former, **sleeping 6**, with a large upstairs kitchen/living/dining room that has glorious views.

A few years ago Wauchope was greatly enlarged. Downstairs, it has a large living room, an adjoining dining room and kitchen, and a bathroom. (There are two divan beds in the living room.) Upstairs, there are four bedrooms with twin beds, and a second bathroom.

Bishopland Lodge, tucked away on its own, has exceptional views towards the castle and of the Girvan Valley. Throughout we noted excellent carpets and rugs, pretty drapes and duvets, attractive pictures and posters, useful bedside and standard lamps.

All have oil central heating. Prices are from around £250 in winter to £800 in summer. Details from the Blairquhan Estate Office, Straiton, Maybole KA19 7LZ. Telephone 01655 770239, fax 770278.

www.blairquhan.co.uk
email: enquiries@blairquhan.co.uk

Dunning, near Perth
Duncrub Holidays

These are absolute charmers. In a superb location for people wanting to explore 'the heart of Scotland' and, say, the Trossachs, sometimes called Scotland-in-a-nutshell, there are two much-admired 19th century chapel apartments, ten minutes' walk from the conservation village of Dunning (easy to locate: just south of the A9 trunk road). *The Tower House* (**'Visit**

Chapel House incorporates original features (as does The Tower House)...

Scotland' Five Stars), the ultimate romantic hideaway **for 2**, has an open plan kitchen/dining/sitting room on the ground floor and, via a narrow stone spiral staircase, an upper floor double bedroom (five foot bed) and bathroom. *Chapel House* (**Four Stars**) in part is modern, incorporating parts of the original chapel. It **sleeps 4** in an ensuite twin (or double) and upper floor double bedroom and bathroom. Visitors can enjoy badminton and table tennis in the chapel nave. Linen and towels are included. TVs, videos, central heating, washer/dryers. Well behaved dogs are welcome in Chapel House. No smoking. Cost: about £320 to £580. Switch/Solo/Access/Visa/Mastercard. Further details from Wilma Marshall, Duncrub Holidays Ltd, Dalreoch, Perth PH2 0QJ. Telephone 01764 684100.

www.duncrub-holidays.com   email: ghc@duncrub-holidays.com

Abade Self Catering is a hand-picked group of quality cottages, lodges and unusual places to stay in the glorious county of Perthshire. Owners with Abade (an old Scots word for abode, or home) aim to give their visitors a really good holiday experience, by not only providing excellent high quality self-catering accommodation in beautiful locations, but also applying that attention to detail that makes all the difference between 'a good time' and a really memorable holiday.

Perthshire is perfect for sightseeing, with everything to offer from a *ceilidh* to a classical concert, gardens to grand castles, golf courses, whisky distilleries, restaurants and much, much more.

You can choose an apartment in a castle, a 19th century chapel tower, a converted mill by a lochside, a charming garden flat in an old clock tower, and others. Most are just an hour's drive from Edinburgh and Glasgow airports. The central part of Scotland is packed with alternatives, from St Andrews, 'home of golf', to a remote highland glen with dramatic scenery, and wildlife the only company.

For that luxury holiday break, a romantic getaway, a really comfortable home from home, or just for your holiday, choose an Abade holiday. (Visit our website to make your choice.)

Details from Wilma Marshall, Abade, Dalreoch, Dunning, Perth PH2 0QJ Telephone 01764 684100. **www.abade.co.uk   email: ghc@abade.co.uk**

Advertisement feature

Balquhidder
Rhuveag

Near the tiny village of Balquhidder, and overlooking Loch Voil, this well situated house is almost surrounded by a mass of trees, azaleas and rhododendrons. We have seen it, and would class it as 'one in a thousand'. In fact, it's on our list of places we'd like to stay in ourselves some time. Used frequently by the owners them-

One of our all-time favourites in Scotland, both for character and location.

selves, it is warm and very comfortable, with log fires, a Rayburn in the kitchen, and a clothes drying room, as well as central heating. Though rural and 'traditional', there is nothing primitive about the house: in a splendid kitchen it has a dishwasher, washing machine, ceramic hob and more. It **sleeps 8**, and has three reception rooms. The house gets water from a burn which flows through its six acres; there is splendid walking, and tenants may use the 'house rowing boat'. They can sail, windsurf and water-ski on Loch Earn, at the end of the glen. There's an award-winning restaurant half a mile up the road – 'very good, but expensive'.

Dogs are welcome, but this is sheep country, and they must be well controlled. Linen and towels are not available. TV. Cost: about £350 to £475. Details from John and Vanda Pelly, Spring Hill, East Malling, Kent ME19 6JW. Telephone 01732 842204, fax 873506.

Kirkmichael, near Pitlochry   map 4/166
Balnakilly Highland Cottages/Log Cabins

Perthshire – so much more accessible than, say, the western Highlands, is hilly, green and beautiful. These cottages ('sensibly priced', unpretentious, comfy, quiet and full of character: **Colour section, Page 2**) are on a 1500-acre estate. You could be 'miles from anywhere', but you're not in fact remote. There are four properties, one of them the traditional stone *Loch Cottage*, two of them Norwegian log cabins, the fourth a two storeyed timber building, fin-

Interior of Rowan, a substantial two-storey timber building that offers traditional 'cottagey comfort'...

ished to a good standard, called *Rowan Lodge*. We have always especially liked Loch Cottage, which all but opens right on to the water.

Sleeps 4 to 7. There's ski-ing in the area in season, and good walking, shooting and fishing are all readily available – on the estate and elsewhere. Dogs are welcome. Linen is provided, towels are available for hire. TV. Cost: £190 to £400. Details from Mr and Mrs Reid, Balnakilly Estates, Kirkmichael, Perthshire PH10 7NB. Telephone or fax 01250 881356.

www.balnakillyestate.co.uk   email: balnakilly@hotmail.com

95

Glen Strathfarrar, Struy, near Beauly
Culligran Cottages

These are superbly well situated, and
we have enjoyed a short stay in one of
the four Scandinavian chalets here.
They are warm, quite spacious, have
picture windows, and **sleep up to 7**.
On a Nature Reserve, but not remote,
and close to a salmon-rich river on a
sporting estate, Frank and Juliet
Spencer-Nairn have five properties,   *This is one of the best places in Scotland*
the other a characterful, traditional   *to observe wildlife in its natural habitat.*
cottage with a blend of 'antiquey', solid and modern furniture – plus a stag's
head! Three chalets have two bedrooms, the fourth three, as has the cottage.
All have a good fitted kitchen, the larger properties having a shower as well
as a bath. We enjoyed the 15 miles of metalled but private road leading up
Glen Strathfarrar, surely one of the Highlands' best kept secrets, 'similar to
Glen Affric but more intimate'. Ideal for biking: bikes for hire. No TV. Trout
and salmon fishing. Guided tours of Frank's deer farm. Dogs welcome. Cost:
about £189 to £489. Open mid-March to mid-November. Details from Frank
and Juliet Spencer-Nairn, Culligran Cottages, Glen Strathfarrar, Struy, near
Beauly, Inverness-shire IV4 7JX. Telephone/fax: 01463 761285.

www.culligrancottages.co.uk and **www.farmstay-highlands.co.uk/culligran**
email: **info@culligrancottages.co.uk**

Dalcross, East Inverness
Easter Dalziel   map 4/189

Unpretentious but lovingly cared-for
and comfortably furnished, this neat
and tidy trio of traditional, stone built
cottages makes an exceptionally
good base from which to explore the
whole of the north, east and west of
Scotland. Surrounded by a large
grassy area, they have a pretty
heather garden to the front and enjoy   *Always a warm and friendly welcome,*
panoramic views of the surrounding   *and unfussily comfortable cottages...*
countryside. On a working farm with beef cattle, sheep and grain, the
jewel in this particular Scottish crown is *Birch*, at one end of the three
adjoining properties. It is thickly carpeted, its pale green soft furnishings
and deep-pile carpets easy on the eye. There's a nice separate dining
alcove. **Sleeps 6**. *Rowan* and *Pine* (**sleeping 4 and 6**) are a little more old
fashioned but comfortable, warm and cottagey. They are reasonably
priced, and open all year. **'Visit Scotland' Three/Four Stars**. TV. Dogs
welcome. Linen and towels included. Cost: about £160 to £510. Details
from Mr and Mrs Pottie, Easter Dalziel Farm, Dalcross, Inverness IV2
7JL. Telephone and fax 01667 462213.

www.easterdalzielfarm.co.uk email: ghcg@easterdalzielfarm.co.uk

Scotland-wide
Scottish Country Cottages*

We're big fans of 'The Trossachs', which has lots of the advantages of the wild Highlands while being more accessible. So we were pleased to hear from readers who picked up on our recommendation last year of a property just yards from the beautiful focal point that is Loch Katrine. *The Old Smiddy* is a fine cottage, with loch views and a woodburner. It's a great place for touring, but close to 'home' you shouldn't miss out on a loch trip aboard the 'Sir Walter Scott'. **Sleeps 6**. Ref UYA.

A recent journey through much of Scotland was memorable for seeing a property that offers a rare chance to stay on the island of Lismore, off Port Appin (*Tigh An Uillt*, **sleeps 2**, Ref UPW). Also a substantial modern conversion (though in keeping with its surroundings) near Ballater, on 'Royal Deeside' (*Braehead Steading*, **sleeps 18**, Ref USY).

High Mains Cottage, on the Ayrshire coast, is one of our personal favourites.

Macinnisfree Cottage, on Skye, is an amazing place by any standards.

In a part of Scotland most outsiders don't know – the Ayrshire coast – *High Mains Cottage,* at Ballantrae, is an attractive traditional cottage, well modernised (but still with an open fire) with panoramic views. **Sleeping up to 6**, it has a big garden and is quietly located. A sand-and-shingle beach and a pub serving food are just a mile. Ref UPC.

A couple of years ago we heard from Buckinghamshire-based readers who stayed in *Macinnisfree Cottage*, on the Isle of Skye. **Sleeping 7**, this looks on to an extraordinary panorama that takes in some of western Scotland's most-loved coastal landmarks and seascapes. Ref SBC.

Any of the cottages on the Ardmaddy Estate, about twelve miles south of Oban, brings together history and fabulous views. There are four extremely well converted cottages, the biggest of which (in terms of accommodation) is *The Stables*, **sleeping 8 'plus 2'**. Ref SBZ.

One of our favourite parts of Scotland is the Kintyre peninsula, and we are very pleased to single out three extraordinary cottages, **each for 2**, once used by lighthouse keepers of the now-automated lighthouse on Davaar Island, near Campbeltown. (Refs SEE/SED/UMG.)

Details and brochures from Scottish Country Cottages, Stoney Bank, Earby, Colne, Lancashire BB94 0AA.

Brochures and bookings: 0845 268 1027.

www.scottish-country-cottages.co.uk

Escape with
EUROPCAR

Wherever you plan to escape, get there in safety, comfort and style with Europcar. Whether you need a bit more room or a bit more vroom Europcar will have a car to suit. All our cars are under six months old, fully maintained, and come with 24/7 breakdown recovery. With the UK's largest rental fleet of 60,000 vehicles, plus a nationwide network of over 250 locations, Europcar combines quality and convenience with great rates.

Planning an escape to the coast or country? Why not save wear and tear on your own car and rent instead? Rent a car with room for all the family, the luggage and that all-important bucket and spade. No need for back-seat drivers: you can share the driving by renting from Europcar. If it's a chic city break why not head off in a nippy hatchback – ideal for a weekend in one of our cultural towns or cities.

Whatever your plans, once you're there, enjoy the freedom to explore at your own pace and to your own itinerary – that's what self-catering holidays are all about!

Alternatively, if you fancy a bit of luxury then indulge in a driving experience from Europcar Prestige. Whether it's a Porsche, Mercedes or a Land Rover, Europcar Prestige has a car for even the most discerning driver.

Renting is easy with Europcar. Simply book with one click at www.europcar.co.uk. Alternatively call our dedicated reservation line on 0870 607 5000 or visit your local branch.

Ecosse Unique*

We have never, in 25 years, had a whisper of a complaint about this agency, which has about 300 properties spread all over Scotland, from the Border country to Orkney.

Being based in the Borders, the agency has been effective in promoting this often overlooked and much underrated region. During a recent visit to the Selkirk area, for example, we admired *The Steading* and *Knowpark Cottage*, amid quiet and idyllic countryside, well away from through traffic. They **sleep 4/5** and **5**.

Most properties, such as *Old Hyndhope*, **sleeping 6**, splendidly situated on a Selkirkshire hilltop, are in peaceful rural or coastal locations. Or, for

Among the many beautifully situated properties on the agency's books is Achduart, **sleeping 6** *and overlooking the tranquil Summer Isles. Just an amazing fifty yards from the sea and only four miles from Achiltibuie, it lies at the end of a single-track road and is completely secluded. With its own private garden, and access to a further five acres of wooded garden, it faces south and has spectacular sea and mountain views.*

stimulating city breaks, where apartments often have the edge over hotels, you could consider 17th century *Peffermill House* (**sleeping 6/7**) in Edinburgh, or one of the agency's rather elegant properties in Glasgow.

There are idyllic cottages in Highland Perthshire, such as *Balvarran Mill* (**sleeping 4**) near Pitlochry, near Loch Tay, and, among the hills near Dunkeld, the spectacularly positioned *Keeper's House* (**sleeping 6/7**).

There are also a number of excellent cottages round Loch Ness, such as *Bunloit Farmhouse* (**sleeping 5**), where the view is jaw-dropping. As well some fine properties, which we've seen, and which a Glasgow reader has praised, on the lovely Lynaberach and Ruthven Estate, near Kingussie.

On the ever-romantic islands of Skye, Mull and (just off the mainland near Kinlochmoidart) the privately owned Eilean Shona, there are excellent shoreline cottages (of all sizes) in locations to die for, while on the mainland there are many traditional Highland cottages set amid equally stunning scenery. For example *Bunallt Eachain* (**sleeping 8**), a fabulous property in a memorable location, *Achleek* (**sleeping 5/6**) on the shores of Loch Sunart, or *Achduart* (**sleeping 6**) which overlooks the lovely Summer Isles, off the west coast.

Do request their brochure: Ecosse Unique Ltd, Lilliesleaf, Melrose, Roxburghshire TD6 9JD. Telephone: 01835 822277. Fax 870417.

Or check their web sites:

www.unique-cottages.co.uk and **www.uniquescotland.com**

email: reservations@uniquescotland.com

Scotland-wide
Large Holiday Houses*

This is an extraordinary organisation, which has had a huge impact in the comparatively few years it has been running. In fact, it's done so well in Scotland that it is now extending very successfully into England (See 'Large Holiday Houses in England', Page 27). We've stayed in and/or visited several properties.

Most recently we drove via quiet roads towards Portmahomack, and the very imposing but nevertheless privately situated early 19th century country mansion called *Pitcalzean House*. We don't have the space here to do justice to this fabulous property, but we remember elegant rooms, fine furniture and paintings, as well as a warm and welcoming atmosphere. It **sleeps up to 23 people, plus 4** in a separate cottage.

There are over a hundred impressive properties (**sleeping from 7 to 37**) spread widely over Scotland on the books of Large Holiday Houses, run by Wynne Bentley, who founded it in 1997. Her own base, *Poyntzfield House*, a Grade A listed Georgian mansion (**sleeping 16 plus 4 under-10s**) near Inverness, is among them. She offers a compelling combination: the romance of great houses and castles, marvellous locations and the huge appeal of properties where extended families or groups of friends can stay together. Several are historically important, such as the 11th-century *Dairsie Castle* (**sleeping 11 'plus 2'**) in Fife, close to St Andrews, and cliff-top *Craighall Castle* (**sleeping 10**) in Perthshire.

Calgary Castle, which enjoys one of the best views on Mull, facing sandy Calgary Bay beyond meadows framed by woods, is more modern, having been built in the 18th century as a laird's house.

We had a delightful stay, ten miles south of Oban, at the secluded *Bragleen House* (**sleeping 7/8**) at the end of a five-mile lane beside Loch Scammadale. The owner, who built it in 1996, ready for his retirement, has combined luxury with comfort – spacious rooms, deep sofas, double-glazing and a fitted kitchen complete with bread-maker. After a walk up the glen at the back, we strolled later in the day down to the loch: perfect!

Details and a copy of the brochure (one of the best we've seen) from Wynne Bentley, Large Holiday Houses Ltd, Poyntzfield House, Poyntzfield, Dingwall, Ross-shire IV7 8LX. Telephone 01381 610496.

www.LHHScotland.com   email: LHH@LHHScotland.com

Lickleyhead Castle, Aberdeenshire. Family owned, never a ruin, it retains much of its original medieval atmosphere. Sleeps 14.

Drumrunie House, Braemar. A great 'good four star' family house, with super gardens and stunning views. Sleeps 12.

Scotland-wide
Little Holiday Houses*

As you might expect from the people behind Large Holiday Houses (see previous page), this is a very judiciously chosen selection of properties.

For example, there's a fine newly available property on the Moray coast called *Steading Cottage*, **sleeping 5**. It is owned by the people who live in the large mansion next door, and among the good things going for it – such as a superb light and bright interior – is access, by arrangement, to the owners' beautiful garden.

If you appreciate fine period houses you will probably like *Lochnagarry*, at Golspie in Sutherland. **Sleeping up to 10**, it is notable for elegant, high ceilinged rooms. There is a Rayburn and an open fire.

Almost any rural property on the stunningly beautiful west coast will appeal to readers of this guide. For example, *Clachan Garden*, near Ullapool, is a top notch property in a fabulous setting, located within one of our favourite features – a walled garden.

Culkein, equally memorable and pristine, is perched on the shores of Eddrachillis Bay, north of Lochinver, and underneath magnificent and famously photogenic Suilven mountain. It has an especially inviting and stylish sitting room, with an open fire. This and Clachan Garden **sleep 8** and **9** respectively.

Another beautifully situated property, in a rather famous location, is *The School House*, at Glenfinnan, famous for its great railway viaduct. Built in 1876, and **sleeping up to 8**, it has *two* woodburning stoves, including one in the master bedroom!

To rival this property is *Kellan Mill*, on the Isle of Mull. **Sleeping up to 7**, it's a beautiful and sensitive conversion of a former mill house. With fabulous views, its location is close to Ulva Ferry, from which there are nice jaunts across the water to the traffic-free island of Ulva.

Details and a copy of the brochure (one of the best we've seen) from Wynne Bentley, Little Holiday Houses Ltd, Poyntzfield House, Poyntzfield, Dingwall, Ross-shire IV7 8LX. Telephone 01381 610496.

www.LittleHolidayHouses.com
email: LHH@LHHScotland.com

Smartly on parade: handsome Clachan Garden is on the shores of Eddrachillis Bay, beneath Suilven mountain...

The School House, Glenfinnan, is on 'the 'Road to the Isles'. With a cosy woodburner, it's rather romantic. Sleeps 8.

'Do this...don't do that'

Some well-meant suggestions for owners and agents:

Do help first-time guests get their bearings. One of the most popular 'add-on' features in cottages is a full-size Ordnance Survey map of the immediate area, framed and hanging in a kitchen or a hall.

Do, if you really want holiday tenants eating out of your hand, provide little but always-appreciated items such as a home made cake, a bottle of wine, something bubbly for the bath.

Do, if you have a woodburner or multi-fuel stove, consider lighting this if the weather's cold and you know when people are arriving: this small act produces more ecstatic reader-responses than anything else.

Do, if you inhabit an ideal world, occasionally stay in the cottages yourselves so you can check out what's right and what's wrong (noisy plumbing, drafts, too-amorous local cats, nosy neighbours).

Do give detailed how-to-get-there instructions. Internet cartographic printouts are useful, and a bit of local information is a bonus ('Turn left *before* The Dog and Flea, not after'...'There's a hand-made sign nailed to the dead oak tree'...)

Do by all means clean cottages to within an inch of their lives, but do leave salt cellars and pepper pots with their contents intact. It's something few tenants think to bring, and their absence has ruined many a fish supper! We'd say leave oil, vinegar and spices too.

Do also provide soap, ideally in both liquid and old fashioned bar form: each has its fans! No soap at all is increasingly common.

Don't get in guests' hair as they try to settle in. Some well-meaning owners spend an hour telling people about eccentric previous guests and which cupboard the board games are hidden in when all the new arrivals really want to do is make a cup of tea and put their feet up.

Do decide whether pets are welcome or otherwise. There are owners who'll accept cats but not dogs, and vice versa, and a number who'll accept everything except tortoises. Leaving the question of pets open to negotiation can mean trying to run with the hare and hunt with the hounds.

Don't hesitate to take a deposit against damage. We wish everyone we feature would do so, but few do. (We've never heard of potential customers saying 'We won't go there because they want a deposit'...)

Tomich, near Cannich
Tomich Holidays

One of our favourite short journeys in the north of Scotland is westwards from Beauly, near Inverness, via quiet country roads bordered by trees, towards sleepy, little known Cannich, and then to end-of-the-road Tomich, a beautiful stone-built place, preserved as a conservation *Even in Highland terms the location is outstanding, and the properties excellent.* village. What we go to see is a delightful arrangement of stone and slate courtyard cottages. There's a snug and cosy Victorian dairy and six two-storeyed timber chalets. The cottages have memorable panoramic views and are highly graded by **'Visit Scotland'**. The Victorian dairy is a stone-built cottage, part of a Grade II listed building. A short stroll away, among trees, are the timber chalets, private but not remote, within 100 yards of another. Each is roomy, simple and 'practical', but comfortable, with balconies for wildlife spotting, birch trees and grassy banks. Most are booked by guests returning for 'endless walks', the cycling, the wildlife, the quiet, and the lovely indoor pool. Dogs welcome. TVs/videos/DVDs. **Sleep 4 to 6**. Cost: £240 to £605. Details from Tomich Holidays, Guisachan Farm, Tomich, By Beauly, Inverness-shire IV4 7LY. Telephone 01456 415332 or fax 415499.

www.tomich-holidays.co.uk   email: admin@tomich-holidays.co.uk

---

It's good to talk

We always recommend telephone discussions with an owner or agent about any properties that appeal, and the more detail you can give about particular concerns and requirements, the better. It is possible to book direct from this guide, and readers often do so late in the season or at short notice, but in general we recommend that readers send off first for brochures and other information. Elements essential to readers' holiday enjoyment and peace of mind should be double checked prior to making any commitment. This applies for example to the number of people a property comfortably sleeps, whether bedrooms are all upstairs, the types of bed ('firm', 'soft', etc), whether en suite, and whether bathrooms have bath or shower or both.

Short breaks

Readers often write or phone about short breaks, and sometimes ask why we don't list the properties that offer these. It's because about ninety per cent do. This can almost be taken for granted, depending on the time of year, and it is usually worth asking about a short break even during the main holiday season. Winter weekends especially can still be a bargain, but are more realistically priced than they used to be, when some owners were happy 'just to keep the places lived in'...

Rural Retreats*
Dumfries/Newtonmore/Plockton

We are fond of the little-known country north of Dumfries where Rural Retreats (see also Page 216) have four properties on the superb green, rolling 3300 acre Crofts Estate. We visited recently, and saw *Marwhirn Cottage*, **sleeping 4**, and *Marwhirn House*. Close together but still private, both are beautifully located half a mile down a private drive. We met holiday tenants installing themelves in Marwhirn House, and loving it.

In another part of Scotland that in our view doesn't get the attention it deserves, *Bishop Cottage* is a 200-year-old, listed property in the centre of Ceres, a village of great character and historic associations. With thick walls and a slate roof, the cottage has been completely restored to a high standard. **Sleeping 4**, with an enclosed garden, and views over the village and countryside, it makes a delightful base from which to explore Fife.

Among several superbly well situated properties is *Borenich*, near

Sitting room of Borenich, a super, detached, recently refurbished property near the popular town of Pitlochry.

Lochenkit, near Dumfries, lies on a private estate, and sleeps up to eight people in comfort and style...

Pitlochry, very close to (though not quite in sight of) Loch Tummel. **Sleeping 6**, with a zip-link double bed in the main bedroom, it has an open fire and stands within an acre and a half of its own grounds. Also in Perthshire, *Gushat* is an extended semi-detached cottage converted from the village shop. **Sleeping 6**, it's right opposite a nine-hole golf course!

And just two miles from Plockton, one of the prettiest and most visited villages in the Highlands, *Achnandaroch Lodge* is a Swiss-chalet style property, **sleeping 9**. Just five miles from Kyle of Lochalsh and the now-free bridge to Skye, it means that that fabulous island is within the scope of, say, a summer evening excursion.

Lochenkit is a 19th century farmhouse on a private estate. Refurbished to high standards, it **sleeps 8** in great comfort. It is on the edge of the moors, with delightful walks. There's a large farmhouse kitchen with an Aga, a sitting room with a log fire, one king-size bedroom with ensuite bathroom, one double and two twin rooms.

Details and a copy of the organisation's impressive brochure from Rural Retreats, Draycott Business Park, Draycott, Gloucestershire GL56 9JY. Telephone 01386 701177, fax 701178.

www.ruralretreats.co.uk   email: info@ruralretreats.co.uk

Kinlochlaggan, near Newtonmore
Ardverikie Estate Cottages

Two summers ago it was a pleasure, not just a duty, to revisit the holiday properties here. For they are surely among the most beautifully situated in the whole of Scotland – which is to rate them very highly!

We met tenants staying in *Gallowvie Farmhouse* and admired spacious rooms, high ceilings, deep sofas, lots of comfort. With, for example, a five-oven Aga, and accommodation for **up to 13**, it has lots of atmosphere. Also, there's an enclosed mature garden. We also revisited *Inverpattack Lodge*, standing on its own on a hillside overlooking the road with good views, **sleeping up to 12**. It has a good sized sitting room, a big dining room and farmhouse kitchen. We have always liked this a lot: a real, rather nostalgic 'family house'.

The estate, rising above and around Loch Laggan, is a kind of microcosm of the extraordinary Highlands. It even embraces a substantial sandy beach that is just one bonus for city dwellers escaping to one of the characterful cottages tucked away in the heart of, or on the edge of, the Estate.

It's well away from any town, a real tonic for people wanting to get away from city cares, but it's not actually in the back of beyond.

There's a good range of sizes and different degrees of seclusion as well as different styles of interior. If you prefer family furniture to MFI and care more about seeing a deer, a hare or a pine marten while you are doing the washing up than about dishwashers and deep-pile carpets, these could be for you. All the houses except *Pinewood*, incidentally, have open fires with free firewood.

Most recently available is *Rowan Brae*, **sleeping 6** and quietly situated close to the water and good walking. We admired the special character of *Ardverikie Gate Lodge* – a listed building this, by a road, best suited to a couple plus, say, one friend or relative. The spiral stair is excellent and fine prints and a particularly good bedroom enhance its appeal further. Pinewood has an especially cosy dining room, gets lots of sun and is indeed among the trees. Not a luxury item but, we thought, welcoming and comfortable. **Sleeps 4**.

Gate Lodge absolutely sets the mood as you approach this memorable place...

Inverpattack sleeps twelve, with masses of space and even more 'character'.

Cost: about £445 to £1450: not expensive if you consider how many the larger properties sleep. Details from Desiree Bruce, The Estate Office, Kinlochlaggan, Inverness-shire PH20 1BX. Telephone 01528 544322.

www.ardverikie.com   email: desireebruce@blueyonder.co.uk

Attadale, near Lochcarron

We recently revisited Attadale, on a glorious summer day. The fabulous gardens that are just one reason for booking a holiday in one of the charming, bright and spacious cottages on the estate were surely at their best.

On a previous and memorable occasion we had taken a train from Kyle of Lochalsh to Inverness, getting off at the tiny station halt ('by request only') that serves the Attadale estate. The line and its surroundings got us reaching for our index of superlatives: 'unforgettable scenery'..'a blissful escape from the everyday world'...'exceptional even in Highland terms'.

By road, the A890 must surely be one of the most scenic routes in the Highlands, especially where it veers westwards from the Ullapool/ Inverness road, and then arrives at Kyle of Lochalsh, across the water from Skye. With panoramic views at every turn, it surely underlines one's belief that Scotland is one of the most beautiful countries in the world.

Across the loch from the elongated, pretty, white-painted village of Lochcarron you take a private drive; with the single track railway and the loch behind us, we reached the owners' impressive mansion, and from there drove out into the estate, passing the beautiful gardens that are open to the public, and finally reached the cottages.

Guests have complete access to the estate, famous for its wildlife and its natural beauty, except from 15th August to 15th October when they are asked to keep to the paths while deer are being culled. Loch fishing up in the hills is available, and following a seven year restocking programme, sea trout and salmon have returned to the River Carron: day tickets are available.

In the cottages we noticed open fires or wood stoves, good beds, lots of lamps, many very attractive pictures (some by the owners' daughter, who is a painter). Here was a delightfully lit alcove, there a congenial juxtaposition of dining room and kitchen.

Such a romantic, 'away from it all' location, with comfy estate cottages...

...in complete harmony with their beautiful and unspoilt surroundings.

Sleep 4 to 8. Well behaved, sheep-respecting dogs welcome. Linen and towels provided. No TV reception. Cost: from £290 to £515. Details and colour brochure from Frances Mackenzie, Attadale, Strathcarron, Wester Ross IV54 8YX. Telephone/fax 01520 722862.

www.attadale.com   email: cottages@attadale.com

Glen Coe
Glen Coe Cottages

On a quiet Saturday morning last year we took 'the old road' up towards Glencoe to revisit one of our all-time favourite Scottish holiday cottage set-ups: *24 years in the guide*, and never a complaint. So close to the mysterious and famous glen, to get to these three neat, tucked away pebbledash bungalows in their leafy enclave overlooking the River Coe you cross a cattle grid and pause beside the mirror-like Torren lochan (featured in a Harry Potter adventure, 'The Prisoner of Azkaban' – filmed in Glencoe). After this you continue along a track to the three cottages, which combine mod cons with just a hint of the outdoor life – the setting is beautiful and not remote and you do not have to have climbing boots to enjoy it. Fishing is available in the owners' two trout lochs and in the river that flows prettily past the doorstep.

A high standard of comfort is achieved despite the comparatively small size and open plan nature of the single-storey buildings. All the cottages have underfloor heating, fired by an eco-friendly woodchip boiler, and dishwasher, and a shared laundry room for those damper days – for this is

The river and the dramatic glen are near: one is memorably 'close to nature'.

The cottages are 'compact', but well planned and notably warm all year round.

'outward-bound country'. There's a large drying room in the laundry building, a TV/video in each cottage, a payphone and internet access.

All three cottages have a good degree of privacy, because they separately face the river through big picture windows and do not look directly at each other. The River Coe is very well fenced off from the properties and there is no danger to little ones. There is a lot of pinewood, well fitted kitchens and sitting-cum-dining rooms.

This is an excellent base from which to tour not only the wild landscape of Glen Coe and Rannoch Moor but, being close to the Corran Ferry, it is quickly accessible to the Morvern and Ardnamurchan peninsulas and, beyond them, the Isle of Mull. Fort William is half an hour to the north.

Sleep 6 to 8, or the whole place can be taken over by a group of **up to 24**. '**Visit Scotland**' Gold Award for Environmental Management; member of ASSC. **Three 'Visit Scotland' Stars**. Dogs welcome, 'wi-fi' is installed (no charge). Discount for couples-only, children under two free, cots and highchairs included free. Cost: up to a maximum of £795, two-night weekends £296. Details from Victoria Sutherland, Torren, Glencoe, Argyll PH49 4HX. Telephone 01855 811207. Fax 811338.

www.glencoe-cottages.com   email: victoria@glencoe-cottages.com

Aultbea, near Gairloch
Shore Croft

This **Five Star** house is in a beautiful part of Scotland, on a peninsula overlooking Loch Ewe, only yards from a pebble beach, and just 20 minutes' drive from charming Gairloch. The fine architect-designed house has the further advantage of memorable views. **Sleeping up to 8** in great comfort, Shore Croft has accommodation on two floors.

The house is quite an attraction in itself, and the location sets it off beautifully...

Downstairs there's a very large kitchen/dining room with dishwasher, range cooker, a large American fridge freezer and microwave. There is a dining table seating eight and French doors opening on to decking with garden furniture and a barbecue, a large sitting room with open fire, satellite TV, DVD and music system, plus a cloakroom. Upstairs, the master bedroom has an en-suite shower room and separate dressing room; there are three further twin bedded rooms and a family bathroom.

Open all year. Cost: about £495 to £1050 per week (Christmas and New Year prices on application). Dogs welcome. No smoking. Contact Hilary Cowan. Telephone 0151 494 1488.

www.shorecroft.co.uk
email: hilary.cowan3@btinternet.com

Kilberry, near Tarbert
Laundry Cottage (Kilberry Castle)   map 4/206

What a memorable location! In the grounds of Kilberry Castle, this lovely three-bedroom cottage has uninterrupted views of the Western Isles, notably of one of our all-time favourites, which is Jura. (Kilberry is mid way between Tarbert and Lochgilphead in an area of outstanding natural beauty with sandy beaches and rocky headlands where you can watch spectacular sunsets.) The cottage's secluded woodland setting guarantees privacy and tranquillity. A short walk via woods takes you

In a 'don't miss' corner of western Scotland, a cosy cottage on the edge of woodland, with fabulous views.

to a lovely sandy beach. The cottage interior is spacious, clean, and comfortably furnished, with beautiful views from all rooms, and the comfortable sitting room has an open fire for cosy evenings. Upstairs are three bedrooms, one double and two twin, and a large bathroom. Details from Kilberry Castle Cottage [Laundry Cottage], Kilberry, near Tarbert, Argyll, Scotland PA29 7YD. Telephone 01880 770217

www.argyll-cottage.co.uk   email: kilberry_castle@hotmail.com

Strontian, by Acharacle
Seaview Grazings

For about twenty years now, this harmonious, easy-on-the-eye arrangement of Scandinavian log cabins has proved to be the makings of a delightful getting-to-know-the-Highlands experience for cottage guide readers. And many of these have become regulars at Seaview Grazings: 70% of bookings are repeats, with many weeks sold out months in advance. When we last visited, the Hanna family who run it were awaiting the arrival of a family who have been coming here for a fortnight's holiday *three times a year for seventeen years*.

The eleven-acre site has seven cabins (**sleeping 4 or 5**) on a lightly wooded hillside facing the loch. Built of real pine-logs, they are available throughout the year, being of permanent-home standard with double-glazing, modern kitchens and full bathrooms, all now with over-bath shower. Each feels private, but many guests like the fact that there are neighbours (and the owners) near at hand. Shops and pubs are only a mile away.

All the cabins, which are regularly refurbished, have large windows to make the most of the lovely views, yet they have a really warm atmosphere inside, with full central heating. The fully-fitted kitchens have four-ring electric cookers, washing machines, fridge/freezers, microwaves and roomy cupboards.

Boat-hire can easily be arranged locally, as can loch fishing – for beginners as well as more experienced anglers – up in the hills. The area is also excellent for all grades of walking. 'Wild glens, peaceful woodlands, beautiful coastal walks and mountain challenges – at the end of a week we'd experienced only a fraction of what was on offer', wrote one reader.

Yet another extraordinary location on the west coast of Scotland! Quite amazing...

Each of the log houses feels private and self contained, but there's no isolation.

Motoring from Strontian is a joy too. We ourselves arrived after a visit to Mull via the 19-mile drive from the pretty ferry crossing at Lochaline.

Blankets/duvets, linen, towels, electricity included. Children's cots and highchairs available free of charge. Three cabins have two bedrooms (double and twin), the others have three (double, twin and single). Cost: from about £280 to £620. Some short breaks available. Details from John Hanna, Seaview Grazings Holidays, Strontian, by Acharacle, Argyll PH36 4HZ. Telephone 01967 402409.

www.seaviewgrazings.co.uk
email: gareth@seaviewgrazings.co.uk

Elgol/Staffin

Over the years we've visited a good clutch of properties on Skye in the hands of the ever more interesting and go-ahead Welcome Cottages organisation. Here are two that retain a lot of their original character and are in scenically impressive locations. In the exceptionally quiet and attractive village of Elgol, near Broadford, a cottage **sleeping 6** (Ref W41104), with an open fire, has the huge advantage for any but the most confirmed lounge lizards of being

At Elgol, near Broadford, this is 'one to remember'. At the end of a beautiful country road, it has spectacular views and an open fire. Sleeps up to six people.

just five minutes from the Cuillin Hills. Further north, at Staffin (Staffin Island is famous for its birdlife) is a handsome, traditional crofthouse (Ref W4138) that makes a comfortable holiday base. **Sleeping 4**, it has panoramic views, a woodburning stove and is handy for visiting impressive Dunvegan Castle.

For availability and bookings, contact Welcome Cottages, Spring Mill, Earby, Barnoldswick, Lancashire BB94 0AA. Brochures/bookings: 0845 268 0945. Properties in France are also available.

www.welcomecottages.com

Stein (Isle of Skye)
The Captain's House

We appreciate almost every corner of Skye, but we especially like the more out-of-the-way places. One such is the quiet, pretty, waterside village of Stein **(map 4/203)**, where nothing is out of place within its row of white houses. They incorporate one of the best pubs and one of the best seafood restaurants on the island. The handsomest house of all,

The Captain's House is an excellent property, a great place from which to explore the whole of Skye...

known for its ground floor art gallery and craft shop, is The Captain's House. The first and second floors of this make up a spacious holiday house (self-contained, private and quiet). We liked the big sitting room, the deep sofa and armchairs and the Victorian tiled open fire. The large kitchen/breakfast room overlooks the loch, as do all but one of the rooms in this appealing property; off it there's a separate dining room. There are two large bedrooms, one double and one twin. **'Visit Britain' Three Stars**. **Sleeps up to 4** (cot available). Non-smoking. Linen, not towels, included. Dogs by arrangement. Cost: about £225 to £390. Details from Mrs Cathy Myhill, The Captain's House, Stein, Waternish, Isle of Skye IV55 8GA. Telephone 01470 592223/592218.

www.the-captains-house.co.uk   email: cathy@the-captains-house.co.uk

Isle of Mull (Carsaig)
Pier Cottage/The Library

This is an unusual and most appealing holiday property. A few yards above the rocky shore on the island's south coast, these two remote cottages convey something of an 'end of the world' feeling as you approach them. Access is along a four-mile narrow wooded lane off the single-track 'main' road, which is one of the most scenic we've ever driven. The single-storey stone *Pier*

Marvellous, we thought, for autumn and winter breaks. (This is Pier Cottage.)

Cottage has a sun-porch where we found two happy visitors watching out for otters and seals over a late breakfast. None appeared while we were there but as a consolation they gave us bunches of delicious grapes from the prolific vine that covered the ceiling. Wood-panelling inside Pier Cottage (**sleeping 3/4**) gives it a cosy feel and there are masses of books. *The Library* – built originally to house more of the owner's books – is a roomy, open-plan log-cabin (**sleeping 4/6**) up the terraced garden. Cost: £325 to £495. Mid-winter weeks often available from £195.

Details from David McLean, The Oasis, 181 Lyham Rd, Brixton, London SW2 5PY. Telephone 020 8671 6663. Mobile 07738 816469.

email: dhmclean@tiscali.co.uk

Dervaig (Isle of Mull)   map 4/207
Penmore Mill

Even during its first year in the guide we had happy reader reports about this. An old watermill (**sleeping 8/9 people**) just outside the village of Dervaig – famous for the tiny Mull Little Theatre – was imaginatively converted by Pat and Iain Morrison, who live in the house behind. We guessed Pat is an artist: the bathroom is a pale turquoise, and each bedroom, two doubles (one downstairs),

Rather a long haul to get there – but, we thought, well worth the journey.

a twin and one with bunks, features its own colour scheme set off by pine floors. A long pine table is the centrepiece of the fitted kitchen – fridge-freezer, washing-machine, dishwasher, microwave, double-electric oven – which has a terracotta tiled floor with cosy underfloor heating and a farm-house atmosphere. It leads into the sitting room with its log-effect stove and deep sofas. A sheltered patio-deck makes a pleasant sitting/eating area. Iain runs the island's Turus Mara boat trips, so most guests go to see Fingal's Cave on Staffa and to the Treshnish Isles, home to a colony of puffins. Cost: about £500 to £850.

Details from 01438 869489. email: info@goodcottageguide.com

Isle of Carna
Isle of Carna Cottage

Having featured this cottage in our guide for two years we actually stayed in it in 2006 – an idyllic short break. You almost have the whole of the little island to yourself: there are just two other cottages, only one of those for holiday letting (see below):

This cottage really is one in a thousand!

hard by the landing stage for the 16-foot boat, with outboard, that comes with your booking. 'Isle of Carna' cottage is two hundred metres along the pretty foreshore from there. For many visitors its appeal is not just the closeness to nature but the fact that there is no electricity. Cooking is by means of a bottled-gas stove, lighting by gas or candle, plentiful heating/water by a Parkray Anthracite stove – we tested it – an open fire and closed stove. There's a large Calor gas fridge.

The beautiful 600-acre traffic-free island lies in the middle of Loch Sunart, between the peninsula of Ardnamurchan to the north and the remote hills of Morvern to the south. The 550 ft rocky peak offers spectacular views (we did the climb!) and there are many rocky inlets and beaches ideal for watching wildlife: seals, herons, cormorants, eagles, buzzards, porpoises, otters, foxes and red deer live here. Originally a shepherd's bothy, the cottage is a cosy, well equipped, tranquil base for trips on or off the island. Caretakers contactable by radio at any time. Cost (including boat): about £575 to £850. Dogs welcome. Linen supplied, but not towels. **Sleeps up to 8,** with two adult sized bunk beds. Details from Timothy and Sue Milward, Pine House, Gaddesby, Leicestershire LE7 4XE. Telephone 01664 840213. Fax 840660. **www.isleofcarna.co.uk email: suemilward@googlemail.com**

Isle of Carna
Carna Farmhouse

You'll probably initially be transported to your holiday accommodation on Carna by one of the Jackson family, who run boat charters and look after both of the letting properties. Closer to the landing stage than Isle of Carna Cottage, Carna Farmhouse is a comfy bungalow,

Looking towards Carna Farmhouse, from beside Isle of Carna Cottage.

sleeping 4 plus 2. Here, there's electric light (only) from a generator. Linen and towels included.

Also available on the mainland: a fine, spacious apartment at Glenborrodale, overlooking Carna (accessed from very steep stairs).

Details from Allison and Andy Jackson, Bruach na Fearna, Laga Bay, Acharacle, Ardnamurchan, Argyll PH36 4JW. Telephone 01972 500 208. Fax 500222. Mobile: 07799 608199.

www.west-scotland-marine.com email: ardcharters@aol.com

Three Mile Water (Fort William)
Druimarbin Farmhouse

Revisited by us one recent summer, this fine, pleasantly rambling family house – just three miles south of Fort William – has marvellous views of Loch Linnhe. We appreciate the home comforts, the character and the location: excellent for touring. Reached via its own drive, and on the edge of woodland, it **sleeps up to 7/8** (in comfortable beds) – though the handsome dining table will actu- *This is a warm and comfortable base for a family holiday in the Highlands, with many gratifying reader reports...* ally seat 12. There is an open fire (logs are supplied) in the drawing room, which is graced by fine paintings, antique furniture, comfortable sofas, old fashioned armchairs. There are lots of good books, the odd bit of tartanry to remind you you're in the Highlands, a very well equipped kitchen, a payphone, Ordnance Survey maps.

TV, video and DVD. Bedlinen included. Walk-in drying room. Dogs possible by arrangement. Cost: £700 to £800 per week. Further details are available from Mrs Anthony German-Ribon, 57 Napier Avenue, London SW6 3PS. Telephone/fax 020-7736 4684.

www.coruanan.co.uk   email: germanribon@googlemail.com

By Fort William   map 4/209
Coruanan Farmhouse

A memorable part of a recent visit to the Highlands was to a house amid lovely, partly wooded country high above the Fort William-Corran road, at the end of a private lane. In the same ownership as Druimarbin (see above) and quite close to that, Coruanan has a partial view of Loch Linnhe and a superb view of Ben Nevis. **Sleeping 6**, it has an intriguing *One of the happiest discoveries of our summer 2006 visit to the Highlands.* history: in 1745, the site was the home of the standard bearer to Lochiel (Clan Cameron Chieftain) during Bonnie Prince Charlie's Jacobite Rebellion. The standard was found at the turn of the century in one of the old buildings here where it had lain since the rebels' defeat at Culloden. It is now at Achnacarry Castle, home of the present Lochiel.

A sitting room with an open log fire, a cosy kitchen/diner, central heating and double glazing, a drying cupboard (for outdoor clothing), telephone, TV, DVD and CD players, a dishwasher, washing machine, tumble drier, microwave and fridge freezer make this a truly comfortable house.

Cost: about £500-£800 per week. Long weekend breaks (winter only) £350. Dogs possible by arrangement.

Details as for Druimarbin, above.

Achahoish, near Lochgilphead
Ellary Estate Cottages

Over the years, one of our greatest pleasures in putting this guide together has been driving westwards and then further westwards on the Scottish mainland. And then, if we're lucky with our itinerary, catching a Caledonian MacBrayne ferry to one or more of the Hebridean islands.

While still on the mainland, the journey to the Ellary estate, via ever narrower country roads, and with ever more impressive panoramic views at nearly every turn, is one of the most memorable for us. It's 25 years since we first came here (*the Ellary cottages have appeared in every edition since our first*) and it seemed appropriate to make one of our occasional revisits one recent summer.

Ellary stands out as a haven of quiet and calm, an antidote to stress. It is one of those places that *guarantees* 'peace, perfect peace'. (Even the nearest shop is 20 minutes' drive!)

The 15,000 acres on the sumptuous promontory between Lochs Sween and Caolisport, in Argyll, belong to the Ellary estate, an ancient family property that is partly farmed (predominantly sheep) yet mostly left wild

Ellary Cottage is a favourite of ours. Sleeping 4, it's the oldest of the cottages.

Location, location, location...it's a pleasure to sit and drink in the scenery.

for recreation purposes. Guests are welcome to wander where they will.

No-one can guarantee that you'll see otter, deer, eagles, peregrines, wildcats or any other estate residents, but they will certainly tell you where and when to look. There are several lovely beaches of white sand, and fishing – trout from the lochs and salmon and sea trout in Lochead Burn. Four of the self-catering units are ranch-type chalets, simply-built wooden structures with wide verandahs overlooking the loch. The cottages, recently much upgraded and without exception havens of comfort and warmth are mostly of stone. *The Lodge* is a particular joy: we loved the spiral staircase! There is an open fire as well as night storage heaters, a double room and two twin rooms. We also admired *Gardener's Cottage* and looked in again to one of our all-time favourites, *Ellary Cottage*.

All this adds up to a peaceful retreat that is also suitable for energetic families, to which many of our readers return year after year.

Sleep 4 to 8. Cost: about £252 to £610. Pets usually possible by arrangement. Details from The Estate Office, Ellary, Lochgilphead, Argyll PA31 8PA. Telephone 01880 770232 or 770209. Fax 770386.

www.ellary.com   email: info@ellary.com

Scotland-wide
Blakes Country Cottages (Scotland)*

There's something about holiday houses in Scotland that seems to inspire nationwide letting agents. And the Scottish section of the Blakes brochure is especially appealing. We've heard from a number of readers that it was after staying in Blakes cottages in England that they were encouraged to 'try Scotland'.

While checking out several properties in the Ullapool area we found ourselves asking for directions in a rural general store. We got talking to people staying in a Blakes cottage nearby, called *Caberfeidh* (**sleeping 6,** Ref 1809). Though it was not on our schedule, we were asked to tea – and, of course, to admire the cottage, a converted croft. We *especially* admired

Seeing Caberfeidh was an unexpected bonus for us: an open fire and great views.

Four Winds: you could spend a week or longer just gazing out of the window.

the fabulous views, the open fire, the seven acres of orchard, the private path to the lochside, and much more. We found ourselves rather envying our hosts and proud tenants.

We've heard from two readers who like the look of a superbly located property at Glenelg, which is easily accessible to the short ferry crossing to the Isle of Skye – a much more romantic way of getting to the island than via the new(ish) bridge. **Sleeping 4,** *Rams Cottage* is a recent conversion that combines comfort *and* character, and is well situated for memorable walking – plus the chance of seeing otters. Ref 14464.

A reader who stayed at *Four Winds*, at St Monans, overlooking the Firth of Forth ('fabulous views from every room, including the loo!') recommends it highly. **Sleeping 4,** it is a traditional end-terrace fisherman's cottage renovated to 21st century standards. Ref B5743.

Most usefully there are three very comfortable (**Four Stars**) apartments superbly located in Oban, a vital jumping off point for the Hebridean islands and some ferry trips that are a delight in themselves. **Sleeping 2, 4 and 6,** these *Esplanade Court Apartments* overlook Oban Bay: such a lot going on! Refs B5888, B5890, B5892.

Further details are available from Blakes, Stoney Bank Road, Earby, Barnoldswick BB94 0AA. Bookings/brochures 0845 268 0944.

Live search and book: www.blakes-cottages.co.uk

Arduaine, near Kilmelford
Arduaine Cottages

We'd not seen these two beauties since a new owner took over. A very skilful upgrading, plus masses of 'TLC', have made both *The Chalet* and *The Post House Cottage* among the most desirable holiday properties on the west coast. We visited recently, and although there are so many good things to single out we especially remember harmonious light, colour schemes, one of the most charming

On Scotland's beautiful west coast, with stunning panoramic seascape views.

and beautifully lit kitchen-diners (in Post House) we have seen, top quality beds and fabrics, expensive and well chosen floorings, lighting and mirrors. The Chalet **sleeps 2 'plus 2'**, with an open plan sitting room/kitchen, double sofa bed and a dining table by a picture window to take advantage of the view of Loch Melfort. The separate bedroom has twin beds. The Post House Cottage has a large kitchen/diner, plus picture-windowed sitting room, and **sleeps up to 5** in two bedrooms, one with a king sized double, the other with a double and a single. TVs, DVDs, videos, stereos. Pets welcome. Linen and towels included. Cost: from about £240. Details from Julie Rowden, Arduaine Cottages, Arduaine, Argyll PA34 4XQ. Telephone 01852 200216.

www.arduainecottages.com   email: arduainecottages@aol.com

Machrie, near Port Ellen/Bowmore   map 4/215
Machrie Hotel Lodges

Islay is one of our all-time favourite Hebridean islands, and the *Machrie Lodges* are superbly positioned near the Machrie Golf Course and the Machrie Hotel. The hotel has a reputation for providing the best food on Islay: a huge bonus for self caterers, and there's an ongoing programme of improvements to its lodges. We visited two of three that have been

You don't have to be a golfer...

upgraded – though they are all acceptable for a holiday base. We found these two delightful: closest of the group of fifteen to the golf links, and with superb views of Laggan Bay (though every property has panoramic views). We admired a spacious triple aspect sitting room/diner/kitchen, cosy bedrooms – two twins, one en suite – an excellent sense of colour co-ordination: we liked the deep-cushioned cane sofa and armchairs in dark green and tartan, the big reading lamps, the plain walls. **Sleep up to 6** (with sofa bed). TV. Dogs welcome in the 'standard' lodges. Linen/towels included. Cost: £180 to £750. Details: the Machrie Hotel, Port Ellen, Isle of Islay, Argyll PA42 7AN. Telephone 01496 302310. Fax 302404.

www.machrie.com   email: machrie@machrie.com

Carradale, Kintyre
Torrisdale Castle Cottages and Apartments

In the summer of 2006 we revelled in a long overdue revisit to a handful of properties that for us encapsulate the charms of one of the most delightful parts of Scotland. For within Torrisdale Castle itself (well down the leafy, rather secret, eastern side of the Kintyre peninsula, just a few minutes' drive from Campbeltown) and on its fine, wooded estate there are respectively spacious, very private, comfortable apartments and individual houses of character and long lasting appeal. *All have featured in this guide for 25 years without a break.*

We revisited most of them. We noted, in the castle, high ceilings, large rooms, comfortable sofas, well equipped kitchens or kitchenettes, and just enough individual little details (like secret alcoves that actually form part of the turrets) to add a touch of character and individuality to each one. The flats **sleep between 4 and 6**, with lots of space for an extra bed, and are **'Visit Scotland' Three Stars**.

The cottages are on a leafy and exceptionally quiet estate, and are all well away from each other. They are not show-houses, but are 'practical' and notably inexpensive. *South Lodge*, which **sleeps 2**, is on the 'B' road that runs the length of the peninsula, but it is mainly used by local and holiday traffic. It has the advantage of overlooking a pretty and sandy bay which is, of course, readily available to all guests here. We actually stayed here when we visited two summers ago: comfy, quiet, nicely self contained. We particularly liked *Lephinbeag Cottage*, at the end of its own rough drive, overhung with tall trees and with a babbling burn rippling beside it. It is quite small (two bedrooms, **sleeping 4**) but one of those places that, with a peat or log fire burning, after a day tramping through the hills, has lots of charm.

Lephincorrach Farmhouse, with its spacious kitchen and dining room, **sleeps 10** in five bedrooms. *Garden Cottage*, **sleeping 4** in two bedrooms – a downstairs double and, intriguingly, an attic room reached by ladder – is beautifully, peacefully situated among trees. *Glen House* is a converted croft house, **sleeping 7** in three bedrooms.

Televisions. Dogs are welcome. Cost: about £150 to £490. Further details are available from Mr and Mrs Macalister Hall, Torrisdale Castle, Carradale, Kintyre, Argyll PA28 6QT. Telephone/fax 01583 431233.

www.torrisdalecastle.com
email: machall@torrisdalecastle.com

Spacious Lephincorrach Farmhouse sleeps 10 in five bedrooms.

The castle, looking out to sea, contains several impressively roomy apartments.

Cumbria and the Lake District

Cottage owners and agents in certain parts of the country look enviously at 'the Lakes', mainly because it comes close to enjoying an all-year-round season. Readers of this guide, and other holiday tenants, seem to be as content in a tucked-away Lakeland cottage during an icy February as during a hot August (we are too, though we insist on a log fire or a glass-fronted woodburner – the best kind). So don't take it for granted that the cottage that has a waiting list in high summer is available in winter. Especially among those idyllic places that are perched above or right beside famous lakes such as Windermere, Coniston, Derwentwater and Ullswater. After a recent visit, we know how they get those so-perfect photographs of looking glass lakes reflecting a cloudless blue sky and the awe-inspiring hills! Seen from above, unforgettable. But we are fond of less well known lakes such as Thirlmere, Bassenthwaite and Esthwaite, and of holiday cottages on the fringe of the Lakes-proper, such as the sleepy Eden Valley, still one of 'England's best-kept-secrets', There is something special about striking off into the empty hills on one of those windswept, bright and showery days of early spring when clouds are scudding across the ever-changing sky, or walking through the grounds of one of the region's great country houses when winter closes in.

Watermillock, near Ullswater
Land Ends   map 8/236

As you approach these cottages, along little-used country lanes, you feel 'a hundred miles from anywhere', but in fact you're just a mile or so from Lake Ullswater. The four log cabins are in 25 peaceful acres of gardens and natural woodland, with streams and exceptional birdlife, on the slopes of Little Mell Fell. Opposite the cabins is "guests' own" lake, with ducks and moorhens and areas of mown grass with seating for walking

Featured by us for many years, these handsome log cabins are deeply rural without actually being isolated.

or relaxing. (Look or listen out for red squirrels, tawny owls and woodpeckers.) Dogs are 'very welcome', and can get plenty of exercise. There is a second lake further down the grounds, and an 18-acre field for strolling in. You are surrounded by dramatic scenery, many attractions and superb hill-walking. The nearest village (Pooley Bridge) is three miles away, but there is a pub serving good food just a mile down the road.

Sleep 2 to 5. TVs. **'Visit Britain' Three Stars.** Linen is included, but not towels. Cost: about £270 to £540. Open all year. Details/brochures from Land Ends, Watermillock, Cumbria CA11 0NB. Telephone 017684 86438.

www.landends.co.uk

email: infolandends@btinternet.com

Kirkland, near Penrith
Kirkland Hall Cottages

'A superb location – a bolthole to escape to from the rigours of life.' ...'Pretty, quiet and comfortable.' ...'We've been coming each year since 1990 – sometimes twice a year.' These were typical of the comments we read in the visitors' book while staying last autumn in Haybarn, one of four attractive cottages created from sandstone farm buildings by Ian and Lesley Howes. They have run the cottages for twenty years and still take immense pride in making them warm and welcoming for their guests.

The location, at the foot of the Pennines in an Area of Outstanding Natural Beauty, is very special. It lies at the end of narrowing roads east from Penrith, ten miles away. Beyond the cottages, hills rise to Cross Fell, nearly 900 metres high. Its summit – a bracing climb: allow anything from two to five hours – looks down over the Eden Valley to the Lake District fells.

In *Haybarn* (**sleeping 6/7** plus cot), the ground floor is taken up by a big sitting-room with dining area and well-equipped farmhouse-style pitch-pine kitchen at one end. Three big sofas surround an enormous sit-in inglenook fireplace with a large log-burning stove where we toasted our toes. From the centre of the room an open staircase leads up to a minstrels' gallery, an en-suite double bedroom, two twin bedrooms and a second

Beck (featured in 'Country Living') is a little gem, a romantic hideaway for two.

Haybarn is a delightful property, with several memorable interior features.

bathroom. A big conservatory with comfy seats opens on to a south-facing patio with extensive rambling gardens beyond and a distant view of unspoilt countryside. When we sat there, small birds provided continuous entertainment as they busily patronised a bird-table just a few feet away. Red squirrels visit too, and the Howes also have a flock of white doves.

Like Haybarn, the other three cottages have central heating to back up wood-burners: logs (free) are on a saw-your-own basis. *Beck Cottage* (**sleeping 2**) which adjoins a tumbling mountain stream has featured in Country Living magazine. *Stables* and *Shearers* cottages (both **sleeping 4** plus cot) each have double and twin bedrooms.

All around there are glorious walks. You can also ride the scenic Carlisle-Settle railway from Langwathby Station, just five miles away.

Cost: about £200 to £700; short breaks in low season. Details: Ian and Lesley Howes, Kirkland Hall, Kirkland, Penrith, Cumbria CA10 1RN. Telephone/fax: 01768 88295.

www.cottagesincumbria.com

email: kirklandhallcottages@hotmail.com

Ambleside and Central Lakeland
Cottage Life and Heart of the Lakes*

Having featured it for nearly 25 years, we've stayed in several of the properties on the books of this important agency.

They do have some real gems. Of course, we only have room to mention a handful of the 330 or so on the organisation's books – last year, for example, we had excellent reader reports of a 'charming, authentic' 17th century cottage called *High Beckside*, near Patterdale (**sleeps 7**), and – we've stayed there – of *Acorn Cottage* (**sleeps 5**), within easy walking distance of Coniston.

Some properties are in quite famous places, and they don't come much more famous than Far Sawrey, one-time home of Beatrix Potter open to the public. There, *Rowan Cottage*, **sleeping 5**, has lots going for it, such as

Big family party? Consider Hart Head Barn, sleeping up to ten and superbly located in famous Rydal...

High Beckside is a rarity even in the Lakes: an authentic 17th century gem.

a multi-fuel stove, views of fields and trees from the back and several good pubs, serving food, just a short walk away.

Hart Head Barn was converted from an old Lakeland stone barn and as you might imagine now offers very substantial accommodation. With wonderful views, in a peaceful location, this outstanding property is situated in the hamlet of Rydal, between Grasmere and Ambleside. **Sleeps 10**.

A ten minute drive from Keswick, in the village of Mungrisdale, *Elind Cottage* is part of a Grade II listed barn, with a wealth of beams and evidence of a flair for interior design. It is full of character, and makes a very comfortable holiday home. **Sleeps 4**.

Just a couple of minutes' walk from the centre of Ambleside is *Wren Cottage*. Newly renovated and upgraded, while retaining many authentic features, this **sleeps 2** and will appeal to couples looking for a village (or perhaps small town) 'pied-à-terre'.

The properties range from **'Visit Britain' Two to Five Stars**, and all include free leisure club membership. Further details of all these and of course many more are available from 'Heart of the Lakes'/'Cottage Life', Fisherbeck Mill, Old Lake Road, Ambleside, Cumbria LA22 0DH. Telephone 015394 32321. Fax 33251.

www.heartofthelakes.co.uk

email: info@heartofthelakes.co.uk

Talkin, near Brampton
Long Byres

Among so many things readers have (over 26 years!) loved about Long Byres is the fact the owners say 'Do bring your children and dogs...'!

Better yet, owner Harriet Sykes (who runs the place and lives adjacent) says 'the more boisterous the better, and as many of each as you like.' She goes on to say, 'the cottages are child- and dog-proof. We are what we are, we know our market and we don't overcharge.' The formula seems to work: there are many repeat visitors.

As well as enjoying forays to such famous places as Windermere, Keswick and Ullswater, guests tend to be people who appreciate this 'serenely wild' corner of the Cumbria/Northumberland border country.

We revisited one recent early autumn, and found that the character of the seven former farm buildings still comes over. The two larger cottages have enjoyed a complete refurbishment, and have been extended to provide three bedrooms, one ensuite, plus a family bathroom. The kitchen/living rooms in both cottages have been redesigned and updated, and look out on to their own gardens and across the farm towards the Lake District.

With their easy access to the Lakes, the Roman Wall country and the Scottish border, these are unpretentious and inexpensive, and have always brought a good response from our readers...

Upgraded interiors are light, bright and thoroughly inviting, while remaining essentially 'practical'.

All the cottages enjoy splendid views. A charming beck ripples along within 50 yards of the property. Talkin Tarn, as pretty as several of the Lakes-proper, is within walking distance; Talkin village, which is half a mile away, has an excellent pub. Brampton, three miles away, is the nearest town. It has a railway station, and the Sykes are happy to meet people from the train.

Dogs are welcome, and children will enjoy the pets' corner, the dogs, the cats, the horses and the newly acquired alpacas. Cost: about £167 to £500, including electricity, hot water, heating, linen and towels. Details from Harriet Sykes at Long Byres, Talkin Head, near Brampton, Cumbria CA8 1LT. Telephone 016977 3435.

www.longbyres.co.uk
email: stay@longbyres.co.uk

Loweswater, near Cockermouth
Scale Hill

These attractively grouped cottages, three **sleeping 2** and three **sleeping 4**, are like a tiny hamlet as they face each other in two rows across a narrow cobbled space. This has access at both ends to the quiet country road which by-passes it and runs past remote Loweswater, a mile away.

Occupying 17th century farm buildings, they were previously part of the Thompson family's highly-regarded hotel before being converted for self-catering. Now they are run with the same welcoming touch by daughter Heather. Indeed many of the hotel's guests continue to return, including a couple who first came 40 years ago and have returned every year since.

Visiting last autumn, we were impressed by the quality of the decor and furnishings, especially the colour schemes. A welcome-basket of local goodies, a bowl of fruit and fresh flowers await the arrival of guests. Heather also collects any letters 'posted' in her antique pillar-box – a nice touch.

At one end of the former hotel building, *Sheila's* (**sleeping 4**) is open-plan with a triple aspect sitting room which enjoys a glorious view over the valley to Low Fell. French windows open on to its own terrace which is surrounded by the large communal garden where there is a trampoline, pond and summer house. It has two en-suite bedrooms. *Barty's*, **sleeping 2**, has a four-poster and spreads across the middle of the building. Its sitting-room has windows front and back.

Four more cottages occupy the converted stone Coach House opposite. One, *Lanthwaite*, is notable for its beams, while *Shell* (named after the petrol pump which once stood outside) has an oak staircase leading to a double-aspect bedroom with a four-poster. Both **sleep 2**. *Howe House*, **sleeping 4**, which started off as a hayloft, has a spacious beamed sitting room and Brackenthwaite occupies the whole of the original loft with rooms looking over Swinside Fell.

Scale Hill (arrowed): how is this for a cottage location? It is quite outstanding even compared with other parts of the Lake District, and our readers have come to love it.

Dogs welcome in some cottages. TVs, VCRs, DVDs, microwaves, fridge-freezers and laundry facilities. Heating/linen included. Cost: £290 to £810.

Further details from Heather Thompson, Scale Hill, Loweswater, near Cockermouth, Cumbria CA13 9UX. Telephone 01900 85232. Fax 85321.

www.scalehillloweswater.co.uk
email: thompson@scalehillloweswater.co.uk

122

Windermere, Ambleside and beyond
Lakelovers*

A succession of guests were collecting keys for properties when we were in this highly regarded agency's busy shop/office in the centre of Bowness-on-Windermere one afternoon last year. It is a personally-run operation, and we sensed how helpful the staff were being. A further sign of its success is that it has recently opened a second office in Ambleside.

We know a good proportion of the 280 properties on its books, which are all within a radius of around ten miles. Its seductive brochure reads almost like a guidebook, clearly describing and illustrating not only the properties themselves but also the area around each one.

During our visit we were delighted to see round *Pullwood Bay*, a large country house in 50 acres of woodland and gardens spread for half-a-mile along the shore of Windermere near Ambleside. Built in 1891, the house was empty for many years until 2000. Now with a matching extension, it is divided into twelve of the most stylish apartments we've seen. **Sleeping 2, 4** or **6**, they are ultra-modern, with cream decor, walnut wood

Roger Ground is an exceptional property, combining history and modern comforts.

Valentine Cottage (not featured) makes a rather special and romantic retreat.

floors and underfloor heating. We admired deep sofas, majestic beds, sleek marble bathrooms and glossy kitchens.

Guests, including those in five cottages (**sleeping 2** to **6**) in the grounds, get temporary membership of the nearby Low Water Leisure Club, which has a pool featuring underwater bubble bursts, showers and waterfalls.

We also admired the views from *Holbeck Lane Cottage*, a handsome stone-built house (**sleeping 6**) in a well-tended garden just south of Ambleside. The clever split-level design makes the most of its hillside position, including a conservatory-style sitting room.

Between Bowness and Ambleside, *Pudding Cottage* is an award-winning property (**sleeping 6**) converted from an 18th-century coach house and stables. Prettily furnished with a large garden, it has enough toys, games and videos to keep even the liveliest families entertained for hours.

For a copy of an outstanding easy-to-read brochure, contact

Lakelovers, Belmont House, Lake Road, Bowness-on-Windermere, LA23 3BJ. Telephone 015394 88855. Fax 88857. Brochures 88858.

Bookable on line: **www.lakelovers.co.uk**

email: bookings@lakelovers.co.uk

123

Elterwater, near Ambleside
Meadowbank/Garden Cottage

We try to be even handed, but have to admit this is one of our favourite three or four properties in the whole of 'the lakes'. In the heart of a sought-after village, with a good pub close, it's of permanent-home standard, with a stylish, spacious, uncluttered interior (we loved the red carpeting and the tartan covers in the main sitting room: see the **Colour section, Page 3**), an impressive, traditional pine kitchen, a medium

This must be one of the finest holiday houses in the Lakes: grab it when you can!

sized, well tended and enclosed garden that gives on to open fields. (We also admired the view from the main bedroom.) **Sleeps 8/10.** Within the garden, but unobtrusively, *The Garden Cottage*, **sleeping just 2** in a double, can be taken separately, or is an excellent addition to Meadowbank for a large family party. Three TVs/videos/Sky film/sports channels.

Bed-linen included. Pets not allowed. Cost: (Cottage) £200 to £370, (House) £550 to £2000. See the website for full details of price, availability and special offers.

Telephone 0161 928 6953

www.langdale-cottages.co.uk email: patricia.locke@btinternet.com

---

Note: we cannot vouch for every property on an agency's books, but only those we have seen. Most agents have a number of modest properties that appeal only to a specific market (for example, fishermen or walkers), or sometimes properties at the extreme edge of the region they deal with that are not typical of what they offer. But in principle the agencies we feature are reliable and conscientious. (We do however strongly recommend that when approaching them readers are as specific as possible about their requirements.)

About 60% of the cottage owners featured in this guide accept dogs, which usually but not always means other pets too (a small number exclude cats). Most owners charge between £10 and £20 per week per dog for the inevitable extra wear and tear on properties. Please don't arrive with more dogs than you have permission to take, and do not sneak a dog into a cottage where it's not welcome. Note that, even when cottage owners say 'No dogs', dog lovers may still find themselves 'among friends': it could be that visiting town dogs don't take very well to cottages surrounded by farmland, perhaps with lots of sheep, or that the owners' dogs don't like strange animals.

Applethwaite, near Keswick
Croftside/Croft Corner/Upper House/Lower House at Croft House Holidays

Only just over a mile from Keswick are five properties, all in peaceful, rural settings, with stunning views to Skiddaw, Borrowdale and the north-western fells. *Croftside*, **sleeping 4**, and *Croft Corner*, a ground-floor apartment **sleeping 2**, are located at Croft House – a handsome Victorian country house. A Croftside visitor

Croft House: an exceptional location and super views, a mile or so from Keswick.

said: 'After 25 years of Lakeland holidays this is the best accommodation we've stayed in.' Said another, of Croft Corner, 'Thanks for the little touches that made us feel so much at home'. A colleague stayed in *Lower House*, **sleeping 4**. She described great views, and 'everything light and open plan'. A visitor to *Upper House*, **sleeping 6,** said: 'Wonderfully equipped, fantastic view'. At *Croft Head Farm*, **sleeping 8** (it's a detached barn conversion with a snooker room) a visitor highlighted 'the serene and picturesque location'. **'Visit Britain' Four Stars.** TVs/videos/DVDs. 'Sorry, no pets'. Linen, towels, heating, electricity, cot/high chair included. Open all year. Cost: £280 to £995. Short breaks from £168. Details: Mrs J L Boniface, Croft House, Applethwaite, Keswick, Cumbria CA12 4PN. Telephone: 017687 73693.

www.crofthouselakes.co.uk email: holidays@crofthouselakes.co.uk

Windermere map 8/254 and Ravenglass

Only a mile and a half from popular Bowness-on-Windermere, a property colleagues have stayed in (Ref W3326), a listed former farmhouse, partly 17th century, **sleeping 5/6**. On a working farm (children can watch lambing, shearing and sheep-dipping) it has an open fire. One of our all-time favourite places is Ravenglass. Just a mile and a half from there, in a high-lying situation with panoramic views of the Irish Sea and, if you're lucky, sunset over

This detached barn conversion near Ravenglass will suit keen walkers.

the Isle of Man, another detached barn conversion **(map 8/253)** combines masses of character with 21st century comforts. **Sleeping 6**, it makes a good base for a short break, and is near a pub. Ref W4359.

For availability and bookings, contact Welcome Cottages, Spring Mill, Earby, Barnoldswick, Lancashire BB94 0AA. Telephone 0845 268 0945. A number of properties in France are also available.

www.welcomecottages.com

Bassenthwaite and the Northern Lake District
Lakeland Cottage Holidays*

This long-established agency, owned since 2001 by David and Jo Burton, has 60 properties scattered around the Keswick area – some in very popular locations, others remotely situated near quiet lakes and fells. They include big houses, terrace houses, farmhouses, white-walled cottages and stone cottages, many with outstanding views. Five are alongside the Burtons' own home, a 17th-century listed farmhouse and converted barn.

During our latest visit we saw *Crown Cottage*, a new addition handily placed in the centre of the village of Braithwaite, which is renowned as a walking centre. The building has been skilfully converted from the former post office and an adjoining barn. **Sleeping 6**, it has a cosy lounge with log burner and separate dining-room.

Similarly well-placed is *Bessy Boot*, a two-minute stroll from the centre of Keswick. This is a surprisingly spacious terraced house on three floors, **sleeping 8** in two twin bedrooms, an en-suite double and a further double. The agency also has two other terraced houses in neighbouring streets, all with unrestricted on-street parking.

Among the reasons we liked Hause Gill, a former quarryman's cottage, sleeping five, are the delightful views.

Not featured. but known to us, The Coppice is also in Borrowdale. It sleeps up to nine people.

Many Lake District properties boast wonderful views, but we think those from *Squirrel Cottage* at Bassenthwaite, which **sleeps 4** in a twin and a double, take some beating. From the cottage's south-facing conservatory and garden, they take in the fells of Skiddaw (an exhilarating five-hour walk to the summit and back) and Bassenthwaite Lake, with the bonus of wonderful sunsets.

In the tiny hamlet of Seatoller in the beautiful Borrowdale Valley where most of the surrounding countryside is owned by the National Trust, *Hause Gill Cottage* (**sleeps 5**) is a former quarryman's cottage. We really liked its views across the magnificent old High Stile oak wood and the stream plunging down from Honister Pass.

Further details and a copy of an informative brochure are available from Lakeland Cottage Holidays, Melbecks, Bassenthwaite, near Keswick, CA12 4QX. Telephone 017687 76065. Fax 76869.

www.lakelandcottages.co.uk
info@lakelandcottages.co.uk

Bassenthwaite
Bassenthwaite Lakeside Lodges

Tucked away down a leafy lane among mature trees, and run with great professionalism, the community of about 60 log cabins/lodges, fifteen of them for holiday let, have been much praised by readers of our guide for about seventeen years. Standards are reliably high.

You don't often hear people say 'We holidayed on Bassenthwaite'. For access to this, one of Lakeland's most beautiful but least-known lakes, is famously quite difficult. These fine lodges, however, border the lake's shore, with easy and immediate access to the water.

We especially admire the most recent properties, **sleeping up to 6,** in a private location on the edge of the development, with the most impressive lake views of all, but were very pleased to spend time in one of our long time favourites, *Overwater* (right by the lake) – and also to see *Broadwater*. This is especially geared to 'wedding day' and honeymoon couples, and we were very impressed by the walk-in closet that's big enough to take a wedding dress in all its glory.

While not for those who want to be lonely as a cloud, this remains the sort of location where visiting children – and adults – will enjoy making new friends, though they can be private too. We noted the care taken in choosing top-notch kitchen and bathroom ranges, likewise comfy sofas more usually associated with up-market traditional holiday houses. We'd say most of the interiors are reminiscent of four star hotels.

As well as generous balconies with gas barbecues and outdoor furniture, the lodges have picture windows, TVs, videos, DVDs/Freeview, wi-fi. There is a free video, books and games library. Nearby you can hire mountain bikes, play tennis and golf, and go horse-riding. Keswick is just ten minutes' drive.

Dogs are permitted only in the category of the smaller Parkland, Lakeside and Woodland Lodges. Linen and towels are, as you would expect here, included.

Cost: about £360 to £1010, depending on which property and when. Short breaks are available. Details available from Bassenthwaite Lakeside Lodges, Scarness, Bassenthwaite, near Keswick, Cumbria CA12 4QZ. Telephone 0845 4565276. Also: 017687 76641. Fax 76919.

www.bll.ac email: enquiries@bll.ac

A rare chance to be based right by the shores of Bassenthwaite – one of the most 'secret' of all the Lakes.

We've always admired the marriage of considerable comfort and the rather rustic style of the surroundings.

Sebergham, near Caldbeck
Monkhouse Hill Cottages

Featured by us for over twenty years, these nine lovingly cared-for cottages are within a 17th-century farmyard with panoramic views, in the quieter, more northerly part of 'the Lakes'. Keswick, Bassenthwaite Lake, Cockermouth, the coast, the Eden Valley and the Northumberland border are all within a pleasant drive. Set back from a not especially busy B-road, they are easy to find but completely rural. Resident owners Jennifer and Andrew Collard run them with pride and professionalism. Having three children themselves, they are well tuned to the needs of families. Thanks to regular upgrading, the cottages are among Cumbria's best, and have won an impressive number of accolades, including Excellence in England's Silver Award and Self-Catering Holiday of the Year from the Cumbria Tourist Board.

When we looked round last autumn, further improvements were in full swing, including the addition of balconies to three properties that enjoy uninterrupted 30-mile views across the Eden Valley.

Three of the cottages have their own saunas. One, *Brae Fell* (**sleeping 8**), also has a chromatherapy bathroom. Another is *Great Calva*, a **Visit Britain Five Star** property built in 2000. **Sleeping 12/14**, it is ideal for three families, as the bedrooms are grouped in three large suites.

Each cottage has its own patio area, complete with barbecue equipment, and guests can play games like croquet, boules and badminton in the two-acre paddock. They also get complimentary membership of the North Lakes Spa (15 minutes' drive) which has an indoor heated pool.

For honeymooners, the Collards offer a package in a cottage for two with four-poster bed, spa bath or sauna, bath robes, champagne, chocolates,

An award winning, absolutely pristine, neat and tidy arrangement of cottages....

...with comfortable interiors, a food ordering service and children's playground.

flowers and aromatherapy oils. Wedding groups are another speciality.

Cost: about £350 to £2340 (inc electricity, linen and towels). On-line ordering for Cumbrian food hampers, three-course suppers, home-cooked freezer meals, local beers, papers and more! All properties have log-stoves, central heating, Freeview TV and DVD/video. Well-behaved dogs welcome in six.

For further information see Monkhouse Hill's comprehensive website: **www.monkhousehill.co.uk**

Monkhouse Hill, Sebergham, near Caldbeck CA5 7HW. Telephone/fax 01697 476254.

email: cottages@monkhousehill.co.uk

Windermere and Ullswater
Matson Ground Estate Cottages

In three locations on family-run farms near Ullswater and Windermere, these seven cottages (**sleeping from 2 to 10**) combine rural solitude with beautiful views. Two of them are modernised 17th-century properties at the end of a 1½-mile gated track in the remote Grizedale Valley. Looking across fields and a stream to the steeply rising Patterdale Common, they make a perfect base for walking, as there are footpaths all around.

Cruck Barn, though only **sleeping 2**, impressed us by its spaciousness. The large sitting-room has exposed stone walls and a smart new kitchen area at one end, all attractively framed by two large 'crucks' – ox-bow beams. Next to it, *Elm How* (**sleeping 10**) retains its original character as a farmhouse with beamed ceilings and an unusual stone spiral staircase. This leads off the large main sitting-room to the bedrooms, which include one **sleeping 4**. Combined, the two properties are particularly suitable for multi-generation family groups. However, neither has any TV reception (a blessing for some!) though they *are* equipped for watching DVDs.

Nearby, above Glenridding village, *Eagle Cottage* (**sleeping 4**) is a traditional stone cottage perched up a steep drive with a splendid view over Ullswater from the garden and main bedroom. Heating is by electric night-storage heaters and an open fire for which fuel is provided.

Though only a mile from Lake Windermere, Helm Farm's four apartments in an award-winning barn conversion are peacefully located. Paths lead directly across the farm's grazing land to a network of walks. *Helm Eden*, **sleeping 4**, and *Helm Mint*, **sleeping 2**, are both on the ground floor, while *Helm Kent*, **sleeping 2 plus 2 children in bunks**, is on the first floor. *Helm Lune*, **sleeping 5**, spreads over both floors. All are fitted out in pine with fitted kitchens and have open wood fires except Helm Mint, which is avail-

We're especially fond of Elm How, which is in a really appealing location...

Cruck Barn: history, original features and mod cons rolled into one...

able at a discount if booked with one of the other three.

Washer-dryers except in Helm Mint. Microwaves, barbecues, cots and highchairs. Linen/towels included. Short breaks usually available. No dogs. Cost: £250 to £1250.

Brochure and details from Matson Ground Estate Company, Estate Office, Matson Ground, Windermere, Cumbria LA 23 2NH.

Telephone 015394 45756. Fax 47892.

www.matsonground.co.uk   email: info@matsonground.co.uk

Buttermere
Bowderbeck

Lake District cottages don't come much more authentic or well located than this.

One in a thousand, it's not hard to see why this is so sought-after. For the character of this picture-book cottage, a classic of its kind, has been well preserved: it has even doubled up as 'Dove Cottage' in a film about Wordsworth. But it now incorporates 21st century comforts, with for example a timber extension at the end of the whitewashed-stone 17th century cottage of a kind Wordsworth would not have known; he'd have appreciated its view of Buttermere, which for many visitors is the most romantic and beautiful lake of all. The lake shore is only half a mile away, and children will love the little beck that runs alongside the cottage. (This makes Bowderbeck unsuitable for children under five.) Specifically, there are rugs on slate floors and a handsome (and original) stone staircase up to a roomy first floor, where there is a spacious main bedroom, a roomy twin, a single, a separate wc, shower and bathroom, plus WC. **Sleeps 7 'plus 1'**. Not suitable for pets. No smoking. Payphone. Linen supplied, not towels. Cost: about £440 to £670. No TV reception. Details from Michael and Anne Bell, New House, Colby, Appleby-in-Westmorland, Cumbria CA16 6BD. Telephone 017683 53548.

www.bowderbeck.co.uk   email: info@bowderbeck.co.uk

Enquire within...

The editors of *The Good Holiday Cottage Guide* welcome personal calls and emails from readers about properties in Ireland or the UK, about things to see and do in the area that is of interest. Every property featured in this guide has been seen by at least one inspector, sometimes two or three of them, and there may be specific questions readers want to ask that are not covered in individual write-ups or round-up agency features. There is no charge for this, nor is the phone number a premium-rate one.

Telephone 01438 869489 email: info@goodcottageguide.com

'Mummy, that man's on fire'...

The very extensive ban on smoking in the UK does not apply across the board to self-catering accommodation: it's still a matter of 'owners' discretion', just as hotels have smoking and no-smoking rooms. However, we are finding that not all owners understand this, and that some assume the question of smoking no longer arises. So dedicated smokers – including a recognisable minority of sufferers from various ailments who 'roll the occasional joint' – should double-check.

Patton, near Kendal
Shaw End Mansion

In a secluded rural setting, just three miles north of Kendal, Shaw End has fine views of the Howgill Fells, and popular lakes such as Grasmere and Windermere are only about half an hour's drive. Up on the hill, Shaw End is a most impressive major restoration of a Georgian mansion. It has a lot of history, with the advan-

Shaw End Mansion: a degree of grandeur, with great views from each apartment.

tages of what is effectively a new building. There are four high ceilinged apartments, all accessed via the impressive main entrance, two on the ground floor, two – reached via a fine, sweeping pine staircase – on the first floor, all with superb interiors, including large sitting rooms with open fires, and exquisite views of the River Mint, in which children love to play. Guests have the run of the 200 acre estate. Three apartments **sleep 4**, one **sleeps 6** meaning that **a total of 18 people** can stay here for, say, a wedding or a family get-together. Trout and salmon fishing (one rod) is available. TV, washing machine, telephone, microwave, linen included, towels available for a small extra charge. Cost: about £230 to £420. Details from Mr and Mrs E D Robinson, Haveriggs Farm, Whinfell, near Kendal, Cumbria LA8 9EF. Telephone 01539 824220, fax 824464.

www.fieldendholidays.co.uk email: robinson@fieldendholidays.co.uk

---

Bailey, near Newcastleton
Bailey Mill Inn

map 8/222

It's coming up to 25 years since we first featured these courtyard apartments, only just inside the English border. All five are in an arrangement of single and two-storeyed buildings in the converted 18th century grain mill, one of them, *The Folly*, **sleeping up to 8**: a bargain for larger groups. Most **sleep 2 to 6**. A ground floor apartment called *The Store* houses the original archway,

Scotland is just a caber's toss away...

dated 1767. There's a jacuzzi, a sauna and meals in the licensed bar. Dogs welcome. Baby sitting. TVs; microwaves. Looking in on the Copelands' handsome horses, riding (and learning to ride) is very much a part of Bailey Mill, and full-day stable management courses are available 10am to 4pm (£30 per day), also full board riding holidays. **'Visit Britain' Two and Three Stars.** Cost: about £178 to £598. Short breaks – out of season – from £108 per cottage for two nights. Further details from Pamela Copeland, Bailey Mill, Newcastleton, Roxburghshire TD9 0TR. Telephone 016977 48617.

www.baileycottages/riding/racing.com

email: pam@baileymill.fsnet.co.uk

Crosby Garrett, near Kirkby Stephen
Mossgill Loft/Mossgill Chapel

What a charming location. Crosby Garrett is a delightful, well spaced out, blissfully quiet village in the Upper Eden Valley, distinguished by a viaduct on the Settle to Carlisle railway, with the fells only a few yards beyond. In the heart of the village, in striking distance of the Lake District, on the eastern edge of Cumbria, these lovingly cared for properties are among our absolute favourites in the north of England.

The location is excellent for walking both long and short distances, being only two miles from the Coast to Coast route and near the Pennine Way. The Cumbria Cycleway is just a mile away, and the Smardale Nature Reserve is half an hour's walk. The market town of Kirkby Stephen has pubs, restaurants and antique shops. A nine hole golf course is nearby.

A Victorian Baptist chapel conversion has created two attractive self-contained holiday lets, furnished to a high standard and with many original features. There's central heating throughout, log fires, off road parking and private sitting out areas. Fuel, electricity and linen are all included. A cot and high chair are available. Dogs welcome, at a cost of £10 per dog per week.

Mossgill Chapel, which we visited for the first time two years ago, has a large tiled kitchen with an oil-fired Rayburn, electric hob, microwave and fridge/freezer. A warm utility room houses a washing machine and tumble dryer and provides plenty of space for drying walking clothes. An upstairs sitting room has an open fire, beams, comfortable furniture and TV/DVD. There are two bedrooms, one twin with en-suite bathroom and one downstairs double with a bathroom next door, including a shower.

Fitting harmoniously into the village scene.   *Lovingly planned and cared-for interiors.*

Stained glass windows are an attractive feature on the staircase. All is light and bright, with a stylish sense of colour and design. Cost: from about £300 to £385. Short breaks at a bargain £65 per night. **Sleeps 4 plus cot**.

Mossgill Loft is approached by a short flight of stone steps. There is a large living/kitchen area, a double bedroom and bathroom. There are lattice windows, beams, an open fire and rugs on wooden floors. Plus an electric cooker, microwave, washing machine, fridge and TV/DVD. The two properties can be taken together – the makings of a memorable family holiday. The owners' tennis court is available on request. Cost: from £200 to £250 per week. Short breaks at £50 per night. **Sleeps 2**.

Furrher details from Clare Hallam, Mossgill House, Crosby Garrett, Kirkby Stephen, Cumbria CA17 4PW. Telephone 017683 71149. **www.mossgill-holidays.co.uk   email: clarehallamuk@yahoo.co.uk**

Wales

Wales feels bigger than many first time visitors expect it to be. Every few miles, every turn in the road seems to promise new things to see, more history to reach out and touch. The language, the terrain and the vast supply of 'tangible' history means the place is packed with interest.

Almost as soon as you're over the border into Wales (say via Ross on Wye, or Ludlow) the magic, the sense of the past and the scenic beauty are all-enveloping. A good number of readers have taken to the Pembrokeshire Coast and, for example, the Llyn Peninsula, in the north. In Pembrokeshire, Tenby is much-loved, while people who discover resorts such as Broad Haven and Newport tend to rave about them. There are lofty peaks and magnificent beaches, and although the most dramatic scenery is around Snowdonia, almost every corner of the Principality is holiday country. There are the rolling, lightly wooded English-Welsh borders, the brown moors of the Brecon Beacons National Park, our own favourite coastline around Barmouth, the rather proud, rather self contained town of Dolgellau and nearby Portmeirion, the architectural fantasy that's like a cross between Portofino and Munchkin-land. (We don't quite buy the 'Italianate' tag – we've never seen anywhere like it in Italy!) There are castles to storm, ponies to trek with, salmon and trout to catch, steam trains to travel on.

Or consider the scenic line that runs from Shrewsbury across to Welshpool, goes over the Mawddach estuary and then via Barmouth up to Harlech Castle and beyond. And there's the Isle of Anglesey: one of our favourite towns in the whole of Britain is Beaumaris, just over the Menai Straits, and the hinterland is as Welsh as anywhere we know.

St David's map 5/276
Beth Ruach

Beth Ruach is a very stylish, comfortable and spacious family house...

We remember these as among the best we've located in west Wales. *Beth Ruach* is on a grand scale, up a private drive, spacious (and pleasantly cool on the hot day of our visit) with a particularly comfortable sitting room. It has a skilful layout of bedrooms and **sleeps (yes!) up to 12 people**. This also has sea and country views from upstairs: but, of course, you would want to explore this fabulous part of Wales, not just look at it! Linen and towels included. TVs. Payphone. Cost: about £395 to £2395. Not yet seen by us are *Hendre Loan*, in a fine, high situation in the St David's conservation area **(sleeping 6)** and *Whitesands* **(sleeping 12)**, a colonial-style bungalow with fabulous sea views.

Details, with an excellent brochure, available from Thelma Hardman, 'High View', Catherine Street, St David's, Pembrokeshire SA62 6RJ. Telephone 01437 720616.

www.stnbc.co.uk   email: enquiries@stnbc.co.uk

Saundersfoot, near Tenby
Blackmoor Farm Holiday Cottages

These quite excellent cottages have been appreciated by our readers for over twenty years. Superbly well situated, they are just two miles from the glorious Pembrokeshire coast, and only a short drive from Saundersfoot's sands and Tenby. Though not 'remote', they are nicely tucked away via winding country lanes. Better yet: Blackmoor Farm is surrounded by its own 36 acres of pastureland, accessible only by a private drive.

Families with children have always praised Blackmoor: indeed, as we arrived on our last visit, young children were playing happily among the trees near these beautifully cared for cottages. They also appeal to people who appreciate purpose-built accommodation in an attractive courtyard location. Resident owners Len and Eve Cornthwaite try to ensure that families enjoy a warm, friendly atmosphere.

Blackmoor Farm has cattle grazing peacefully, and the old stables in the spacious gravelled farmyard contain resident donkeys that children can enjoy rides on most days. (Be warned: more than one adventurous child has asked if next time the family can book one of the well appointed, discreetly situated mobile homes!)

There are just three cottages, south facing, side by side in a courtyard setting. Accommodation is two-tiered. Downstairs there are two bedrooms (each with full size twin beds, which can convert to bunk beds) and a well fitted out bathroom with bath *and* shower. Upstairs there is a large open-plan room containing the kitchen/dining section and comfortable living area leading on to a small patio balcony. A sofa bed allows the cottage to **sleep a maximum of 6**. The single-storeyed *Stable Cottage*, a converted farm building, **sleeps 2,** and has an appealing triple aspect living room. The decor and furniture are modern, comfortable, simple but attractive. Each cottage is well equipped, heated by storage heaters and, with double glazing and good insulation, cosy in the early and late seasons.

Cost: about £316 to £520 (less than this for Stable Cottage). TVs. Linen is provided, towels available for a charge. Laundry facilities. Games room. Not suitable for dogs and other pets. More details from Len and Eve Cornthwaite, Blackmoor Farm, Amroth Road, Ludchurch, near Saundersfoot, Pembrokeshire SA67 8JH. Telephone/fax 01834 831242.

www.infozone.com.hk/blackmoorfarm
email: ltecornth@aol.com

South-facing balconies, each with a table and two chairs for alfresco meals.

Stable Cottage – just right for 2, and a modestly-priced introduction to Wales.

Walwyn's Castle, near Little Haven
Rosemoor

Twenty-five years with us can't be wrong! Tucked neatly away in the Pembrokeshire Coast National Park, well away from any main roads, the quiet and attractively situated Rosemoor cottages have featured in this guide since it first appeared in 1983.

The sandy beaches of Little Haven and Broad Haven, which has a handy supermarket, are within three miles' drive and Haverfordwest, the old county town, is about six miles away. And Walwyn's Castle? It's the remains of a Norman castle superimposed on an Iron Age fort.

The cottages, all annually graded by **'Visit Wales'**, were created from the red sandstone outbuildings of the large Victorian house in which the Dutch owners live. Each cottage is described in detail, with floor-plans, in Rosemoor's brochure. The estate extends for 34 acres, 20 officially designated as a nature reserve. Walking trails lead through woodland and around the picturesque five-acre lake. For naturalists and bird-watchers, it's a delight.

Each time we've visited we've been impressed by their variety as well as their very high standards. Six are grouped round a large three-sided open courtyard which has a central lawn; at the back they look on to wooded countryside. These include the spacious combination, with internal connection, of *Peace* (**sleeping 4**) and *Apple* (**sleeping 6**). Apple has three bedrooms and two bathrooms, one of which is en-suite to a ground floor bedroom, professionally designed for disabled use. *The Coach House*, nearby (**sleeps 5**), is capped by a small belfry and has a patio on to a walled garden, while *Holly Tree* (**sleeps 3**) has a view of the lake.

Most of the cottages have dark slate floors topped by attractive rugs, with underfloor heating. We also admired the polished dark grey Welsh slate

The three-bedroomed Coach House is distinctively capped by a small belfry. It is of course just one of Rosemoor's several 'characterful' properties here in rural West Wales. It is handy for beaches and lovely countryside, but not remote.

working surfaces in the fitted kitchens and liked the smart modern bathrooms tiled in black and white. A newly installed wood fired CH boiler is part of the owner's drive to have as little environmental impact as possible.

Cost: about £170 to £1485. Dogs welcome. Home-cooked meals available. Linen supplied. Laundry facilities. Four cottages have extra woodburners. Games room and playground. Brochure from John M and Jacqui Janssen, Rosemoor, Walwyn's Castle, Haverfordwest, Pembrokeshire SA62 3ED. Telephone 01437 781326. Fax 781080.

www.rosemoor.com   email: rosemoor@walwynscastle.com

Llanfallteg, near Whitland
David's Farm

At the centre of a working farm that children will love (lambs, calves, rabbits to meet, and ancient woodlands to explore), this is a particularly quiet and spacious arrangement of cottages. It has featured in this guide for many years, with lots of enthusiastic reader responses. The focal point here is the owners' handsome Georgian home. Adjacent to the main house are *The Coach House* **(sleeps 4/6)** and *Butler's Cottage*

A reliably warm welcome at this very quiet, spacious and comfortable place.

(sleeps 2/3), which can be linked to make one bigger property. Across grassy open ground, but still part of the original farm, stand *The Old Barn* and *Tower Cottage*, **sleeping 6** and **2/3** respectively, and also combinable. Our favourite has always been the roomy, stylish Coach House, with a triple-aspect sitting room/diner and central heating. **'Visit Britain' Four Stars**. No smoking. TV. Well behaved dogs by arrangement. Linen (not towels) and heating included. Cost: £125 to £450. Details and brochure from Angela Colledge, Gwarmacwydd Farm, Llanfallteg, Whitland, Carmarthenshire. Telephone 01437 563260; fax 563839.

www.davidsfarm.com email: ghg@gwarmacwydd.co.uk

Cenarth Falls, near Cardigan Bay map 5/289
Penwern Fach Cottages

Not yet seen by us (to be remedied in 2008) Penwern Fach Cottages come recommended for all sorts of good reasons, including the fact that they are situated in ten acres of beautiful countryside, with glorious views across the rolling landscape of the Teifi Valley and Preseli Hills. The five cosy cottages, converted from traditional stone farm buildings, still with exposed beams, are ideal (at any

Very comfortable, deeply rural, each with its own distinctive character and charm.

time of the year) for romantic breaks **for 2** or for family holidays. Each cottage has all the home comforts you'd expect, plus wood-burning stoves. There are spacious gardens, a children's games room, a football field and a 250-yard golf practice area. The cottages also have their own patio areas. Discounted rates are available at a nearby indoor pool and leisure club. Just six miles away are the beautiful beaches of Cardigan Bay, along with spectacular cliff-top walks and lots of outdoor activities for all the family.

Contact Yvonne Davies, Cenarth Falls Holiday Park, Cenarth, Newcastle Emlyn, Ceredigion SA38 9JS. Telephone 01239 710345. Fax 710344.

www.penwernfach.co.uk email: enquiries@cenarth-holipark.co.uk

Coastal Wales
Quality Cottages Cerbid*

Featured in this guide every year since it first appeared in 1983, Leonard Rees's own 'Cerbid Cottages' are located in an idyllic, quiet backwater of deeply rural Pembrokeshire. Better yet, you'll find them down a little sleepy lane.

The high standards here tend to be reflected by the quality of Leonard Rees's agency properties, ninety per cent of which are within five miles of the sea – a huge selling point.

For example, just a few minutes from Newgale beach, which consists of over a mile of golden sands, is *The Red Hen House*. A superb barn conversion with sweet-smelling honeysuckle over the door, it is idyllically set in a secret valley conservation area complete with a private south-facing garden and a nearby trout lake. The feature stone fireplace makes it a good bet for the shoulder season.

If you want a dramatic coastal location, you will be impressed, as we were, by *Craig Yr Awel*, on Whitesands Bay, just a few yards above the beach. We could enjoy a week here just watching the ever-changing sea

The Cerbid cottages effectively form a hamlet of their own – utterly peaceful, each cottage with a high degree of privacy, everything beautifully cared-for.

The Red Hen House is an admirable barn conversion, and is marvellously well situated. It has 'honeysuckle round the door', and an open fireplace...

below. During a most enjoyable visit we noticed lots of books to read, comfortable leather armchairs. There's an open fire which is an absolute delight when the sea mist comes down or autumn nights close in, and a glazed patio with, as you would imagine, spectacular views. **Sleeps 10**. Dogs are welcome here.

In the beautiful lush and wooded Gwaun Valley between Fishguard and Newport, *Pontfaen* is a most impressive Victorian country house which **sleeps 11**.

A handsome full colour brochure, which also contains details of the Cerbid properties, can be obtained from Leonard Rees, Cerbid (GHCG), Solva, Pembrokeshire. Telephone 01348 837871. Freephone 0800 169 2256.

www.qualitycottages.co.uk

email: info@qualitycottages.co.uk

Penrallt, near Boncath
Clydey Country Cottages

A reader from near Shrewsbury wrote to us during 2006 about Clydey's 'extraordinary location' and its 'clever marriage of what appeals to children and adults alike'.

There are ten cottages, all beautifully converted from original outbuildings. Dewi and Jacqui Davies took over the 20-acre estate in 2003, giving up high-powered jobs in the City of London, because they wanted to enjoy bringing up their young family in a much more pleasant environment, particularly as Dewi comes from Wales. They have certainly found a lovely spot, on high ground deep in the Pembrokeshire countryside and boasting glorious views.

There's a luxurious indoor heated swimming pool with a sheltered sun terrace from which there are stunning views, plus sauna, gym and games room to complement the existing outdoor hot tub. For further relaxation, beauty treatments are now on offer in the comfort of your own cottage.

The decor and furnishings of the cottages (**sleeping 2 to 10**) have been chosen to complement the age and style of the buildings. They retain their beams and stone inglenooks and feature farmhouse-style kitchens and fireplaces with multi-fuel stoves. Most have four-posters and/or king or 'super king' sized beds and dishwashers. All have DVD players and satellite TV.

A nature trail leads down into woods and there's a playground area that includes a Wendyhouse, rope swing and sandpit. There are two resident-ponies, a small flock of sheep and numerous chickens and ducks. (Not just a treat for breakfast but also a wonderfully de-stressing time for adults with

This is indeed 'a haven of outstanding natural beauty, peace and tranquillity'...

...in twenty acres of grounds, with a heated swimming pool, and much more.

toddlers is the daily excitement of the children animal-feeding and 'golden yolked' free range egg-collecting.) The nearest shop is a couple of miles away and there's a pub and micro-brewery, the Nag's Head, which is 'child-friendly and highly rated for its food'.

Welcome pack is provided of tea, coffee and milk, together with fresh flowers, local home-made preserves and a basket of logs. Shared laundry room. Highchairs and cots available. Portable barbecues. Sorry, no pets. Cost: approximately £400 to £1400. Details from Dewi and Jacqui Davies, Clydey Country Cottages, Penrallt, Lancych, Boncath, Pembrokeshire SA37 0LW. Telephone 01239 698619; fax 698417.

www.clydeycottages.co.uk   email: info@clydeycottages.co.uk

Rhyd-Yr-Eirin, near Harlech

For - yes! - *24 years* we've had a special fondness for this cottage. We love its character and its unforgettable location. When we say it's isolated, we mean *isolated*! It's full of atmosphere. You are 900-feet up, sheltered by hills to the north and east, in an oak-beamed, three-bedroomed, 17th century farmhouse with an unusual stone staircase, original sitting-room window, antique fur-

Splendid isolation, lots of atmosphere.

niture and a wide-ranging Welsh-holiday library. There is an open fire in the inglenook (coal/wood provided) and each room has a storage or wall heater. The all-electric kitchen, bathroom and shower-room are up to a very high standard. Harlech and the glorious, sandy beaches are only fifteen minutes away by car, allowing for gate-opening! There's a concealed TV/DVD player, radio/CD player, telephone, double-oven cooker, microwave, fridge-freezer, dishwasher, washing machine, spin-dryer.

Sleeps up to 7. Cost: £150 to £650 (discounts for two-week bookings). Well-trained dogs welcome. Details of the house and garden from Mr Chris Ledger, 7 Chelmer Road, London E9 6AY. Telephone 020 8985 1853.

www.rhydyreirin.com   email: info@rhydyreirin.com

Llanbedr, near Harlech
Nantcol   map 5/313

Another extraordinary location. From this 14th century stone built Welsh longhouse, five miles from Llanbedr village up a narrow valley road, you can walk straight up into the hills. It is perfection for walkers, bird watchers and lovers of the countryside: a spectacular location, spectacular views. In other words – it's one in a hundred! You can explore Snow-

What should we show – the house itself or the fabulous view?

donia, relax on sandy beaches or play golf at Royal St David's, Harlech, a championship course. As we walked in, it was a joy to see real log fires burning at both ends of the living room. This oak beamed cottage is filled with many interesting pieces of old Welsh furniture. The spacious farmhouse kitchen was just as welcoming, with a large oak table and, yes, an oil-fired Rayburn stove. Another bonus: no TV! **Sleeps 7** plus cot. Linen not provided. Open all year. Short breaks possible. Pets by arrangement (small charge). Cost: from about £400. Details from Stephanie and John Grant, Bollingham House, Eardisley, Herefordshire HR5 3LE. Telephone 01544 327326.

www.north-wales-accommodation.co.uk
email: grant@bollinghamhouse.com

Uwchmynydd, near Aberdaron
Talcen Foel

It would be hard to find a more away-from-it-all spot than this old Welsh farmstead cottage. It is in the hamlet of Uwchmynydd, below the summit of Mount Anelog, at the western tip of the Lleyn Peninsula.

After a scenic drive along approximately seventeen miles of country lanes from Pwllheli, we eventually found it up a gated track which climbed around a hillside bordered by heather and gorse before ending along the edge of a field.

In ten acres of pasture, it's a fine comfortable cottage (**sleeping 2 to 4**) with wonderful sea and mountain views. On a clear day the Irish coast and Wicklow Hills beyond are clearly visible and also the mid-Wales coast. Inside, the interior has been sympathetically rebuilt and modernised while retaining its original character. To make the most of the views, the spacious lounge – originally a cowshed – has windows on three sides, but is kept cosy in cooler weather by a woodburner in an attractive fireplace. Up a couple of steps you reach the kitchen-dining room which has a flag-stone floor and large inglenook with an oil-fired range. The fully-fitted galley kitchen area includes a microwave and washing machine. Both bedrooms, a double and a twin, are at the front and the double offers sea views from the comfort of its bed. Above the kitchen-dining room, an open 'crog loft den' on a balcony reached by a wooden ladder provides a perfect place in which to sit and read.

A super addition to the 'cottage guide' family, with fabulous views...

Ideal for honeymooners, 'stressed out' couples, walkers and birdwatchers.

When we called there, two readers from Hertfordshire were enjoying a mid-morning coffee on the patio. 'We've been coming regularly ever since it was converted in 2001', they told us.

The cottage is on the Pilgrims' Way coastal path, two miles from the sea-side village of Aberdaron (shops, pub and beach) and one from the excel-lent seafood restaurant at Penbryn Bach, near Sanctuary Cottage. Available July/August, first week of September, Christmas and New Year. 'Sorry, no pets'. TV, video. Linen not provided. Friday to Friday book-ings. Cost: from about £450 inclusive of electric and storage heaters (win-ter) with reductions on fortnightly bookings.

Details: Roger Jones, Roger's Retreats, The Old Granary, Tremadog, Gwynedd LL49 9RH. Telephone 01766 513555.

email: jenny.roger2002@virgin.net

Tal-y-Bont, near Conwy
Pant Farm

We like the way one goes along a private, gated track to get to this. The main part of the farmhouse dates back to the 16th century, but restoration includes every 21st century creature comfort. It has a good-sized 'farmhouse' kitchen/breakfast room with a dishwasher, a microwave and pine furniture. There's a utility room with washing machine, a dining room

In ten acres of pastureland, this is one of our all-time favourites in North Wales.

with massive inglenook fireplace and a sitting room featuring inglenook, bread oven and TV/video, sympathetically extended with French windows to the garden. Upstairs there's an elegant master bedroom (king sized bed), a twin-bedded room with washbasin and a third bedroom with two single beds. The bathroom has a bidet, and a second bathroom comprises shower, toilet and washbasin. (There's also a downstairs loo/washroom.) The house has double glazing, gas fired programmed central heating during winter lets, a woodburner. Not suitable for dogs. **Sleeps 6**. Cost: £295 to £550. Available main season and bank holiday weeks only. Linen not provided. Details: Roger Jones, Roger's Retreats, The Old Granary, Tremadog, Gwynedd LL49 9RH. Telephone 01766 513555.

email: jenny.roger2002@virgin.net

Tal-y-Bont, near Conwy
Robyn's Nest map 5/331

Across the drive from Pant Farm, though self contained, *Robyn's Nest* shares a remarkable situation in ten acres of land, overlooking the River Conwy and positioned perfectly for the coast (ten miles) and the heart of Snowdonia. The house offers split level accommodation with a king sized bed in the main (ensuite) bedroom and a dining area and big sitting room on the first floor, overlooking

It's just across the drive from Pant Farm, and enjoys the same remarkable location.

the valley. Better yet, there is a woodburning stove, as well as programmed central heating available at an extra charge. The ground floor contains a modern fitted kitchen, separate bathroom and toilet and a twin bedroom. There's an old stable door out on to a private paved patio area.

TV/video. **Sleeps 4** (ideal for two couples or families with children over ten). Not suitable for dogs. Cost: £450. Available main season/bank holiday weeks only. Linen not provided. Details: Roger Jones, Roger's Retreats, The Old Granary, Tremadog, Gwynedd LL49 9RH. Telephone 01766 513555.

email: jenny.roger2002@virgin.net

141

Aberdaron
Sanctuary Cottage (Bryn Du Farm)

Tucked away along narrow lanes on the Llyn Peninsula, this has sandy beaches within a mile and a half and a network of footpaths leading to the sea. The large sitting room has an inglenook fireplace with multi-fuel stove, an old dresser with Willow Pattern plates, TV/video and dining table. Open stairs lead to the first floor, with one double bedroom, one twin bedded room and a third bedroom with bunk beds. All the rooms are small and cottagey, with rural

Well situated for sea-fishing and walking: delightfully, there's coastal-path access over the garden stile...

views. The bathroom has an electric shower over the bath. There's a well-modernised kitchen/diner with cooker and microwave. A utility room off the kitchen houses the fridge/freezer, washing machine and dishwasher. Fronting the length of the cottage is a large conservatory with cane furniture and dining table and chairs. Windows are double-glazed. **Sleeps 6**. Cost: £295 to £550. Available all year. Not suitable for dogs. Linen not provided. Details from Roger Jones, Roger's Retreats, The Old Granary, Tremadog, Gwynedd LL49 9RH. Telephone 01766 513555.

email: jenny.roger2002@virgin.net

Pwllheli   map 5/314
Gwynfryn Farm Holidays

This impressive 100-acre organic farm on the Lleyn Peninsula is looked after at every stage by the owners themselves, including the dozen WTB **Four and Five Star** cottages created here from original barns. They **sleep from 2 to 8.** Prices

Very family orientated, a great location.

include the use of an indoor pool, a gym, tennis court and playroom, family bikes and more, and electricity, towels, bedding and heating are also 'all-in'. There are 'no hidden charges'. And children will love the pigs and chickens to feed, and the cows to watch being milked. There are wood-burning stoves, dogs are welcome, home-cooked meals are available. The newest properties are *Glaslyn* and *Crafnant*, both graded **Five Stars**. They have tiled floors, leather furniture and two bathrooms. B&B is available in the farmhouse. Pwllheli and the sea are just a mile away, part of a stretch of 'heritage' coast noted for its sandy bays and rocky headlands. Cost: about £250 to £975. Details are available from Alwyn and Sharon Ellis, Gwynfryn Farm, Pwllheli, Gwynedd LL53 5UF. Telephone 01758 612536.

www.northwales-countryholidays.com
email: frank@gwynfryn.freeserve.co.uk

Portmeirion, near Porthmadog
Portmeirion Cottages

We recently stayed (one night: it was all too brief) in this enchanting hillside village created by the distinguished architect Sir Clough Williams-Ellis. Begun during the 1920s, its higgledy-piggledy sugared-almond buildings make staying there a real experience. We strolled on the lovely sandy beach at the foot of the village and bought some of its famous pottery. **Sleeping from 2 to 8**, there are fourteen cottages, each one a picturesque gem

An extraordinary 'village', with a very special place in our readers' affections.

(some have small gardens). The cottages are cosy, 'lived-in', deceptively spacious. We spotted antiques, good beds, well-equipped kitchens and often superb views from upper windows. Newspapers, bread and milk are available from a shop and guests have free use of the Portmeirion Hotel's heated pool by the sea from May to September. You can also eat there – in style – or in the hotel by the village entrance. Cost from £602 to £1381; three/four night winter breaks from £281 to £649. Satellite TV, heating, towels and linen. Details from Portmeirion Cottages, Portmeirion, near Porthmadog, Gwynedd LL48 6ET. Telephone 01766 770000.

www.portmeirion-village.com   email: hotel@portmeirion-village.com

---

Llanrug, nr Llanberis
Bryn Bras Castle   map 5/326

Wales is indeed 'a land of castles', and one of the most memorable is a castle in which self-caterers can actually stay. As indeed have many readers during the 26 years in which we have featured Bryn Bras. Within the castle is a selection of beautifully appointed, spacious, *In this guide for 26 happy years!* warm and comfortable apartments, each with a suite of rooms of distinctively individual character, set off with antiques. The Regency castle (Grade II* Listed) lies among the Snowdonian foothills, in 32 quiet acres, with landscaped gardens, woodlands and its own panoramic hill-walk overlooking the sea and Snowdon. Centrally situated for exploring the charms of North Wales and Anglesey, with excellent restaurants and pubs nearby, Bryn Bras is a much loved home and guests appreciate the historic surroundings, peaceful grounds and degree of care in the castle apartments (sleeping 2 to 4). Flexible start/departure days. **'Visit Wales' Five Stars**. Dogs are not allowed, nor are children. Short breaks all year round. Fully inclusive cost: £500 to £900; short breaks from £195 (two people, two nights).

Details from Mrs Gray-Parry, Bryn Bras Castle, Llanrug, near Caernarfon, North Wales LL55 4RE. Telephone/fax 01286 870210.

www.brynbrascastle.co.uk   email: holidays@brynbrascastle.co.uk

Maesycrugiau and Llandeilo

In a super location in the valley of the River Teifi. the first of these properties (Ref W8409) is actually the wing of a larger house. It has a woodburning stove and **sleeps 6**. There is a four poster bedroom and an attic bedroom that our own children would have loved when small. You're only about five miles from the Brechfa Forest, where there are mountain bike trails, and a pub/-restaurant is only a mile away. And at Capel Isaac, near Llandeilo, we

Near Llandeilo, this quite exceptional farmhouse is full of character and lies amid delightful surroundings.

discovered a delightful 17th century detached farmhouse notable for original features such as an inglenook fireplace and flagstone floors. **Sleeping 5/6**, it has lovely surroundings: there's an orchard, and the River Dulas runs through the farm. Ref W3478. Here one is well placed for exploring the River Towy, the National Botanic Garden of Wales and the Brecon Beacons.

For availability and bookings, contact Welcome Cottages, Spring Mill, Earby, Barnoldswick, Lancashire BB94 0AA. Properties in France available too. Telephone 0845 268 0945.

www.welcomecottages.com

The Gower Peninsula map 5/345
Crwys Farm/Tankey Lake Livery

A quartet of quite notable properties, rejoicing in **Five Stars** from **'Visit Britain'** and **sleeping 8, 8, 4 and 4** respectively, make a fine base from which to explore the much-loved 'Gower'. A good number of original features at Crwys Farm have been preserved, blending in sympathetically with 21st century comforts. Refs ONQ, ONR, ONT and ONS. At Tankey Lake Livery, Llangennith, nestling in 31 acres of the owner's

Oak Barn is one of the larger properties at Crwys Farm: a super family house.

small working farm, are two single-storeyed cottages called *Bluebell* and *Buttercup*, conversions from a 16th century barn. One **sleeps 2**, the other **sleeps 4**, and both are suitable for wheelchair access. Refs JYW/JAM. Outdoor pursuits include surfing, windsurfing, canoeing, pony trekking, bird-watching, fishing, golf, hang-gliding and caving.

Further details available from English Country Cottages, Stoney Bank Road, Earby, Barnoldswick BB94 0AA. For bookings and brochures, telephone 0845 268 0942.

www.english-country-cottages.co.uk

Brecon Beacons and around
Brecon Beacons Holiday Cottages*

Recently chosen as 'The Best Small Business in Wales', Liz Daniel's agency is remarkable, with over 270 cottages and farmhouses in and around the Brecon Beacons National Park. The properties range from a tiny cottage in a lovely setting with a high level of comfort for 2, to spacious farmhouses sleeping – really! – up to 50. We remember *Crofftau*, whose beautifully-furnished upstairs sitting-room/dining room revels in a steep beamed ceiling, wood burning stove

Duffryn Beusych (not featured) is a cosy charmer. The owner will prepare a meal for guests on arrival 'at cost'. Sleeps 3/4.

and spectacular mountain views on both sides. **Sleeps 8**. Cost: £820. Also *Dovecote Cottage*, with a hard tennis court and three miles of fishing on the River Usk, in a most beautiful location. The impressive sitting room has heavy oak beams, a large wood-burning stove in an inglenook fireplace and comfortable sofas and chairs. **Sleeps 8**. Cost £690.

Details from Elizabeth Daniel, Brecon Beacons Holiday Cottages and Farm Houses, Brynoyre, Talybont-on-Usk, Brecon, Powys LD3 7YS. Telephone 01874 676446. Fax 676416.

www.breconcottages.com email: enquiries@breconcottages.com

Abergwesyn map 5/337
Trallwm Forest Cottages

At the heart of a working forest, in a deeply rural part of mid Wales, this is a clutch of cottages converted from former farm buildings. **Colour section, Page 4**. All are **'Visit Wales' Four Stars**. *Siskin,* a detached stone cottage, is **for a couple** (non-smokers). *Nant-Garreg* is full of character, has oak beams, an inglenook fireplace and

Quiet but not isolated, the Trallwm properties are comfortable and warm.

sleeps 4. Two cottages, *Kestrel* and *Red Kite*, are two-bedroomed and very comfortable. *Trallwm Farmhouse* **sleeps 7**, has a large lounge/diner and a blend of rustic and modern, with one of the three bedrooms downstairs. *Magpie* is a cosy cottage for a non smoking couple. *Trawsgyrch*, a large, traditional Welsh stone farmhouse overlooking hayfields, is well equipped for the **9/10 it sleeps**. Cost: from about £237, fully inclusive, for 2 people. One well-behaved dog is welcome by arrangement (in Nant-Garreg, Siskin and Trawsgyrch). TVs throughout and phone in Nant-Garreg, Siskin and Trawsgyrch only, plus payphone for general use. Details from George and Christine Johnson, Trallwm Forest Lodge, Abergwesyn, Llanwrtyd Wells, Powys LD5 4TS. Telephone/fax 01591 610229.

www.forestcottages.co.uk email: trallwm@aol.com

Sennybridge, near Brecon
Cnewr Estate

Over the years the Brecon Beacons National Park has become one of our favourite corners of the whole of Britain, and we can hardly think of a nicer spot from which to enjoy this rather underrated national park than the holiday houses on the Cnewr Estate. We sometimes happen on houses or cottages that fit perfectly into their surroundings and give immediate access to much treasured corners of the country: we would include these. (As would a number of cottage guide readers who have quite fallen for the Cnewr properties.)

You can choose between a big 1890 farmhouse and a shepherd's cottage, both of them on the 12,000-acre estate (owned and farmed by the same family since 1856), and all much praised by readers over the years.

The whole area is ideal for walking, and you could spend a day on the mountains without leaving the estate. There is fly-fishing on the estate's Cray Reservoir, *one of only four in Wales with wild trout*, as well as the hill streams.

Cnewr Farmhouse, which **sleeps 12** in five twins and one double, has a long dining table big enough to seat everyone comfortably in the huge well-equipped kitchen. The main sitting room has unspoilt views down the valley and there is also a TV-lounge/children's room, two bathrooms and shower room. The owner's private dining room is available by arrangement for special occasions. There's lots of warmth and a good number of 'country antiques'.

The other property is beside the Sennybridge to Ystradgynlais road but the windows facing it are double-glazed, though there is little traffic. *Fan Cottage* overlooks Cray Reservoir, having been built as a shepherd's cottage to replace a house lost when the reservoir was built. It has one double and two twin bedrooms, bathroom, sitting room, dining room and large kitchen. It **sleeps 5/6**.

Each property has an open fire (logs provided free), payphone and TV. Well-behaved dogs welcome. Linen and towels provided. Cost, including heating and electricity, from about £200 to about £750. Short-breaks are available at less busy times of the year.

Detailed brochures are available from the Cnewr Estate Ltd, Sennybridge, Brecon, Powys LD3 8SP. Telephone 01874 636207. Fax 638061.

www.cnewrestate.co.uk

email: cottages@cnewrestate.co.uk

Cnewr Farmhouse can accommodate twelve people. It's a comfortable, rambling place of great character...

Fan Cottage, where we have stayed briefly, overlooks peaceful Cray Reservoir, amid fine scenery...

The West Country

Among other good things from holidays in Cornwall and Devon we remember marvellous sunsets, luscious crabs, clotted cream, Cornish pasties, coastal footpaths and ancient castles. John Betjeman was one of Cornwall's best-loved advocates ('Safe Cornish holidays by the sea'...), but it seems that every corner of the West Country has lots going for it – the proximity of child-friendly beaches, the wild moors, the two national parks (Exmoor and Dartmoor), great stately homes. Notably, and uniquely in England, Devon revels in two separate (unlinked) coasts – a north and a south. On the borders of Devon and Somerset, Exmoor is pony trekking and walking country, where wild ponies and deer roam freely. Exmoor has a stretch of coast it can almost call its own, and some spectacular views. In Somerset, Cheddar Gorge and Wookey Hole are memorable. Over the border in Dorset, it is easy to find country houses off the tourist beat and holiday resorts full of history and charm (Lyme Regis is a delight). And the best of Wiltshire is the essence of rural England, unchanged for hundreds of years. It is dotted with ancient pubs, and half its holiday cottages seem to be thatched!

Botelet, near Herodsfoot
Manor Cottage   map 6/348

With its origins mentioned in the Domesday Book, oak beams, flag-stone floors and open fireplaces, this 17th century listed longhouse is – not surprisingly – a real favourite among cottage guide readers. The dining room doors open on to a private walled garden created from earlier ruins, and the kitchen features a cov-ered floodlit well (a first for us!).

A spacious traditional farmhouse, suitable for family groups and couples.

Coupled with this is a flair for design for which Richard Tamblyn has been featured in Elle Decoration. The cottage has been furnished to a standard that makes guests instantly feel at ease: they often choose to stay twice a year. Brass beds are made up with antique linen, the fire is lit and the table laid; with 300 acres, with a neolithic hill-fort, fields, lanes and a woodland walk, there is plenty to explore. The Tamblyn family have been on the farm since 1860 and the present generation live in the Georgian farmhouse across the cobbled courtyard.

Sleeps 5 in three bedrooms (double, twin, single); one bathroom, one shower room. Linen is supplied. Dishwasher, fridge/freezer, washing machine, dryer, microwave, TV, video, CD/tuner. Woodburning stove. Babysitting. Dogs by arrangement. Cost: £270 to £970. Please note that a further cottage (*Cowslip*, not yet seen by us) is available. Further details from Julie Tamblyn, Botelet, Herodsfoot, Liskeard, Cornwall PL14 4RD. Telephone/fax 01503 220225; fax 220909.

www.botelet.co.uk
email: stay@botelet.co.uk

Duloe, near Looe
Trefanny Hill

The cottages here, each one with its own special character and each, we've noticed over 26 years of featuring 'Trefanny', with its own following, are very special. One couple told us they booked a cottage here with the aim of making it their touring base for a week. 'But', they said, 'we never left "the village", as we came to know it. It is such a retreat from everyday cares, so peaceful and nostalgic.'

It's hard to believe that over 40 years ago, when the Slaughter family first discovered Trefanny Hill, it was a desolate ruin. Nestling above a tributary of the West Looe River, this ancient farming settlement was at one time a thriving, medieval smugglers' hamlet which in the last century was granted its own school, smithy and chapel. Even today, Trefanny Hill retains a village atmosphere. The cottages are lovely, their stone or white-

There is a village atmosphere at Trefanny Hill. The cottages are well spread out and enjoy a feeling of independence.

Each cottage has its own individual character. They range in size from those for 6 to mini cottages just for couples.

painted walls draped with ivy, roses and other climbers and looking just like everybody's idea of what a country cottage should be. Each has bags of character, and reveals the Slaughters' amazing eye for detail. There are seventeen cottages in all—well spread out, each with its own garden.

There are five different sizes of cottage, appropriate to the size of your family, ranging from a cosy cottage just for **2** (either with an antique brass double bed or four poster, or king-size/twin beds) to a three-bedroom for **6** (7 with a cot). Among the little extras you will find are plenty of books (including a set of coffee table items on wild flowers, trees, birds). There are video recorders, hairdryers, electric blankets, hot water bottles, alarm clocks. The kitchens are fully equipped with filter coffee makers, spice jars, wine coolers, microwaves, dishwashers and extras galore. All the cottages for 3 or more also have a washing machine/tumble dryer installed, while the smaller ones without this have access to washing machines and dryers in a traditional Cornish building nearby.

Each garden has chairs, a table, a parasol and a good barbecue so you can enjoy fine weather to the full. Standing in 75 acres, Trefanny Hill is surrounded by rolling greenery and commands a wide panorama over the Looe Valley. Among the permanent residents are the ducks on their pond, the chickens, doves, cats, Jacob's sheep and shire horses. The wild flowers in springtime are particularly magical. There are no half-hidden eyesores that detract from the peaceful atmosphere. The interiors of the cottages are like private homes. The furniture is good, old and varied. Each cottage is different; some have Laura Ashley and Sanderson wallpaper and fabrics, most have oak beams up to 400 years old, and log fires.

Perhaps the most memorable part of our most recent visit was strolling downhill past the heated outdoor pool that is accessible to all Trefanny's guests – it is amazingly scenically situated, and always warm – and then through fields towards a wooded stream where we discovered *Tregarrick Millhouse*, another of those substantial family houses that make these journeys so worthwhile. We do not have the space to convey all its delights, but noted most appealing reds and greens in the decor and, outside, large grounds with a stream and a mill pond. **Sleeps 6**.

A tea and coffee tray greets every arriving guest, and all linen – crispy white, generous in size – is provided. Shared amenities include that beautiful heated swimming pool, a children's play area, a grass lawn with badminton net, a golf net for driving practice and more. There is an attractive lake with wildlife, a full size tennis court, and an enchanting bluebell wood.

Most unusually, cottage guests at Trefanny Hill have their own cosy little inn, which is much enjoyed for drinks, snacks and full meals.

In this attractive setting, people staying at Trefanny Hill have ready access to one of the most impressively situated outdoor pools in Cornwall!

The tiny inn within the hamlet is also a popular feature, where you can relax in a cosy, informal atmosphere for drinks or candlelit dinners. Dishes are cooked to order using fresh local produce (freshly caught local fish and organic steaks being the specialities of the house), or alternatively you can eat in the privacy of your own cottage by choosing from the full and varied menu offered by a home cooked meals service.

More fishing (lake, river and sea), windsurfing, including hire and instruction, riding, golf, sailing and many more activities are all available in the area. Each cottage has an information folder and relevant Ordnance Survey maps. We wish this was universal!

A typical comment culled from the visitors' books in the cottages reads 'For a long time we have looked for a holiday that offers top class hotel accommodation with the freedom of self-catering – at last we have found it'. Said one Lancashire visitor, 'it's the most honest brochure I have seen in many years'. And a Surrey couple have been to stay – yes! – 41 times!

Cost: about £150 to £1945. Children and well behaved pets are welcome. Details from John and Suzanne Slaughter, Trefanny Hill, Duloe, near Liskeard, Cornwall PL14 4QF. Telephone 01503 220622.

www.trefanny.co.uk
enq@trefanny.co.uk

Treworgey Manor, Liskeard
Coach House Cottages

A late summer Cornish journey in 2007 took in an early evening revisit to this peaceful family-run estate. We could have settled down for a week there and then – it has that sort of effect. In the same family for over 500 years, now under the stewardship of Jeremy and Jane Hall, Treworgey Manor is a charmer, and the holiday property conversions have been done with sensitivity and style, combining character and comfort.

Even the large heated outdoor pool seems to blend in well with the ancient clock tower, the symbol of the easy-on-the-eye group of 16th century courtyard cottages. An all-weather tennis court, games room and boules pit complete the outdoor attractions.

Re-discovering this beautifully cared for Cornish oasis of comfort and style on an early evening visit in 2007 cheered us up a lot!

Well suited as it is to a big family or a group of friends, we love *The Coach House*. **Sleeping 8**, it even has a half size snooker table in the huge sitting room. There is one double bedroom with en suite bathroom, a further double bedroom, one twin-bedded room, a bunk-bedded one, a bathroom and a separate shower room, making it ideal for two families, or for those bringing grandparents. *Paddock View* and *Deer Park* both **sleep 6**, but vary in the distribution of bedrooms and also in decor, each being delightfully distinctive, with good use made of original beams, paintings, ornaments and objects of interest from the old manor buildings.

Middle Barn **sleeps 4** in a double bedroom and a twin, and has an upstairs bathroom. Pets are accepted in this property. Dogs will certainly appreciate the walks, the Manor being tucked into 100 acres of pasture and woodland. Children will also have fun exploring the nooks and crannies around the courtyard, not least the mysterious priest's hole.

With a roaring log fire for company there is every temptation to stay put in your own little world. Which is where short breaks, weekend parties – renting all four cottages – come into their own. Each garden has a table and chairs, plus barbecue.

Electricity and calor gas are included, and also an initial basket of logs (each property has an open log fire); linen is supplied, except beach towels; there is a laundry room, payphone and TVs with DVD players. Cost: about £160 (three night short break) to £1180. Details are available from Jeremy or Jane Hall, Coach House Cottages, Treworgey Manor, Liskeard, Cornwall PL14 6RN. Telephone 01579 347755. Fax 345441.

www.treworgey.co.uk   email: info@treworgey.co.uk

Pelynt, near Looe
Tremaine Green

We certainly see some delightful corners of Britain during our travels. The cottages at Tremaine Green, which we have known and admired since 1983, effectively make up a cosy hamlet in a quiet part of Cornwall (nicely inland, but only a short drive from Looe), and are absolute charmers. Better yet, they hold the 'Best Conservation Garden' and a 'Green Acorn Award for Sustainable Tourism'.

In this group of traditional craftsmen's cottages, the whole family will appreciate the games room with table-tennis, pool, darts and other games. They'll also appreciate the lovingly kept, award-winning gardens. Good beaches are a short drive away, as is 'quintessential' Polperro. Also, there's a hard tennis court, putting green, swing-ball, pigmy goats, ducks, miniature ponies etc to feed. Hamlet, the owners' blue Great Dane, completes the picture.

Every building is named after its original use, such as *Blacksmith's*, *Carpenter's* and *Miller's*, and each is decorated with interesting pictures and artefacts. Leather hobnail boots and saddlery are interesting reminders of *Ploughman's* history, while *Cobbler's* boasts relics from a shoemaker's.

We love the fact that Tremaine Green's cottages are private and self-contained...

...but are at the same time part of a tucked away hamlet, 'part of a whole'.

There are eleven cottages altogether (**sleeping 2 to 6**), each with its own individual charm. Most have exposed stonework and many have an antique four-poster or half-tester bed at least in the main bedroom. Cots and occasional single beds are available in most cottages. The kitchens in cottages **sleeping 4** or more have dishwashers and fridge-freezers. We liked the comfortable settee/deep armchairs in Ploughman's and the inglenook fireplace with the original cloam (bread) oven, also *Dairymaid's* antique half-tester bed, the pretty fabrics and the open fire. *Tinner's*, which has a bunk bedroom and shower downstairs, plus two doubles upstairs, is popular with families, as children sleeping in the bunks can feel independent.

The double glazing and the oil-fired central heating make all this cosy in winter. (Four cottages have real fires as well.) Videos and DVDs are available for rent. Tickets for the Eden Project (14 miles away) are for sale to avoid queuing at the ticket office there. Dogs and other pets welcome. Linen provided. TVs, videos and DVDs for rent. Cost: about £188 to £974. An excellent brochure is available from Justin and Penny Spreckley, Tremaine Green Country Cottages, Pelynt, near Looe, Cornwall PL13 2LT. Telephone 01503 220333; fax 220633.

www.tremainegreen.co.uk   email: stay@tremainegreen.co.uk

Duloe, near Looe
Treworgey Cottages

For all its usefulness, the **'Visit Britain'** grading scheme doesn't accord cottages special credit for being in idyllic locations. So in our book (literally) these are **Five Star**-plus, with all the comfort and style that implies *and* a memorable situation.

High above the River Looe, with spectacular south-facing views over patchwork fields and the river itself, they are outstanding. Better yet, owners Lynda and Bevis Wright have landscaped the prettiest of individual private gardens for each cottage, with masses of flowers.

Each cottage exudes good taste and is individually styled, mostly with family antique furniture, original paintings, wool carpets, oriental rugs, plenty of lamps and books. Bedrooms have exceptionally attractive four posters or beautiful brass beds with really comfortable mattresses, antiques, lace and fresh flowers.

Add to this a delivered candlelit dinner (from Treworgey's mouthwatering menu) by your roaring log fire, a good video from the Wrights' comprehensive library and you'll think you have died and gone to heaven! (Don't worry about the washing up – the dishwasher will do it!)

There is plenty to do here too (the Eden Project, for example, is only half an hour away), and the landscaped outdoor pool is stunning. Readers are full of praise about that: 'really warm...open and steaming as late as October, when the weather allows'... There is excellent riding available on site, an all-weather tennis court, indoor and outdoor playground with wendy house and more, and a delightful collection of animals: the goats

Unusually for this sort of set-up, every property has its own cottagey garden...

Such a lot of style and attention to detail has gone into every one of the interiors...

and Bramble the pony spend most of their time befriending guests.

Short breaks are welcome out of season. With log fires and ample central heating, Treworgey is very popular in winter and for Christmas and New Year. (By the way Treworgey is easy to get to by train – there's even a tiny toy station down the lane at Sandplace.)

Cost: from about £275 per week to £2071, according to cottage size and season. **Sleep from 2 'plus baby' to 8**. Children are welcome. Telephone 01503 262730. Fax 263757.

www.cornishdreamcottages.co.uk

email: treworgey@enterprise.net

Looe Valley
Badham Farm Holiday Cottages

There are not many 'deeply rural' properties you can still reach by train.

But this is one, via Causeland Halt on the scenic Looe Valley Line – a most charming feature that Jan and Pauline Scroczynski plan to make more of as they expand and add facilities to the site. Newly completed *Oak Cottage*, **sleeping 4**, *Ash Cottage*, **sleeping 5**, and *Larch Cottage*, **sleeping 6**, have been built to suit less mobile guests, with all accommodation on the ground floor and level access. Car parking is

Both 'deeply rural' and near the sea – a powerful combination in holiday houses.

adjacent to each cottage. All nine cottages have modern kitchens and bathrooms with power showers. All neatly complement the other six cottages, **sleeping between 2 and 10** (in the *Farmhouse*). Bonuses include an animal and bird paddock, a coarse fishing lake and tennis court, along with a convivial bar and a gym and jacuzzi.

Dogs at £20 a week. Cost from about £200 to £1300 including heating; also short breaks. Contact Jan and Pauline Scroczynski, Badham Farm Holidays, St Keyne, Liskeard, Cornwall PL14 4RW. Telephone/fax 01579 343572. **www.badhamfarm.co.uk email: badhamfarm@yahoo.co.uk**

Coverack, near Helston
Trevarrow Cottage map 6/360

This is rather special. The quaint Cornish fishing village of Coverack, very well located on a south easterly corner of the Lizard peninsula, is the kind of place that photographers drool over. And this idyllic looking cottage looks as good as any you might see on chocolate box lids or jigsaws. Also, Trevarrow would surely win the prettiest-holiday-cottage-in-the-village award on account of its pastel-pink walls and thatched roof. Better yet, it was once a smugglers' hideaway. Though it has been properly modernised, it still has its original shipwreck beams and inglenook fireplace. It has an excellent and well-equipped kitchen with microwave, washing machine/tumble dryer. Electricity is included, as are bed-linen and towels. Friday to Friday bookings. Sorry, no pets; no smoking.

One of the prettiest houses in a much sought-after coastal village: on the sea-front, with front and back gardens.

Sleeps 6. Cost: about £395 to £875. Further details are available from Amanda Wiseman, Shenstone Court, Court Drive, Shenstone, Lichfield, Staffordshire WS14 0JQ. Telephone 07980 370373.

email: wisemanaj@googlemail.com

Praa Sands
Sea Meads Holiday Homes

It had long been our ambition to stay in one of the holiday houses in this extraordinary spot, and in the summer of 2007 we did just that. We revelled in the space, the high-ceilinged bedroom, the amazing late-evening and early morning light, the sea views. It's one thing to be 'by the sea', but at Sea Meads you can not only see and hear the waves, you can almost touch them. (One recent reader wrote: 'When the children were unruly we let them sit by the window at bedtime; they were as quiet as mice, and toddled off to bed on their own'.)

Almost hidden from the little cluster of buildings above the beach, Sea Meads is a group of six detached houses, each with its own garden facing the sea, spacious lounges with large sliding patio windows through which to enjoy those views, dining areas with serving hatch from modern kitchens equipped with dishwashers, fridge-freezers, cookers with extractor hoods, microwaves, washing machines, bathrooms with heated towel rails and wall heaters – everything to permanent-home standards.

*Solmer, Sunwave, Sea Horse*s and *Sunraker* are all similar. On the ground floor there is a twin-bedded room with en-suite bathroom and toilet, and a small room with double bunk beds. Upstairs are two large bedrooms (one double, one twin) – each has a small balcony with magnificent sea views, and a second bathroom with shower unit. The ambience is one of brightness and light, with comfortable furniture and charming touches. There is plenty of space, a private garage to each house, room in the garden for ball games, all-in-all a recipe for a memorable family holiday. **Sleep up to 8**.

The other two houses are situated between the Estate Road and the sea. In *Four Winds*, **sleeping 5**, we loved the big, comfy sitting room and the linked sunlounge overlooking the sea. Also the different-level dining area with adjacent kitchen and the en suite bedroom with impressive sea views. At first floor level there are two further bedrooms and an adjoining bathroom. In *Sandilands*, **sleeping 6**, all of the Four Winds attributes apply, but it has two double bedrooms en suite and a further double and bathroom.

Cost: approximately £295 to £1145, depending on which property and when you go. TVs/videos. Dogs are welcome. Linen is included, towels available. There's a games room with table tennis, pool and darts.

Further details from Best Leisure, Old House Farm, Fulmer Road, Fulmer, Buckinghamshire SL3 6HU. Telephone 01753 664336. Fax 663740. **www.bestleisure.co.uk**

How's this for a memorable bedroom-balcony view? The sound is nice too!

We admired the semi-tropical gardens and the spacious, light, bright interiors.

St Austell
Bosinver Cottages

We're not surprised 'Bosinver' won the accolade of 'Self Catering Establishment of the Year' in the Cornwall Tourism Awards for 2007, making it a hat-trick. For sometimes we come across holiday cottage owners whose sheer delight in what they do adds a magical ingredient to what they offer. Pat and David Smith are such people: they have made Bosinver into something quite extraordinary.

Having revisited in 2007, ahead of the awards, we can confirm that Bosinver gets better and better. Among the nineteen cottages, people have been completely bowled over by *Coliza*, a lovely thatched two-storey cottage (**sleeping 4** plus cot). It looks and feels old, yet it's only been completed during the last couple of years. The old thatched farmhouse **sleeps 12**, *Laburnum* and *Jacks Barn* both **sleep 8**, and the combinations possible make it easy for groups wanting to celebrate special occasions. Most are totally private and overlook meadows teeming with wildlife and friendly farm animals.

The cottages are scattered among trees, gardens and meadows around the 30-acre estate, just three miles from the sea and a five-minute stroll from Polgooth's village shop and pub. Pat furnishes each one individually, with antiques, local materials and traditional crafts.

Bosinver has a Green Tourism Award, but also provides plenty to do, including an adventure playground with trampoline, slides, rope bridge and climb-on tractor, and a fabulous 'play barn'. In a glorious south-facing position, one end is glass and oak from floor to ceiling, incorporating an 'R and R'

A 'Green Tourism' Award and more (see above) from the Cornwall Tourist Board.   *...and plaudits from us for a massive upgrading during recent years.*

area for mums and dads, and a small 'gym area'. There's also a heated outdoor pool (April to September), sauna, tennis court, coarse fishing and games room with pool, darts and table football. Bikes can be hired.

All cottages have baby cutlery and crockery; cots and highchairs, stairgates, bed-guards and booster seats are available. Dogs by arrangement. No smoking. Some properties Friday-Friday, some Saturday-Saturday. Short breaks November to April. Cost: from about £250 to £2000 per week from the smallest, **sleeping 2**, to the largest, **sleeping 12**. Details from Pat Smith, Bosinver Farm, St Austell, Cornwall PL26 7DT. Telephone/fax 01726 72128.

www.bosinver.co.uk   email: reception@bosinver.co.uk

Fowey
Fowey Harbour Cottages*

Specialising in Fowey Harbour, on the south Cornish coast, this long-established agency is run with style. Cottages include *Sideways Cottage*, a semi-detached property **sleeping 6** in three bedrooms. **Visit Britain Three Stars**. *The Penthouse*, in the centre of Fowey, is a four-storey town house with parking space and a roof-top terrace from which there is a 360° outlook over the harbour (three bedrooms, **sleeping 6**: **'Visit Britain' Three Stars**). *17a St Fimbarrus Road*, Fowey, is an apartment in a tall Victorian terrace house with windows overlooking the whole harbour (two bedrooms, **sleeping 4**: **'Visit Britain' Three Stars**) and there's a selection of stone-built cottages in the village of Polruan on the other side of the harbour, including *Rose Villa*, a pleasant cottage in Polruan, opposite Fowey, with a patio garden. It **sleeps 5** in three bedrooms. **'Visit Britain' Two Stars**. Most **sleep 4 to 6**. Dogs welcome in most, all have TV. Linen for hire. Cost from £175 to £1200. Short breaks at certain times. Details from David Hill, 3 Fore Street, Fowey, Cornwall PL23 1AH. Telephone 01726 832211. Fax 832901.

Sideways Cottage is located right in the town centre, but nicely away from any traffic noise.

www.foweyharbourcottages.co.uk   email: hillandson@talk21.com

---

Looe map 6/366
Wringworthy Cottages

On a perfect late-summer day in 2007 we turned off the Looe to Liskeard road into an enclave of neat, tidy, pristine cottages looking like a rural hamlet. All eight cottages, once part of a stone farmstead, have been lovingly converted by the most welcoming and efficient owners to retain many original features.

Family orientated, rural but near the sea.

They can be taken in their entirety by carefully vetted groups. Among so many good things we especially remember the warm heated pool, safe play areas, outdoor games, barbecues and more. There are tame farm animals, and a games barn, and one cottage is wheelchair-adapted. Each with **Four Stars** from **'Visit Britain'**, the cottages (which hold a 'Green Acorn' Award for sustainable tourism) **sleep from 2 to 8**, and have the big advantage (often referred to by readers of this guide) of resident owners. Cost: about £146-269 to £399-1065 per week. Short out of season breaks. Linen and towels included. No smoking. Pets welcome.

Details from Michael and Kim Spencer, Wringworthy Cottages, Morval, Looe, Cornwall PL13 1PR. Telephone 01503 240685, fax 240830.

www.wringworthy.co.uk   email: holidays@wringworthy.co.uk

Helford River and Falmouth
Cornish Holiday Cottages*

On a warm autumn day in 2007 it was no hardship to visit/revisit a few of the very best Cornish cottages we know. Better yet – because many of our readers like the sense of security and the ease of organisation this entails – they are in the hands of a charming family-run agency we've featured for ten years. There are just 60 or so hand-picked properties, and the team running the agency know every stick and stone.

We briefly revisited *Tregullow*, in Maenporth, a modern bungalow **sleeping 4**. It occupies a wonderful clifftop position overlooking Falmouth Bay, and the sumptuously comfortable L-shaped sitting room makes the most of the view. It's extremely popular: you'll need to book well ahead!

New to us was *Bosryn*. An extraordinary place! We could hardly tear ourselves away. Fronting on to Port Navas creek, with its own quay and water frontage, private and quiet, it's a tonic for stressed-out city people. **Sleeps 8**. But, so conveniently, it's only six miles from Falmouth.

Less exalted but nonetheless charming and in fact more rustic, *Inow Cottage* is close to Port Navas creek. An early 19th century cottage with its beamed ceilings and inglenook, it **sleeps 4**. And we admired *Pheasant*

The Garden Wing (not featured) is part of The Sanctuary, a beautiful Georgian former rectory at Mawnan. Sleeps eight.

We were bowled over by Bosryn, and the location is memorable. Though deeply rural, it's just six miles from Falmouth.

Cottage, on the north bank of the Helford River. **Sleeping 6**, it is close to the National Trust's Glendurgan Gardens: a delightful outing.

In a leafy residential area is *Helford Point*, a property of high quality **sleeping up to 8**. It is a four-bedroomed bungalow in a large garden, with stunning views of the mouth of the Helford River and Falmouth Bay.

Closer to Falmouth – in fact, just two minutes' walk from the High Street – *6 Jane's Court*, **sleeping 4/6**, is in Packet Quays, with views from the two bedroomed apartments over Falmouth Harbour. Built in 1985, it is part of an architect's award winning complex. So expect high standards.

Cost: from about £175 to £1950. Dogs and young children welcome. Further details available from Emily Boriosi, Cornish Holiday Cottages, Killibrae, Maenporth, Falmouth, Cornwall TR11 5HP. Telephone/fax 01326 250339.

www.cornishholidaycottages.net

email: Info@cornishholidaycottages.net

Cornwall – countywide
Forgotten Houses

Even in terms of the often remarkable properties we see on our travels, some of these are extraordinary. It would take many weeks to visit all of what the brochure (full of historic and architectural details) calls 'these unusual holiday homes' – largely in Cornwall – a modest way of saying that they all benefit hugely from their location, architecture or history. Which as Stephen Tyrrell, the brains, and occasional renovator behind this extraordinary concept says, means most are listed, and many have been carefully modernised. This also means that some, by necessity, 'do not meet the modern standards of use or convenience'.

Nor will he budge from this formula, telling us during a recent visit that his strict criteria meant turning down some properties rather than create a suburban version of the countryside. Instead, most properties – about 35 in all – are built of stone, with walls two feet thick under slate roofs. Nearly all have fireplaces or stoves with wood supplied as part of the rent – as well as television and washing machines, books and games.

The approach is perhaps best summed up by the most famous house, *Mellinzeath*, close to the Helford River. Thought to have been rebuilt after a fire in 1665, it **sleeps 4/5**, with a Land Rover ride for guests and their luggage to the house – a 600 metre walk from your car! 'Return to the roots and get back to basics,' urges one guest. 'A beautifully restored cottage, and a fireplace that takes six-foot logs has been burning continuously for six and a half days.'

Most have two, three or four bedrooms, but there are also a few larger properties – such as *Manorbier Castle*, Pembrokeshire, **sleeping 12** plus cot. Fascinating, but with walls and towers you should keep a careful eye on the children.

Last year we took a fresh look at *Lower Bosvarren*, one of six houses in the hamlet of Bosvarren, up a tree lined drive just ten minutes' drive from Falmouth. A listed Elizabethan farmhouse, redecorated in 2002 and 2004 and fun for families, it retains original features, including the roof of small 'scantle' slates and two granite bread ovens. It **sleeps 8** in four double bedrooms, plus cot, and is oil fired centrally heated.

Previously we saw *Bosbenna*, a spacious house with three big bedrooms and a 'Heidi' attic up a ladder. *Badgers* (Helston), **sleeps 4/6,** and likewise has a gallery loft with two beds reached by ladder for two adventurous children. 'Having been to Cornwall many times we can honestly say Badgers is the loveliest cottage we have stayed in,' wrote one guest.

Bosvathick Lodge, near Falmouth, **sleeping 4,** though the smallest of all the properties, has its own little drive, lawn and large garden. Like most others it accepts dogs, and, again like so many others, it seems, is close to a prize-winning pub.

For a copy of a functional, not glossy but detailed brochure, with floor plans, contact Forgotten Houses, Bosvathick, Constantine, Falmouth, Cornwall TR11 5RD. Telephone 01326 340153. Fax 340426.

email: Info@Forgottenhouses.co.uk

Or see the well regarded website: www.forgottenhouses.co.uk

St Martin, near Helston
Mudgeon Vean Farm Holiday Cottages

On her glorious newly produced brochure – some memorable photos – owner Sarah Trewhella neatly conveys the charms of Mudgeon Vean, so prettily situated near the Helford River. The two cottages, *Swallow* and *Swift*, are identical, **sleeping 2 to 4**, plus cot/zed-bed. Nicely converted from the former dairy, they have a cosy open-plan sitting room/dining room/kitchen around an open fire. The third, *Badger*, **sleeping 2/6** plus cot, is attached to the

There's an outdoor play area, a table tennis room, and a private woodland walk.

farmhouse. The small arable/orchard farm has inspiring valley views and produces apple juice and cider. The farm, with **Three Stars** from Southwest Tourism, is bordered by a beautiful National Trust walk to the Helford River, and the coves of the Lizard and the beaches of North Cornwall are in easy driving distance. Cost: about £150 to £450. Dogs by arrangement (£10 pw). Linen included. Details from Mr and Mrs J Trewhella, Mudgeon Vean, St Martin, near Helston, Cornwall TR12 6DB. Telephone 01326 231341.

www.mudgeonvean.co.uk
email: mudgeonvean@aol.com

St Tudy, near Wadebridge
Chapel Cottages map 6/385

Twenty years in this guide, many enthusiastic reader reports (including lots of return visitors). Original stable front doors, beamed ceilings, polished slate floors, window seats and (in three) large granite fireplaces with cloam ovens amount to 'masses of character'! *Chapel Cottages,* which we revisited recently, are a group of four listed stone-built cottages on the edge of the quiet village of St Tudy (a

Twenty years with us, a visitor-friendly base from which to explore Cornwall.

shop and an inn are a short walk away). Each cottage has a character of its own, with good bedrooms – one with a double and a single bed, the other with twin beds – and everything on hand. The pine kitchens are attractive, with individual washing machines. In easy reach are Bodmin Moor, the Eden Project, the Camel Trail to Padstow, and the beaches of Trebarwith, Polzeath and Daymer Bay. Cost: about £150 to £445 per week. TV. Linen, cots and high chairs are included. Private parking. Not suitable for pets. Details from Clifford and Margaret Pestell, 'Hockadays', Tregenna, near Blisland, Cornwall PL30 4QJ. Telephone/fax 01208 850146.

www.hockadays.co.uk

South West Cornwall
St Aubyn Estates

There's no shortage of holiday houses of character and charm in Cornwall, but all eight of the St Aubyn properties are remarkable. We can hardly think of more stylish homes anywhere (full of 'TLC', it's as 'homes' that we think of them). During a 2007 re-visit we first saw a new addition to the St Aubyn 'family', namely *Tregarthen*. At Marazion, it's an exquisite, rather romantic hideaway, with a view of St Michael's Mount from the secluded garden. Among many good things there's a bespoke oak kitchen, a very cosy sitting room and a spacious master bedroom with a six-foot double bed. **Sleeps 4**.

Also at historic Marazion, we love the spaciousness of *Venton Farmhouse*, the high standard of the accommodation, with no loss of character. We liked the view across the water to St Michael's Mount and the private path to the rocky beach below. With **Five 'Visit Britain' Stars** (no surprise), it **sleeps 10**.

Then we headed westwards into deeply rural and coastal Cornwall, revelling in the special diamond light of the Cornish coast, the fields, rarely-seen wild flowers, the sparkling sea. Within a few minutes' drive of Land's End, towards the sea at Porthgwarra, we loved *Higher Rokestal* for its quietness, its views, its lovely family atmosphere. **Sleeps 6.**

Also at Porthgwarra, *Three Chimneys* is a complete renovation of two hill-top cottages, **sleeping 8**, and is a recent addition to the portfolio.

Newly available Tregarthen (Five Stars) is a very special property.

We loved Higher Rokestal for its quietness, its views, its atmosphere.

Literally yards from Porthgwarra Cove, *Corner Cottage* and *Cove Cottage* are little gems. In Cove we admired a well planned combined kitchen/dining room/sitting room, and an unusual basement with a glassed-over stream below. **Sleeps 4** in a double (ensuite) and a twin. In Corner we liked the double brass bedstead, the expensive pine floor. **Sleeps 2**. Each has central heating.

We'd not previously seen *Bosistow Farmhouse*, at Nanjizaal. Very private-seeming, spacious, light and bright, it's a beauty, and **sleeps 7**. Perhaps our own favourite: but that's a hard choice! More remote, but also charming, is *Faraway Cottage* at Nanjizal, **sleeping 4**.

Details and brochure from Clare Sandry, St Aubyn Estates, Manor Office, Marazion, Cornwall TR17 0EF. Telephone: 01736 710507. Fax 719930.

www.staubynestates.co.uk email: godolphin@manor-office.co.uk

adwins Farm, Suffolk. Unfailingly high standards, great views, a pool and sauna. And the
...y cottages have been described by more than one reader as 'little showhouses'. Page 34.

...d Farm Cottages, Norfolk. Rural style and
...nfort, but near the Broads. Page 51.

Clippesby Cottages, Norfolk. Appealingly,
both rural and not far from the sea. Page 55.

...rfolk Holiday Homes. Some real gems on the books of this fine agency. These are (left)
...uper beach-side property at Hunstanton, and one near the sea at Heacham. Page 52.

...rsyde Farm Cottages, North Yorkshire. These have so much going for them, such as
...ses to ride and easy access to sought-after stretches of the Yorkshire coast. Page 69.

Colour section, Page 1

Fold Farm Cottages, North Yorkshire. It's the genuine article: a real 'village idyll'. Page 70.

Dalegarth/The Ghyll, North Yorkshire. Cottage excellence deep in the Dales. Page 72.

Peak Cottages, Derbyshire. A much-loved part of England, reliable cottages of character. Page 76.

Bee Cottage, Northumberland. 'Traditional' charm, handy for Holy Island. Page 90.

Blairquhan, Ayrshire. Properties of great character, long-term favourites of ours. Page 93.

Loch Cottage, Perthshire. Many years in this guide: a quiet, rural Scottish classic. Page 95.

Amazing even in 'cottage guide' terms, much-admired Large Holiday Houses in Scotland...

...includes for example Cul Na Craig (left) and Auchinroath (above). Page 100.

Colour section, Page 2

...lligran Cottages, Inverness-shire. A classic ...ghland location, good fishing. Page 96.

Torrisdale, Kintyre. Go down the beautiful peninsula: it's 'a world away'. Page 117.

...n Coe Cottages, Argyll. One of the most ...azing of all cottage locations. Page 107.

Attadale, Wester Ross. Even in terms of the Highlands, a fabulous place. Page 106.

...adowbank, Cumbria. This is definitely one ...ur Lake District 'top ten'. Page 124.

Long Byres, Cumbria. Twenty-four years with us: a 'serenely wild' spot. Page 121.

...semoor, West Wales. 'Family-orientated', ...r good beaches, deeply rural. Page 135.

Portmeirion, Gwynedd. A fantasy-world by the sea, cottages a delight. Page 143.

Colour section, Page 3

Clydey, West Wales. Readers have often praised these cosy, very welcoming cottages. Page 138.

Pant Farm, North Wales. Gorgeous: a woodburner and central heating. Page 141.

Trallwm Forest Cottages, Mid Wales. Quiet, not pricey, 'deeply rural' but not remote. Page 145.

Brecon Beacons Holiday Cottages, Mid Wales In or near a fine National Park. Page 145.

Tregeath, Cornwall. Unpretentious, comfy, sensibly priced: since 1983, a reader-favourite. Page 183.

Treworgey Coach House, Cornwall. Comfort style, lots to do, a hundred acres. Page 150.

Pollaughan, Cornwall. Surely, if we counted, this would be one of our 'UK Top Ten'. Page 173.

Gullrock, Cornwall. A little-known sandy beach just a short stroll away. Page 174.

Colour section, Page 4

efanny Hill, Cornwall. Private, well spaced out, lots of individual character. The place is like a ˙mlet in its own right, and even has its own country inn, serving excellent food. Page 148.

sinver, Cornwall. Delightfully, it's both rural and handy for the sea. Energetic, welcoming ˙ners have turned these properties into some of the best in Cornwall. Page 155.

˙dgeon Vean, Cornwall Very much geared ˙amilies, very informal. Page 159.

Mineshop, Cornwall. Twenty-four years in this guide, an amazing location. Page 175.

˙ Meads, Cornwall. We've recently stayed in one of the spacious, light and bright properties ˙e. With the sound of the waves and perhaps a flaming sunset it's a magical place. Page 154.

Colour section, Page 5

Marsdens Holidays, North Devon. An exceptional agency, in a much loved but never overrun part of the West Country, and known for its quite superb brochure. Page 180.

Wooder Manor, Devon. You can hardly get closer to the heart of secret, ancient Dartmoor than in one of these fine properties, long admired (and visited) by our readers. Page 187.

Compton Pool, Devon. Close to the sea but completely rural, these well converted and most attractive cottages are especially popular among families with small children. Page 194.

Horry Mill, Devon. A rare 'traditional' cottage, a fine wooded location. Page 182.

Fursdon, Devon. Enjoy the flavour of life in a fine English country house. Page 197.

lpful Holidays – Devon, Cornwall and beyond. This West Country specialist is virtually a usehold name. They feature some real beauties, including houses right beside rivers...

r (much sought-after) the sea, spacious country houses with gardens, hidden-away perties where you'll hardly meet a soul during your stay and a number of big houses.

eing the West Country, there are many traditional thatched cottages, some even with roses und the door, and quite a few places with historical or literary associations. Pages 191-193.

rtmouth Holiday Homes, Devon. Super ws from many properties. Page 195.

Salcombe Holiday Homes. Reliable places in one of Devon's most-loved resorts. Page 189.

English Country Cottages (main feature, Pages 222/223, also covers Scotland and Wales (there's a separate brochure for Scotland). The organisation is now virtually a household name...

Above and above right, there's an extraordinary collection of cottages and fine houses that seem to su up the best of what's to be had, for example, in Cornwall and the Cotswolds...

Their Welsh programme is appreciated by the tourist board, and they've secured many 'traditional' cottages, as above. Also above, right: a charming North Yorkshire cottage.

All over the British Isles, their range is huge, but they are known for their properties of character, historic interest and comfort. These two are in Cornwall and Dorset...

addon Cottages, Devon. A dependable, uceful escape from every-day cares. Page 186.

One of our favourite 'Marsdens' cottages is high above impressive Lee Bay. Page 180.

Swiss Chalet, Herefordshire. An impressive d unusual property: readers love it! Page 213.

Buckland, Worcestershire. It's in one of our favourite Cotswold villages. Page 218.

es, East Sussex. 'Incomparable', say ders. Also 'unique...great fun!' Page 206.

Owlpen, Gloucestershire. An unforgettable place:'rural England stands still'. Page 212.

Old Dairy, Gloucestershire. The cottage is a joy, the view 'something to behold'. Bring binoculars cameras, and postcards so as to be able to write home about it. Page 215.

Colour section, Page 9

Blakes Cottages – main features on Pages 115 and 226/7 – is one of the three or four most prominent agencies in the country. It has 'properties with facilities', many rural jewels...

...and several places ideal for extended families, such as this (above left) in rural Somerset and (above right) near the sea in Wales. This one sleeps up to twenty!

Among so many properties of character is this beauty near Barnard Castle, in underrated County Durham and (above right) this property in nostalgically rural Norfolk.

In rural Suffolk you can stay in the wing of a handsome country house, above, and, in Derbyshire Peak District, among so many possibilities, this charmer in the Hope Valley.

Colour section, Page 10

...d Hall Cottages (Page 188) are widely known for their 'picture-postcard' (dare I say 'chocolate box'?) holiday properties, mainly in Devon and Cornwall.

...especially like the way so many of their cottages take holiday tenants right to heart of the rural English idyll and encourage them to support village life.

...n some of the names of the villages where (or near where) you'll find many Toad ...l Cottages sound like a checklist for nostalgia-buffs...

...ch as (included here, but not in the order they appear on the page) ...tlemouth, Newton Ferrers, Slapton, Thurlestone, Bigbury and Ashprinton.

Country Holidays (main feature on Pages 224/225) have a bigger selection of individual cottages than any other operator, so holidaymakers needing variety tend to be regulars.

They appreciate this fine mill in North Yorkshire, adjacent to a waterfall once sketched by J M W Turner, and thisrural property near Portreath, near Redruth, in Cornwall.

Among people's dreams-come-true are such places as (above left) a well-booked cottage in mid-Wales and, right, a beauty near Cheriton Bishop, in rural Devon.

There's this superbly well situated cottage in the West of Scotland, close to a sandy beach, and a delight in Naunton, near Bourton-on-the-Water, in the Cotswolds (also marketed by Blakes).

Roseland Peninsula
Roseland Holiday Cottages*

This fine medium-sized agency has an impressive range of different types of cottage. There are 66 of them, dotted around the idyllic semi-tropical Roseland Peninsula, whose southerly point is postcard-pretty St Mawes. Most are by, or very near, the sea. All are described in a stylish brochure – a real armchair 'voyage of discovery'. On our most recent visit we noted two that were totally different: *Martha's*

Martha's Cottage is thatched, Grade II listed, and near a super family beach!

Cottage (**sleeping 4**), an old Grade II listed thatched house at Treworthal, four minutes' drive from Pendower Beach, and *3 Tregarth Cottages* (**sleeping 6**), one of three smart new terrace houses on the hillside above St Mawes, five minutes' walk away. Its lounge (upstairs) opens on to a balcony with lovely sea and river views. At Gerrans, the old village chapel near the harbour has been divided into two imaginatively designed houses: *Sunday House East* (**sleeping 8/10**) and *Sunday House West* (**sleeping 6**). Details/brochure from Roseland Holiday Cottages, Crab Apple Cottage, Portscatho, Truro, Cornwall TR2 5ET. Telephone/fax: 01872 580480.

www.roselandholidaycottages.co.uk
email: enquiries@roselandholidaycottages.co.uk

Portscatho map 6/355
Pollaughan Cottages

It's no surprise that these fine cottages (**Colour section, Page 4**) have received a string of awards. Such as a Green Tourism Gold Award, and first place in the 2006 'Sustainable Tourism Cornwall' awards and (The Accessible Holiday of the Year' scheme. The latter is important: Pollaughan is suitable at the highest level for people with disability. (Said

See Page 8 for more information about Pollaughan's approach to Green Tourism and to high accessibility standards.

one wheelchair-bound guest we met in *Owl Cottage*, **sleeping 2**, 'It's wonderful here. I trust it won't be our last visit'.) Like *Willow Barn*, which **sleeps 6**, it is geared for accessibility, though as with *Farm House*, a Victorian charmer, **sleeping 5**, with antique pine furniture, and *Swallows Barn*, **sleeping 2**, the main thrust is in providing a home from home. The latest addition is *Meadows*, a detached property **sleeping 6**, with jacuzzi and woodburner. Typical of the caring approach of the owners are the provision of a welcoming cream tea and a basket of toys for children. Unsuitable for dogs. Linen and towels included. Short breaks. Cost: about £300 to £1030. Valerie Penny, Pollaughan Cottages, Portscatho, Truro, Cornwall TR2 5EH. Telephone 01872 580150.

www.pollaughan.co.uk email: info@pollaughan.co.uk

Port Gaverne, near Wadebridge
Gullrock

Long a favourite among cottage guide readers, these are superbly well situated: close to the sea, but not buffetted by it, in a charming little seaside village that has somehow remained self contained and is never overrun by visitors. Better yet, these cottages, just two minutes' stroll from a sandy beach, are rich in local history.

Half-hidden away nicely down a narrow lane the cottages are on three sides of a grassy courtyard with flower borders. The building was originally constructed about 200 years ago to cure and store the fish catches landed in the cove, and was used for this until the turn of the century.

The cottages are sensibly priced (particularly good value outside the main season), 'unpretentious and practical' units in what can sometimes be an expensive corner of the West Country. We particularly liked the bigger, *Seaways*, which **sleeps 6** in three double or twin rooms, with a spacious sitting room and a pleasant outlook on to the courtyard at the front and trees at the rear. The charming and cosy flat called *Creekside*, looking in part over the courtyard, is cleverly arranged to **sleep 6** in four bedrooms.

Each unit has a dishwasher, microwave, fridge-freezer, Freeview 26-inch IDTV and DVD/HDD recorder, plus computer with Broadband, CD/radio cassette and full central heating. An outbuilding houses washing/drying machines, a payphone and an assortment of garden furniture. The grounds

Even by coastal Cornish standards, this is an exquisite little place.

And the cottages themselves are in a pretty and rather historic courtyard.

include not only the courtyard, but an outer garden with barbecue and picnic area, and there is a parking space for each cottage. The beach, just 75 yards from Gullrock, is very sheltered, providing safe bathing and fascinating rock pools. The coastal path crosses the head of the beach, leading over the westward headland to the village of Port Isaac, and east along wild and remote clifflands to Trebarwith.

Visitors' pets are welcome, and Gullrock's resident pets are all friendly. Sample prices, which include electricity and heating, are: £200 February, £440 May, £750 August. Discounts are available to parties of three people or fewer from April to October, except in the summer school holidays.

Full details from Malcolm Lee, Gullrock, Port Gaverne, Port Isaac, Cornwall PL29 3SQ. Telephone 01208 880106.

www.goodcottageguide.com/self_catering_accommodation/gullrock.html
email: gullrock@ukonline.co.uk

Crackington Haven
Mineshop Cottages

You could hardly holiday more closely to some of the most dramatic coastal scenery in Cornwall than in one of these pleasant cottages. As you go from one tiny, hidden lane into another (shortly after you turn west off the A39 Camelford-Bude road and come, finally, to leafy Mineshop) you feel a million miles from the workaday world.

During our last summer revisit, Mineshop's wandering ducks were being fed by guests sitting contentedly on the verandah of *The Old Shippon* in the cool of the evening. They (the guests, not the ducks, although the latter may have tried to accompany them!) planned to walk down the green and tranquil footpath to the beach at Crackington Haven (where there is an excellent pub and coffee shop). In one of the lodges, in the same green and generally sunny location, a couple were brewing up and simply enjoying the view of the garden.

Mineshop has a strong following among people, including readers of this guide, who like getting 'away from it all' without feeling isolated: the owners of the Mineshop cottages live in the centre of what is effectively a private hamlet. More than half of each year's visitors have been here before, and one family has been 30 times!

Effectively under the same ownership, but elsewhere in this dramatically striking corner of North Cornwall, is a quite excellent cottage, beautifully located high on a headland, and very private. This, *Cancleave*, has dramatic views of the famous bay. There are comfortable sofas and lots of pine. Outside, there is a big lawn adjacent to the coastal footpath. **Sleeps 8** in four bedrooms.

Cost: approximately £150 to £768 per week, according, as usual, to size and season. Short breaks from £100. Bedlinen is supplied in all the cottages. (Cots provided.) TVs, laundry room. Obedient dogs are allowed.

For further details please contact Mr and Mrs Tippett, Ref: GH, Mineshop, Crackington Haven, Bude, Cornwall EX23 0NR. Telephone 01840 230338.

www.mineshop.co.uk

email: info@mineshop.co.uk

The exceptional Crackington Haven beach, notable even for North Cornwall, is just a short walk from the cottages...

...one of which is the spacious and private Old Shippon – where on one visit we met guests feeding the ducks.

175

Cornwall – countywide
Cornish Traditional Cottages*

The longest-established cottage letting agency in Cornwall, 'Cornish Traditional', has become one of the most highly regarded in Britain. From little acorns, indeed: after the directors bought and renovated a derelict cottage in Padstow for family use, they found that other people wanted them to let their properties, and never looked back.

Since its beginnings the agency has prided itself on its personal service. You can speak to 'a real person' (not a machine) between 9 am and 9 pm seven days a week. Then there is the 'smiles' system of rating properties – generated entirely by customers from the grading the company asks them to give a cottage's fittings, furnishings and equipment.

We certainly smiled last autumn when we came across two cosy charmers in a cobbled street close to the National Trust harbour of Boscastle. Here

Carveth is yet another of the agency's properties that enjoys a superb location.

Bridge Cottage, sleeping 6, is in the highly sought-after village of Boscastle.

the agency offers two character cottages, each sporting three smiles. *Bridge Cottage* (**sleeps 6**), though completely renovated, retains its period charm, with a view overlooking the river leading to the harbour mouth from the king size double bedroom, one of three upstairs.

Likewise, *Millstream Cottage* offers a double fronted cottage whose front door opens on to a small sitting room with beamed ceilings, windows to the lane and looking to the headland at the harbour mouth. **Sleeps 4**.

Superbly well located, at the head of a tidal creek on the River Fowey (from the comfort of your cottage you can watch the ebb and flow of the tide, probably putting the cottage into the 'we hardly left the place for a week' category so beloved of cottage guide readers), *Pont Quay Cottage* **sleeps 4/6** – including a double-bunk room suitable for children.

It's just a mile by car and car/pedestrian ferry to Fowey or – even more appealingly – half a mile by boat on the Pont Pill creek. (Guests can make arrangements to bring their own boats.)

Enjoying remarkable views, *Titania* is a spacious detached bungalow, **sleeping 6**, in two twins and a double, in a quiet residential cul-de-sac just a mile from St Ives and about a fifteen minute walk to the beach. At the rear, a gently sloping path leads up to a raised terrace with patio furniture and a beautiful garden with a large lawn, apple tree and flower borders.

On the approach road to Mousehole (remember to pronounce it 'Mousel'), *Carveth*, **sleeping 4**, is the upper part of a detached house with good sea views from a double and twin bedroom and, even more notably, with views of the splendid St Michael's Mount – from a bright and sunny sitting room with five big windows. Opposite the cottage there's a footpath to a stony beach and a rockpool and – a first for us – a children's seawater bathing pool, exposed at high tide.

Garden enthusiasts will love the cottages at Tregrehan, which has a famous collection of camellias, rhododendrons and conifers. The walls of the estate's old grain mill enclose a secret garden (guaranteed in our experience to appeal to visiting children) at the entrance to *The Coach House*, which has a bunk room and a king size bedroom, both with an additional single bed. *Sprys Cottage* is tucked away from the main courtyard and **sleeps 2** in a double room. *Gamekeepers Cottage* is the end cottage in the old carriage house and **sleeps 4** in a king size double and a twin room. There is a spacious walled garden. The cottages here are graded 'two-smiles'. The Eden Project and Carlyon Bay's golf course are less than ten minutes' drive away.

Pilsamoor Cottage makes a handsome base for a traditional Cornish holiday.

Pentire Cottage, on Pentire Farm, has an open fire and memorable views...

At the end of a rough track – but enjoying spectacular views over the Camel Estuary – is Pentire Farm, with one-smile properties. These include the *Farm Wing* (**sleeps 6 to 8**), with four bedrooms, one with substantial bunk beds, and *Pentire Cottage* (**sleeps 4 to 6**) with a working open fire. Beamed farm-style kitchen. One bunk room downstairs, a double and a room with two pine singles upstairs.

Not yet seen by us, but very promising, is *Pilsamoor Cottage*, a recently converted detached stone barn that was originally a milking parlour and hayloft. With an upstairs living room (to take advantage of the rural views) the house, **sleeping 8,** has lots of good things going for it. There are four ground floor bedrooms: two twin bedded rooms, a five-foot-double bedroom and a fourth bedroom that has that seriously luxurious item: a zip-linked six-foot 'super-king' bed.

Pets are welcome in about a third of the agency's properties.

For further details and an excellent brochure, with a clear and attractive illustration of each property, contact Cornish Traditional Cottages, Blisland, Bodmin, Cornwall PL30 4HS. Telephone 01208 821666, fax 821766.

www.corncott.com
email: info@corncott.com

Blisland
Hockadays Cottages

Here's another super location. For people who want to slow their pace of life, yet still be within fifteen minutes' drive of the spectacular coast, about 25 minutes from the Eden Project and handy for the Camel Trail to Padstow, these two charming cottages could be 'just the job'. In

Such a lot of care and attention goes into these 'two-plus-baby' cottages...

deeply rural North Cornwall, approached delightfully via leafy lanes, *Demelza* and *Rowella* are looked after by caring and conscientious owners. Each is within a converted 17th century barn that feels very private, and each is a wonderful hideaway **for 2** plus a baby. Among the details are white painted walls setting off oak beams, wall lamps, some original features such as wooden lintels, small paned windows, and cottage doors. Each has a living room, a separate well equipped kitchen, double bedroom and bathroom. One is an 'upside down' house, with the bedroom downstairs. There is a big garden, parking and excellent views. The nearby Blisland Inn is a 'Campaign for Real Ale' award winner. TV. Linen is included. Regrettably, they are not suitable for pets. Cost: about £150 to £335. Details from Margaret Pestell, 'Hockadays', Tregenna, near Blisland, Cornwall PL30 4QJ. Telephone/fax 01208 850146.

www.hockadays.co.uk

St Issey, near Padstow
map 6/405
Trevorrick Farm Cottages

With ducks to feed, a well equipped outdoor play area, a games room and a heated pool, these well-run cottages appeal especially to families, but are cosy for couples too. Melanie and Mike Benwell have created a really caring atmosphere here. The six barn conversions, refurbished in recent years, are in an Area of Outstanding Natural Beauty, close to sandy

Easy access to some of North Cornwall's many sandy beaches is a bonus here...

beaches and the Eden Project, and within walking distance of Padstow. *Lily Pad Cottage* (with four-poster) and the popular *Old Round House* are cosy hideaways **sleeping 2**. Single-storeyed *Serendipity* (**sleeps 2 to 4**) is suitable for people with limited mobility. *Owl's Roost, Curlew Cottage* and *Badger's Way* **sleep 4**. All have an individual character, with a log burner or an open fire. TV plus video and DVD. Log burners/open fires. **Four Stars**. Cost: £240 to £995. Out of season short breaks. Dogs welcome in some cottages, linen included; baby-sitting and B & B available. Details from Melanie and Mike Benwell, Trevorrick Farm Cottages, St Issey, Wadebridge, Cornwall PL27 7QH. Telephone 01841 540574.

www.trevorrick.co.uk   email: info@trevorrick.co.uk

Cornwall and beyond
Farm and Cottage Holidays*

We first became aware of this long-established family run agency when a reader praised *Old Holcombe Water Farm*, at Clatworthy, five miles inland from Watchet, in North Somerset. It has three delightfully converted barns (**sleeping 2 to 4**) across lawns, and an orchard across from the 17th century farmhouse. Children delight in helping with collecting eggs and milking, as well as enjoying the farm's clotted cream and

Near Boscastle, in North Cornwall, this lovely house (not featured) sleeps 8.

occasionally ice cream! A regular reader has her eye on *Destiny Cottage*, near Port Isaac, in North Cornwall. On a working farm, **sleeping up to 5**, it is of a high standard and offers excellent walking. But these are just samples of over 850 properties in Cornwall, Devon, Somerset and Dorset, **sleeping from 2 to 22**. Details/brochures from Farm and Cottage Holidays, Victoria House, 12 Fore Street, Northam, Bideford, Devon EX39 1AW. Telephone 01237 459894.

www.holidaycottages.co.uk
(up to date availability and secure on-line booking)
email: enquiries@holidaycottages.co.uk

Scorrier, near Truro
The Butler's Cottage   map 6/362

Among the many charms of this property, it's the thoroughbred horses that graze in the park fronting the elegant main house that readers tend to mention. It's very much our kind of place – stylish, sensibly priced, quiet and inviting. Butler's is a comfortable, spacious, recently renovated wing of 'the big house'. We admired the terraced garden at first floor level, the well equipped flagstoned kitchen, the antiques, the excellent paintings and prints, the first floor sitting room with beautifully chosen sunflower yellow sofa and armchairs, the long bath in the excellent bathroom. All is stylish

This is one of our personal favourites in Cornwall – quiet, comfortable, stylish.

and elegant, but not uncomfortably so: you can put your feet up here and unwind. All in all, this is a gem: the only thing lacking is the butler to wait on you. With an open fire in the sitting room, central heating, books and board games, this makes a good base in the autumn, winter or spring.

Sleeps 4. TV/video; payphone. Pets possible by arrangement. Linen/towels included. Breakfast pack. Cost: about £250 to £360. Weekend breaks. Details from Richard and Caroline Williams, Scorrier House, Scorrier, Redruth, Cornwall TR16 5AU. Telephone 01209 820264. Fax 820677. **email: rwill10442@aol.com**

Croyde and beyond
Marsdens Cottage Holidays*

We see some impressive cottage brochures, but Marsdens' is exceptional. It's one of four or five that gets us turning away from the computer, pouring a cup of coffee and having a browse and a day-dream. It's a reflection of the company's reputation for absolute integrity and properties of a very high standard. We've featured them for 25 years, and had *nothing but praise*.

The staff all have an intimate knowledge of North Devon; all properties are inspected annually and have **'Visit Britain'** star gradings. Around half the 300 or so properties are in and around Croyde, a small village of much thatch, with dunes between it and Croyde Bay's wide sandy beach. The rest are scattered across the area from the small sandy resort of Instow around the coastline to Exmoor.

From the terrace of Devon Fudge you can literally hear a 'babbling brook'.

The Stables has, in turn, views out to sea and along famous Woolacombe Sands.

The memorably named *Devon Fudge*, for example, **sleeping 4**, has been lovingly converted to create a fine countryside retreat. From the hallway you go down a step to the comfy, open plan living room, kitchen and dining area. French doors open on to a terrace from which you can hear a 'babbling brook' as it meanders through the nearby field. Two bedrooms are located one step up from the entrance hallway, the double having an ensuite shower room and the spacious twin room having an ensuite bathroom with corner bath, both with terracotta tiled floors.

For a cosy and romantic hideaway retreat at the heart of Exmoor, you'd find it hard to beat *Keepers Cottage*, **sleeping 2**, a mile from the village of Brendon. Detached, on an eighteen-acre estate, it's a stylish barn conversion, with beams, a woodburning stove and French doors on to the terrace and garden. The spacious bedroom on the first floor has views over the river and fields and an ensuite bathroom. A private patio terrace leads to a lawn overlooking the river (the cottage is not recommended for toddlers).

The Stables is an outstanding detached house enjoying views out to sea and along Woolacombe Sands. Stylish and designed to top specifications, this does indeed offer 'something a little bit special'. Light, bright and modern, with tones and textures reflecting the natural coastline, it **sleeps 8** in two doubles and two twins. There is a large, paved terrace from which to enjoy those views and two living rooms (satellite TV DVD, further TV and Play Station 2).

There are two properties on the outskirts of Berrynarbor, in the lovely Sterridge Valley. *Derrivale*, a large, detached cottage, provides plenty of space **for 6**, both inside and out. Delightfully, it backs on to its own two-acre private natural woodlands. There is a small patio, a level lawned area and a pretty stream-fronted cottage garden to the front. We've admired

Derrivale has its own two-acre private natural wood, and an inglenook fireplace.

Meadowside Barn has a memorable outlook over gardens and meadows.

flagstone floors, an inglenook fireplace, a range cooker, bedrooms with vaulted ceilings and beams, a super-king (zip link) bed in one bedroom, a five foot iron bed and ensuite shower room in the master bedroom.

In an idyllic location down a lane, surrounded by lush meadows, *Meadowside Barn*, **sleeping 4**, is a fabulous detached barn conversion. A country lane to the entrance is shared with the neighbouring stud farm, and once past the entrance your own driveway takes you to the private grounds of the cottage. The open plan living room, for example, has a beautiful feature window overlooking the garden and meadows beyond.

At the end of a long woodland track, *Modbury Cottage* is the typical picturesque thatched 'chocolate box cottage'. With a wealth of character features, it is up to the moment with furnishings and a brand new kitchen. At Buckland Filleigh, deep in rural Devon, it has its own secluded gardens. **Sleeps 4** in a double and a twin. It has a water supply from its own well.

Keepers Cottage is a stylish barn conversion on an eighteen-acre estate.

Modbury Cottage is a thatched 'chocolate-box' delight, with its own well.

For further details of these and the many others in that outstanding brochure, contact Marsdens, 2 The Square, Braunton, Devon EX33 2JB. Telephone 01271 813777, fax 813664.

Full on-line availability and booking on the website:

www.marsdens.co.uk   email: holidays@marsdens.co.uk

Langtree, near Great Torrington
Stowford Lodge Holiday Cottages

Well away from any traffic, accessed via narrow, high banked lanes typical of this part of Devon (we had to check our map carefully when we first visited!) these four properties have proved very popular with readers. They **sleep 6, 4, 4** and **4**, and have been converted from farm buildings with style and skill. *Warren* and *Halcyon* are suitable for wheelchairs. A special feature is the indoor heated swimming pool: lovely warm

Deep in rural Devon: new owners ready to make 'cottage guide' guests welcome.

water, curtained windows; wall pictures/hangings, underwater lighting. The cottages stand in six acres, surrounded by beautiful, rolling Devon countryside: a peaceful, quiet, relaxing location. There is a well equipped children's play area, with plenty of space for them to burn off excess energy! Dogs are welcome (small charge). Linen provided. **'Visit Britain' Three Stars**. Cost: £260 to £600. Details and brochure from Rich and Diana Jones, Stowford Lodge, Langtree, Torrington, North Devon EX38 8NU. Telephone 01805 601540, fax 601487.

www.stowfordlodge.co.uk email: enq@stowfordlodge.co.uk

Hollocombe, near Chulmleigh   map 7/445
Horry Mill Cottage

For starters, the location is marvellous: among woods, close to a lake, basking in peace and quiet. There are 30 acres of privately owned woodland, mainly mature oaks, and notable for bluebells. Exuding 'tender loving care', Horry Mill is an increasingly rare example of a traditional cottage. An open log fire for which, delightfully, 'unlimited' logs are supplied gets our vote! Linen

This is very much our sort of cottage.

and towels are included, there's a Rayburn, oil fired central heating and continuous hot water. Sleeps 4 in a double and a twin, with a cot provided. The fully equipped bathroom has a free-standing electric shower. We admired the huge inglenook fireplace and bread oven in the sitting room, also the small south facing sun parlour with grapevine. There is a well equipped kitchen and the dining room seats six, plus high chair. A glass-fronted dresser boasts a splendid array of glass-ware and pretty china. TV, stereo/CD player. DVD player. One dog by arrangement. No smoking. Cost from £310 to £580. Details from Sonia and Simon Hodgson, Horry Mill, Hollocombe, Chulmleigh, Devon EX18 7QH. Telephone 01769 520266.

www.horrymill.com email: sonia@horrymill.com

Tintagel
Tregeath

This traditional farmworker's cottage has proved popular with readers ever since we first published in 1983. We revisited last year, and confirmed that in its way it's a real charmer. Quietly situated on a little-used country road, it is 'unpretentious', with a degree of character. There's a small rear patio, ideal for lazing in the summer sun, listening *Not far from Tintagel, this does not claim to be a show-house, but we like it, and have always had good reader reports.* to very little except the sound of sheep from adjoining farmland. About a mile from Tintagel, and one and a half from the surfing beach at Trebarwith Strand, this is no showhouse, more a sensible family home with a very convenient galley-kitchen, a combined sitting/dining room and stairs up to two bedrooms (note that one has a 4'6" wide bed; the other a 4' wide bed). There's a good-sized single room that's adjacent to the sitting room, a washing machine and separate tumble dryer, and a pleasant enclosed and safe garden. **Sleeps up to 4** plus cot. **'Visit Britain' Three Stars.**

Cost: £110 to £410. TV/video in each bedroom. Payphone. Single dogs welcome. Further details from Mrs E M Broad, 'Davina', Trevillett, Tintagel, Cornwall PL34 0HL. Telephone/fax 01840 770217.

Stratton/Pyworthy, near Bude
Lovers Retreat/Hopworthy Farm   map 6/399/400

As far as we're concerned, any comfortable, quiet, warm and well run property near Bude is immediately 'in the frame': it's one of our favourite places in the whole of the West Country. In Stratton, a mile and a half from the resort, three-storeyed 200-year old *Lovers Retreat* has a five foot wide 'sleigh' bed and a woodburning stove. **Sleeps 3**, **Four Stars**, Ref 17925. In a more rural sit- *Lovers Retreat, sleeping three, is handy for Bude, and in a historic village...* uation, you can even bring your own horses to Hopworthy Farm, a short drive from Bude and in striking distance of Dartmoor. Graded with an admirable **Five Stars** from '**Visit Britain**' it offers stabling, livery and the use of an indoor school. Impressively, and in line with much current demand, *Hopworthy Farmhouse* **sleeps up to 18** – Ref 18016.

Details from Blakes Country Cottages, Spring Mill, Earby, Barnoldswick BB94 0AA. Brochures and bookings: 0845 268 0944.

Live search and book: www.blakes-cottages.co.uk

Countisbury
Kipscombe Farm

Most usefully **sleeping 8** (recommended by two of our readers), *Kipscombe Farm* (Ref HTU) is a spacious, self contained wing of a fine 17th century farmhouse, with its own secluded garden. There's a woodburning stove in an inglenook in a big, beamed sitting room and – for that touch of rural farmhouse authenticity – an Aga in the spacious modernised kitchen. The location is 'a delight'. Guests (the house **sleeps 8**) have access to 640 acres of National Trust farmland, and there are coastal footpaths direct from the property, with some spectacular views: on a clear day you can see across the Bristol Channel to Wales. The 'twin' coastal villages of Lynton and Lynmouth, possibly our own favourite resorts in the whole of Devon, are under three miles away, and we'd always recommend a boat trip from Ilfracombe to Lundy Island.

It's a spacious, self contained main wing of a beautifully situated farmhouse.

Details from English Country Cottages, Stoney Bank Road, Earby, Barnoldswick BB94 0AA. Bookings and brochures: 0845 268 0942.

www.english-country-cottages.co.uk

We'd never have guessed, all those years ago, how popular open fires and woodburning stoves would be in the 21st century...

Brendon, near Lynmouth
Rockford Lodge

Over twenty years in this guide, many enthusiastic reader reports: it's one of our own all-time favourites too, particularly for its location.

For it's a special pleasure for us to leave our car in the main part of the hamlet of Rockford (just a pub and a handful of cottages) and walk a few yards over a footbridge across the tumbling River East Lyn to see Rockford Lodge again and, sometimes, to meet the contented people staying in it.

They tend to be people who like places that ramble a bit, and have something of a farmhousey character. Tucked away in a secret, wooded valley on the edge of mysterious Exmoor, Rockford has a big kitchen with a cosy Aga, fitted carpets, lots of books, paintings and a very big carpeted upstairs bathroom. The river that rushes past the garden fence does not do so loudly enough to keep one awake! The footpaths in the beautiful woods outside the conservatory-like 'river room' beckon one for walks. Described over the years by readers as 'a genuine home from home' ... 'wonderfully well equipped' ... 'the setting is marvellous', the cottage is used quite frequently by the owners themselves. **Sleeps 6** plus cot.

Dogs are welcome but not cats. TV. Cost: about £400 to £695. Further details available from Mrs Lucy Casella, 68 Westover Road, Downley, High Wycombe HP13 5HX. Telephone 01494 461051 or 07707 024371.

email: lucycasella@hotmail.co.uk

Many years in this guide, Rockford Lodge has a most unusual situation ...

... whereby you park your car and then cross a river via a footbridge. Delightful!

Please note: we cannot vouch for every property on an agency's books, but only those we have seen. Most agents have at least a handful of modest properties that appeal to a specific market (for example, fishermen, walkers and stalkers), or sometimes properties at the extreme edge of the region they deal with that are not typical of what they offer. But in principle the agencies we feature are reliable and conscientious...

Ashwater, near Holsworthy
Braddon Cottages and Forest

We have long admired these six properties, all separate and detached.
Close to the Devon/Cornwall border,
they are surrounded by hundreds of
acres of meadow and woodland that is
part of the owners' imaginative
broadleaf planting scheme. All have
woodburners and fine views over the
well stocked three-acre fishing lake.

Fishing is free, reserved for residents,
and there's a newly built three mile
foot and cycle path. *The Linhaye* and

*Notably, all the properties are heated by
renewable energy.*

Lake House are large, purpose-built houses **sleeping 12 plus 2**, each convertible into two self-contained, sound-proofed apartments. Microwave,
dishwasher, washing machine, dryer, gas central heating, double glazing,
barbecues. There's an all-weather tennis court and a games room with a full
size snooker table. TV/videos, payphones. Linen/towels provided. Well
behaved dogs welcome. Open all year. **'Visit Britain' Three/four Stars**.
Cost: £195 to £1580, all prices inclusive of electricity and heating, bargain
breaks from £140 2ppn. Details from George and Anne Ridge, Braddon,
Ashwater, Beaworthy, Devon EX21 5EP. Telephone 01409 211350.

www.braddoncottages.co.uk email: holidays@braddoncottages.co.uk

Near Brendon/Near Bude   map 7/426

We like the way many North Devon
properties offer the chance to
explore much of the best of North
Cornwall, as well as certain parts of
Somerset and Exmoor. In the
appealingly named village of
Welcombe, a mile from Welcombe
Bay and well placed for some of the
most spectacular places along the
North Devon and the North
Cornwall coast, eye-catching *Chapel
Cottage* (Ref W40147, **sleeping 7/8**)
has the makings of a memorable

*This striking house at Welcombe is
exceptionally well situated in terms of
things to see and do...*

family holiday. It has a woodburning stove. And only a short walk from
Bideford, a substantial detached house on a working farm at the end of a
long private drive provides a 'deeply rural' experience without isolation.
It **sleeps 9** in five bedrooms, has two woodburning stoves, and welcomes
one dog. The famous golden sands at Westward Ho! are just a short drive
away. Ref W41242.

Welcome Holidays, Spring Mill, Earby, Barnoldswick, BB94 0AA.
Brochures and bookings: 0845 268 0945.

www.welcomecottages.co.uk

Widecombe-in-the-Moor
Wooder Manor

Good self-catering on Dartmoor is rare, but our readers love this neat grouping of properties converted from an old coach-house and stables. And with the Bell family's home close by (a working farm amid 170 acres of woodland, moor and granite tors), guests are guaranteed a personal welcome. Widecombe-in-the-Moor is a mere half mile away. (See *Dartmoor is magical, and these properties, open all year, are at its heart.* Colour section, Page 6, for the view from Wooder Manor.) *Wooder House* itself **sleeps 12** in five bedrooms; its ambiance comfortable and relaxing. Two cottages **sleep 6**, the others **sleep 4**. Ideal for walking, fishing, canoeing, cycling or riding. Central heating and a laundry room; bed linen by arrangement; all is clean and well equipped. Cots and highchairs free; log fires in *Honeybags* and Wooder House. **'Visit Britain' Three/Four Stars**. Cost: from £200 to £500, £280 to £540 or £700 to £1200, **sleeping 4, 6 or 12** respectively. Ample parking. Details from Angela Bell, Wooder Manor, Widecombe-in-the-Moor, Newton Abbot, Devon TQ13 7TR. Telephone/fax 01364 621391.

www.woodermanor.com   email: angela@woodermanor.com

Higher Clovelly/Bradworthy
Lundy View/Tamar Lodges   map 7/438/432

We love cottages with good views, and here are two that as well as having lots of other good things going for them, have a notable outlook both over countryside and coast. With memorable views of Bideford Bay and Lundy Island, *Lundy View* (Ref 17431) is one of a number of properties within a converted Grade II listed barn. Unusually, the main bedroom has its own spiral staircase leading to a 'viewing room'. **Sleeps 6**. At Bradworthy, on the Cornish *Very well situated for exploring both North Devon and North Cornwall, located half a mile from a village.* border, two unusual (in cottage terms) Scandinavian-style lodges – Tamar Lodges – have comfortable open plan sitting rooms, pine panelling and exposed beams. They have the further advantage of open plan gardens. Both *Willow* and *Pine* (Refs 50281/50280) **sleep 4** in a double and a twin.

Details from Country Holidays, Spring Mill, Earby, Lancashire BB94 0AA. Brochures and bookings: 0845 268 0943.

To 'look and book': www. country-holidays.co.uk

187

Devon: coast and country
Toad Hall Cottages*

Featured by us without a break for nineteen years, people seem to love Toad Hall Cottages because of their romantic retreats, seaside villas and picture-postcard hideaways, all in sought-after locations throughout Devon, Cornwall and Exmoor.

A visit to Thurlestone, South Devon, confirmed this impression. Dotted along the main village street are archetypal thatched or character cottages with flower-strewn gardens. Among them, close to the village pub and shop, is charming 17th century *Bay Tree Cottage*, which **sleeps 6**, and *Jasmine Cottage*, **sleeping 8**, providing charming places to return to after a busy day seeing the delights of the South Hams. Add to these the nearby *Whitegarth*, **sleeping 6**, a sumptuous, spacious detached bungalow with a jacuzzi bath and steam room and elegant top of the range *Stable Cottage*, **sleeping 6/8**, and you have the measure of the place. The beach is about 15 minutes' walk from all these.

There's also *Higher Furlong*, a spacious detached family house, **sleeping 10**, on the exclusive Yarmer Estate with sweeping views of the bay. Along with *Warren House*, **sleeping 9**, with superb gardens. The splendidly situated *Seamark Cottages*, just 500 yards from Thurlestone beach, have far reaching sea views and an indoor pool.

Smugglers, a 400 year old thatched four-bedroomed cottage with its own quay, enjoys a unique and secluded location on the estuary beach at Dittisham, on the River Dart. Another charmer, *Alice Cottage*, **sleeping 6**, in a fairytale valley near Blackpool Sands, Start Bay, was the home of the real life Christopher Robin, of Winnie the Pooh fame. Further east, *Idehill Cottages*, near Honiton, consist of three attractive barn conversions with their own 18 holf golf course, exclusively for the use of guests.

Every cottage on the agency's books is known to at least one member of the Toad Hall staff. About half the properties accept dogs and many have open fires.

Check their meticulously detailed, fully comprehensive website with instant online availability and booking – www.toadhallcottages.co.uk or telephone 01548 853089 for a brochure or further information. Toad Hall Cottages, Elliott House, Church Street, Kingsbridge, South Devon TQ7 1BY.

www.toadhallcottages.com

email: thc@toadhallcottages.com

There are several gems in pretty Thurlestone. This is Bay Tree Cottage...

...and this is stylish Stable Cottage, handily sleeping up to eight people.

Salcombe, South Devon
Salcombe Holiday Homes

With great bonhomie and a gift for promoting the considerable charms of Salcombe, Tim and Ginny Windibank delight in promoting local properties that match their own expectations: this means exacting standards, with members of staff visiting each property prior to every arrival.

Closely associated with sailing, fishing and fabulous beaches, this delightful South Hams resort also enjoys a local climate that's especially pleasant even by West Country standards. (There are 150-plus properties, including many cosy cottages and flats **for 2/4 people** and fifteen properties **sleeping from 10 to 18**).

One of the Salcombe landmarks is *The Custom House*. Fronting on to Custom House Quay, this substantial three storey house is next to the lifeboat station and has staggering views over the main anchorage. **Sleeping 10**, the property is a memorable holiday spot for two families who want to be right at the centre of things. *Snapes Loft*, **sleeping 7**, is higher up the town but retains the nautical feel in a huge upstairs room with polished wood floors and a vaulted ceiling with ships' mast supports. One end is all glass, allowing panoramic views over the town.

The Custom House gets our vote. What a beauty, and it sleeps ten people!

We'd happily spend a week just gazing out from the balcony of Wellingtons.

Tucked away up a narrow lane, close to the town's main car and boat parks, is *Gwen's Cottage*. This is an ideal peaceful hideaway for a family (**up to 6 people**) with a dog as, although the property is close to town, the lane leads up to a track skirting the banks of one of the pretty creeks with 360° views over the estuary.

With views as our theme we must mention *Wellingtons*, a beautiful two bedroomed apartment with leafy surroundings situated above the town and looking out to the mouth of the harbour and the sandy beaches at East Portlemouth on the other side of the estuary. The layout and furnishings are of the highest standard. For a colour brochure, contact Salcombe Holiday Homes, Orchard Court, Island Street, Salcombe, Devon TQ8 8QE. Telephone: 01548 843485.

www.salcombe.com email: shh@salcombe.com

See also the sister agency: Dartmouth Holiday Homes, 1a, Lower Street, Dartmouth, Devon TQ6 9AJ. Telephone 01803 833082.

www.dartmouthuk.com email:dhh@dartmouthuk.com

Membury, near Axminster
Cider Room Cottage

We regret the gradual passing of this sort of cottage. 'Traditional', with much of its original character intact, it lies deep in the rolling Devon/ Somerset border country, next to the family-in-residence but with plenty of privacy – we like it very much. The location is rural and peaceful, but not isolated, and the cottage is neat and attractive: it will suit people who prefer an individual cottage to being part of a complex. The views

Very reasonably priced indeed, but certainly worth its Four Stars grading, this cottage is cosy and traditional...

of green, hilly farmland are delightful, and there are ducks, dogs, cats and pet Vietnamese pot-bellied pig to delight small children. The cottage has a spacious, comfortable stone-flagged and carpeted sitting room, two pretty bedrooms, lots of beams, rustic stone walls (there is a shower-room, not bath). We spotted lots of books and fresh flowers.

TV. **'Visit Britain' Four Stars**. Dogs by arrangement. Cost: £180 to £305. Details from Pat and David Steele, Hasland Farm, Membury, Axminster, Devon EX13 7JF. Telephone 01404 881558. Fax 881834.
email: davidsteele887@btinternet.com

Modbury, Ivybridge
Oldaport Farm Cottages

We like cottages that are 'miles from anywhere', especially if there's a quiet beach a mile and a half away. So do many others, as last year's visit to this property, tucked away in the South Hams, confirmed. One couple have been back 15 years running! Cathy Evans runs the four cottages and the 80-acre farm (**map 7/435**) overlooking

Much appreciated by readers, and by us: we will be revisiting during 2008...

the beautiful Erme estuary. Much thought and care has gone into the conversions. Three cottages, **sleeping 2/4, 6** and **6**, were created from the old stone cowshed and dairy. The fourth, *Orchard* – single storeyed and **just for 2** – overlooks the paddock where miniature Shetland ponies graze beside chickens and ducks. Latch doors, pine furniture and comfortable furnishings convey the right mood, and there are games and books. The farm is famous for its championship Lleyn sheep. The South Coastal footpath is nearby, as is Dartmoor. **'Visit Britain' Four Stars**. Laundry room, payphone. TV. Bedlinen included. Cost: £240 to £640. Dogs welcome except end July and August. Short breaks, low season. Details from Miss C M Evans, Oldaport Farm Cottages, Modbury, Ivybridge, Devon PL21 0TG. Telephone 01548 830842. Fax 830998.

www.oldaport.com   email: cathy@oldaport.com

The West Country
Helpful Holidays*

This is a remarkable organisation by any standards, and happily still very much a family concern. It's no exaggeration to say that the agency is known throughout the travel and leisure industry for its uncompromisingly high standards. We feel a special bond, as (in 2007) *The Good Holiday Cottage Guide* celebrated its first quarter-century at the same time as 'Helpful'.

The Bowaters famously believe in saying what properties are really like, warts and all, and have an exceptional variety, from boathouses and 'beach houses' to historic country houses and picture-book thatched cottages.

Their properties are spread all over the West Country, from Land's End to Somerset and Dorset – seaside and inland. And a glance at their unconventional brochure, detailing approximately 530 cottages, underlines their 'truth will out' philosophy.

The company was, for instance, closely involved in the design of *Great Cleave* (**sleeping 8,** Ref A16), formerly a threshing barn and one of a group of three located down a long lane, with wonderful Dartmoor views, close to Drewsteignton. The 'upside-down' look, with the upstairs living/dining room rising high to the apex, with fine beams and tresses, works a treat. *Old Orchard*, **sleeping 4**, Ref A18, got our stamp of approval for its freshness and rural charm, as did *Little Cleave,* Ref A17, fractionally smaller but also **sleeping 4**. All share eight acres of pastureland, a fenced pond with ducks and chickens, an indoor heated swimming pool, a sauna and a games barn.

Half a mile from open moorland, and just three from the ancient small town of Chagford, is a beautiful Grade II listed 14th century longhouse, in 30 acres of farm and parkland on the edge of the Teign Valley. *Northill* is a superbly comfortable and sympathetically renovated property, with a fine collection of antique furniture, high quality fittings and soft furnishings in all six bedrooms, four bathrooms, drawing and dining room and modern kitchen – all with good views over the grounds and the moor. **Sleeping up to 10**, Ref A66, the house provides a superb base for a family gathering, walking holiday or just sheer relaxation all year round; with large open fires for winter and a perfect *al fresco* area for summer.

Five miles from Cullompton, *Halsbeer Farm* incorporates four thatched cottages, three adapted for wheelchair user, that happily retain the distinc-

Northill is a Grade II listed 14th century Devon longhouse in 30 acres. Ref A66.

The charming Boat House is a stunning and harmonious hideaway. Ref C617.

191

tive flagstones and original timbers. *Cider* and *Swallow* both **sleep 6,** while *Haybarn*, which we looked over, has a sturdy Elizabethan style four poster and a galleried landing. **Sleeps 7**. The fourth property, *Apple*, is next to the farmer's fine thatched farmhouse. **Sleeps 3**. A huge barn, converted into a conservatory, can seat gatherings of up to 25; an indoor swimming pool is complemented by a children's play area. Refs G4-G7.

One delightful journey of discovery led us to *Lower Elsford*, near Lustleigh. It is a classic rural Devonshire enclave, four skilful barn conversions adjacent to the owners' house in 35 acres of garden and farmland, from which at certain points it is possible to see the sea. Refs A135/136/137/139.

Among many good things, we admired deep sofas, woodburners, high ceilings, good quality rugs and table lamps, and many charming personal details. A well heated indoor swimming pool in a converted piggery (we loved the piggy murals!) even has an open fire: a first for us! There are lots of animals for children to make friends with. **Sleep 2 to 6.**

Beside the River Avon, on the South Devon coast, and on an excellent and varied stretch of coast (sandy beaches, coves, cliffs, golf courses, pretty thatched-cottage village centres) is the charming *Music Room*. Ref L249. This stunning retreat **sleeps 2** under its vaulted stucco ceiling, with four massive arched windows running the length of the room. The Music Room was once the home of concerts and recitals, but now has a new life as a superb holiday home for a couple wishing to explore the stunning coastline and countryside.

Helpful is increasingly strong on large houses for large parties. These

Many Helpful properties are 'amazing'. This beauty is at East Portlemouth, in the 'South Hams'. Ref L213. Sleeps twelve.

Close to the western edge of Dartmoor, at Lydford, this fine house sleeps up to six people in comfort. Ref A51.

include a brilliantly converted barn (with an impressive tally of ten bedrooms and ten bathrooms) which has superb views of the River Dart, and a former hotel superbly situated in St Agnes on Cornwall's north coast of sandy surfing beaches.

Extraordinary *Sandridge Barton*, **sleeping 12**, Ref C618, which 'Helpful' describe as 'sensational', is a fabulous Georgian mansion in a secluded location overlooking the Dart Estuary, with a mosaic-lined indoor swimming pool any middle-ranking Roman emperor would have been proud of.

Other supremely well sited, very high quality sea-view houses, **sleeping 10 or more people**, are near Prawle Point, Salcombe, in southernmost Devon, and in Salcombe itself.

High on the Exmoor National Park, with stunning views to the sea and across the varied landscape of the moors, is a magnificent fifteen-bedroom, 19th century house. *Porlock Vale*, Ref F30, at the gateway of the great outdoors, is a truly breathtaking holiday home for all the family. It **sleeps up to 31** and there are even stables for guests to bring their horses. Twelve acres of grounds and gardens surround the house, full of mature trees, huge lawns (croquet, play area) and rhododendrons, all managed for maximum wildlife habitat; wistaria cascades from the verandah, with the pebbly beach only two fields away. Inside, the house has a wonderful mixture of comfort, elegance and space, with comfy leather sofas, two sitting rooms and an elegant staircase for grand entrances.

Helpful have more than twenty holiday properties on or near Exmoor, which is probably *our* own favourite National Park. Access to the sea is appealing, as is the wildness of the moors combined with the charm of tucked-away and unspoiled villages.

In Somerset, they have cottages, farmhouses and a superb country house on Exmoor and on the slopes of the Quantock Hills. These include a Grade II listed miller's house in the county's lush farming centre, and a converted cider barn from which you can walk to the tops of the Mendips.

Naturally, Helpful have many cottages in and around Chagford, their very popular little 'home town' on Dartmoor's edge, and in its neighbour, Drewsteignton, a village above the dramatic River Teign valley, near amazing Castle Drogo. Here there are four classic thatched cottages. All of these have the considerable attraction of open fires or woodburners.

Euan and Su Bowater are owners themselves. Slumbering under a traditional thatched roof in the Teign Valley below Castle Drogo is their picture-postcard *Gibhouse*, Ref A14, in peaceful gardens by a stream, with superb views of rolling hills.

Weekly prices range from about £131 to £7875. Dogs are welcome in many properties. Details are available from Helpful Holidays, Chagford, Devon TQ13 8AW. Telephone 01647 433593. Fax 433694. Or have a look at their website:

Gibhouse is an idyllically located cottage near Castle Drogo, above. Note: it gets booked up early! Ref A14.

www.helpfulholidays.com

email: help@helpfulholidays.com

Near Torbay, Sandridge Barton (at Stoke Gabriel) sleeps twelve. Ref C618.

Porlock Vale makes a super holiday home for a big family. Sleeps up to 31! Ref F30.

193

Compton Pool, near Torquay
Compton Pool Farm Cottages

In the autumn of 2007 we met the (to us) new owners of these absolutely pristine cottages, which are in a location that readers – especially families – rave about: only ten minutes' drive from the centre of Torquay, but entirely rural, with Dartmoor only a short drive away. They can be quite hard to locate, which we rather like!

They have featured in this guide for 23 years, with nothing but praise from readers. We visited on a Saturday morning, and met contented guests packing up after their stay. We spoke to one: 'It's our first time here, but we'll be back. It ticks all the boxes'.

We noticed exterior details that give a clue to the superlative standards here: manicured lawns, perfect rockeries, well ordered paths and parking.

There are far too many good things for us to describe here, but, for example, there are marble floors to kitchen/dining areas, the well appointed bathrooms and shower rooms with power showers, the hand crafted contemporary furniture produced in the UK. Everything is 'just so'.

There are expensive king size beds in all double bedrooms and full size singles in twin rooms (no bunks), the best quality soft furnishings, with all bedding and towels included, flat screen digital TVs, DVD players and Bose HiFi systems (plus extra TVs in all double bedrooms). There is a super indoor swimming pool to enjoy, and a tennis court on site.

Hot on the heels of achieving **Five Stars** for all the cottages and the *Gold Award* for the best tourism website in the South West, Compton Pool Farm enjoys yet another accolade: it was the first Five Star self-catering establishment in Devon to be awarded the *Green Tourism Award*, relating to energy use, waste management and care for the local environment. In fact it was a key objective for the farm to be a fully sustainable business. See also Page 8 for more information.

Absolutely top-notch accommodation in the care of new, on-site owners that is winning prestigious awards and also gets the vote of many 'cottage guide' readers...

There are nine cottages, namely *The Farmhouse* (**sleeping 10/11**), *Ambrook* (**sleeping 8**), *Arch* (**4**), *Bidwell* (**6**), *Bow* (**2**), *Crazy Well* (**6**), *Kester* (**4**), *Redlake* (**4**) and *Wray* (**4**). Each cottage has a private and secure garden with good quality garden furniture, and independently controlled central heating.

Details from Compton Pool Farm, Compton, Devon TQ13 1TA. Telephone 01803 872241. Fax 874012.

www.comptonpool.co.uk   email: info@comptonpool.co.uk

Dartmouth
Dartmouth Holiday Homes

Chic, beautifully cared for Dartmouth is rather special. With the sun sparkling on the sea, packed pleasure boats puttering up the river, and cream and brown trains transporting people on the restored Dart Valley Railway, it's not surprising the resort is so popular among self caterers.

There are a good number of holiday homes right in the town (some self-contained houses, many apartments), the best of which are looked after by the highly professional and welcoming Ginny and Tim Windibank and their staff. Ginny and Tim also own the successful Salcombe Holiday Homes.

We've seen a good cross section of what's available, mostly places with the sort of view that could keep one sitting quietly in a bay window or on a balcony – just gazing at the river and the town – for hours on end.

Sleeping 10, *36 Clarence Street* is a spacious period townhouse close to the heart of the town. It has fabulous views from the feature attic sitting room. From the kitchen is an atrium with glazed roof, terracotta floors and comfortable seating. The property also benefits from garage parking and a pretty terraced, part lawned garden at the rear with views to the harbour.

Properties in Above Town nearly all benefit from views over the river and towards Kingswear. *Bell Cottage* is just such a property. Full of character and decorated to a high standard, this four storey house, **sleeping 4**, has 180 degree panoramic views from all the main rooms, patios and a pretty conservatory. *13 Above Town* is a delightful four storey house **sleeping 6**, which is surprisingly roomy and has a pretty garden with wonderful views. Again the property has a Dartmouth relative rarity: a garage. The cosy *Flat 1* in *Speedwell House* does not have views but is ideal for those who want to be a very short, level walk to the centre of town and close to the Lower Ferry which provides a regular connection with Kingswear.

Numbers 9, 11 and *25 Sandquay Road* **sleep 6, 4 and 4** respectively, and

In a quiet location just above the new Dart Marina, 9 Sandquay Road sleeps six.

Bell Cottage (sleeps four) has 180-degree panoramic views from all the main rooms.

are a short walk up river from the central shops and quays. All are comfortable, well equipped and in a quiet location just above the smart new Dart Marina with restaurants, bar and river access, close to the Higher Ferry to Kingswear. With coastal and country walks, nearby beaches, fine shopping and super restaurants. Dartmouth is great all year round.

Details and brochures from Dartmouth Holiday Homes, 1a Lower Street, Dartmouth, Devon TQ6 9AJ. Telephone 01803 833082. Fax 835224.

www.dartmouthuk.com email: dhh@dartmouthuk.com

Rattery, near Totnes
Knowle Farm

On a warm summer day in 2007 we negotiated typically narrow high-hedged country lanes to revisit this delightfully tucked-away and quiet enclave of cottages. It represents one of the finest family-orientated places we know, not just in the West Country but anywhere.

Children love to spend their time with Knowle's collection of chickens, ducks, pigs, rabbits and donkeys, then move on to the outdoor play areas and one of the best indoor playrooms for under fives we have seen, including a ballpool, slide and toys. But there's a high degree of privacy, and adults without children love the cottages too, converted as they are from stone and slate barns, with the big advantage of woodburning stoves.

Moncks Green **sleeps 6** plus cot, with a double, twin and bunk rooms downstairs, plus bathroom/wc with shower. Upstairs is a large living-room that has a high ceiling and exposed trusses, commanding impressive views, also

In 44 acres, the farm has an exceptional playroom and a whole host of pets...

...as well as swimming for all the family in a most inviting indoor pool.

a dining-room and shower-room/toilet. *Applecross*, **sleeping 4** plus cot, has double and bunk rooms downstairs with bathroom/toilet with shower. Again there are good views from the upstairs living/dining room. *Clematis*, **sleeping 2** plus child or cot, is a cosy single-storey cottage with a wood panelled ceiling in the living/dining room area, full of character like the others. *Woodbine* (**sleeping 8** plus cots) is suited to two families. Downstairs it has an open plan kitchen/dining area alongside a galleried living area with a high ceiling, exposed beams and trusses, and a double bedroom with en-suite facilities. The first floor gallery sports a gorgeous sitting area, a double and bunk room, plus bathroom/wc with shower. *Foxglove* and *Cow-mumble* both **sleep 4 plus cots**, with double and twin bedrooms downstairs, along with bathroom/wc and shower. The living/dining and kitchen areas upstairs have lovely views.

The farm, in 44 acres, also offers a 34 by 17 foot heated indoor pool, tennis court, and indoor table tennis and pool table. Dartmoor is about five minutes away, the coast about half an hour. Not suitable for pets; electricity and heating by meter; duvets (with linen) supplied. TV. Highchairs, cots and stair gates. Cost: from about £265 to £1675.

Details from Lynn and Richard Micklewright, Knowle Farm, Rattery, near Totnes, Devon TQ10 9JY. Telephone/fax 01364 73914. There's lots more information on the website, including prices and current availability:

www.knowle-farm.co.uk

Fursdon, near Exeter
Fursdon

Astonishingly, and it's exactly the sort of thing that appeals to readers of this guide, the 700-acre estate in the Exe Valley in rural mid-Devon has been the home of the Fursdon family since 1259. The present generation, David and Catriona, let out two apartments on the first floor of their handsome manor house, whose origins date from the 13th century.

Garden Wing (**sleeping 3**), which opens on to the walled rear garden, has a large double bedroom, a small single and a cosy sitting-room, with the much loved advantage of an open fire (logs supplied) and enough books to keep the most avid reader happy for months.

Park Wing (**sleeping 6**), which enjoys magnificent views over the landscaped parkland at the front of the house, has a large ensuite double bedroom. Two further (twin) bedrooms are at the back and share a shower room. The spacious lounge, again with masses of books, and the large kitchen both enjoy the front view too. Catriona, who masterminds the decor, chooses furnishings and colours that suit the age of the rooms. Both apartments have good-sized kitchens with dining-tables and are equipped with gas-cooker, dishwasher, fridge-freezer and microwave.

We were not at all surprised to learn that one family has been coming here regularly for twenty years. and that another has visited several times from Alaska. Guests can make use of the extensive gardens and woodland and are welcome to join a guided tour of the historic house on any Open Day

Not just another holiday booking, but a chance to savour a fine country house...   *...in which the advantages of good-quality kitchens are not forgotten.*

or enjoy a freshly made cream tea in the Coach Hall. Young visitors particularly enjoy getting to know the three friendly ponies and Catriona¹s flock of black Welsh Mountain sheep.

TV, DVD, CD player. Washing machine and dryer in courtyard. Linen and logs provided. Cot and highchair available. Bookings Friday-Friday. Cost: about £325 to £785 per week. Short breaks available. Not suitable for dogs.

Details from Catriona Fursdon, Fursdon, Cadbury, Exeter EX5 5JS. Telephone 01392 860860. Fax 860126.

www.fursdon.co.uk

email: holidays@fursdon.co.uk

Beer
Jean Bartlett Cottage Holidays*

A highly regarded fixture in this guide for many years, concentrating very astutely on a specific and very popular area, this medium-sized agency has been described in glowing terms by many of our readers, *with never a complaint.*

'Jean Bartlett' handles properties from Honiton to the coast of East Devon and West Dorset: some grand, some modest and inexpensive. We have visited about a dozen, most in sight of the sea and one or two right on it.

On our most recent visit we looked at *Hope* and *Creole* cottages, both former fishermen's houses with beautiful gardens, right in the centre of Beer village, and at *The Belvedere* and *The Look Out*, spacious and most appealing apartments, with sea views, also right at the heart of Beer.

Hope and Creole (**sleeping 5/6**) are furnished to permanent home standards and are much admired by passers-by. They have good sized sitting rooms with deep sofas and chairs, upholstered window seats and an original beamed fireplace. Both have modern kitchens, three bedrooms and a bathroom (Creole has an additional *ensuite* bathroom) plus the benefit of a private parking space.

For guests who are seeking absolute top-of-the-range accommodation, the agency offers several **Five Star** standard properties. For example, there is *Steppes Barn* – a spacious barn conversion near the River Axe, which has plenty of space for guests who wish to take advantage of the location and bring a boat.

Picture-book villages such as Branscombe are a short drive, as are the resorts of Sidmouth and Lyme Regis. Near Branscombe, for example, *Rockenhayne Farmstead* has a delightful stone-built cottage and a stunningly well restored barn that retains its original 16th century oak beams. For people happy with more basic accommodation there is also a static caravan, commanding superb views of the wooded valley.

Costs range from about £160 to £2000. Dogs accepted in about half the properties by arrangement. Details/brochures from Jean Bartlett Holidays, Fore Street, Beer, Devon EX12 3JA. Telephone 01297 23221. Fax 23303.

www.jeanbartlett.com
email: holidays@jeanbartlett.com

Hope and Creole Cottages offer a rare chance to be based in the heart of Beer.

Steppes Barn is one of several 'Jean Bartlett' Five Star properties: Lovely!

Corfe Castle
Scoles Manor

The location is remarkable: the view of Corfe Castle, framed between the Purbeck Hills, has inspired many a painter. Close to the castle, these three cottages have been imaginatively created within a long barn/ dairy. They have large windows, pine *The Purbeck Way footpath to Corfe Castle* furniture, smart kitchens and such *or to the sea passes right by the property.* features as exposed stone walls and oak beams. Owners Peter and Belinda Bell live in the adjoining manor house. The thirty-acre estate, enviably located at the end of a 600-yard farm track, is home to ducks, gamefowl and doves. There are sandy beaches at Studland and Swanage, a short drive, or you can walk to small coves. All are **'Visit Britain' Four Stars**. Single-storeyed *Dairy* has four double rooms and two bathrooms, *Great Barn* three double rooms (two bathrooms), *Little Barn* two bedrooms (one with bunk beds). Central heating, bedlinen, payphones, starter pack of groceries, babysitting. Open all year. Cost: £225 to £1030. Short breaks. Further details from Peter and Belinda Bell, Scoles Manor, Kingston, Corfe Castle, Dorset BH20 5LG. Telephone 01929 480312. Fax 481237.

www.scoles.co.uk   email: peter@scoles.co.uk

The Isle of Wight   map 7/483/484
No 3 Coastguard Cottages/Greystones

Good quality self catering properties on the Isle of Wight are at a premium. Planning restrictions are very tight, so cottages tend to have permanent residents. Close to the beach at Freshwater Bay, *No 3 Old Coastguard Cottages* (Ref W8342) is a gem, a pretty terraced Victorian cottage **sleeping up to 5**. It's located in a quiet lane with a lawned garden, *One of the most desirable holiday houses* and, delightfully, you can walk from *on the Isle of Wight, this former* the gate just the short distance to the *vicarage, Greystones, sleeps up to ten.* beach. Among other 'Welcome' properties is an excellent detached house called *Greystones*, on the edge of Freshwater village, close to a sandy beach and most usefully **sleeping 9/10**. Very much a family house, it used to be a vicarage. Ref W8158.

For availability and bookings contact Welcome Cottages, Spring Mill, Earby, Barnoldswick, Lancashire BB94 0AA. Brochures and bookings: 0845 268 0945.

www.welcomecottages.com

Lyme Regis, Charmouth and around
Lyme Bay Holidays*

During 2007 we visited the smart new offices of this much-liked, highly professional agency. It's notable - and well known – for the fact that most of its properties are within ten miles of quiet, sandy, slightly old fashioned Charmouth, which we'd call one of Dorset's best kept secrets, and of the genteel seaside resort of Lyme Regis.

Some properties stick in our mind for their real character. One is *Pound House Wing* (**sleeps 4 'plus 1'**), close to Hawkchurch, rich in atmosphere and full of intriguing corners. This is a happy property, geared to the present day but furnished in sympathy with its history as the converted wing of a 14th century farmhouse. It even has its own priest-hole, discovered during renovation. There are exposed beams and flagstone floors.

The property, in twelve acres of grounds, is a quarter of a mile from the road but accessible along a well maintained track suitable for most family cars. It's only fifteen minutes from the coast at Lyme Regis.

We're keen on a picture-postcard thatched cottage tucked prettily away in a secret, miniature valley and called *Sunshine Cottage*, in which on a blustery day a couple were very cosily installed (it sleeps **just 2**). Dating back in part to the 16th century, this charming property has a third of an acre garden. We also liked a spacious detached family house called *Penderel*, **sleeping 7 'plus 1'** plus cot. We appreciated the big rooms, the open fire, the quietness – even though Charmouth's high street is only a matter of yards away. It has now been upgraded to **Four Stars**.

We also admired a row of pastel-coloured properties on Marine Parade, all distinctly different but enjoying unique sea front views. 'An outstanding location' said **'Visit Britain'** of one. Two of the most appealing are *Benwick Cottage*, pictured below, and *Library Cottage,* which features a south-facing terrace that has an unobstructed view of the exceptional bay.

Dogs are welcome in over a third of the 200 to 210 properties. For a copy of the brochure, with good colour photographs and precise descriptions, write to David Matthews, Lyme Bay Holidays, Wessex House, Uplyme Road, Lyme Regis, Dorset DT7 3LP. Telephone 01297 443363, fax 445576. Freepost RLYG-GZSA-CEYA, Lyme Regis, Dorset DT7 3BF. There's a very comprehensive website, with internal photographs and on-line availability and booking:

www.lymebayholidays.co.uk   email: email@lymebayholidays.co.uk

Pretty Benwick is likely to have been familiar to Jane Austen, who loved Lyme.

This pretty thatched cottage makes a cosy hideaway for two people...

Coastal Dorset
Dorset Coastal Cottages*

On an autumn morning in 2007 we drove from Weymouth to visit the people behind this much-loved agency and to look at a cross-section of properties.

Their stock-in-trade is that they concentrate purely on traditional cottages, most dating from the 17th, 18th or 19th century. To insist that they should also be *within ten miles of England's important World Heritage 'Jurassic Coast'*, between Studland and Lyme Regis (most are within five), is an even greater challenge. But it has paid off, which says a lot about the charm of this part of the country and the persistence of Charles and Jennie Smith in pursuing their idea of the perfect country cottage. Many are thatched, with open fires.

Our first visit was to *Riverside View*, a cosy delight with a woodburning stove that's adjacent to the owners' house in Winfrith Newburgh, but detached. With rugs on wood floors, deep sofas and thoughtfully arranged lighting, it **sleeps 2**. Also in Winfrith Newburgh, we were very taken with *Milton Cottage*, a traditional thatched cottage, **sleeping 4**, with two-feet-thick walls and distinctive 'eyebrow' dormer windows.

In nearby East Chaldon, we loved spacious *Shepherds Cottage*, **sleeping 8** in four bedrooms. On the little village green, it has most inviting main rooms, a very big and inviting kitchen/diner, and a good-sized garden. And on a narrow country lane, on the edge of East Chaldon, beside lovely open country, handsome *Long Barn* is no draughty conversion but warm and inviting for **7- 'plus'**.

There are around a hundred properties in the portfolio. Some can accommodate large groups, such as *The White House*, at Kimmeridge. This not only has direct access to the Coast Path and sea views, but with five bedrooms and five bathrooms, it **sleeps 10 plus cot**.

In the Bridport area, *Medway Farm*, Askerswell, tucked down a private road in a rural setting, has accommodation for **up to 10/12 people**. This is shared between two stone barn conversions, *Coombe Barn* (**sleeping 4 plus cot**) and *Haydon Barn* (**sleeping 6 plus cot**). Many cottages take pets; most are available for short breaks. *All include linen and towels, as well as electricity, gas and oil.* Details from Dorset Coastal Cottages, 3 Station Road, Wool, Wareham, Dorset BH20 6BL. Telephone 0800 980 4070. Fax 01929 460125.

www.dorsetcoastalcottages.com   email: hols@dorsetcoastalcottages.com

The agency has three properties at Seatown and Golden Cap: memorable!

Milton Cottage, Winfrith Newburgh, has two attractively beamy bedrooms.

South and West
Hideaways*

We often direct readers who ask about renting a holiday cottage in Wiltshire, Dorset or Hampshire to 'Hideaways'. For with a handful of notable exceptions we'd say the agency has on its books the best holiday houses in these rather hidden-away but very appealing counties.

Many are picture-book places 'suspended in time': a chance to catch the flavour of some of England's most unspoilt corners.

Based between Salisbury and Shaftesbury, Hideaways also extends into Cornwall, Devon and Somerset, with a good selection of properties in the Heart of England, and more besides.

During a brief 2007 visit we came across two real gems. Firstly, on a warm and sleepy afternoon in the village of Tarrant Keynston, near Blandford, in Dorset, *The Old Rectory Cottage*. **Sleeping 3** (or **2 plus a**

With its handsome old beams, and accommodation all on the ground floor, Drovers Barn appeals to us a lot.

Used occasionally by the owners themselves (a good sign), Shedrick slumbers in deeply rural Dorset.

cot), it is one of those increasingly rare traditonal gems one associates with quiet rural English backwaters. Built in the 18th century it is Grade II listed, with a thatched roof, thick cob walls and an interior that exudes character, charm and 'tender loving care'. We noticed, for example, a miniature cottage garden, an open fire and rather steep stairs.

Off the A303 near Buckland St Mary, in Somerset, we located *Grange Cottage*. This is a rare delight, hidden among trees, at the end of a private drive, secluded and well away from the sound of traffic. Tucked away behind a manor house of 1656, in complete seclusion, this beautifully renovated cottage is situated at the north edge of the Blackdown Hills on the borders of Somerset, Devon and Dorset, in an Area of Outstanding Natural Beauty. Originally the gamekeeper's cottage for the Estate, the cottage has been extended and lavishly modernised inside, while retaining every ounce of its charm. We thought it an out and delight, and would rate it among our favourite ten properties in this guide. **Sleeps 5/6**.

A rare instance of a quite excellent cottage in the Forest of Dean, where (in one of England's best-kept-secret places) really good self catering is thin on the ground, *The Old Pumphouse* is outstanding. **Sleeping up to 6**, it is approached by a woodland track and stands on its own in a clearing by a trout pond. A real 'hideaway' indeed! Another is tucked away in the New Forest. *The Lodge,* near Fordingbridge, is a sunny three-bedroom thatched cottage which shares the owners' three-acre landscaped woodland garden. With distant views over the Forest from its balcony and terrace, this is another 'hideaway'. **Sleeps 6/7.**

Dorset is true thatched cottage territory, and recently we visited *The Owl Box* in the hamlet of Throop, twelve miles from Dorchester. This cosy Grade II, ultra-romantic cottage lies deep in the countryside. Once a thatched brick and cob barn, lovingly converted to a cottage with a spacious, open living-room, original beams and timber cladding, this is heaven-sent for those who dream of the ultimate bolthole. **Sleeps 2.**

On a previous Wiltshire-Dorset visit we were impressed, among others, by *Shedrick*, a 17th-century thatched cottage situated on its own deep in the Dorset countryside near Chard, which lost none of its character (oak beams, low ceilings) when it was modernised. So it has a cosy atmosphere and the convenience of a large fitted kitchen. The three bedrooms (**sleeping 6**) are a double with ensuite shower room/wc, a double with a brass bed, and a twin. The garden has a secluded patio area and barbecue.

Kate's Cottage, Winterbourne Kingston (**sleeps 5**), is over 200 years old

The Old Stable, in pretty Rockbourne, in Hampshire, is one of our favourites. It has an open fire and several antiques.

The Old Rectory Cottage, near Blandford, is a chocolate-box delight, with modern comforts and character.

and lies along a track on the village edge. It is well placed for visiting some of the most spectacular stretches of coastline in England.

We have also admired *The Old Stable,* **sleeping 4**, a traditional thatched cottage in the meandering village of Rockbourne, on the northern edge of the New Forest. Romantic *Garden Loft* (**sleeping 2**), also in Rockbourne, is a cosy studio flat tucked away beyond a wrought iron gate and up a flight of steps. In a nearby village, *The Coach House,* standing opposite the former village rectory, incorporates a particularly impressive, heavily beamed and timbered bedroom with sloping ceilings. **Sleeps 2 'plus 2'.**

Sleeping 4/6 plus cot, *Drovers Barn,* at Shrewton, makes an ideal base for visiting Wiltshire's best known historic sites, including Stonehenge, Avebury and ever-enigmatic Silbury Hill. The accommodation is all at ground floor level, with oak beams, reclaimed pine floors and a particularly stylish interior decor. The property looks out on to a two-acre garden.

The Lodge, near West Wittering, West Sussex, with its origins in the 18th century, is an enchanting cottage within the grounds of the owners' Georgian farmhouse. It **sleeps 3, or 2 'plus cot'.**

Details of these and other properties from Hideaways, Chapel House, Luke Street, Berwick St John, Shaftesbury, Dorset SP7 0HQ. Telephone 01747 828000, fax 829090.

www.hideaways.co.uk email: enq@hideaways.co.uk

Poole
Fisherman's Quay

With its uninterrupted views of Poole Harbour (said to be the second largest natural harbour in the world), from which car ferries run to the Channel Islands and to France, this three storeyed house is in a spectacular location. We've had so many ecstatic reader reports, and sometimes think we could do with a week here ourselves, just gazing at the view!

We could do with a week here ourselves, just enjoying the fantastic views.

Looking down over the impressive Fisherman's Harbour, two balconies offer an extraordinary vantage point from which to watch every type of waterborne activity – not least, the skills of the pilots guiding huge ships to their berths near Poole Quay – itself bustling with smaller craft and pubs, restaurants, galleries, shops and museums. There are two double rooms, one ensuite, and one twin, main bathroom (both bathrooms have showers), a first floor sitting room with those panoramic views, a well fitted kitchen, dining area, a ground-floor cloakroom, patio and barbecue. Not suitable for pets, infirm or very elderly people, or very young children. Non smokers preferred. Parking space and integral garage. Central heating is included. Cost: £350 to £750. Details from Dr D Halliday, 1 Grange Drive, Horsforth, Leeds, West Yorkshire LS18 5EQ. Telephone 0113 258 4947.

'Do this...don't do that'

Some well-meant suggestions for owners and agents:

* Do take a deposit against damage and dirt. We wish everyone featured in this guide would do so, but few do. (We've never heard of potential customers saying 'We won't go there because they want a deposit'...)

* Do include a folder with information about local pubs, restaurants and shops. Not just menus from smart places and glossy brochures from commercial attractions, but 'the nitty gritty': which fish and chips shops serve fresh, not frozen fish, which pubs have rude landlords, where there's an old fashioned ironmonger's that will sell you six odd nails when you don't want that plastic pack of 100...

* Don't say 'Short walk to beach', if that beach really consists of rough scree and boulders, and the nearest one to play ball games on is a fifteen minute drive.

* Do give detailed how-to-get-there instructions. Internet cartographic printouts are useful, and local colour is a bonus ('Turn left *before* 'The Sheepshagger and Dog', not after'...'There's a hand made sign by the old chestnut tree'..)

South and South East

You have to work at it, but it's still possible to find 'peace, perfect peace' in the south east of England. Much of rural Hampshire, Kent, Sussex and Surrey have gone into the 21st century surprisingly well preserved. We associate the best of those counties with the smell of wood-smoke on autumn days, hop fields, 'tile hung' cottages, sleepy red-roofed villages beneath wooded escarpments, manicured topiary gardens. Within easy reach of several of the cottages featured in this section are Winston Churchill's Chartwell, near Westerham, Knole House, at Sevenoaks, Sissinghurst Castle, the celebrated Pantiles, in Tunbridge Wells – perhaps the most elegant 'shopping precinct' in England – the historic Cinque Ports. It's scattered with castles of the toy-fort kind – Bodiam, Hastings, Arundel, Leeds, Hever – and great cathedrals such as Winchester, Chichester and Canterbury (we'd also include Guildford's: 1930s plain-Jane from the outside, exquisite inside). It is also the most fruitful corner of Britain for antique-hunters, with a good sprinkling of old-fashioned tea shops, many in gabled old towns that have defied the depredations of developers. And we have noticed readers now include Paris in their 'interesting days out' list – for it's an easy matter to pick up a train at Ashford and have lunch in Montmartre instead of, say, Midhurst.

Milford-on-Sea
Windmill Cottage   map 2/478

This is a modern, clean and tidy house with everything you could need to give you a virtually chore-free holiday...

A long-term favourite among readers of this guide, this is a neat, tidy, modern, Georgian-style red brick property that's pleasantly in keeping with the rest of Milford-on-Sea, whose village green and 'character shops' maintain a sense of bygone and rather genteel charm. The house is a joy, with good quality carpets, and is pristinely clean and well cared for. The through sitting/dining room has a bow window to the front and French windows to the enclosed back garden. Every electric appliance is to be found in the brand new kitchen, including a washing machine, dishwasher, fridge-freezer, tumble drier and microwave. There are three bedrooms (one double, one twin, one a small single). **Sleeps up to 5**. There is a modern bathroom, and ample parking space plus a garage in a nearby block. The New Forest, Lymington and Bournemouth are all within easy reach. Village shops are a six minute walk, and cliffs, together with a pebbly beach, are three minutes by car. Cost: about £230 to £545. TV. Dogs welcome at £11 each. Linen, heat and lighting included. Incoming telephone. **'Visit Britain' Three Stars**. Details/brochure from Mrs S M Perham, Danescourt, Kivernell Road, Milford-on-Sea, Lymington, Hampshire SO41 0PQ. Telephone 01590 643516. Fax 641255.

www.windmillcottage.info

email: michaelperham@btinternet.com

Chiddingly, near Hailsham
Pekes

This is remarkable. Very much 'our sort of thing', and our readers'. For the Tudor manor house that is the focal point of the estate and a clutch of extremely characterful holiday houses were first renovated in 1550!

During our most recent visit, accompanied by the owners (Mrs Morris is the grand-daughter of the man who bought the estate in 1908), we looked inside three of the five distinctively different properties in and around that fine Tudor house. They enjoy the jacuzzi, a sauna, and an indoor swimming pool. There is a tennis court and lawn badminton.

Mounts View has stunning views from the good sized sitting room, off which there is a dining alcove. It also has a 'barrel sauna' on the terrace. **Sleeps 6 'plus 2'**. The humblest property is cosy, tile-hung *Gate Cottage*. Up the steep staircase are a double and a twin, with space for 2 on a bed-settee.

All the cottages have well equipped kitchens: washing machines, tumble dryers, mixers and dishwashers. *Tudor View* is close to the main house, has an open fire and a smart kitchen/diner. The twin bedroom leads into the double bedroom, with a door on to the patio and garden. **Sleeps 5 'plus 2'**.

We have always liked *The Oast House*, which has its own private 'state of the art' jacuzzi in a cabin in the grounds. Its porticoed entrance leads into a biggish hall and a large, circular dining room. The kitchen has a table big enough for the largest get-together; the sitting room has French windows on to the garden. The green-covered stairs and big landing lead to the master bedroom with an enormous four-poster bed. There is a second large circular family room with a double and two singles, a twin bedroom and a very small single. **Sleeps 7 'plus 5'**. *The Wing* is unusually shaped, with a smart kitchen and several inter-connecting rooms. **Sleeps 5**.

Cost: Oast House £1340 to £2000; Cottages and Wing £406 to £900. Mounts View £865 to £1145. Short breaks: Oast House £900. Cottages and Wing £258 to £536. Mounts View £500 to £710. (Different prices apply to Christmas and New Year.) TVs. Children welcome, also dogs, especially in the three cottages. Central heating and open fires or open-front wood-burners. Linen for hire. **'Visit Britain' Three/Four Stars**. Details from Eva Morris, 'Pekes', 124 Elm Park Mansions, Park Walk, London SW10 0AR. Telephone 020 7352 8088. Fax 020 7352 8125. Also 01825 872229, Saturday to Monday.

www.pekesmanor.com   email: pekes.afa@virgin.net

A fine Tudor manor house, with a non-Tudor swimming pool and tennis court.

We've always liked the Oast House, especially its large, circular family room.

Appledore
Ashby Farms Cottages

Many years in this guide, Ashby Farms Cottages offer the chance to get to grips with a largely unsung corner of England that most outsiders never discover. For example, the Weald of Kent and – happily within striking distance – the hauntingly beautiful Romney Marsh.

Roughlands, outside Woodchurch, is a conventional detached bungalow, quite roomy and blissfully quiet, with pleasant open views and gardens back and front. Fully fitted modern kitchen and bathroom. There is a twin and double-bedded room, with a bed available for a 5th person.

Only a hundred yards away but completely hidden in woodland, the specially designed and pine built *Fishermen's Lodges* (**sleep 6**) reminded us of Scandinavia, even down to the setting, close to two isolated fishing lakes. The familiar A-shape encompasses a large double bed sleeping area reached by an open rung wooden ladder. On the main level are two twin bedrooms, bathroom and a modern well-fitted, galley-style kitchen. Sliding patio doors open on to a large wooden verandah. There are pinewood walls and furnishings, full carpeting, and the lounge/dining area benefits from the full height of the lodge.

Numbers 2, 3 and 4 Spring Cottages, in the adjacent small village of Kenardington, are within a terrace of brick-built dwellings (a shepherd lives in the other one). Each **sleeps 5** in three bedrooms reached by steepish stairs. They are simply furnished, but bright and attractive, have modern kitchens and bathrooms, fitted carpets and TVs. Fine rural views from the rear. Pretty front gardens.

On the road leading into Appledore is a semi-detached cottage called *65 The Street*, unpretentious but with a good-sized kitchen and a modern bathroom. Modestly furnished, **sleeping up to 5** in three bedrooms, it is well placed for those who like to be close to shops and pubs. There is a neat garden at the back, and attractive rural views.

Cost: about £120 (for a short break) to £450. Dogs welcome. Fishing permits are available at £40 per week for a family of 4 (also by the day), and rough shooting at £12.50 a day. Linen and towels for hire. Further details from Ashby Farms Ltd, Place Farm, Kenardington, Ashford, Kent TN26 2LZ. Telephone 01233 733332. Fax 733326.

www.ashbyfarms.com
email: info@ashbyfarms.com

Fishermen's Lodges: Scandinavian flair, close to two isolated fishing lakes. Easy-to-maintain interiors.

Spring Cottages: No frills, but clean, tidy and bright.

Eastwell Manor, near Ashford
Eastwell Mews

The nineteen individually styled cottages or courtyard apartments in the grounds of the sumptuous Four Red Star Eastwell Manor Hotel are quite exceptional. An indication of the sort of standards they achieve is the new nine-hole golf course now available for the exclusive use of hotel and – yes – cottage guests. That's a first for us.

The hotel, an ivy-clad Jacobean-style stone mansion with turrets, tall chimneys and arched leaded glass windows, lies in 62 acres of parkland and landscaped gardens surrounded by a working estate of 3000 acres.

Everyone staying in the cottages or apartments has use of all the hotel's extensive facilities as if they were a hotel guest. Indeed, the cottages and apartments are sometimes used to provide extra bedrooms when the main building is full, so they are equipped and furnished to the same standard.

With one, two or three bedrooms – each en-suite and with its own TV – they have been cleverly converted from the old Victorian stables. Each apartment or cottage has spacious accommodation with kitchen, dining and living areas. All of them are superbly furnished, with top-quality fab-

With the fine hotel (and all its impressive facilities) as a focal point...

...these stylish and comfortable cottages really do offer 'the best of both worlds'.

rics and linen. They are a short walk from the hotel and its convivial bars and award-winning wood-panelled restaurant (AA 'Two Rosettes').

The hotel's Pavilion leisure complex is even closer. It has a brasserie restaurant, a cocktail bar, a 20-metre heated pool, a 'Dreams' beauty therapy salon and a spa that incorporates steam room, sauna, jacuzzi and hydrotherapy pool. Upstairs is a state-of-the-art gymnasium.

A further advantage is that the Eurostar station at Ashford is only a few minutes' drive away and the Eurotunnel terminal just 20 minutes' drive. So you're well-placed for a day-trip to France.

The cottages and apartments can be rented on a self-catering basis or hotel-bedroom basis. All have satellite TV, video, fax and ISDN. Well-behaved dogs welcome. Costs on a weekly basis from about £440 to £1100. Short breaks also available.

Details and brochure from Eastwell Manor, Eastwell Park, Boughton Lees, Ashford, Kent TN25 4HR. Telephone 01233 213000.

www.eastwellmanor.co.uk

email: enquiries@eastwellmanor.co.uk

Cotswolds, Heart of England, Welsh Borders, Home Counties

Is it real, or perhaps a Hollywood film set representing a fictional or long-gone English idyll? No – it's just down the road from, say, Cheltenham, or Oxford, or Stratford-upon-Avon. It's 'The Cotswolds'. How can this corner of England have survived intact and so all-of-a-piece for so long? About a hunded miles from London, 25 from Birmingham, lies a fairy-land of old walled gardens, honey-coloured villages snug within rolling green valleys, clear rivers and shallow trout streams and sturdy manor houses. Roughly, the Cotswolds stretch all the way from Gloucester and Herefordshire in the west to Bath in the south, and to Oxford in the east, passing close to the fertile Vale of Evesham. Probably the most popular village is Bourton-on-the-Water; less commercialised are the Slaughters (Upper and Lower), Moreton-in-Marsh, the straggly village of Blockley, imposing Broadway, Winchcombe. There's Cirencester, with its Roman amphitheatre, and Stratford-upon-Avon is closer than you might think. To the west and the north is country known as the 'Heart of England'. You'll see ruined abbeys, castles, half timbered buildings, cider-apple orchards. To the east are the Chilterns, the upper reaches of the Thames, rural Hertfordshire and a range of undiscovered country that is 'so near but so far'.

Tintern, near Chepstow
Riverside Cottage   map 9/510

Though you can't see the join, this property is technically just inside Wales. It stands (memorably) about as close to the River Wye as you can be without actually getting your feet wet, close to the road that runs alongside the river. Detached, stone-built, most attractive to look at (though the best view is from the far side of the river), the house is within easy walking distance, alongside the river, of Tintern Abbey: throbbing with visitors during summer week-

We saw this cottage on a bright, sunny Saturday in early summer, with the sun sparkling on the River Wye.

ends, more 'moody' at other times. And there is much excellent and more serious walking beyond. With stone walls, exposed beams, rugs on a tiled floor, the house **sleeps 4** in a double and a twin; the L-shaped sitting room has an open fire. Ref ODA.

Note: there is a terrace adjacent to the river where after cottage-visiting on a busy summer Saturday we were pleased to lean and put our minds into neutral. But – though there are railings – children should be watched. In fact, the property is 'unsuitable for small children'.

Details from English Country Cottages, Stoney Bank Road, Earby, Barnoldswick BB94 0AA. Brochures and bookings: 0845 268 0942.

www.english-country-cottages.co.uk

Stanton Lacy, near Ludlow
Sutton Court Farm Cottages

Grouped congenially around a courtyard, these skilfully converted stone farm buildings have long been a favourite among 'cottage guide' readers. Although this is no longer a working farm, it is surrounded by farming activity. (The lambs in the paddock in springtime are a reliable source of entertainment.) The cottages enjoy peace and quiet in an idyllic situation close to the owners' timbered farmhouse and provide an exceptionally comfortable base for exploring the quiet Shropshire countryside and the historic market town of Ludlow only five miles away. Many varied attractions are within easy reach: ruined castles, black and white villages, gardens, farms, shops and markets.

The six cottages (*Barleycorn, Woodsage, Sweetbriar, Hazelnut, Holly* and *Honeysuckle*, **sleeping 4, 6, 4, 4, 2 and 2** respectively) are comfortably furnished, with wood burners in Barleycorn and Woodsage. Each bathroom has an overbath shower, and there are TVs, videos and CD music systems. There are fitted carpets, night storage heating and electric blankets for the winter months. Holly is all on the ground floor, and has additional features suitable for accompanied wheelchair users. Honeysuckle is a first floor apartment, **cosy for 2**, with chairs outside to enjoy the evening sunshine. They all enjoy **'Visit Britain's'** highly desirable **Four Stars** classification.

There is an information room, payphone, laundry facilities and a children's playroom. Horse riding, cycle hire, trout fishing and golf are nearby. Cream teas and home cooked evening meals may be provided given at least 24 hours' notice. Christmas and New Year are special here, with Christmas trees, decorations and mince pies awaiting visitors, a remarkable number of whom return here time and time again.

This excellent place is comfortably within our and our readers' top twenty in the British Isles, and probably in the top five in the Heart of England/Welsh Border country...

The cottages are open all year round and also offer bed and breakfast and short breaks from two nights. Well behaved pets are welcome in some cottages, at an extra charge. Cot and highchair available. Cost: from £220 to £499 (linen, towels, electricity and logs included). Details from Jane and Alan Cronin, Sutton Court Farm, Little Sutton, Stanton Lacy, Ludlow, Shropshire SY8 2AJ. Telephone 01584 861305, fax 861441.

www.suttoncourtfarm.co.uk

email: enquiries@suttoncourtfarm.co.uk

Frampton-on-Severn, near Gloucester
The Orangery

One of our most memorable recent re-visits was, on a glorious late summer day, to this extraordinary Grade II listed 18th century 'garden house'. We have known and loved it for many years, as have dozens of readers, and were agog to see the major upgrading of a number of rooms within the seductively beautiful building.

We took time to re-acquaint ourselves with the exterior, strolling beside the lily-strewn, carp-rich, ornamental canal that sets it off so handsomely. That's part of a Grade I listed garden, but guests have a double bonus in the form of their own private garden too. A note to new arrivals: though the entrance is at the side of the property, they should contrive to see the building from the front before they go in, though as side entrances go, it's a delight, as it gives on to the meadow-like village green.

In a lovely sheltered spot on the east bank of the River Severn, Frampton is known for its traditional rural scene, with summer cricket on the green and the famous Frampton Country Fair in the autumn. For nearly a thousand years the Frampton Court Estate has been at the heart of this ancient settlement, where splendid buildings around the green include the Orangery.

This is a rare delight, a real treat for people blessed with a sense of history.

Every single room is a gem, but this is no museum piece, and is to be 'lived in'.

We used to describe the interior as fascinating and comfortable rather than grand, being much impressed by the tiled fireplaces in the (south-facing) drawing room and dining room, by the spiral staircase, by the fabrics based on the Frampton Flora painted by five sisters in the 1800s. But the careful restoration and decoration of the last couple of years have lifted much of the interior on to a new plane, with the kitchen a special delight, in which the rare, original 18th century limestone walls of the building have been exposed. *All* the rooms are now pristine and beautiful, with antiques set off nicely by well chosen fabrics and, in the drawing room, a charming wall painting.

Cost: about £650 to £1075 per week.

Sleeps 8. Short breaks possible. TV/video/DVD. Central heating. Details from The Secretary, Frampton Court Estate Office, Frampton-on-Severn, Gloucestershire GL2 7EP. Telephone/fax 01452 740698.

www.framptoncourtestate.co.uk
email: clifford@framptoncourt.wanadoo.co.uk

Owlpen, near Uley
Owlpen Manor Cottages

Readers often ask if and when we've stayed in the cottages we write about. We've stayed twice at Owlpen, which we have a special affection for, as it has featured in this guide since our tentative beginnings in 1983. We stayed most recently during a golden late summer, in light, spacious *Manor Farm*, at the very heart of the estate.

With its softly enfolding hills, its mellow buildings, its woods and pastures, Owlpen is an amazing survivor, a thousand miles from the rat-race, a small corner of England preserved at its most nostalgic and unspoiled.

The nine cottages, and fine Tudor manor house where owners Nicholas and Karin Mander live, complement the idyll. The cottages are scattered throughout the many-acred valley, along a lane here, up a track there, in sight of the main house, or tucked away in the woods. *Grist Mill* (**sleeps 8/9**) – we've stayed in it: a remarkable historic survivor – and *Woodwells* (**sleeps 6**), are favourites. But on a late summer day we also admired *Summerfield* (**sleeps 2**), *Marlings End* (**sleeps 5**), *The Court House* (**sleeps 4**), *Peter's Nest* (**sleeps 2**), *Tithe Barn* (**sleeps 2**), *Manor Farm* (**sleeps 4**) and *Over Court* (**sleeps 5**). The latter two can be let as one large family house **sleeping 9**, with an internal door from one to the other.

The Grist Mill is a historic building skilfully adapted to modern use...

...but it's just one of several properties of great character in an amazing location.

We can also recommend the cosy restaurant, where visitors to the manor house rub shoulders with cottage guests. In a converted old cider house, this feels like a cross between a smart restaurant for an occasion and an upmarket pub. There's an excellent, sophisticated menu, and good wines.

The Manor House and three of the properties are officially 'listed' as buildings of architectural and historic interest, but their intrinsic charm is enhanced by contemporary comfort and cosiness, and an exceptional flair for decor, fabrics and furnishings. There are remote control TVs, videos, radio/alarms, antiques, telephones, hairdryers and food mixers (some have dishwashers, microwaves, freezers, washing machines, log fires and four-posters), and an on-site laundry service. All the cottages have **'Visit Britain' Four Stars**. They have central heating, and are set off by well chosen paintings, deep sofas, good quality fabrics and some king-size beds.

For a copy of the most attractive colour brochure, contact Nicholas and Karin Mander, Owlpen Manor, near Dursley, Gloucestershire GL11 5BZ. Telephone 01453 860261. Fax 860819.

www.owlpen.com   email: sales@owlpen.com

Canon Frome, near Ledbury
The Swiss Chalet

On a warm late summer day, needing to check the local map even though we had been here before, it was a pleasure to rediscover this (really!) unique property, recently repainted and 'freshened up'. By a weir on the River Frome, The Swiss Chalet is a most delightful and amusing holiday cottage. It has the makings of a romantic stay **for 2**. From a comfortable but naturally not large, double

This is one of the most romantic places we know: you can hide yourselves away!

bedroom, on the ground floor, you ascend a 'ship's ladder' to the first floor where you can hide yourselves from the world. From a balcony overlooking the water you will probably see kingfishers, and in late autumn see salmon jumping the weir. There are deep and comfortable sofa/chairs, a kitchenette with dining bar, lots of warmth, a high beamed ceiling: all this adds up to a remarkable holiday retreat.

TV. Dogs by arrangement. Cost: about £200 to £400. Linen provided. Further details from Julian and Lorna Rutherford, Mill Cottage, Canon Frome, Ledbury, Herefordshire HR8 2TD. Telephone 01531 670506 or 07901 667474.

email: julianrutherford@hotmail.co.uk

Fairford/Chedworth
The Mill Cottages/Littlecote map 9/519/529

The Mill Cottages, at Fairford, are two little gems within a handsome Grade II listed Mill House. Just a short walk from Fairford's peaceful market square, one is bordered by water on three sides and both have open fires. **Sleep 6 'plus 1' and 7 'plus 1'**. Refs NQL and NXE. Also, quite near the fabulous Chedworth Roman Villa (stunning mosaics) pretty, detached *Littlecote* makes a handsome small base for exploring the area. Or you could just stay put and unwind in comfort. (The living

Millstream Cottage (the two gables, above) is one of 'The Mill Cottages'. A reason for its popularity among readers is its proximity to the centre of Fairford.

room, for example, has an open fire and rugs on a flagstone floor.) **Sleeps 3 'plus 1'** in a zip-link twin and a single plus a second single bed. Ref NW6.

Details from from English Country Cottages, Stoney Bank Road, Earby, Barnoldswick BB94 0AA. Brochures and bookings: 0845 268 0942 .

www.english-country-cottages.co.uk

Docklow, near Leominster
Docklow Manor

The location is a delight: very quiet, though not isolated, amid peaceful countryside, and with views towards the Black Mountains and Brecon Beacons. Most recently, on a perfect late August morning, we turned off the Bromyard to Leominster road and then along a tree lined private drive to revisit one of the consistently best loved cottage enclaves we know: it has featured in this guide every year *since it was first published in 1983.*

Docklow is in easy reach of Ludlow, one of the handsomest towns in England. There are National Trust mansions and gardens nearby, and the cathedrals at Hereford and Worcester are easily accessible.

We met the fairly new owners for the first time. They, Jane and Brian Viner, have retained and refurbished two of the original seven cottages. We looked at both, and met very contented guests – in one case, readers of *The Good Holiday Cottage Guide.*

Specifically, *Yewtree Cottage* has two double bedrooms, a comfortable kitchen/living-room, and a private back garden with access to a secluded orchard. *Manor Cottage* is a romantic hideaway, with a four-poster bed. Like neighbouring Yewtree, it overlooks an ancient stone cider press: a picture-postcard setting.

Each cottage has a TV, video recorder, and books, videos and games. The more energetic can enjoy the manor house's five acres of formal gardens and woodland, or play table tennis and table football in the Victorian con-

Staying at Docklow is like being part of a traditional English village.

Cottage interiors are comfortable, warm, quiet and have plenty of character.

servatory. Guests are encouraged to feed the free-range bantams, and play with Fergus, the golden retriever. (Note: well behaved dogs are welcome.) Children are welcome: the Viners have three, who deliver occasional treats to the cottages such as home-made ice-cream. The Viners also offer dinner either in their manor house or, pre-prepared, supplied to the cottages.

Cost: from £175 for three nights in Manor Cottage in low-season to £475 for a week in Yewtree in peak season. **'Visit Britain' Three Stars**. Linen included.

Details from Docklow Manor, Docklow, Leominster, Herefordshire HR6 0RX. Telephone 01568 760668. Or you can book through the website:

www.docklow-manor.co.uk
email: enquiries@docklow-manor.co.uk

Cleeve Hill, near Winchcombe
The Old Dairy

Houses with fabulous views sometimes rest on their laurels, but not
this. With apologies to 'Visit Britain',
we'd say both are worth Five Stars.
For not only is The Old Dairy a
delightful *tour de force* done to a
superb standard (**'Visit Britain'
Four Stars!**), it also has an amazing
180-degree panorama over the
Severn Vale to the Black Mountains.

One of our long-time Cotswold favourites.

Off the Winchcombe/Cheltenham road, you snake past the owners' house,
then climb higher. We love the huge sitting room, its woodburner and oak
floor, the vaulted ceiling, the gallery at one end. Downstairs, from that
main room you go through to a stylish kitchen. A good-sized bathroom
leads to a pristine double bedroom (ensuite). Upstairs are two twin rooms,
and another bathroom. The house is light and heated partly by solar panels.
Sleeps up to 8 (including a futon). TV/video/DVD/CD. Linen/towels
included. Not suitable for pets. Cost: about £370 to £1200. Details: Rickie
and Jennie Gauld, Slades Farm, Bushcombe Lane, Cleeve Hill,
Cheltenham, Gloucestershire GL52 3PN. Telephone/fax 01242 676003.
Mobile 07860 598323 and 07764 613284.

www.cotswoldcottages.btinternet.co.uk
email: rickieg@btinternet.com

Poole Keynes, near Cirencester
Old Mill Farm   map 9/524

We really like these quietly situated
converted barns – at the end of a
series of meandering country lanes.
On two sides of the not-very-busy
farmyard are four cottages **sleeping
from 2/3 to 7**. We've stayed in
Thames Cottage: it backs on to the
stream that is the infant River
Thames. Stylish, comfortable, light
and bright, it has some exposed stone
walls, lots of pine. It has a double

*These are charmers: well hidden away in
peaceful countryside, but not remote.*

room downstairs, and the main (gal-
leried) double has a five foot bed. Next door is *Granary*, the littlest, also
with a five foot double and backing on to the stream: both cottages have a
little balcony. We didn't see *Tuppenny Cottage* but met a family enjoying
their stay in single-storeyed *Stable*, with french windows on to the yard and
the biggest sitting room/diner. Dogs welcome. TVs. Linen, not towels
included. Dishwashers in the larger cottages. Cost: £195 to £700. Details
from Gordon and Catherine Hazell, Ermin House Farm, Syde, Cheltenham,
Gloucestershire GL53 9PN. Telephone 01285 821255. Fax 821531.

www.oldmillcottages.co.uk
email: catherine@oldmillcottages.fsnet.co.uk

The Cotswolds and beyond
Rural Retreats*

We seem to pick up more reader responses about Rural Retreats than any other agency. Perhaps it's that the particular style of the organisation matches most closely what we try to do.

The distinctive Rural Retreats style (always properties of character, often with historical associations, very well cared-for, a fine attention to detail) seems to suit them particularly well.

Among properties we've recently had glowing reports about happens to be one of our own favourites. On the edge of the deeply rural village of Wingfield, in Suffolk, *Red Roofs* is a 16th century, Grade II listed long house overlooking rolling farmland. Sympathetically restored, **sleeping 8**, it retains all of its original character and charm and lies in half an acre of enclosed garden that's ideal for children. Ref SU014.

Based at Moreton-in-Marsh, Rural Retreats are particularly strong in the Cotswolds, but their selection of over 400 properties now extends all over England, Scotland and Wales, from Cornwall to the Scottish Highlands.

On arrival, you'll be greeted with a complimentary hamper sitting on the kitchen table, a bottle of wine chilling in the fridge, and often a log fire waiting to be lit. Many of the properties are several hundred years old, so you can expect to find plenty of character too. And there are invariably nice interior touches like handsome table-lamps, expensive curtains, good quality rugs, pretty bedspreads and complimentary toiletries.

Another bonus is that at any time of the year you can choose which days of the week you want to arrive and leave (minimum stay is often only two nights). TVs, bedlinen, towels, electricity, fire logs and cots/highchairs are all included in the price.

The fine brochure simplifies the task of choosing where to stay by having very clear maps and an index which lists the properties by size, by whether they have ground-floor bedrooms and by whether dogs are allowed. And an 'activity' index shows those suitable for guests who want a swimming pool, a hot tub, tennis, fishing or cycle hire.

Some of the most interesting properties, thanks to Rural Retreats' partner-

The Pendeen Lighthouse properties are an experience, not just 'a place to stay'!

Watermill Cottages: a great location, and each property with its own character.

ship with Trinity House, are former lighthouse-keepers' cottages. Three of them, all single-storey, are in a group of four at the foot of the famous Pendeen lighthouse, just six miles north of Lands End. Built in 1900, it was automated in 1994, but an attendant who lives in the fourth cottage conducts brief tours for the public four days a week, Easter to September. And you must be prepared for the fog-horn to sound when necessary! *Vestal* and *Solebay* cottages both **sleep 4**, *Argus* **sleeps 3**. Ref CW-032/3/4.

Two lighthouse-keepers' cottages ideal for keen golfers are situated beside the Cromer lighthouse on the north Norfolk coast, adjacent to the 18-hole Royal Cromer course. *Valonia* **sleeps 6** and *The Link* **sleeps 2**. Ref NO-034 & 051.

There are in fact now twelve sites, from Yorkshire to Cornwall and the Channel Isles, that feature lighthouse keepers' cottages.

Among Rural Retreats' many lovely old properties in the Cotswolds, the aptly-named *Cotswold Cottage* at Tetbury is a period semi-detached stone building, **sleeping 5,** with TV in each of the three bedrooms. Its gardens are unusual in that the front one has a pond and small waterfall and the rear one has a hot tub (for year-round use). Ref CO-163.

In the Peak District, walkers appreciate *Memorial Cottage* at Eyam as an ideal location. **Sleeping 2** plus a child, it is a Grade II listed stone terraced house a few minutes' walk from the centre of the beautiful unspoilt village, high in the moors of the National Park. Ref DE-024. Nearby, in a restored 18th-century cotton mill on the River Derwent, a spacious ground floor apartment **sleeping 4/6** is available. Each room is south-facing and has lovely views. Ref DE-025.

We've had glowing reports of, for example, *Sparrow Cottage*, **sleeping 10**, one of the 'Watermill' cottages, in a notably pretty location – which is really saying something – in rural East Suffolk. In the Deben valley (the River Deben at Woodbridge being one of our favourite places in England) there are two other properties – *Tarka* and *Bluebell*, each **sleeping 4**. Refs SU023, SU022, SUO24.

And one regular readers has said he 'will definitely book' 200-year-old *Nuthatch* (Ref SH020) **sleeping 6**. Beautifully situated in an Area of Outstanding Natural Beauty in Shropshire, with views of Clunbury Hill, it has an open inglenook fire and many original features. Ref SH020.

Holcombe is near Hemyock, which has a pub, a post office, a shop and a 'chippie'.

Lochenkit is in a desirably remote setting on the edge of moors near Dumfries.

Further details from Rural Retreats, Draycott Business Centre, Moreton-in-Marsh, Gloucestershire GL56 9JY. Telephone 01386 701177.

www.ruralretreats.co.uk

email: info@ruralretreats.co.uk

Exhall, near Alcester
Glebe Farm

There's a skilful use of the available space in the conversion here of one-time barns that stand around three sides of a traditional farmyard. Of the ten properties, five are single storeyed cottages, *The Stable* is a sizeable, two storeyed, and chintzily comfortable house with lots of beams and lots of warmth (shower only, not bath). One of the cottages, *Mill Meer,* is suitable for people with limited mobility. Most recently

Neat and warm cottages well placed for Shakespeare Country and the Marches. There are two good pubs in the village, both serving food, and others just a short drive away...

available, within a handsome converted barn, are *Duck Pond* and *Goose,* deliberately made for flexibility. There are two apartments done to a very high standard in a separate, detached, one-time cartshed, called *The Granary* and *The Cart Hovel.*

One dog per cottage welcome. TV. All linen and towels, electricity and heating included. Cost: about £150 to £500. Details from Roger Arbutt, Glebe Farm, Exhall, Alcester, Warwickshire B49 6EA. Telephone/fax 01789 772202.

www.glebefarmcottages.net

email: enquiries@glebefarmcottages.net

Buckland, near Broadway   map 9/534
Hillside Cottage/The Bothy   Colour section, Page 9

Buckland is one of our half dozen favourite Cotswold villages At the end of its picture-postcard street (it's a no-through-road) you continue uphill to locate three comfortable, private, self contained properties. Two are 'upside down' (first floor sitting rooms, from which you look down on the outer reaches of this leafy, honey-coloured village), the new one – *The Nook* (**sleeps 2***)* – is on the ground floor, and

A lovingly cared for duo of properties.

can intercommunicate (to suit a larger family or a group of friends) with *Hillside* (**sleeps 4**). All are adjacent to but have separate entrances from the owners' home. We like the beamed ceilings, the open fires, the comparative roominess, the comfy sofas. One of the bedrooms in *Bothy* (also **sleeping 4**) has a four-poster. There is a good sized indoor heated pool available all day, and a garden with barbecue. A bonus for walkers: the Cotswold Way is yards from the cottages. TV with teletext. Linen/towels included. Dogs welcome. Cost: about £280 to £560. Details from Bob Edmondson, Burhill, Buckland, Worcestershire WR12 7LY. Telephone 01386 853426. Mobile 07811 353344.

www.burhill.co.uk   email: bob.e@tesco.net

The Cotswolds
Manor Cottages and Cotswold Retreats*

Enviably based in the heart of sought-after Burford, 'Manor Cottages' are known for dealing almost exclusively with properties that offer 'the true Cotswolds experience': places of real character and, sometimes, historical associations, as well as picture-postcard locations.

Happily, a recent addition to the agency's portfolio is a splendid property in Burford itself. *Wysdom Hall*, **sleeping up to 20,** combines history (the fine house dates back in part to the 15th century) with 21st century comforts. It's understated and stylish.

We looked at a handful of typically chic properties, absolutely pristine inside and out but very much in keeping with their surroundings. Four of these stand together in the Oxfordshire-Cotswolds in the quiet village of Lyneham, near Burford. As neat and pretty as (four) maids-in-a-row, **sleeping 2, 3, 3 and 4**, they are contained within the building that was once the village school, and are little jewels.

'Maids in a row', in sleepy, little-known Lyneham, near Burford.

Gable Cottage, in Lower Quinton, is a classic of its kind, and sumptuous inside.

At Luckington, in Wiltshire, we saw *The Forge*. This is also quietly situated, with owners conveniently at hand and with all the accommodation on the ground floor. **Sleeping 4**, it is expensively ultra-modern, with for example surround-sound TV and a cosy corner-sofa. Booking days are flexible.

We have also visited a couple of the agency's houses in the village of Lower Quinton, between Stratford-upon-Avon and Broadway. *Elmhurst (***sleeping 9***)* and *Gable Cottage* (**sleeping 7**) are real charmers, though different in character. The latter is a plushly comfortable jewel, a real no-expense-spared *tour de force*, in which the powerful (and very recent) combination of a specialist builder and an interior designer is a delight to see. Elmhurst is more farmhousey in character. We like the big family kitchen, the spacious bedrooms in most cases, the country antiques.

Properties are situated throughout theh Cotswolds, and most sleep from **2 to 4/6**, with a number of places that will take **7/9**, and a sprinkling that sleep **10-plus**.

Dogs and other pets are welcome in about half the properties. Brochure/details from Chris Grimes, Manor Cottages and Cotswold Retreats, Priory Mews, 33A Priory Lane, Burford OX18 4SG. Telephone 01993 824252. Fax 824443.

www.manorcottages.co.uk
email: chris.grimes@cottagesetc.com

Swerford, near Chipping Norton
Heath Farm Cottages

These are almost 'in a class of their own'. We revisited two seasons ago, and, having inspected the latest property to become available, came away even more full of admiration. For this is a superlatively comfortable and thoughtfully equipped group of five cottages, which make an excellent base from which to explore the whole of the unspoilt Cotswolds, the glories of Oxfordshire and, further afield, Shakespeare Country.

There's a pretty, flower-filled courtyard with a mature water garden, 70 acres of meadows and woodland readily accessible, extraordinary views of large tracts of rural Oxfordshire from the courtyard and some windows of the five golden ironstone cottages, and exceptional interiors.

David Barbour, who with his wife Nena has created such a haven of comfort at Heath Farm, is a master craftsman with his own joinery business. For example, all the interior doors and the windows, the kitchen units and much of the furniture is hand-made *on site*: a joy to see. (In one of the larger properties, attached to the Barbours' own house, we admired handsome handmade high backed dining chairs in elm from the farm itself.)

Beechnut and *Hazelnut* **sleep 2**, but both also have sofabeds. They are compact, comfortable and private, with rugs, expensive small sofas, cosy lamps, a skilful use of space. Across the courtyard are *Chestnut*, **sleeping 2** (but it also has a sofabed), and *Walnut,* **sleeping 4**. They are exceptional by any standards, with lots of space, a six foot double bed in the latter, rugs on slate floors. Walnut is a little palace, with a big sitting room, ceiling to floor windows, fabulous views (it's on two floors), a magnificent dining table, exposed stone walls, handsome beams, a superb bathroom/perhaps the most impressive shower-room we've ever seen! The most recently available cottage is *Cobnut*, **sleeping 4** in two ensuite twins/doubles (that is, zip-link beds). Among so many good things, there are extraordinary views from the master bedroom and a top of the range power shower.

All have open fires for which logs are provided. Cobnut is **'Visit Britain' Five Stars**, the others are **Four Stars**: we'd have thought Five throughout. Electricity, central heating, linen and towels included. Non smokers only. 'Sorry, no pets.' Cost: £276 to £658 (Christmas/New Year cost extra). Credit cards accepted. Details/brochure from David and Nena Barbour, Heath Farm, Swerford, near Chipping Norton, Oxfordshire OX7 4BN. Telephone 01608 683270/683204. Fax 683222.

www.heathfarm.com   email: barbours@heathfarm.com

Award-winning properties, effectively all 'Visit Britain' Five Stars...

...are outstanding, among much else, for the craftsmanship of the interiors.

Sedgeberrow, near Evesham
Hall Farm

We know these properties well, and have stayed several times, always appreciating the tea tray, with scones and jam. Plus wine!

We've stayed here several times: loads of 'tender loving care' and good for touring.

The seven cottages are exceptionally sympathetic barn conversions that benefit from their quiet village location (a shop/post office, a good pub) on the edge of the Cotswolds, a few minutes' drive from busy Evesham. Each retains a number of original features. The cottages are fully equipped to a high standard, and the rather cosy interiors (good beds!) include a number of antiques. Guests can relax in an acre of gardens, or use the owners' heated outdoor pool, only a five minute walk away. **Sleep 2 to 6.** Cost: about £225 to £750, including linen, towels, heating and electricity. TV, video, DVD in all cottages. Washer/dryer and dishwasher in all the cottages. Pets not accepted.

Details from Rebecca Barclay, Hall Farm Cottages, Sedgeberrow, Evesham, Worcestershire WR11 7UF. Telephone 01386 881243.

www.hallfarmcottages.net
email: enquiries@hallfarmcottages.net

East Hagbourne
The Oast House   map 9/548

Another 'cottage guide' fixture for over 20 years, *The Oast House* is quietly situated. On the edge of the village of East Hagbourne, below the Berkshire Downs and half-way between the 12th century church and the farmhouse where the owner lives, it is more spacious than its creeper-covered appearance suggests, and has five bedrooms. (The one on the

Very much a family house, with a tennis court by arrangement.

ground floor can be used for alternative sleeping arrangements.) The master bedroom has a five foot bed. The living room has a Victorian style gas fired stove as an appealing back-up to the central heating. On the ground floor there is also a separate dining room, a modern kitchen which includes a dishwasher, and a utility room with washing machine and drier, a shower and a third loo. **Sleeps 6/8.** TV/DVD/video plus satellite TV and freeview. Plus internet access. Not suitable for dogs. **'Visit Britain' Four Stars.** Details are available from Robin Harries, Manor Farm, East Hagbourne, Oxfordshire. Telephone/fax 01235 815005.

email: manorfarm.easthag@virgin.net

English Country Cottages*

The cottages on the books of this extraordinary organisation, which include over 2500 that are available all year round, are spread over Scotland and Wales as well as England. Whatever your preference – big or small, by the sea or up a leafy lane, from Cornwall to Caithness – you are bound to find something to please you.

Well-equipped kitchens and bathrooms, cosy bedrooms and relaxing living-rooms are the essentials that have won 'ECC' such a high reputation since it was set up thirty years ago. Its stated aim was to provide 'superior and beautifully well-equipped holiday homes'.

Our most recent visit was to Morland Hall in Cumbria, eight miles southeast of Penrith, where two large apartments, *Torbock* and *Shorrock* (**sleeping 7/8 and 7/10**), are available. Both have spacious rooms decorated and furnished to the highest standards. With decanters of sherry to welcome guests, and open fires, they suggest a country-house lifestyle at its most gracious.

In a lovely, less famous corner of Cumbria, Morland Hall offers two very comfortable apartments. Ref LYX, LYY.

West Lynch, near Porlock in Somerset, is set amid stunning landscape and has far-reaching views. Ref EJL.

Indeed it is hard to imagine that the 1861 building, after being used as a Red Cross hospital in the Second World, stood derelict and roofless until 1999 when new owners restored it with loving care and finesse.

The apartments are linked by an interconnecting door so together are suitable for larger groups and there is also a third property in the grounds, the *Coach House* (**sleeping 8/10**). Equally spacious, it includes a remarkable double-height lounge furnished in white with white floor and open fire. All three properties are **Visit Britain Five Star** rated and have use of an outdoor heated pool. Ref LYX, LYY & LYZ.

Also in Cumbria, *Yew Bank* (**sleeping 10**) is a handsome Lakeland house near Windermere. Built in 1880 on the edge of the Grizedale Forest and close to the attractive village of Hawkshead which has connections with both Wordsworth and Beatrix Potter, it stands in a large mature garden where a small stream tumbles down a mini-waterfall. Big windows ensure that guests enjoy the lovely view of Esthwaite Water and the fells rising beyond it. Ref LWE.

We ourselves had an idyllic week in Somerset staying with a group of friends at West Lynch, a beautiful thatched farmhouse at Allerford, close to Porlock. Owned by the same family for over 300 years, its rambling interior (**sleeping 11**) is interestingly furnished with antique and modern table-tennis and ideally located for walking on Exmoor or beside the sea. Ref EJL.

Greenwood Grange Cottages, at Higher Bockhampton, in Dorset, are in the heart of the countryside where Thomas Hardy set his tales, just two miles from Dorchester (his 'Casterbridge'). Many of the 16 cottages have been converted from barns which his father built in 1849. **Sleeping 2 to 8,** they stand in four acres of peaceful grounds with two all-weather tennis courts, badminton and croquet lawns, a children's play area and Wendy house. Indoor facilities include a 32ft x 18ft heated Roman-style pool (overlooked by a mural depicting an emperor and his handmaidens!), sauna, solarium and games room. Ref DGY-DUC.

We find North Wales wonderfully far from the hustle and bustle of city life, a feeling that becomes even stronger if we cross the Menai Bridge on to Anglesey. One of ECC's twenty or so properties on the island is *West Lawn,* a spacious detached bungalow (**sleeping 7**) with direct access from its garden to Rhosneigr's vast sands. The beach offers safe swimming as well as canoeing, windsurfing and sand-yachting. Riding, golf and sailing are available nearby too. Ref JAC.

Tuckenhay Mill, in South Devon, offers 21 properties to choose from. This is the shared outdoor pool. Ref FUB.

Yew Bank is a house of great style and character close to Hawkshead, at the heart of the Lake District. Ref LWE.

One London couple we know has so much faith in ECC that they don't even bother to read the property descriptions. Instead they simply take it in turn to shut their eyes, open the brochure at random and put their finger on one. The first time either of them lands on a property sleeping two, they book it. Last summer they picked on *Burns Cottage* at Drumnadrochit, very close to Loch Ness and 12 miles from Inverness. It's a 200-year old single-storey stone cottage, now comfortably furnished with all mod cons and featuring a four-poster bed. While there they did lots of walking, went pony-trekking, played golf and ate most evenings in the local pub, just 200 yards away. Ref UZM.

In the Cotswolds, *Hill Mill Cottage* (**sleeping 4**) was originally a water-mill. Part of a six-acre estate with a lake, it is a great place for wildlife watching, especially from the rowing boat that guests can use. The accommodation includes two beamed bedrooms and a basement games room. For walking, the Cotswold Way long-distance path is a mile away. Ref NRR.

Further details from English Country Cottages, Spring Mill, Earby, Barnoldswick BB94 0AA. Telephone 0845 268 0942.

www.english-country-cottages.co.uk

Country Holidays*

The Country Holidays 2008 brochure (an extraordinary 668 pages!) really does include 'something for everyone'. It features literally thousands of properties of every shape, size and age, spread all over England, Scotland and Wales, plus a few in Ireland, France, Spain, Italy and Croatia.

To help you make your choice, the properties are divided into regional sections, each beginning with interesting suggestions for days out in the area. Many accept pets and many are available for short breaks. Furthermore couples are offered a 20% discount on week-long stays before May 31st or after September 30th and this applies even if they take a child aged up to 5 with them.

Each property is inspected annually and graded to the Visit Britain standards and criteria which go from the 1-star 'Acceptable overall level of

Grade II listed Luntley Court, sleeping up to fifteen, is one of the finest houses in Herefordshire. Ref 13708.

Just outside the beautiful village of Burwash, in the High Weald of Sussex, this peaceful place is Ref 16700.

quality; adequate provision of furniture, furnishings and fittings' up to 5 stars for 'Exceptional overall level of quality; high levels of decor, fixtures and fittings, together with an excellent range of accessories and many personal touches'.

In addition some properties have been given a Gold Award. Totally independent of the Star gradings, these are awarded solely because holiday-makers have rated them as 'excellent overall' in customer satisfaction surveys.

So what could be better than staying in a top class Five Star/Gold Award property? One of them is *Rowan Cottage,* at Bideford, in North Devon. **Sleeping 4**, it's a former Grade II listed coachhouse, now with its own sauna and spa bath. Local activities include playing on sandy beaches, boat trips to Lundy Island, walking or cycling along the Tarka Trail, watersports, golf and fishing. Ref 18386.

Another Gold Award property **sleeping 4** is *Milk Lodge*, in the Ancient High Weald of Sussex. Graded 4-star, it is well placed for exploring the 1066 country or visiting the many National Trust castles and gardens in the area. As Eastbourne, Bexhill and Hastings are all within 20 miles, this is a good spot to combine a countryside holiday with days out by the sea. Ref 16700.

Old Chapel Cottage at Tindale Fell lies in an Area of Outstanding National Beauty on the Cumbria/Northumbria border, 15 miles east of Carlisle. Originally part of an old chapel, it is now a comfortable 3-star cottage **sleeping 2/3** and ideal for couples who enjoy an active holiday, perhaps walking (the Pennine Way passes within 100 yards), fishing, climbing or birdwatching on the nearby RSPB reserve. Ref NC63.

Chickens, pigs, sheep, goats, geese, ducks and horses help keep visitors entertained on the 10-acre *Werngochlyn Farm* at Llantilio Pertholey, near Abergavenny, in South Wales. Riding is available too (with instruction if desired) and also stabling for those who want to bring their own horse – and there's an indoor swimming pool. Accommodation is in four interesting barn conversions, all 2-star, **sleeping from 2 to 6**. Ref 6252/5.

For families with lively children, *Whitmuir Hall,* near Selkirk, in the Scottish Borders, is ideal. (We have stayed, with a seven and a nine year old.) Originally an Edwardian manor house, its outbuildings have been converted into cottages and apartments **sleeping 2 to 6**. The 32-acre grounds include an indoor heated pool, sauna and games room. Ref 5309.

In the heart of the Norfolk Broads, *Deerfoot,* at Horning, is a comfortable 4-star detached house **sleeping 9** on the waterfront. It has a small garden with

At Deerfoot, on the Norfolk Broads, you can fish directly from the garden, and moor a boat to boot. Ref 19794.

Werngochlyn Farm has an indoor pool, and there's even stabling for visiting horses. Sleeps from 2 to 6. Ref 6252/5.

a decked seating terrace leading on to the river and a first-floor decked verandah. Fishing is available from the garden and a day cruiser (bookable in advance) can be moored there. There are plenty of walking and cycling trails nearby, and Norwich is just 11 miles away. Ref 19794.

In Scotland the *Old Lock Keeper's Cottage,* in the pleasant small town of Fort Augustus, is perfectly situated for watching the boats going to and fro on the Caledonian Canal. From the sitting room you can see them just a few yards away, with a view down to Loch Ness at the end of the road. Inverness is a scenic 33-mile drive along the Loch's north bank. Graded 4-star, the building **sleeps 4**. Ref 18717.

Country Holidays also has good choices for those who simply want a quiet retreat sleeping 2, or to escape alone – like a friend of ours who regularly seeks a little hideaway to work on her TV scripts. 'All I need is a bed, microwave and my laptop', she says. Her current favourite is the *Old Cider Mill* (3 stars) at Tarrington, near Hereford. Lovingly converted, with an open-plan kitchen/lounge/dining room downstairs and bedroom with low beamed ceiling and bathroom above, it suits her perfectly. Ref 13166.

Details from Country Holidays, Spring Mill, Earby, Barnoldswick, Lancashire BB94 0AA. Brochures and bookings: 0845 268 0944.

www.country-holidays.co.uk

Blakes Country Cottages*

Whether you want a cosy cottage for two or a grand house suitable for a family gathering, you should have no difficulty in finding it amongst Blakes's vast selection of properties. Its hefty 668-page brochure covers everywhere from Lands End to the Orkneys, together with a few in France, Spain, Italy and Croatia.

England, Scotland, Wales and Ireland are divided into 22 regions, making it easy to locate a cottage in a particular area and the indexing is helpfully designed to simplify finding a large property or one with a swimming pool. Moreover many are still at 2006 prices.

In addition each section starts with information about the area and tips for days out, including a specific recommendation from one of Blakes' local team. The brochure also shows whether a property is available for short

Delightful Ninham House, at Shanklin, a family house set in a wooded valley, is close to sandy beaches. Ref 19270.

This is one of our Yorkshire favourites. Comfortable, with a 'traditional English cottage' flavour. Ref B5065.

breaks and - if so - for how many nights and at what times of the year. Header bars against each property's details highlight important features such as those that accept pets.

Every property has been quality assessed using the Visit Britain criteria. Five Stars mean 'exceptional' while, at the other end of the scale, 1-star cottages suit those, perhaps on a tighter budget, who are happy with somewhere simpler but still want to be assured of cleanliness and comfort. In addition, irrespective of their star rating, some properties have also been honoured with a Gold Award because holidaymakers have rated them as 'Excellent overall'.

For lovers of the sea, one of the Gold Award winners is within 100 yards of the beach at Downderry, near Looe on Cornwall's south coast. It's the 3-star *Coastguard Cottage*, a cosy, compact terraced building (**sleeping 5**) which has a comfortable sitting room with a picture window and a garden overlooking the beach. Ref 50100.

A Gold Award property ideal for train lovers of all ages is a first-floor 4-star apartment (**sleeping 5**) in Kingsley & Froghall station, close to the lovely Caldon Canal about 10 miles east of Stoke-on-Trent. This replica Victorian building is on the Churnet Valley line which recreates the ambience of a 1950s rural railway with trains hauled by gleaming steam locomotives. It's great for train buffs: there are special Thomas the Tank Engine days and even occasional 'ghost trains'. Or a little further away, Alton Towers and the glorious Peak District National Park are both within a short drive. Ref 17343.

Even closer to the sea, another Gold winner stands at the top of the wall above the sandy beach at Walcott, in Norfolk, 18 miles from Norwich. This 2-star detached timber holiday bungalow (**sleeping 4**), named *Heyhoe,* is well placed for visits to Cromer. Ref AB38.

At Erbistock near Llangollen, a converted water mill **sleeping 10** enjoys a spectacular setting on the banks of the River Dee, graded 3-star. Surrounded by natural woodland, it boasts spiral staircases and a balcony. In Scotland, *Kilpatrick Farm House* is a spacious 3-star building **sleeping 7** on a working farm at Pinmore in Ayrshire. Most guests are content to enjoy walking in the beautiful countryside or fishing for trout or salmon, but the seaside at Girvan is only six miles away, with championship golf at Turnberry just beyond it. Ref 18964.

Ideal for lovers of the Yorkshire Dales, three characterful 4-star cottages have been created from *Grange Farm,* a pleasant 17th-century stone

Gold Award property, The Mill, on the banks of the Tyne in Northumberland, is a haven of peace. Ref NN15.

Railway enthusiasts will enjoy staying in this property on the Churnet Valley line near Stoke-on-Trent. Ref 17343.

farmhouse in the quiet village of Draughton just outside Skipton, with a fourth cottage just across the road. **Sleep from 4 to 10**. Ref B5065.

Watersports enthusiasts and nature lovers are well catered for at the Cotswold Water Park, an area of 150 lakes covering 40 square miles on the outskirts of Cirencester. Four honey-coloured modern houses (**sleeping 6 or 8**), modelled on the style of local villages, are available beside it in Lower Mill Village and four New England-style lodges (**sleeping 6**) at Isis and Spring Lakes. All are 4-star rated and ideal for families with teenagers who want an active holiday, whether sailing, water-skiing, riding or cycling. *Lower Mill* has a heated outdoor pool (Easter to October). Ref 19713/6 and 19709/12.

On the Isle of Wight at Shanklin, *Ninham House* (**sleeping 8/9**) is a delightful family home set in a picturesque wooded valley with a decorative lake. Built in 1904 it has been upgraded to provide tastefully-furnished but comfortable accommodation (graded 4-star).

Guests have access to a heated outdoor swimming pool, toddlers' pool and games room provided for the nearby caravan park. Ref 19270.

Details from Blakes, Spring Mill, Earby, Lancashire BB94 0AA. To book, telephone 0845 268 0944.

www.blakes-cottages.co.uk

Welcome Cottages*

Looking at the impressively wide range of Welcome's cottages, it's hardly surprising to learn that the agency turns down around two-thirds of those offered to it. Yet its properties, which are spread all over England, Scotland, Wales and Ireland, plus an interesting selection in France, Spain, Italy and Croatia, remain notably affordable.

Welcome also provides the advantage of its own clear and simple colour-coded grading system to help you assess each property to the full. This has four well thought out categories: Comfortable ('plenty of creature comforts'), Good Quality ('well appointed and well furnished'), Lovely ('handsome, harmonious and tasteful') and – best of all – Beautiful ('beautifully decorated and furnished').

Handy for the Norfolk Broads, this little thatched gem sleeps 2. The North Norfolk coast is within easy reach. Ref W3645.

This bungalow near Amble, Northumberland, has a full size snooker table and a whirlpool bath. Ref W1766.

'Pets go free' is another reason why this is such a successful agency (most of its properties accept them). Moreover if you book to go with your pet between October and the end of March, you get £25 off the cost of your holiday.

For couples, many properties offer a 20% discount on holidays between October and May, including those accompanied by a baby or child up to the age of 5.

Among many attractive places to stay in the West Country, *Sithney*, near the ancient town of Helston, is a luxurious farmhouse (**sleeping 9/10**) with an indoor pool, games room, lawned garden and patio looking on to farmland. Graded as 'Beautiful', it also has the advantage of being wheelchair-friendly; two of the six bedrooms (a double and a single) are on the ground floor and have head and foot lift electric beds. The sea is within three miles and you are on the doorstep of the lovely Lizard Peninsula and not too far from Falmouth, Penzance and Lands End for days out. Major attractions nearby include Flambards Theme Park and the Goonhilly Down visitor centre, which explains all about satellite communications. Ref W8405.

Another property rated 'Beautiful' is *Cwm Main*, a 16th-century Grade II listed farmhouse **sleeping 8** near Bala in North Wales. It's on a 100-acre farm where pheasants and ducks are reared. Lovingly restored, the building's original character is now combined with modern facilities throughout. There's a wealth of huge beams and oak wall panels, two inglenook fireplaces and an impressive wooden spiral staircase. Ref W2399.

A considerable number of thatched properties are on Welcome's books, including a charming old cottage with a pretty garden in the village of Ludham, 13 miles from Norwich and seven from the sea. The wildlife and windmills of the Norfolk Broads can be explored in day cruises from nearby Potter Heigham and Wroxham. Other attractions around range from bird and seal colonies to stately homes and steam railways. Graded "Good Quality', the property **sleeps 2**. Ref W3645.

Just on the English side of the Welsh border, 22 miles south-west of Shrewsbury, *Hyssington* is part of a 17th-century timber-framed barn converted into modern holiday accommodation (**sleeping 7/8**). However, it has retained its original charm and character so successfully that it is graded 'Beautiful'. The traditional country-style interior includes a farmhouse kitchen and large lounge with woodburner. A children's playground is close by and there's hillwalking, cycling and bird-watching. Ref W40143.

Sithney is a super family house in an exceptional location. Sleeping up to ten, it's only about three miles from the sea.

Original character blends with 21st century facilities in this listed Welsh farmhouse near Bala. Ref W2399.

One of our own most memorable holiday experiences ever was waking up in the Ring of Kerry in south-west Ireland. When we looked out of the bedroom window, the scenery was breathtaking. *Wheatfield*, an L-shaped house at Muckera, seven miles from Kenmare, is well placed for exploring the whole area. The interestingly designed split-level accommodation (**sleeping 6**) makes the most of the spectacular view of Killarney Bay. Ref YMF.

Eight miles north of Banbury, an open-plan studio apartment **sleeping 2** is available in the grounds of a private home in the beautiful conservation village of Wormleighton. Graded 'Good quality', it's on the first floor above a games room with table-tennis. Quiet and secluded, the property has a shared patio/lawned garden and boasts stunning views of the surrounding countryside beyond the Oxford Canal, a mile away. Ref W8300.

An artist friend of ours reckons that north-west Scotland is unbeatable for seascapes and mountains to paint, but its attraction for us is the scope for bird-watching and walking. At Laide, near Gairloch, a 'Beautiful' property (**sleeping 6**) is only yards from the shore and a small sandy beach. Built in the 1700s but lovingly renovated, it has original wood panelling in several rooms, a four-poster style box bed and even its own sauna. Ref W143.

For availability and bookings, contact Welcome Cottages UK, Spring Mill, Earby, Barnoldswick, Lancashire BB94 0AA. Tel 0845 268 0945.

www.welcomecottages.com

Ireland

There's definitely something addictive about Ireland. Of all the holiday destinations we feature, this seems to be the one that gets people wanting to go back. We've often heard self-caterers say 'The more I see of it, the more I like it.' It's probably Ireland's age-old charms that make this one of the most appealing destinations in Europe. We remember strolling through Killarney after dark, listening to traditional music being played in what seemed like every other pub, the sun setting over the bleakly beautiful coast of Connemara, and finding 'b and b' en route between cottage visits in a faded but still grand Georgian mansion. We think of the green of the countryside bordering the coast of North Antrim, of the mystical quality of the early-morning light over Lake Killarney, and of the wild blue mountains of Connemara. We remember anglers' eyes lighting up over a candlelit dinner in romantic Delphi Lodge, among the hills on the Galway-Connemara border, when describing their day's battles with salmon. We hear from readers who enjoy 'two-centre' Irish holidays. One family, regular users of the book but first-time visitors to Ireland, stayed first in a thatched cottage at Kinvara, nicely poised for explorations of Galway and the Connemara National Park, and then a week within the Ring of Kerry.

Note: when telephoning Ireland you should dial your own international prefix (eg 00) then 353 followed by the area code (eg 51, not 051), then the number. Within Ireland, however, you should prefix the area code with '0', eg 051. Note also: a small number of contact phone numbers in this section are UK ones.

Killarney, Muckross   map 10/562
Killarney Lakeland Cottages

Killarney is the most popular tourist destination in Ireland, and usually buzzes with life. Brian O'Shea's landscaped, well-spaced, villagey arrangement of white-painted and traditional-style cottages is in a quiet parkland setting seemingly miles from the town centre (though that's actually quite close). In two separate groups, each is surrounded by trees, a well planned distance from its neighbours. Every one has a peat fire. The number each

A great location, close to a famous town.

property sleeps varies **from 4 to 7**. There is access to two hard tennis courts, a good games room, bikes, and in each cottage TV with multi-channel reception and direct dial telephone. Not suitable for dogs. Cost: about €200 to €1000. Details/colour leaflet from Brian O'Shea, Killarney Lakeland Cottages, Muckross, Killarney, Co Kerry. Telephone (outside Ireland) – your international code plus (353) 64-31538, fax (353) 64 34113.

www.killarney.cottages.com

email:info@killarneycottages.com

Bansha
Lismacue Coach House

In a superb location for touring (the Glen of Aherlow, Tipperary, historic Rock of Cashel, and beautiful Cahir beyond it, Killarney, the Dingle Peninsula, Co Clare and more besides), here is a skilfully converted two storeyed coach house conversion attached to the owners' grand

We loved this cosy converted coach-house attached to a Georgian mansion.

listed Georgian mansion, where very up- market 'bed and breakfast' is available. **Sleeping up to 7** in one double, two twins and a single, it has the advantage of a wood-burning stove and even a sauna. The single bedroom, conveniently for older or less able people, is on the ground floor. There is a covered garage.

Among comments from people who have stayed. Adam and Lucille Pauley, of Cambridge, Massachusetts, write 'a wonderful week in peaceful and scenic surroundings', and William Koyle of Orangeville, Ontario, said 'To look out on the Galtee Mountains from Lismacue has to be one of the best views in Ireland'.

Not suitable for dogs. Linen and towels included. Details from Kate Nicholson, Lismacue House, Bansha, Co Tipperary. Telephone (62) 54106.

www.lismacue.com

Ballina   <small>map 10/563</small>
'The Holiday House'

Used occasionally by the Suffolk-based owners, this neat, modern, semi-detached house, just 45 minutes from Knock airport, makes a *notably inexpensive* base from which to explore much of the glorious west of Ireland. A town property but quietly situated on a little-used road that runs alongside the River Moy, it

It's a pleasant fifteen minute walk into lively Ballina alongside the River Moy.

sleeps 5 in a double, a twin and a single. It is well carpeted through-

out, and as well as central heating there are *two* open fires – a great bonus for those so-enjoyable spring and autumn breaks. There is easy access to the river and walks along it (a fifteen minute walk to the town centre) and it's just eight miles from the fabulous sandy beach at Enniscrone. Fishermen will love this: among much else there's salmon fishing on the Moy from February to September. Cable TV, small 'music centre'; large storage shed for housing fishing gear. Not suitable for pets, and there are no special facilities for babies or small children. *Costs are very reasonable.* Details from Mr and Mrs Burke, 57 Head Lane, Great Cornard, Suffolk CO10 0JS. Telephone 01787 311626.

email: m.burke@amserve.com

The South of Ireland
Country Cottages in Ireland*

No wonder so many holidaymakers keep going back to Ireland. 'Deserted silver sands, isolated cliff tops, secluded woodlands, exquisite seafood, famous greens, the friendliest people on earth' as the organisers behind Irish Country Cottages put it.

Couples have the advantage of being able to book some of its larger properties for added comfort at a 20% discount when they stay at least a week between September 1st and May 31st (except half-term and bank holidays). This applies even if they take a child under five with them.

Near the south-east corner of Ireland, *The Farmhouse* is a handsome 16th-century white building (**sleeping 8**) in a quiet position on a working sheep farm with a duck pond and sanctuary. It has a sun room and pleasant garden, with beaches, country walks, tennis, riding, sailing and fishing all within three miles and five golf courses within twenty miles. The ferry terminal at Rosslare from Fishguard is an hour's drive. Ref ZF5.

Further north on another sheep farm, handily placed for visiting Dublin (15 miles), three bright but cosy single-storey apartments, *The Stables*, have been created from barns at Ashbourne in Co Meath. **Sleeping 2** each, they share a garden and are only 12 miles from the sea. Ref 31532.

Remotely situated on the island of Achill, Co Mayo, this spacious modern house is just 50 yards from the sea. Ref YBBE.

The Old Monastery is an elegant Victorian property in secluded gardens at Cahersiveen, Co Kerry. Ref ZO3.

One of the remotest properties is *Aitin Aoibhinn* on the west coast island of Achill in Co Mayo. Though accessed by a bridge, the island has an 'away-from-it-all' charm which often lures artists and writers. The property is a smart modern house **sleeping 8** with big windows to ensure that everyone enjoys the views of the mountains and the sea. Ref YBBE.

For a large group, *The Old Monastery* at Cahersiveen in Co Kerry **sleeps 16**. Built in 1840 as a merchant's house, it still has its old wood floors and stained-glass windows. Ancient castles, prehistoric burial grounds, standing stones and medieval crosses all wait to be explored nearby. It's also a good area for activities – walking, cycling, climbing, watersports, riding, tennis, golf and every sort of angling. Ref ZO3.

For a brochure or to make bookings, contact Irish Country Cottages, Spring Mill, Earby, Barnoldswick BB94 0AA. Telephone 0845 268 1029.

www.irish-country-cottages.co.uk

Bantry
Whiddy Holiday Homes

On board a small passenger ferry you cross beautiful Bantry Bay, fringed by green hills, to Whiddy Island. Ten minutes on the water, a world away. Depending on which of the three most appealing cottages is yours (usefully, their owners live on the island in summer), you might be driven a couple of miles along a bumpy track, past a freshwater lake

An outstanding quartet of spacious and comfortable cottages, with Shannon airport just an hour away.

with a rowing boat freely available to cottage guests, past hedges of scarlet fuchsia that are a summer trademark of the west of Ireland. All three are utterly quiet, all with sea views 'to die for'. Rowing on the lake, exploring every nook and cranny of the island by bike or on foot, climbing to the eerily beautiful, deserted Napoleonic fort, would fill a happy week or, in good weather, a fortnight of serious unwinding. Fishing and sailing can be arranged without difficulty. Linen and towels included. TV. Dogs welcome.

Booking details available from Greta Steenssens, Roddam 83-2880, Bornem, Belgium. Telephone: 00 32 3 889 61 11. Fax: 00 32 3 889 41 71.

email: walco.pottery@skynet.be

Ballyvaughan   map 10/573
Village and Country Holiday Homes

With the special combination of a charming village that happens to be surrounded by an exceptional landscape (the limestone hills of the Burren and the shores of Galway Bay), these are some of the best self catering properties we know in the west of Ireland. The enclave of well appointed cottages (each with its own garden, quiet and private) is located in a courtyard. The owners also have two apartments, bright, deceptively spacious, within a few yards of the court-

A rather pleasant decision for visitors to make: in the village or by the sea? Both sets of properties are quite outstanding.

yard cottages. All the properties have quality fabrics and furnishings, easy-on-the-eye colours, well equipped kitchens. The houses **sleep 6, 4 or 6** (there are two styles, plus the apartments). Cost: about €310 to €830. Further details from George Quinn, Frances Street, Kilrush, Co Clare. Telephone (outside Ireland) – your international code plus 353 65 90 51977.

www.ballyvaughan-cottages.com
email: sales@ballyvaughan-cottages.com

Delphi, North Connemara
Boathouse Cottages/Wren's Cottage

We've stayed here twice, and would recommend it wholeheartedly as a place to unwind in beautiful surroundings. We love it, and would rate it among our favourite half dozen places in this guide.

Delphi is in a beautiful mountain setting, reminiscent of a idealised classical 18th century landscape: great looming hills, misty valleys, rushing rivers, dark woods.

Serious fishermen probably know Delphi, and walkers should consider it. It is a wildlife paradise, known for wild flowers, otters, peregrine falcons, pine martens and badgers. You will find it where western Mayo nudges into Connemara, a few miles north of Leenane.

Almost adjacent to elegant Delphi Lodge, the original four cottages (Boathouses) are very cosy, quite unpretentious, with deep chairs and sofas, lots of antique pine, big open fires (making them a most appealing choice for an autumn or winter break), traditional stone floors with rugs downstairs and carpets upstairs. These four are most attractively bordered by shrubs and old stone walls; two **sleep 4** in two twins, the other two **just 2** in a double bed.

During our most recent visit we saw a newly restored cottage, Wren's. On the approach road to Delphi Lodge, overlooking Finlough, in the Delphi Valley, it has a greater degree of privacy, and has been furnished and equipped to a very high standard. It **sleeps 6** in three bedrooms.

Boathouse Cottages are full of character and charm. We have met people in residence, and they have all loved their cottage and its romantic location.

Wren's Cottage, newly renovated, is the pride and joy of the Delphi ownership. Idyllically, it overlooks the lough, and is bound to attract a following of its own.

Linen/towels included. All cottages have telephone. Wrens has Sky TV. Not suitable for very young children or dogs. Cost: about €800 to €900 (c £533 to £600). Wrens €1250 (c £833). Details: Delphi Lodge, Leenane, Co Galway (postal district). Telephone 353 95 42222. Fax 42296.

Note: Excellent bed and breakfast accommodation is available in Delphi Lodge, and cottage guests may sometimes have candlelit dinners here, usually on a communal basis: such a bonus for lone travellers or people from overseas wanting to make new friends.

www.delphilodge.ie
email: stay@delphilodge.ie

Ireland Directory
Welcome Cottages*

Whatever size or style of property you fancy in Ireland, you are likely to find it in Welcome's selection of around 500 cottages, each usefully graded as 'Beautiful', 'Lovely', 'Good Quality' or 'Comfortable'.

In Co Cork – close to Mizen Head, Ireland's most south-westerly point – *Seascape*, at Ballydehob, is a superb architect-designed house (**sleeping 8**) in a wonderful position overlooking Roaring Water Bay and a myriad of tiny islands. The conservatory enjoys a panoramic view and grounds leading down to the shore. No wonder it's rated 'Beautiful'. Watersports, boat trips, golf and riding, walking are all available nearby. Ref YSH.

On the east coast, three small stone cottages (all Irish Heritage listed) are surrounded by beautiful mature parkland on the Fortgranite Estate at Baltinglass in Co Wicklow. They are the *Stewards House*, *Doyles Lodge* and *Lennons Lodge*, **sleeping 4, 2** and **2** respectively. Free trout fishing is within walking distance and golf only three miles away. The Wicklow mountains offer walking or pony-trekking, and no one should miss a drive on the lonely and narrow military road through them; we did it a couple of years ago and chalked it up as one of the great experiences of our week's stay in the area. Ref YWK, ZVA, ZVB.

A former farmhouse, comfortably refurbished to **sleep 5**, near the village of Woodford between Galway and Limerick, is particularly well placed for those who want an active outdoor holiday. Golf, riding and pitch and putt are all within easy reach; a nearby oak forest nature reserve and the Slabh Aughty mountains provide plenty of possibilities for walkers; and the Shannon (six miles) and Lough Derg offer boating, watersports and fishing. Ref W31233.

In Co Cork, this handsome cottage (not featured) is only four miles from a Blue Flag Beach. Sleeps six. Ref W31134.

Just outside Woodford, this is well placed for self caterers wanting an active, even 'sporty' holiday. Ref W31233.

Eight miles from the centre of Dublin yet occupying a tranquil location among rolling hills and pine forest, two properties at Tibradden are ideal for a holiday that combines rural life with easy trips into that world-class city. *Heather Cottage* **sleeps 8** and *The Loft* apartment **sleeps 4/6**. Ref ZEX/YDK.

For availability and bookings, contact Welcome Cottages, Spring Mill, Earby, Barnoldswick, Lancashire BB94 0AA. Telephone 0870 268 0945.

www.irelanddirectory.co.uk

'Do this...don't do that'

Some well-meant suggestions for owners and agents:

Do help first-time guests get their bearings. One of the most popular 'add-on' features in cottages is a full-size Ordnance Survey map of the immediate area, framed and hanging in a kitchen or a hall.

Do, if you really want holiday tenants eating out of your hand, provide little but always-appreciated items such as a home made cake, a bottle of wine, something bubbly for the bath.

Do, if you have a woodburner or multi-fuel stove, consider lighting this if the weather's cold and you know when people are arriving: this small act produces more ecstatic reader-responses than anything else.

Do, if you inhabit an ideal world, occasionally stay in the cottages yourselves so you can check out what's right and what's wrong (noisy plumbing, drafts, too-amorous local cats, nosy neighbours).

Do give detailed how-to-get-there instructions. Internet cartographic printouts are useful, and a bit of local information is a bonus ('Turn left *before* The Dog and Flea, not after'...'There's a hand-made sign nailed to the dead oak tree'...)

Do by all means clean cottages to within an inch of their lives, but do leave salt cellars and pepper pots with their contents intact. It's something few tenants think to bring, and their absence has ruined many a fish supper! We'd say leave oil, vinegar and spices too.

Do also provide soap, ideally in both liquid and old fashioned bar form: each has its fans! No soap at all is increasingly common.

Don't get in guests' hair as they try to settle in. Some well-meaning owners spend an hour telling people about eccentric previous guests and which cupboard the board games are hidden in when all the new arrivals really want to do is make a cup of tea and put their feet up.

Do decide whether pets are welcome or otherwise. There are owners who'll accept cats but not dogs, and vice versa, and a number who'll accept everything except tortoises. Leaving the question of pets open to negotiation can mean trying to run with the hare and hunt with the hounds.

Don't hesitate to take a deposit against damage. We wish everyone we feature would do so, but few do. (We've never heard of potential customers saying 'We won't go there because they want a deposit'...)

Good news from far countries

Readers of *The Good Holiday Cottage Guide* who stay in self catering properties abroad as well as in the UK were among the first to encourage us to widen our horizons, as did the noticeable number of UK cottage owners who *also* have properties to let overseas. For the moment we've confined ourselves to France, Italy and Spain, with a nod to northern Germany, Malta, Poland and New England. We'd be pleased to get more reader reports and recommendations of self catering properties in those and other countries.

Among our best recent discoveries were self-catering cottages on the Baltic islands of Bornholm (Denmark) Goland and Öland (Sweden) Åland (Finland) and Saaremaa (Estonia), which provide the same high standard of accommodation as those on the Scandinavian mainland.

The islands are memorable for their delightful scenery and fine bathing beaches. Except for Öland, which is connected to the Swedish mainland by a four and a half mile bridge across the sea, a holiday on the islands involves a ferry trip through one or more of the beautiful Baltic archipelagoes – a delight in itself...

More details from **www.visitdenmark.com**

Denmark

Island of Fyn
Hindemae Mill

This is a lovely introduction to Denmark.

We meet people who are intrigued by Denmark but never quite manage to get in a visit. Well, we can't think of a better introduction to the country than this. We stayed in the summer of 2007, and loved it: it's strongly recommended. On the island of Fyn, the converted 200 year old mill, with an attached miller's cottage, provides comfortable and centrally heated accommodation for **up to 12 people** in six bedrooms, with three bathrooms. We liked the new dining room/kitchen. There's a washing machine and dryer. There is a cosy sitting-room off the dining/kitchen and a huge octagonal family room with squishy sofas and open fire. This room covers the entire ground floor area of the old mill. There's a games room. satellite TV, video games and small office with internet access. There is large garden surrounded by beechwoods, with lovely country walks. Two adult bikes are provided. Fyn has many sandy beaches, the nearest about five miles away. Access: via Copenhagen (90 minutes by motorway and road bridge) and Esbjerg (ferry from Harwich) also 90 minutes via motorway. By air from Stansted to Esbjerg. Cost: about £600-£1600 per week. Contact Victoria Sutherland: telephone 01855 811207. Fax 811338.

email victoria@torrenglencoe.com

Vence (Alpes Maritimes)
Villa Paradise

Recently constructed Villa Paradis (**sleeping 8**) has all the advantages of
new fittings, uncluttered space and yet still with charm and character
from the unusual furnishings, some from Morocco and many of them
hand-cast pieces of unique wrought-iron. The bathrooms and showers
are all tiled with hand-made tiles, and the wardrobe doors are North
African hardwood, specially imported.

The house is on the outskirts of Vence, where there is a medieval walled
'cité', and, close by, other perched medieval villages such as St Paul de
Vence and Tourrettes sur Loup. Sightseeing in the area reveals spectacular views along the Gorge du Loup. Within easy access to Nice, Cannes
and the whole of the Côte d'Azur, the villa provides comfortable living,
peaceful surroundings, unrestricted views and good accessibility.

Largely open plan on the main living area, there is a spacious salon with
full width patio windows opening on to the pool terrace. French satellite
TV, CD and DVD. New kitchen with maplewood and stainless steel fit-
ments. On the same level are two bedrooms, one twin with shower
room/WC en suite and a master double with views to the swimming
pool. The first floor has two further bedrooms.

email: azuruk@boltblue.com

Vence/Grasse (Alpes Maritimes)
Villa La Salamandre

This villa (**sleeping 5 to 6**) is situated just outside Vence and ten minutes from St. Paul de Vence, with its famous restaurants, *jeu-de-boules*
court and art galleries. It has a splendid view over the hills towards the
mountains. The villa lies in a calm residential area and has its own private grounds with automatic gates and large private pool. The garden is
immaculately maintained, and has a most beautiful rose garden.

The villa itself is on two levels. The main entrance door gives access to
a hall with access via French doors to the living room on one side and
the hall to the bedrooms on the other side. The living room has a sitting
area with comfortable sofas and chairs around an open fire place with a
TV with satellite and music system. On the other side is a large wooden
dining table that seats six people with access to the covered veranda and
garden. The kitchen is exceptionally well equipped.

On the same floor there are two bedrooms, each with a double bed.
They share a bathroom There is also a study that can be made in another
bedroom with single bed. On the upper floor there is another bedroom
with a large comfortable single bed and nice views over the garden.

email: azuruk@boltblue.com

Hérault
Magalas

A fast, easy drive from Montpellier airport (80 km, much of it via motorway) brought us early on an October evening to the – for us! – unexpectedly ancient and absolutely charming hilltop village of Magalas. The origin of the name in the old local dialect is said to mean 'a pile of old stones'. But don't let that put you off: it's a delight, full of narrow, spiralling alleyways with sudden views of distant wooded hills and vineyards. It's especially deserted, silent and full of atmosphere after dark, with cats in the shadows and, if you're lucky, shafts of moonlight illuminating the half-hidden courtyards of 500-year old houses.

We knew our villa was in a small, new, residential development, but had assumed it was some way out of Magalas. In fact, it's just a very pleasant five minute walk from the house up towards the market square, close to which there are restaurants, bars, small shops, two bakers and a pâtisserie.

Though it's essentially 'practical' and designed for easy living and maintenance, it has certain very appealing features. For example, we

Easy, uncomplicated modern living on the edge of a fascinating ancient village...

...with a really inviting sitting room that at any time is 'so nice to come home to'.

liked the good sized sunken sitting room, more than adequate for the eight people the house sleeps. The October weather was very mild, but we eyed the (safely enclosed) fireplace with satisfaction, remembering the pleasures of other houses in rural France and the scent and instant heat from stores of olive wood: get it when you can. We also liked the first floor twin room (extra privacy, and an ensuite shower to boot), a bath and shower in the main bathroom, boules court at the rear, the swimming pool, by all accounts a serious sun-trap in summer. There's a spacious paved terrace with an awning. There's good touring from Magalas to, for example, the coast at Sète and Mèze, to the attractive town of Pezenas and the lower reaches of the Massif Central.

Cost: approximately £180 to £950. Further details from Tim and Jo Gray, Kembroke Hall, Bucklesham, near Ipswich, Suffolk IP10 0BU. Telephone 01394 448309.

email: tdgray@msn.com

Nérac
Moncaut

We stayed here recently, and were delighted by it. It's a 'Maison de Maître', which sits well back from a moderately busy road and is in fact hardly disturbed by traffic. It's a real family house, which is used from time to time by the owners themselves. and therefore functions properly! There's plenty of heating,

A fine, spacious, comfortable house of character, with an excellent pool and very well tended gardens.

instant hot water (two actual baths), a well equipped kitchen, a big out-door pool – with shade – kept in tip-top condition by the efficient care-taker. He also looks after the six acres of grounds, within which there are separate sitting-out areas: we loved our *al fresco* meals on the shaded paved terrace outside the kitchen. The main, first floor bedrooms are spacious, even elegant. And the hall and the staircase are a joy. **Sleeps 10**. Ref DL22.

Though the surrounding scenery is not dramatic, it's pleasant, and we were deeply impressed by the virtually traffic-free minor roads. The country town of Nérac, fifteen minutes away by car, is a charmer, with lots of cafes and restaurants, plus boat trips and a preserved-railway jaunt. Details from Dominique's Villas: Page 249.

Dinan (Brittany)
Moulin de Lorgeril

A reader from Suffolk who joined a family party staying in this 'really comfortable, really romantic' con-verted mill thinks 'cottage guide' readers will love it. The surround-ings are peaceful – mainly wood-land, fields and lakes. The main part of the house has a large sitting room cum diner with a stone fireplace and french windows, two bedrooms, a

Loads of character, and easily accessible from the UK while still 'very French'...

well equipped kitchen and separate stairs from the kitchen to that boon in wet weather – a games room. But the real attraction is the tower. On three levels, it has a sitting room with woodburner and french windows and stairs that lead to a double bedroom. From that there are further stairs to a fourth double bedroom with a sunken bath.

Cost: about £600 to £800. Details from Mrs P Lintern:

Telephone/fax 01749 342760.

Dordogne
Souillac Country Club

Readers quickly caught on to this much-admired enclave of properties, which we have featured for the last three years. Nestling in the hilly forests of the picturesque Dordogne valley, near the river/town of Souillac, this young-family-orientated club is a favourite all-year-round holiday destination for British and French alike. We know it well, and have found the staff, both English and French, most welcoming, with good suggestions of what to do and see in the region.

The scenery in this part of France is breathtaking, with deep gorges and castles perched on cliff-tops. It's most impressive in October, when mists rise up from the deep river valleys and the trees take on a multitude of colours. This is the land of foie gras and truffles, of honey and umpteen varieties of bread and mushrooms: British first-time visitors to the weekly market in nearby Sarlat are amazed by the local produce.

The detached houses (all privately owned and managed by the club when the individual owners are not in residence) have views of the eighteen-hole golf course and surrounding countryside. They are all spacious and fully equipped, with large patios, where in peaceful surroundings we enjoyed watching the sunset over a glass of wine.

The houses are in small well separated hamlets, with private swimming pools, and residents can also use the many central amenities, including two swimming pools, tennis, boules, golf, and in July and August the children can join in the fun at the Kids' Club. The excellent restaurant provides a welcome change from cooking at home, and the bar is a friendly meeting place after a game of golf or tennis. The whole region

The detached houses have views of the golf course and the surrounding country.

In a peaceful situation, 'they are all spacious and fully equipped'...

is a popular holiday destination. Apart from that beautiful scenery, medieval market towns and the numerous restaurants for which Périgord is famous, there's extra-good walking and horse-riding.

More information is available on 00 33 (0) 565 27 5600.

www.souillaccountryclub.com
email:rentals@souillac-countryclub.com

France – countrywide
Large Holiday Houses in France*

Much valued both by visitors to France and people in the industry, and from the same stable as the hugely successful *Large Holiday Houses in Scotland* (see Page 100), this is an impressive collection of chateaux, villas and farmhouses. It's an organisation larger groups should definitely check out.

For example, the medieval village of Vouvent, recently voted the most beautiful in France, is only about seven miles from *Les Tilleuls*, a lovely family home in the Vendée. Only an hour's drive from Poitiers (home of Futuroscope) and the coast, the setting is perfect for a secluded holiday.

Among its many charms this lovely family home stands in a private two-acre garden. The 14m x 6.5 metre heated pool is surrounded by a

Les Tilleuls: quiet and secluded, in a lovely area, with a super floodlit pool.

Inside, it's spacious but comfortable, with the makings of a fine family holiday.

large patio area with mature palm trees. The pool is floodlit at night, making it an idyllic location for alfresco dining. **Sleeps 13 'plus 8'.**

In the ever-popular Dordogne, *La Colombière* (**sleeping 15**) is well suited for family holidays, reunions, conferences, weddings, parties, in a beautiful, vine growing area. A big swimming pool is set off by a newly constructed sun terrace. The small poolside summer kitchen provides a variety of light regreshments and drinks (at a small cost) as well as an area to prepare snacks and salads should lunch by the pool be the order of the day. There's lots for children to do, along with a small football pitch, volley ball net, croquet on the front lawns plus a selection of bikes for hire for exploring the surrounding area.

There are also two other gites available to rent:

For more of these, plus some simpler properties, visit the website:

www.LHHFrance.com

email: LHH@LHHFrance.com

Telephone 01381 610496

[All properties are inspected by, and carry the seal of approval of, Large Holiday Houses Ltd, but are booked direct with the owners.]

France – countrywide
The France Directory*

Full of beguiling photographs, Welcome's French brochure comes with a set of eight peel-off labels to stick on properties that attract your interest. Neat! Appropriately, each has 'Perfect' and a tick on it, but we soon found we needed many more than eight as so much appealed.

Altogether there are over 1000 cottages, gites and villas, all helpfully grouped into the country's different regions. Many can be booked for weekend breaks and 10 or 11-night holidays as well as the traditional week or fortnight. Monday or Thursday starts are often available too.

Handy for Calais (12 miles), so ideal for those who prefer not to have a long drive after stepping on to French soil, a charming two-bedroom single-storey cottage (**sleeping 4**) with a central open fire lies in a peaceful country lane in the little village of Landrethun les Ardres. The nearby coast has sandy beaches, cliffs and interesting resorts such as Hardelot and Le Touquet. Ref W12368.

In the Vendée, always a favourite area of ours because of its excellent sunshine record and endless sandy beaches, a stone cottage (sleeping 4) tastefully created from a 16th-century barn is available at Le Tablier, near La Roche-sur-Yon. The lounge opens on to an attractive enclosed garden and the large decorative stone open fire, bread oven and beams ensure a homely feeling. The attractive resort of Les Sables d'Olonne is about 25 miles away. Ref W9161.

Some impressive, sensibly priced properties, a skilful geographical spread.

Included in the portfolio are places we'll see for ourselves during 2009.

In the heart of Biarritz, a traditional Basque villa is well placed for those who like to combine a beach holiday with the attractions of a lively resort. **Sleeping 8**, it has four en-suite bedrooms, a large lounge and kitchen/dining area. Ref W11305. In the south-east corner of France, a delightfully situated villa (**sleeping 5/6**) is tucked away at Montseret, near the beautiful village of Lagrasse. The villa has its own pool and the Mediterranean beaches are only 18 miles away. Ref W12534.

Welcome Holiday Cottages in France, Spring Mill, Earby, Barnoldswick, Lancashire BB94. 0AA. Telephone 0870 242 3856.

www.welcome-france.co.uk

France – countrywide
'Chez Nous'

Celebrating its Silver Jubilee this year, Chez Nous covers everything from chateaux to mobile homes, all privately-owned. Its 400-page brochure invites you to 'Live the real France – languid late breakfasts of *pain au chocolat* and *café au lait*; watching the old guys play boules in the square whilst sipping a glass of local vin rouge'.

The brochure is divided into seventeen geographical sections, each beginning with an enticing description of the region and year-round temperature chart. Also there is a very useful map on every second page showing the relevant area. And the company's website has extra photos of most properties.

Altogether Chez Nous has over 7000 on its books. A telephone call or email to the English-speaking owner enables you to find out everything you want to know about it and the surrounding area, so you quickly get a real feel of the place. Then having booked your accommodation, the Chez Nous travel service can arrange your journey.

One of our favourite parts of France is the Atlantic coast north of Biarritz. It gives you the choice of rolling waves pounding on the endless sandy sea beaches or the calmer waters of large inland lakes, also with sandy beaches. In the attractive little town of Hossegor, an attractive trio of modern beach apartments (**sleeping 2, 4 or 6**) with use of a pool is available beside the sea. Feasting on the fresh fish sold on the

La Boursaie, Calvados, offers restored cider farm cottages in 100 acres of woodland, meadows and orchards. Ref 4485.

Close to Biarritz and sandy beaches, this modern villa with its own pool is in Hossegor and sleeps 12. Ref 11850.

quayside in the picturesque little port of Cap Breton nearby is one of our many happy memories of holidays there. Ref 9634.

In the Vendée, another area we particularly like, a spacious modern detached house with pool and large garden leading to a lake is tucked away in a quiet hamlet near St Vincent sur Graon, about 11 miles south of La Roche-sur-Yon and a similar distance from sandy beaches. It **sleeps 10/12**, including two in a basement annexe which has its own kitchenette and games area with snooker, table-tennis and darts. So the property is ideal for three generations holidaying together and as it has its own swimming pool, should keep all ages entertained. Ref 13976.

In the Hautes-Pyrenées at the elegant little spa town of Bagneres de Bigorre, a characterful 18th-century farmhouse **sleeping 10** has five large bedrooms (two king-size and three twins) and a heated swimming pool. Pony-trekking, white-water rafting, canoeing, fishing, mountain-biking, birdwatching and golf are among local activities. Ref 15370.

Within an hour's drive of the Channel Tunnel and ferries at Calais is a pretty south-facing six-bedroom country house (**sleeping 11**) at Doudeauville with a wealth of exposed beams. It overlooks a garden with a stream, one of the sources of the River Course. An unspoilt beach is half-an-hour away and Crecy, Agincourt and Le Touquet only a little further. Ref 12161.

A large private south-facing terrace with stunning views of the Mediterranean, harbour and mountains is one of the delights of a luxurious modern first-floor air-conditioned apartment in the fishing port of Port Vendre, a few miles north of the border with Spain. Only five minutes walk from the beach, it **sleeps 4**. Just a mile north beyond a headland, another charming port, Collioure, has been a magnet for artists since Matisse settled there in 1905; it's also renowned for its anchovies - and we're talking about fresh ones! Ref 10307.

The Chez Nous range also extends to Corsica where we have enjoyed several very happy holidays. Still largely untouched by mass tourism despite its many sandy beaches, the island has some superb scenery and you can take a breathtaking train ride through the mountains.

Among several interesting properties there, *A Pinarella* is a massively-

Fabulously placed on the French Riviera, this villa sleeps 8, and has terrace, pool, and panoramic sea views. Ref 11182.

A Pinarella at Monticello, on Corsica, has breathtaking coastal views to Cap Corse, big grounds and pool. Ref 15505.

beamed stone house at Monticello, about 15 miles up the coast from Calvi in the north-west part of the island. **Sleeping 10**, it enjoys magnificent sea and mountain views, and the grounds include a pool, covered terraces for outdoor living and over an acre of walled garden with oak, pine, citrus, olive, aromatic shrubs and sculptural boulders. There's a village shop within ten minutes' walk, and the sea is under three miles away. Ref 15505.

For a free copy of the Chez Nous directory, telephone 0870 242 3813; or go to **www.cheznous.com**

email: enquiries@cheznous.co.uk

France
Quality Villas

This is a really impressive French specialist. Now in its 22nd year, Quality Villas describes itself as 'large enough to offer an unrivalled selection of villas throughout France and small enough to give you that personal service larger companies cannot match'. Their portfolio of luxury villas, farmhouses and chateaux have all been hand picked and personally inspected.

The lavishly-illustrated brochure is a joy. Page after page is filled with colourful photos and detailed descriptions of truly lovely properties, including many suitable for families or groups of a dozen or more. Moreover, the reservations team know each one personally so can advise about it and nearby towns and villages.

For example, holidaymakers who prefer not to have a long journey after

Maison Pastorale is a fabulous house in Lot et Garonne (Ref PR651). It sleeps 8/9.

It's real, and you can stay here! It's the Château de la Rivière, in the Dordogne.

crossing the Channel, a château and farmhouse at St Maclou-la-Campagne can be booked separately or together. *Château de la Haye* **sleeps 12/14** (including 2/3 in a former carriage house), having been completely renovated to combine classic features with modern furnishings. *Ferme de la Haye* (**sleeping 10**), in the same grounds, has been totally rebuilt, retaining only the original wooden frame.

Because of the château's historic importance, the grounds are open to the public on Saturdays. Here you're well placed for visiting the D-Day landing beaches, the Bayeux tapestry and Monet's house and garden at Giverny. Ref 543/8.

An infinity pool with lovely views from its sun-terrace is one of the delights of *La Vieille Ferme*, an old French farmhouse (**sleeping 6**) near the village of Saussignac, nine miles from Bergerac, in the Dordogne. Lovingly converted, it has beamed ceilings, stone walls, terracotta floor tiles and antique furniture, paintings and tapestries. Ref PR541.

In Provence, *Domaine des Anges*, near Uzes, is a luxury property (**sleeping 18**) arranged around a wonderful garden courtyard amid vineyards and fields of wheat and sunflowers. It was built in 1840 but has been renovated bydecorated in a traditional but comfortable style. Ref PR557.

A reader of *The Good Holiday Cottage Guide* was inspired by a description in a previous edition of *La Californie* (Ref PR293), on the Côte d'Azur. It seems she persuaded friends to make the booking, and joined them for a few days. She described fabulous views over Cannes, and exceptional gardens. **Sleeps 10.**

Lovers of Art Deco are entranced by *Villa Mont St Clair*, in Sète, on the Languedoc coast, which **sleeps 6/7**. A spacious villa with green tiled roof, it has marble floors, Italian style ceilings and a grand staircase. The indoor heated pool and garden overlook the sea. Ref PR620.

At the southern end of the same coast, the long-established resort of Biarritz is famous for its beaches, fine shops, casino, aquarium and sea museum. *Brise Marine* is a traditional Basque villa **sleeping 4/5** on the cliffside at Bidart, five miles south, close to the Spanish border. Each room enjoys a magnificent sea view and there is a large deck above the small terraced garden which has direct access to the sandy beach below. The area is a golf and surfer's paradise. Also available are wind-surfing,

Villa Paradou, with 17th century origins, is near Arles, and sleeps six.

Villa Elegant, near Monte Carlo, is amazing even in Quality Villas terms.

kite-surfing, hang-gliding, horse riding, mountain biking and hiking, or you can simply pamper yourself in one of the numerous thalassotherapy centres. Ref PR569.

Among recommendations that have come our way, we're very keen to see the beautifully named *Chanson de la Mer*, **sleeping 8**, a luxurious villa with sea views. Right on the dramatic scenic coastline between Nice and Monaco, this modern property is 'very special'. *Each room has magnificent south facing sea views*. Terraces on each of the three levels make full use of the stunning views. There's a relaxing ambience: what better place to sit and unwind with a glass of wine! Energetic may enjoy the gym equipment and sauna.

Note: it is usually possible for properties to offer maid service, a cook, a chauffeur and handle requests such as helicopter/yacht hire, hampers, massages, tennis lessons and more. Further details and a copy of that superb brochure from Quality Villas, 46 Lower Kings Road, Berkhamsted, Hertfordshire HP4 2AA. Telephone 01442 870 055.

www.quality-villas.com

Note: Quality Villas also has properties throughout Italy and Morocco:

www.qualityvillasitaly.com and www.quality-villas-morocco.co.uk.

Haut-Jura
Les Rousses Farmhouse Apartment

Roger Jones's Welsh properties (see Pages 164-166) have featured in this guide for many years, and he has brought the same energy and concern for his guests' comfort to his properties in mainland France and in Corsica – see below. Les Rousses, very close to the Swiss border, is compact but comfortable, at one end of a farmhouse now divided into five apartments. Charmingly, there is access via a wooden staircase to a garden area,

We see some fabulous locations in this job, but this really is something. And it's pretty nice in summer too!

and there are uninterrupted panoramic views across a wide valley to Les Rousses Lake, in a location known for its Alpine wild flowers. There's lots to do, including walking nature trails into Switzerland, golf (two 18-hole courses within sight of the apartment), exceptional ski-ing, fishing and sailing on the lake. And Les Rousses itself has restaurants, bars and shops. **Sleeps up to 4** in a double and a twin. Linen/towels not provided. TV/video. Bathroom with shower only. Cost: from about £195. Accessible by train and taxi, or about eight hours' drive from Calais. Details from Roger Jones, Flat B, The Old Granary, Tremadog, Gwynedd LL49 9RH. Telephone (01766) 513555.

Corsica
Calvi – La Reginella

If a picture's worth a thousand words, we can relax for a moment: the view on the right is what you see from the balcony of this town centre apartment, which is on the third (top) floor of a building overlooking the bay and mountains beyond. Calvi is a chic place, with shops, restaurants and boutiques in

Just add a glass of local wine, sit back and relax: this is the view from the balcony.

walking distance of the apartment. Most appealingly, you can pick up a train here on a narrow-gauge railway that links coastal villages and beaches, with connections to Ajaccio, in the south, and you are just ten minutes' walk from the ferry point from where there are connections to Marseilles, Nice, Toulon and the Italian sea-ports.

Specifically, the apartment **sleeps 4** in a double and a twin, with a combined sitting room/diner and a balcony with a table and chairs, and those marvellous views. TV/video. Bathroom with bath and shower. Very well equipped kitchen: oven, microwave, fridge, freezer, washing machine, dishwasher. Cost: from about £195. Further details from Roger Jones, Flat B, The Old Granary, Tremadog, Gwynedd LL49 9RH. Telephone (01766) 513555.

France – countrywide
Dominique's Villas

Dominique's Villas is a medium-sized agency created 20 years ago by Dominique Wells. The agency is notable for its stylish and beautifully illustrated brochure that's highly professional but also has some charming personal touches. Its great strengths in the Dordogne, Provence and the Côte d'Azur – so much loved by Brits – help towards its popularity.

During a 2004 visit to a number of houses in the Lot et Garonne region, we were much taken with two that are somewhat different in character and location. First, we saw an isolated, utterly quiet, rambling, many roomed and beautifully restored house being spruced up, as it happened, for the owners due down for their own holiday. Gorgeous! **Sleeps 10.** Ref DL72. Then, in a busier location, in an extraordinary situation beside an ancient bridge and a dramatic weir, we visited an exceptional property that use to be a well known rural restaurant and hotel (there's a huge 'professional' kitchen'). **Sleeps – yes – 13.** Ref DL34.

We also stayed in a handsome traditional house (that is, not a conversion) **sleeping 10**. See Page 240.

During a 2004 visit we were much taken with 'Property No DL72', near Nérac.

Open the wine and get the cook-books out! This is the kitchen in 'Property No NR21'.

We remember a house in a hamlet on a hill that overlooks the Lot Valley – a comparatively little-known part of the country. There's a pleasant pool and 'country' furniture, along with antiques. Ref DL60. **Sleeps 6**. Just across the Channel, within easy reach of the ferry ports at Caen and Le Havre, we came across a gem. It's a beautifully renovated 18th-century farmhouse (**sleeping 9/10**) with idyllic views. Sandy beaches at Deauville and Trouville are within fifteen minutes' drive. Ref NR21. And, handy for the Cherbourg ferries, there's an enchanting 17th-century chateau (**sleeping 15**) in the village of Yvetôt-Bocage, just outside Valognes. It's perfect for children, as the grounds include a child-size manor house, a games room, swings and sandpit. A heated pool is a recent addition. Ref NR18.

Details/brochure from Dominique's Villas, The Plough Brewery, 516 Wandsworth Road. London SW8 3JX. Telephone 020 7738 8772.

www.dominiquesvillasco.uk

France Countrywide
French Country Cottages*

Over the past thirty years French Country Cottages has built up a truly remarkable choice of places to stay. From Brittany to the Languedoc, from Alsace to the Côte d'Azur, it has over 1200 cottages, villas and farmhouses, each selected for its own special character and charm.

In a remarkable brochure that bursts with colour, each property gets a detailed write-up and is illustrated with uniformly excellent photos. Plenty of local information highlighting nearby beaches, towns and attractions is included too. Also, the brochure is helpfully split into thirteen colour-coded regional sections, each prefaced with a short description of the area and its highlights.

For couples an attractive new offer has been introduced this year at many properties. When just two people are staying before 31 May or after 1 September, a discount of 20% kicks in.

Anyone who enjoys staying in a building of real character would be as enchanted as we were with *Les Manis,* near Vimoutiers, in Normandy, handily located just 25 miles south-east of the ferry port of Caen. This beautifully restored half-timbered three-storey house (**sleeping 6**) has exposed beams and stonework throughout. Step into the garden and you are met by extensive grounds with a heated pool and glorious views over the surrounding Pays d'Aude. For days out, Bayeux with its famous tapestry and museums and the D-day beaches provide plenty to interest for all ages. **Sleeps 6**. Ref F61114.

Le Pressoir is a most interesting conversion in the 'private and silent' grounds of a chateau. Surrounding the property itself are well kept lawns, a dovecote and a lake...

Down in the south-west corner of France, we've had a couple of delightful holidays in the little fishing port/resort of Capbreton, 15 miles north of Biarritz, where *Villa le Havre* is a traditional-furnished Basquaise house (**sleeping 6**) standing in a large shady garden. A lovely sandy beach is close by, and all sorts of watersports are available on the calmer waters of the large lake at Hossegor (3 miles). We have played golf and tennis, and visited the casino at Biarritz. Ref F40104.

On the outskirts of Chamonix, in the Alps, *Chalet Galicia Les Lacs* (**sleeping 8/10**) overlooks Lake Gailland and has wonderful views of Mont Blanc. The main bedroom has a king-size bed and balcony. A lawned garden at the back is equipped with sun loungers and a barbecue. For a memorable trip, you can catch a train just across the road on the railway that runs through the Chamonix valley, often on hair-raisingly narrow ledges, or take the rack railway to Europe's biggest glacier. Ref F74132.

For real luxury, nothing beats a really top-class property on the French Riviera. *Soleil du Midi* (**sleeping 6**) is a beautiful three-storey villa built in the 19th century, very close to Monte Carlo and ten miles from Nice. It nestles on a hillside in the Basse Corniche, facing the Mediterranean and the delightful village and bay of Roquebrune Cap Martin. Decorated and furnished to a very high standard, with marble or parquet floors throughout, the rooms are bright and airy and all have sweeping views of the sea. Each of the three bedrooms has its own bathroom. Outside there is a pretty terrace and swimming pool. Ref F06236.

In the Loire, eight miles from *Le Mans*, St Paul (**sleeping 15/17**) is an elegant chateau with landscaped grounds that include a lake, tennis court and swimming pool. Marble fireplaces, polished wood floors, a living room with two pianos and plenty of bathrooms add to its appeal, especially for large family groups. For a day out, Le Mans has a superb cathedral, medieval streets, a car museum and excellent shops. Ref F72109.

Just east of the Vendée, a region where we have enjoyed several sun-blessed holidays, you can stay in the Chateau de Puy Chenin (**sleeping 12/14**), 13 miles north of Niort, a lovely12th-century building surrounded by moats and lovely gardens with ponds. Indoors there are huge original stone fireplaces, antique wooden floors and old beams. One of the six bedrooms has a 4-poster. For swimming, there is a pool or nearby lakes with beaches. Ref F79135. *Le Pressoir*, a beautifully converted cider mill in the grounds of a private chateau, 15 miles east of Abbeville, is in the lush countryside of Picardy. It still has its original ancient wooden beams, now set off by tasteful decor and modern home comforts. The chateau's tranquil grounds feature well-tended lawns, a lake and stone dovecote. **Sleeps 4**. Ref F 80103.

Chinon is a first-floor apartment in what was a 15th century ecclesiastical enclave.

Les Manis stands in extensive grounds with breathtaking views over countryside.

At the other end of the size scale, *Le Bastit* is an elegant house (**sleeping 20**) in the small village of St Medard, deep in the Dordogne, about 17 miles north of Bergerac. Nicely furnished, it has ten en-suite bedrooms (5 double, 5 twin), two living rooms and a dining-room which is big enough to seat everyone – with a cook available if required. It stands in a lovely garden with mature trees and large swimming pool (shared with another property). Ref 24181.

For a copy of an impressive brochure or to make a booking, telephone 0845 604 3998. French Country Cottages, Spring Mill, Earby, Barnoldswick BB94 0AA.

www.french-country-cottages.co.uk

Tuscany
Tuscan Holidays

This hugely successful agency (a number of our readers go back to book with them year after year) is run by the people behind 'Heart of the Lakes/Cottage Life'. That much-admired Cumbrian organisation has featured in every edition of *The Good Holiday Cottage Guide* since it first appeared in 1983.

'Tuscan Holidays' has been operating for over 20 years, and offers over 100 villas and apartments in prime locations within a region of out-standing beauty that is also a treasure-trove of history and culture. A good number are either in or on the fringes of Chianti, perhaps the region's most beautiful area. The landscape is magnificent, with its rolling vineyards, olive groves and medieval hilltop villages. Some

There are two apartments in the beautiful Casa Leopoldo, 20 miles from Pisa.

Part of La Sughera: a very flexible arrangement of apartments, a super pool.

readers like to stay put, especially when it's hot, but most include trips to the ancient cities of Florence, Pisa, Lucca, San Gimignano and Siena in their holiday.

Among places readers have enthused about are a beautiful 18th century manor house called *Palazzo Rosadi* (Ref 490). **Sleeping up to 12**, it has fabulous panoramic views and a super swimming pool. The owner also offers a guided wine tour, and a chef can be hired to provide exceptional Tuscan cuisine. *La Villetta* (Ref 270), **sleeping up to 6**, also comes highly recommended. Near Castelfiorentino, it sits in a beautiful, peace-ful location, with views to the Apennine Hills.

Cottage-guide readers based in Suffolk had wanted to be away from it all: 'somewhere unpretentious and, especially, quiet\. They were charmed by *Casa Leopoldo* (Ref 150), **sleeping 2**, with its lovely big fireplace and spacious interior, and only 20 miles from Pisa.

Just 2.5 miles away from the delightful small town of Montespertoli, and 22 miles from Florence, *Il Mandorlo* (Ref 310) is a very good quality detached and restored barn. It is a beautifully furnished property amid stunning landscape, with great views from the property and a delightful pool, **sleeping 6 'plus 2'**.

For a larger group, *Podere San Giovanni* (Ref 230) is a spacious detached property about 25 miles from Pisa and 30 miles from beaches.

As well as being the most delightful place in which to relax, San Giovanni is well placed for visits to all the main 'must-sees' in Tuscany. Amazing views and a large swimming pool for barbecue parties guarantees a good time! **It sleeps up to 12,**

Another delightful property **for 2**, and rather romantic to boot, is *Casa Maria Luisa* (Ref 410) in the wonderful location of Chianti, which is about 19 miles – a pleasant drive – from San Gimignano. Built of mellow stone, this cottage is part of a beautiful old farmhouse. There is a conservatory-style sitting room which leads into the main sitting/dining room and kitchen with a lovely Tuscan fireplace. The bedroom overlooks the lovely private garden where you can enjoy a glass of wine at the end of the evening in the warm summer nights.

A very good property in central Tuscany is *La Sughera* (Ref 90-94). Two carefully restored farmhouses set in a wine and olive oil producing

We've stayed at cosy Casa Fabia, and loved the absolute peace and quiet.

La Murelle is on the outskirts of the most attractive small town of Palaia.

estate are within driving distance of Pisa, Florence, Siena and the old towns of San Gimignano and Volterra. The five apartments **sleep from 2 to 8** and have beamed ceilings, terracotta floors, open fires and central heating. The swimming pool, pizza oven and barbecue will make for the perfect holiday.

A tucked nicely tucked-away but not remote property where we ourselves have stayed is *Casa Fabia*, amid good walking country and handy for the small town of Palaia. **Sleeping 4**, it's quiet and cosy, on a 20-acre farm with vineyards and olive groves.

Tuscan Holidays are able to advise on the most suitable property for your needs, as they have visited each property, liaise daily with their representatives in Tuscany and are on personal terms with the property owners.

Their representatives in Tuscany are on hand throughout your stay if needed and many of the helpful and informative property owners are delighted to offer advice on what's available in the local area to make your holiday even more special.

Telephone.015394 31120,

www.tuscanholidays.co.uk info@tuscanholidays.co.uk

Fisherbeck Mill, Lake Road, Ambleside, Cumbria LA22 0DH.

Italy, France, Spain and Croatia:
Interhome 'Selection'

For its 'Selection' brochure, Interhome's local experts have searched through the most beautiful regions of Italy, France, Spain and Croatia to locate romantic country houses, sumptuous villas, authentic farmhouses and regal residences and castles. But the brochure is only a taster, as there's an even wider selection online, on the easy-to-use Interhome website.

The properties are rated with 3 to 5 stars as a guide to their features, and each has an on-the-spot keyholder to attend to your every need, such as booking a personal chef. With 43 years' experience in dealing with holiday homes, Interhome can be depended on for reliability and service.

La Granadella is a very special property indeed. Better yet, it sleeps up to twelve.

Les Clémentines is just about an hour's drive from St Tropez. It sleeps eight.

In Spain, on the popular Costa Blanca at Javea, *La Granadella* (**sleeping 12**) is a fabulous house spread over several floors, with panoramic views. On a steep slope, it has a large open-air dining area, sun terrace, pool and even a waterfall. Two of the six double bedrooms are in a separate guest house just a few steps from the main building. Ref ES 9710.155.1.

Air-conditioning is one of the features of *Villa Carlina*, a comfortable two-storey white stone house (**sleeping 8**) in north-west Croatia. Though built as recently as 2006, it has plenty of character thanks to rustic style furnishings and exposed beams. There are peaceful views of hills and the sea and the garden includes a swimming pool. Ref HR2453.501.1.

About 35 miles north of St Tropez, in the south of France, *Les Clémentines* is a super modern detached house **sleeping 8**. Three of the four bedrooms have the advantage of opening on to the terrace and a garden with pool. A sandy beach is 18 miles away and golf within eight miles. Ref FR8493.140.1.

Deep in Umbria, one of our favourite parts of Italy, lies Bettona – mid-way between Rome and Florence. The 5-star *Villa Paolotti* (**sleeping 12**) was built about 150 years ago. Renovated in 2003, it has frescoes and period features as well as modern facilities and a pool. Ref IT5516.820.1.

More information, and the Selections brochure, are available from Interhome Ltd, Gemini House, 10-18 Putney Hill, London SW15 6AX. Telephone 020 8780 6633.
www.interhome.co.uk   *Castello la Rocca:* Ref IT5293.820.1

Tuscany: Casentino
Canova

This spacious farmhouse, recommended by a previous printer of this book, is close to the pretty town of Casentino. In spacious grounds among peaceful wooded and olive tree clad hillsides, and with its own secluded swimming pool, it **sleeps up to 12** – either as a whole or via two separate apartments **sleeping 4 and 8** people respectively. Specifically, there are two separate living rooms, six bedrooms and two bathrooms.

Though very pretty, this part of Tuscany, remarkable for its mountain scenery, is comparatively little known. But there is easy access to all the Tuscan 'favourites' such as Florence and Siena.

Details from Rebecca Rawlings. Telephone 020-7482 1663.

email: rebeccarawlings@hotmail.com

Tuscany/Umbria
Vintage Travel

Vintage Travel's Italian portfolio is concentrated in two popular regions, with access too to some famous places.

In Tuscany and Umbria there are about a dozen properties. In the former, Vintage Travel have taken the extraordinary medieval hilltop town of San Gimignano as their focal point. In the latter, most properties are within easy access of Perugia. We know these parts of Italy quite well, and 'Vintage' have the essence of them: almost without exception each property fits prettily into its surroundings, and panoramic views from the properties themselves are quite common.

As noted on other pages, the company's quite outstandingly good brochure is more like a coffee table book than a conventional brochure: quite inspiring. Though there is one modern house (25km from Perugia) that **can sleep up to 22**, most properties tend to be rustic and family-sized rather than palatial. Several have swimming pools – but this is the sort of villa/cottage collection in which the pool serves the property rather than the other way round. Altogether, very impressive.

Further details and a superb are brochure available from Vintage Spain Ltd, Milkmaid House, Willingham, Cambridge CB4 5JB. Telephone 01954 261431. Fax 260819.

www.vintagetravel.co.uk
email: holidays@vintagetravel.co.uk

Tuscany: Versilia
Il Castoro

Readers have recommended this, a rare chance for people who want to be in Tuscany to have a base by the sea. *Il Castoro* is situated on a small development just outside the village of Torre-del-Lago. It is one of the most appealing seaside resorts along the coast of Versilia – not a sleepy hideaway, but a lively resort likely to appeal most to youngish people. And if the occasionally frenetic atmosphere gets you down you can always escape into the hills or take a trip to easily accessible Florence, Lucca, San Gimignano and Siena.

The house **sleeps up to 7** in three double bedrooms and there is shared access for all residents on this complex to a swimming pool and tennis courts. (Music lovers should note that Torre-del-Lago is the place where Puccini wrote all his operas, which are performed every summer in an open air theatre.)

Cost: £350 to £700. Details from Mr N Castoro. Telephone 07979 528955. For a brochure: fax 020 8458 1394.

Tuscany: Posara
Watermill

Five separate apartments in a very sympathetic conversion of this old mill.

Somewhat off the beaten track, only just outside the walled medieval town of Fivizzano in the district of Lunigiana, this privately owned watermill (it really is picture postcard stuff) stands beside the River Rosaro, in the small village of Posara. It's almost too good to be true: in a peaceful wooded valley with a background of rolling hills and mountain peaks, it has the big advantage of being within easy access of the sea – don't forget that inland Tuscany can get very hot in high summer – and the principal tourist attractions of this much loved region.

Specifically there are five self-contained apartments within the mill and it's possible to rent more than one at a time, so a group of **up to 16** can take the whole place.

There are secluded gardens extending for about a quarter of a mile beyond the millstream and around the mill there are grapes and vegetables for the use of guests. Add to this sunny terraces and millstone tables under the vines for eating outside.

Please note: during May and September there are painting courses based here. Further details of those or simply the accommodation from Bill Breckon or Lois Love. Telephone/fax 01466 751111.

Costa Blanca/Javea

It will be interesting to see whether our increasingly hot and dry summers will have any effect on the British love of 'the Costas', which is mainly driven by the weather. It has been reported that 60% of people in the UK would like to live all or part of the year abroad, and something like 50% of that number said they would choose to be on Spain's Costa Brava or Costa Blanca.

'Cottage guide' readers Eileen Robinson and Sally Martin have recommended a number of properties in this inescapably popular 'honeypot'. Not a place to get away from it all but as a colleague put it 'quite a good place to start getting to know holiday-Spain'.

1. Villa Alicia

Just five minutes' drive from Javea – shops, restaurants, discos and fine, sandy beaches – this is detached, comfortable and quietly situated among orange groves and its own well cared for gardens. There is a small but private swimming pool, a sitting room with satellite TV, a separate dining area and a very smart kitchen. **Sleeps 7**. Cost: £400 to £750.

Details from Mr Thomas McConkey. Telephone 0034 965 79 59 70.
email: tjmcconkey@yahoo.com

2. Villa Torre Wombata

This elegant stylish and extremely comfortable villa has been described

Villa Torre Wombata has been said to have the best view on the south coast...

...and they've said some pretty nice things about the interior too!

as having the best view on the whole of the south coast. Though it looks huge, it does in fact only **sleep 6**, so it has the advantage of a degree of intimacy as well. South facing, with several terraces, a large floodlit swimming pool, a solar heated jacuzzi and sauna (all with the view of fishing port, the marina, Javea bay and mountains beyond), it has been furnished with great care and is, not surprisingly, unavailable to children under 12. Cost: about £625 to £1250.

Details from Liane Webster. Telephone 01273 833072.

Among other property recommendations that have come our way are:

*Casa Tranquila and Casa Barranca (Javea)

Both in the same ownership, these excellent properties have a big following among Brits wanting to be close to this popular resort but with a good degree of privacy as well. The former is in spacious gardens in very peaceful surroundings, just 1km from Javea. **Sleeping up to 7** in a double and two twins, it has a particularly charming and shaded good sized swimming pool. The latter is most impressive, **sleeping up to 11** in three doubles and two twins with a particularly appealing sitting room with satellite TV, a dining room just made for convivial get-togethers and a 'last word' kitchen.

Cost: (Casa Tranquila) £400 to £1050: Casa Barranca £600 to £2400. Details from Brian or Angela Liddy. Telephone 0115 989 9118.

*Casa Gisela (Jesus Pobre/Javea)

This is superbly well situated in the foothills of the Montgo mountains among pinewoods, vineyards and almond groves. Just ten minutes' walk from the famous but still very attractive classically Spanish village of Jesus Pobre, it is also just 8km from Javea. **Sleeping up to 10** in two doubles and three twins (and, note, three bathrooms), it has a pool side patio and terraces. Babysitting possible by arrangement; satellite TV; barbecue. Cost about £435 to £1150.

Details from Sheelagh Massey. Telephone 01904 468777.

*Villa Babar/Casa Felix (Benitachell)

Here are two absolute charmers, the first in a quiet new development, with fabulous views and with the advantage for wheelchair users of being all on one level. There's a south facing terrace and a private pool (which the master bedroom gives straight on to). **Sleeps 4**. Details from 01346 515262. The latter also has great views, and the advantage of a feature open fireplace. **Sleeps 4**. Details from 0034 96 6493074.

Casa Barranca sleeps up to eleven. There are manicured gardens and memorable views...

Casa Gisela is just ten minutes' walk from Jesus Pobre, but it's private too. It sleeps up to ten people...

Kaprun, near Zell am See
'Haus Fischer' (Interhome)

We look back fondly on a week spent here. After a false start, when we found ourselves in the wrong apartment in the heart of this famous ski resort (all round skiing on the fabulous, dramatic Grossglockner, but lots to see and do hereabouts in the summer), we detoured 'up the hill' to the correct building. Excellent! It's always nice to be a bit 'out of town', to have your own space. With good views of the mountains and easy access to the village, this was a spacious, reasonably priced delight.

With Zell am See just ten minutes by car, cable cars within three minutes and the one that transports you to the peak of the Grossglockner just ten, it was a good find. We walked for many miles on mountain paths, cycled on hired bikes round the lake at Zell, went on a round-the-lake boat tour.

Specifically, our first floor apartment (**Sleeps up to 6.** Ref A5710/222B) had a spacious double-aspect double-bedded sitting room, a good sized twin room, the option of a further twin, a kitchen-diner and – yes – a bathroom. For some people this is important, and it's not automatic. Soakers must check the small print: only a minority of holiday properties in Austria (and Bavaria) have a bath rather than or as well as a shower. Not that there's any shortage of water around! There's a shared balcony, use of a garden, with some outside seating, and, at the back of the property – which contains other apartments, though all with a good degree of privacy – there's easy access to a charming country lane that, with rural views all around and a panoramic one of most of Kaprun, takes one down into the (large) village centre. In the village there are a good dozen restaurants and an excellent public swimming pool.

In the same ownership, and in the main street of the village, a newly and smartly renovated apartment house is better suited to people who don't want to trek up the hill. There are two apartments, each **sleeping 6.** Refs A5710/230B and A5710/230C.

Further details available from Interhome Limited, Gemini House, 10-18 Putney Hill, London SW15 6AX. Telephone 020 8780 6633. Fax 6631.
www.interhome.co.uk

Summer and winter, Austria is a playground for 'bon viveurs' and outdoor types alike...

Mecklenburg/West Pomerania
'Engelbert Humperdinck lives'

If I hadn't met a Belgian who owns holiday apartments (*writes Bryn Frank*), and been invited to a birthday party nearby, I might have missed out on Germany's best-kept Baltic secrets.

I went via Berlin. I usually enjoy the bus trip from Tegel airport to 'Zoo' station and the raw edge of Berlin's city centre (though little Tegel's now a Cinderella, pushed into the shade by new-look Schönefeld), but this time I'm tired and irritable. Tired because I got up so early for my flight, irritable because on an unusually crowded bus I'm next to somebody wearing the sort of headphones that invite everybody within ten feet to sing along to the music. Or resort to violence.

'Please release me, let me go'. I recognise the tinny sound seeping out. It's 'Engelbert Humperdinck', who used to be called Gerry Dorsey and whose career was going nowhere until his manager thought lifting the name of a half forgotten German composer might kick-start it: it did. I was to remember those headphones later in the day.

I also have an eye on my watch, because I have to catch a train to Neustrelitz, an hour and half due north of Berlin. I won't be done out of my Berlin-fix, though. I'll not return to Stansted until I've had a mooch around Berlin's stunning Ka De We – a bit like our Fortnum and Mason, Selfridges and Harrods rolled into one – and strolled through the Brandenburg Gate and then up Unter den Linden. I won't miss a lunchtime plate of Thüringer sausages and potato salad at a favourite pub, called *Zur Letzten Instanz*. And that's *before* I meet up with Berlin-based friends.

I have two minutes to spare before my train. In fast-paced Berlin, two minutes counts as quality-time. At a quick-snack counter I grab a coffee and a slice of plum cake. I buy a newspaper (hoping that people on the train won't see my lips moving as I read the difficult bits). With a swing-

Deutsche Bahn's double-decker Regional Expresses offer – at no extra charge! – panoramic views of Germany's landscapes.

Stralsund may have the status of a UNESCO 'World Heritage Site' but it's low key and surprisingly little known.

ing travel bag I spill some of my coffee as I jump at the last moment on to a double-decker train, almost splashing a grizzled and grinning passenger sitting opposite.

Direct as Berlin natives often are, he eyes my over-stuffed shoulder bag.

Even I can pick up his Berlin accent. I wonder if it's a bit like Glaswegian might sound to Germans taught only 'BBC English'. He asks 'Where are you off to?'

I tell him I'm going to a place called Neustrelitz to take a look at holiday apartments. 'Ah, nice old place – you should go for a walk in the park.' Which I find strange. Is a walk in the park the best Neustrelitz can offer? Then I tell him I'm also going on to a special birthday party in Stralsund. For over 30 years ago I lodged for nine months in a small town near Bremen with a Frau Dellinger. She was born and brought up in Stralsund, moved westwards ahead of the Soviet sweep into Germany in 1945, and returned after Germany's re-unification in 1990. On this very day she is celebrating her 90th birthday. We kept in touch, though only just, via the occasional postcard. Relatives have traced me and invited me to a celebration dinner in a restaurant in Stralsund's Old Town. My fellow traveller approves ('A beautiful old town – you'll like it'). He even knows the restaurant ('Try their special mixed fresh pan-fried fish with smoked fish')

At Neustrelitz, once the schoolchildren chirruping like exotic birds and milling around the buses outside the station have gone home, the place falls silent. I park my bag and walk into town. I come to a spacious market place with no fewer than *eight* roads spidering off it, said to be unique in Europe. This dates from the creation of a new town in the 1730s to serve the castle, whose best known occupant was Luise, Queen of Prussia. The castle was burned down by Soviet troops in 1945, leaving just a park.

By chance I find I'm close to Neustrelitz's municipal museum. Expecting to kill half an hour I end up finding it hard to leave. Alone in silent rooms, I am transported back to what seems to have been a gentler world. A child's sampler, a dinner service 'last used in the castle in about 1860'. There are ancestral portraits on the first floor, and oval gold-framed miniatures of the young Queen Luise, who died nearby in 1810. Even allowing for the portraitist's flattery, she's slight and pretty, with a soulful gaze.

Stralsund's 'worth the detour' for its delicately restored old buildings, a jaunty maritime flavour, and much more.

Small two-coach local trains offer both a way to meet-the-locals and to get around Rügen without a car.

Walking back to where I'll find the apartments I pass handsome old buildings, but stop outside one called 'Luisenhof', on the market place. I have, admittedly, had two glasses of the local beer in a corner cafe, so I need to peer again. What on earth is this? A plaque on a house announces that this is where, on September 27th 1921, 'the real' Engelbert

Humperdinck died. The original one-hit *wunderkind*, composer of Hansel and Gretel. The coincidence is uncanny. I think of the headphones on the 109 bus from Tegel and try to get the strains of 'Please release me, let me go' out of my head. I'm just able to summon up the treble voices that trill the catchy beginning of the children's nicely scary opera.

I find the apartments, charmingly done out, if a bit small. They'll suit. They overlook a corner of the Schlosspark. Some park! I see what my Berliner meant about taking a walk. So I go the long way back to the station, along the park's main walkway. In a light drizzle, in this historically troubled corner of Europe, it's romantic and sad, with many sculptures as well as ancient trees. It was laid out in about 1730.

An almost empty single decker train pulls in to the station. It's an hour and three quarters to Stralsund. Trees silhouetted against silvery light on the horizon are leaning away from the wind, and there are shafts of sun from gaps in the dark clouds. Friesian cattle are grazing on wide, scrubby pastures. It's a raw, living-on-the-edge sort of beauty that reminds me of wide-skied Flemish-school paintings. It seems I'll be seeing Stralsund at dusk, and probably in the rain too. Which sounds depressing, but it turns out to be a treat. When we arrive, there's enough reddish light left in the sky to silhouette a high rise church-spire and a tall crane by the river.

Frau Dellinger's family have booked me into the *Hotel am Jungfernstieg*, a hundred yards from the station. It's a little jewel, all pale wood and soft colours, receptionists all smiles. I *think* my room has a good view but won't know till morning. It's a nice stroll from here to my assignation in the Old Town, walking on cobbles wet and shiny in yellow lamplight. It's a Tuesday evening in April, dark and quiet, but there's a cheerful glow of table lamps in the frosted window of the restaurant. On opening the door I hear music and laughter. I recognise Frau Dellinger, the focus of a group of a dozen people, looking a bit like Queen Victoria in her later years. Cherubic, smaller and rounder than I remember, but still with the same bright blue eyes. I hand her a birthday present. It's an album of old photos of Mecklenburg and Western Pomerania I've put together over several weeks. It goes down well, and sparks off nice reminiscences.

'I taught you to cook German things,' she remembers. And she did: *Eintopf, Bauernfrühstuck, Sauerbraten, Labskaus*. I chat with a nephew and niece I remember as small children. They have in mind a walking tour of the city for me, and we should meet by the harbour. They also ask if I'm going across to Rügen, and laugh when I say yes, but only for an afternoon, to look at holiday apartments. 'You need a week for Rügen. We'll invite you back!' For most people Stralsund is the jumping-off point for the holiday island,

Frau Dellinger leaves, still in good form. She lives in sheltered housing. Some of us stay very late. Back in my hotel I nurse a sore head, but make it for the grand tour they have sketched out, though I want to do it at my own pace, via the old marketplace and the elaborate town hall of - yes, in part - 1371. This seems to symbolise the self-confidence of this Hanseatic-league town that among other goods traded Russian furs with England.

I poke among houses in side streets that would grace any of Germany's world-class townscapes, browse in antique shops (there are still bargains to be had in 'the old east') and in a bookshop that would sit well in a university town. I also have an hour in the sea-life centre, more impressed by phantasmagorical denizens of the Baltic deep than the more exotic fish swimming there. And, having taken a couple of aspirins for my hangover, I climb the tower of the Marienkirche in the New Market for a seagull's eye view of the town and of Rügen.

I manage both an afternoon and evening on Rügen, by double-decker train to the little seaside resort of Sassnitz, via green woodland, with sudden glimpses of the sea. At Sassnitz the sun is sparkling on the water and there are, even in April, people bathing. In a first-floor seafront bar I point this out to a waiter. 'Some people are crazy', he says. 'It's much too cold. It takes weeks for their nipples to unharden'. The town is all pale blue and bright white, with handsome small hotels and guest houses of the old fashioned kind. In England, there'd be shops selling buckets and spades. A miniature beer festival is under way on the esplanade by the water, though it seems to be more of a brewery promotion. I join about a hundred assorted customers tucking into *Eisbein* (pigs' trotters) and am told that a striking Brünnhilde among the barmaids has won a competition for the number of litre glasses of beer she can carry, and will go to the national championships in Munich.

And so, the following morning, it's back to Berlin. After two energetic days I find myself dozing in the well heated, three quarters empty carriage, even at one point dreaming: of the unlikely pairing of the two Engelberts, of a former landlady who's turned into Queen Victoria, of a miniature seaside resort like something out of *Monsieur Hulot's Holiday*. The train fills up at Neustrelitz. I straighten up, slowly get back into Berlin mode, all the better however for Baltic breezes. I'm cheered en route by a text message from Frau Dellinger's family, who confirm the invitation to go back. They'll show me the real Rügen, they say, and there's no mention at all of bathing.

Holiday houses and apartments, Neustrelitz: mostly on the outskirts of town, Details from the tourist office: +49 (0) 3981/253-153 Fax 03981/2 39 68 70

touristinformation@neustrelitz.de   www.neustrelitz.de

Also **email: taverner1@yahoo.co.uk**

Among holiday apartments in Stralsund, try the Hotel Altstadt Apartments: +49 (0) 3831 – 200 500 Fax +49 (0) 3831 – 200 510

email: info@hotel-zur-post-stralsund.de

Also recommended in Stralsund (not self catering): Hotel am Jungfernstieg

www.hotel-am-jungfernstieg.de +49 (0) 3831 4438-0

Tourist Information Stralsund/Rügen: Alter Markt 9, 18439 Stralsund

+49 (0) 3831/24 69 0 Fax: +49 (0) 3831/24 69 22

email: info@stralsundtourismus.de

Holiday apartments Rügen (Sassnitz): **www.kaul-fewo.de**

Pick me up in Poland

All those smiling waitresses, all those sensibly-priced plumbers. And that's just scratching the surface. They say there are 250,000 recently arrived Poles aged between 18 and 35 working in Britain, making a new life but – surely? – a bit homesick too.

It's easy to strike up a conversation. Recognising the accent, knowing Krakow, Poznan, Zakopane and Warsaw a bit, I sometimes ask 'Where do you come from?' With a faraway look, perhaps wistful about their vast homeland of meandering rivers, wildflower meadows and ancient castles, they tend to mention nice-sounding places I've not heard of.

When colleagues and friends rang to say they were getting up a summer trip to Poland and would I like to join them, of course I said Yes.

That would be walking in the Tatra Mountains? Perhaps visiting the German-border cities of Szczecin, Wroclaw, Posnan? Or taking a look at Gdansk, which I'd never seen? Or maybe a nostalgic revisit to Warsaw?

'Er, no, not exactly...' As part of a cultural exchange they'd been invited to 'the Poland nobody knows' (apart from people who live there, of course). The last place in Poland to get its very own official tourist office, that is the region of Kuyavia and Pomerania, taking in Bydgoszcz and ancient Torun and a generous handful of other places that might in their low-key way be just the job for introducing first timers to this underrated, Anglophile country of great charm and much history.

And of course, as is the way, it was an eye opener. They took us to Bydgoszcz and its Old Town – as you do, in Poland – and a night-time floodlit trip on the river that snakes through the inner-city. We drank in a pub where famously there's good jazz on Wednesday nights, took a Sunday morning stroll through the town while it still slept, admiring art deco buildings, caught bits of an open-air pop concert in as fine a town square as any in provincial Poland, which is saying something.

Torun lies directly on the River Vistula, which runs like a silver thread through the great tapestry that is Poland's history. We climbed the steps of the town hall tower, admired the great cathedral and ancient and beautifully preserved ancient houses, including the one where Nicolaus Copernicus was born in 1473.

Bydgoszcz is especially attractive at night, well lit and full of life...

...and its market square is one of the finest in the whole of Poland.

But as ever, it's the little off-beat moments that linger in the memory Such as a side trip to a botanical garden and smokery where leather-aproned calibans produced fat and juicy smoked trout, still warm. That was followed by open-landau rides beside a river. And as part of a what seems to be an elaborate series of magic spells by which Poland seduces visitors, a double-harp recital in a miniature palace at Ostromecko. In the golden light of a late-afternoon, we half expected Chopin to sidle in unannounced and sit at the unattended grand piano,

The Polish countryside quickly worked its charms. We strolled along woodland paths in warm sun, admired slightly faded grand houses. It's flattish country, but not dull: forests set off by flower meadows, cranes nesting on top of elaborate churches, crimson and gold sunsets in vast skies, factory chimneys, distant church spires.

Our hosts had something else up their sleeves. How did we feel, they asked, about a *real* pick-me-up? Ah, a new-flavoured vodka perhaps? A boat trip on the Vistula? No: we would uncover for ourselves two of the best kept secrets in this part of Poland. That is. health spas, where in a tranquil setting of manicured lawns, flower beds and stucco'd pavilions our minds would be eased and our bodies pampered. All is based around natural springs rich in minerals, and a range of treatments are available to outsider at prices that can seem embarrassingly low to westerners, as are accommodation costs.

So in Ciechocinek and Inowroclaw we allowed ourselves to be pummelled and cossetted in massage rooms, salt water jacuzzis, mud baths. 'Chilling out' was literally that, in soothing salt chambers where time is strictly limited: the taste of salt on your tongue means 'enough is enough'. All this put a spring in our step. So, fighting fit, ready for all-comers, we undermined it all with a valedictory feast in a wood panelled restaurant of ten traditional Polish dishes in a row, plus dessert. No Melba toast, but vodka toasts galore... **BF.**

*Further details (including information about limited but gradually increasing self catering accommodation) from the Municipal Tourist Information Office, Stary Rynek1/1, 5-105 Bydgoszcz .

www.it.bydgoszcz.pl Telephone +48 52 321 45 95

Inowroclaw may seem an unlikely destination for first-time visitors...

...but it's a charmer. The gardens are as much a tonic as the treatments on offer.

Make mine Malta

You could say Malta's got the one thing that every holiday destination would give the whole of its marketing budget for. That's to say: 'The Lot'. Hot weather if that's what you need, lots to do and see – especially if you take a trip to the island of Gozo – so much history that you literally, if you don't watch your step when visiting excavated pre-historic sites, risk falling over.

And you get 'English as she is spoken'. Or, rather charmingly, as she used to be spoken: there's something about Maltese English that's elegant, rather old fashioned, lacking in some modern idioms and all the more appealing for that.

The islands are English-enough for show-biz stars to have had holiday houses there, where they could enjoy a bit of recognition without being overwhelmed. They included Frankie Howerd, Ernie Wise, Tommy Cooper. English-enough for there to be red post boxes and buses that used to look as if they belonged in London's Home Counties. Though getting the colour wrong is a social *faux pas*. 'That lovely apple green' I announced at a cocktail party the first day of a recent trip. An awkward silence. A sympathetic voice at my shoulder: 'When were you last here?'. 'Er...fifteen years ago...Why?' 'Well, the colour was changed. For very complicated reasons.'

You probably won't get *haute cusine*, though the Hotel Fortina comes close, but steak can be melt-in-the-mouth, and fusion food that's sporadically all the rage in Mayfair and Manhattan comes naturally to the Maltese. Think Mediterranean plus a bit of Arabic, a vast variety of shellfish and fresh fish, some of it seasonal, a good dollop of British. If that all gets too much, there are tea shops with gingham tablecloths, slabs of fruit cake on the ferry to Gozo. But beware the culture shock of the cheesy lunch (sheep's cheese in different forms for all three courses), which I experienced at The Citadel, on Gozo, which, as a one-time populated fortress, is roughly the island's equivalent of Malta's Mdina.

Gozo's Citadel, famously windswept, never crowded, with memorable views, is a must-see, as is Malta's ancient capital, Mdina. The Mdina is less exposed to the elements. On a warm mid morning, with virtually no traffic, you seem to leave the real world far behind. Some say it's best in the evening. Along with the language, the Mdina is a tangible link with Malta's Moorish history, just another piece in the jigsaw puzzle that this extraordinary place is, accessible in more ways than one.

Though there are some fine hotels, fiercely competitive at certain times of the year, Malta is very much self-catering territory, and its popularity with UK visitors keeps standards high.

Self catering on Malta:

www.ownersdirect.co.uk/Malta-Gozo.htm

www.holiday-malta.com/

HIDDEN EUROPE

When writer Nicky Gardner (pictured below) bumped into Susanne Kries on a remote quayside in the Faroe Islands a few years back, an interesting partnership was born. It wasn't long before the two women had teamed up in a venture that documents some of Europe's remotest communities. As *The Good Holiday Cottage Guide* caught up with Nicky and Susanne (staying at a cottage in Yorkshire), the travelling duo were just back from a windy excursion to England's wildest railway stations: Dent and Garsdale, on the Settle to Carlisle route. 'Not quite our usual territory,' commented Nicky, for whom a Yorkshire afternoon out is normally just a bit too tame for comfort.

In their magazine *hidden europe* Nicky and Susanne report on much wilder spots. From the Urals to the Azores, from islands in the Russian Arctic to remote villages in the Balkans, *hidden europe* cuts through the glitz and the gloss that surrounds most travel reporting. It's all about good prose, with a wildly eclectic take on Europe's unsung corners and new perspectives on well trodden trails. An annual subscription is £27 and makes for great reading.

For details, go to **www.hiddeneurope.co.uk**, email Nicky and Susanne at **editors@hiddeneurope.co.uk** or call them at their Berlin office on 0049 30 755 16128.

Barnard, near Woodstock
Seven Hills (New England Country Homes*)

It was interesting, two summers ago, to test the famously smooth organ-
isational skills of the people behind this company, which is in the same
stable as the much admired English Country Cottages. Having booked a
handsome-looking house half hidden among wooded hills a few miles
north of Woodstock, Vermont, we travelled via Boston to so-chic
Lennox, in Massachusetts, then spent a few days in rural New
Hampshire, before venturing into the real life picture-postcard that this
little light-under-a-bushel state is.

Vermont had been a long-time 'must see' for us. We'd *expected* to find
weatherboarded houses and delicate timber framed churches bright
white against emerald village greens, leaves just beginning to turn, tumbling rivers. We hadn't expected the horse-drawn buggies, the home
made ice-cream, the maple syrup fountains, a pace of life that makes
rural Ireland seem positively hectic.

Seven Hills was a delight: very quiet, very
private, with great sunsets to admire.

Another Vermont charmer: West Hill
Meadows, just outside the town of Ludlow.

Conveniently for the purposes of this guide it was our holiday house
that was the star of the trip. It's called *Seven Hills*, after the view from
the back of the house. Though after a few glasses of local applejack – a
roughish calvados – on the porch we always counted more. Actually, we
counted more even while quite sober. Seven Hills (Ref WR02), however
accurately named, was a delight, and if anything rather undersold in the
thoroughly inspiring New England Country Homes brochure.

A nearby bonus was the country store in the hamlet of Barnard: on a
cool, rainy Sunday morning the stove was warm, the bacon and eggs a
must. In continual use since 1830, the photogenic store was a reporting
centre for boys joining up to fight in the Civil War, in which Vermont
lost a higher percentage of its troops than any other state in the Union.

In this southern half of Vermont there are several exquisite properties in
the agency's portfolio, such as *Vista View*, at Killington (Ref GM112),
West Hill Meadows, at Ludlow (Ref LW061), and *White Birches*, at
Wilmington (Ref 070).

Details from **www.newengland-countryhomes.co.uk** 0870 192 1764.

Special Categories (UK/Ireland)

A quick reference

We're pleased when readers call us for extra information about cottages we feature. They ask all sorts of intriguing questions, but mostly it's things like 'This cottage looks nice, but can you confirm it has a swimming pool?' ... 'How far away is it from the sea?' ... 'There seems to be a railway station quite near, but are there taxis or will the cottage owners pick us up and take us back?' Listing such items as this is not, however, a value judgement, as many of our very best cottages scarcely score at all in these lists. **Please note that agencies are not included, as it is assumed that most of them can offer properties that include some or even most of the facilities featured.**

1. *In or on the outskirts of a village or town.*
2. *Beside a lake, a loch, a lough, a river, the sea.*
3. *Within about five miles of the sea.*
4. *Deeply rural and/or fairly remote.*
5. *Home cooked food available (including freezer food).*
6. *Access by rail or owner will collect from train.*
7. *Owner/manager living on site or immediately adjacent.*
8. *On working farm.*
9. *Suitable for people with limited mobility.*
10. *Suitable for the disabled (using ETC or RADAR criteria).*
11. *Big houses, suitable for two or more families (say, 9/10).*
12. *Swimming pool on site or immediately adjacent.*
13. *Open fires/coal or woodburning stoves.*
14. *Tennis court on site.*
15. *Special play/entertainment facilities for children.*

* Asterisks mean the facility applies to some properties only.

NB: Some readers ask us to indicate cottages that are available for short breaks, but our records show that four out of five owners or agents offer this facility. It is worth phoning about short breaks even at the height of the season.

East Anglia/E Midlands/Shires	1	2	3	4	5	6	7	8	9	10	11	12	13	14	15
Blue Barn Cottage			✓	✓			✓	✓			✓		✓		
Bones Cottage	✓		✓				✓								
Bramble & Hawthorn			✓				✓		✓				✓		
Brancaster Farms Cottages			✓				✓	✓		✓•	✓•		✓	✓	
Carpenters Cottages, No.6	✓		✓												
Clippesby Holiday Cottages			✓		✓		✓		✓•	✓•		✓	✓•	✓	✓
Corner Pightle			✓										✓		
Gladwins Farm				✓	✓	✓	✓		✓			✓	✓	✓	
Grove Cottages, The			✓				✓								
Highland House		✓									✓				
Ivy House Farm				✓			✓	✓	✓	✓•	✓	✓	✓		✓
Jenny's Cottage	✓		✓										✓		
Little River View	✓	✓					✓								
Margaret's Cottage				✓	✓		✓					✓	✓		✓
Middle Cottage	✓		✓										✓		
Northernhay		✓										✓			
Orchard Cottage	✓												✓		
Peddars Cottage	✓						✓						✓		
Potash Barns				✓	✓		✓		✓		✓		✓		✓
Stubbs Cottages			✓•	✓			✓	✓	✓•				✓•		
Vere Lodge				✓	✓		✓		✓		✓	✓	✓•	✓	✓
Vista/Carpenters Cottages	✓	✓											✓		
Willow Fen	✓	✓				✓									
Willow Lodge	✓	✓				✓			✓		✓				
Wood Lodge			✓									✓	✓		
Yorkshire and The Peaks															
Beech Farm Cottages	✓						✓		✓•		✓	✓			✓
Cherry Tree/The Old House	✓•												✓•		
Cliff House	✓				✓		✓					✓	✓•	✓	✓
Cotterill Farm Cottages						✓	✓						✓•		
Dalegarth & The Ghyll Cottages	✓						✓	✓		✓	✓		✓		
Dalehead Court	✓			✓		✓	✓								
Dinmore Cottages							✓		✓	✓			✓		
Farsyde Mews Cottages		✓	✓		✓•		✓	✓				✓•	✓•		
Fold Farm Cottages	✓			✓			✓	✓					✓		
Hartington/Courtyard Cottages	✓												✓		
Hayloft, The				✓			✓						✓		
Headon Farm Cottages				✓			✓						✓		
Hillside Croft	✓			✓	✓	✓			✓		✓		✓		
Knockerdown Farm Cottages	✓			✓			✓		✓		✓	✓	✓•		✓
Sarahs Cottage	✓					✓	✓								
Sawdon Country Cottages	✓												✓	✓	
Shatton Hall Farm Cottages				✓			✓						✓	✓	
Shepherd's Cottage				✓									✓		
Swaledale Cottages	✓•			✓•			✓•				✓•		✓•		
Thiernswood Cottage	✓			✓•			✓•		✓		✓•		✓•		
Townend Cottage	✓						✓						✓		

	1	2	3	4	5	6	7	8	9	10	11	12	13	14	15
White Rose Holiday Cottages	✓		✓•			✓	✓•		✓•				✓•		
Wrea Head House Cottages			✓			✓	✓		✓	✓	✓	✓			✓
York Lakeside Lodges		✓					✓			✓•					✓
Northumberland and Durham															
Akeld Manor & Cottages				✓	✓		✓				✓•				
Blue Bell Farm Cottages	✓	✓	✓			✓	✓	✓•							✓
Cresswell Wing			✓				✓				✓		✓		
Farne House	✓	✓									✓				
Holmhead Cottage	✓	✓			✓	✓	✓	✓		✓					✓
Old Smithy, The				✓			✓	✓	✓				✓		
Outchester & Ross Farm Cottages		✓	✓	✓			✓	✓	✓•				✓		✓
Pele Tower, The							✓						✓		
Shepherd's Cottage		✓	✓		✓	✓	✓	✓					✓		
Stables, The & The Byre			✓	✓	✓	✓	✓	✓					✓		
West Lodge/Stables/Coachhouse/Bee Cott		✓	✓	✓			✓				✓		✓		
Scotland															
Arduaine Cottages	✓		✓			✓									
Ardverikie Estate Cottages	✓•		✓			✓	✓•				✓•		✓•		
Attadale			✓	✓	✓	✓	✓				✓		✓		
Balnakilly Log Cabins/Cottages	✓		✓			✓	✓	✓•	✓•	✓	✓	✓	✓		
Blairquhan	✓		✓			✓	✓	✓•			✓•		✓		
Bothy, The	✓		✓			✓							✓		
Captain's House, The	✓	✓	✓										✓		
Carna Farmhouse	✓		✓										✓		
Coruanan Farmhouse	✓		✓		✓	✓		✓					✓		
Culligran Cottages	✓		✓			✓	✓								
Druimarbin Farmhouse		✓	✓		✓			✓			✓		✓		
Drumblair	✓							✓							
Duncrub Holidays			✓	✓	✓	✓	✓•	✓•					✓•		
Duns Castle Cottages	✓		✓	✓		✓					✓		✓•	✓	
Easter Dalziel Cottages			✓		✓	✓	✓	✓							
Ellary Estate Cottages	✓	✓	✓			✓	✓						✓		
Glen Coe Cottages	✓	✓	✓					✓							
Isle of Carna Cottage	✓	✓	✓										✓		
Laundry Cottage	✓		✓										✓		
Machrie Hotel Lodges	✓		✓	✓		✓		✓							✓
Millstone Cottage	✓		✓			✓									
Penmore Mill	✓		✓			✓					✓				✓
Pier Cottage/The Library	✓		✓										✓		
Rhuveag	✓		✓								✓		✓		
Seaview Grazings	✓														
Shore Croft	✓		✓	✓				✓					✓		
Speyside Holiday Houses	✓	✓						✓			✓		✓		
Tomich Holidays			✓			✓	✓					✓			
Torrisdale Castle Cottages	✓	✓	✓			✓	✓	✓•			✓•		✓•		

	1	2	3	4	5	6	7	8	9	10	11	12	13	14	15
Cumbria/Lancashire															
Bailey Mill Cottage		✓		✓	✓	✓	✓	✓	✓	✓	✓	✓			✓
Bassenthwaite Lakeside Lodges		✓										✓			
Bowderbeck		✓	✓												
Croft House Holidays	✓•						✓•		✓•				✓•		✓•
Field End Barns		✓•		✓			✓		✓		✓		✓		
Kirkland Hall Cottages				✓			✓				✓		✓		
Land Ends		✓		✓			✓	✓							
Long Byres				✓	✓	✓	✓	✓							
Loweswater Holiday Cottages	✓•	✓•		✓			✓		✓•				✓•		
Matson Ground Estate Cottages				✓•			✓•				✓•		✓•		
Meadowbank/Garden Chalet	✓								✓•		✓		✓		
Monkhouse Hill Cottages						✓		✓	✓•	✓•	✓•		✓•		✓
Mossgill Loft & Chapel	✓						✓						✓	✓	
Old Coach House, The	✓								✓						
Wheelwrights	✓						✓		✓•			✓	✓•	✓	✓
Wales															
Beth Ruach		✓				✓			✓		✓				✓
Blackmoor Farm Holiday Cottages			✓				✓	✓							
Bryn Bras Castle			✓				✓								
Bryn-y-Mor		✓		✓					✓		✓		✓		
Clydey Country Cottages															
Cnewr Estate		✓•		✓				✓			✓•		✓		
Gwynfryn Farm			✓		✓		✓	✓				✓	✓•		✓
Nantcol			✓	✓							✓		✓		
Pant Farm & Sanctuary Cottage		✓	✓•	✓			✓	✓					✓•		
Penwern Fach Cottages			✓				✓					✓	✓		
Portmeirion Cottages	✓	✓	✓									✓		✓	
Quality Cottages, Cerbid			✓	✓•			✓•	✓•	✓•				✓•		
Rhyd-yr-Eirin		✓	✓	✓									✓		✓
Rosemoor		✓			✓	✓	✓		✓	✓	✓				
Talcen Foel			✓	✓									✓		
Trallwm Forest Cottages			✓	✓	✓	✓	✓				✓•		✓		
Victorian Barn		✓		✓			✓					✓	✓	✓	
Y Bwthwn		✓		✓			✓					✓	✓	✓	
Y Llaethdy		✓		✓					✓			✓	✓	✓	
West Country															
Badham Farm Holiday Cottages		✓	✓	✓		✓	✓		✓•		✓•			✓	✓
Bosinver Cottages			✓			✓		✓	✓•		✓•	✓	✓•	✓	✓
Braddon Cottages		✓		✓			✓				✓		✓	✓	✓
Butler's Cottage			✓	✓			✓	✓					✓		
Chapel & Hockadays Cottages	✓•		✓•	✓•		✓	✓•						✓•		
Cider Room Cottage				✓	✓		✓	✓							
Coach House Cottages				✓	✓	✓	✓					✓	✓	✓	✓
Compton Pool	✓	✓	✓	✓			✓		✓			✓		✓	✓
Dairy Cottages			✓	✓			✓	✓	✓•	✓•		✓			✓
Draydon Cottages			✓												

272

	1	2	3	4	5	6	7	8	9	10	11	12	13	14	15
Fursdon				✓			✓	✓					✓	✓	
Gullrock		✓	✓	✓			✓		✓						
Horry Mill Cottage				✓			✓	✓					✓		
Knowle Farm		✓•					✓•	✓•			✓•	✓•	✓•	✓•	✓
Manor Cottage				✓	✓	✓	✓						✓		
Mineshop Holiday Cottages		✓•	✓	✓			✓				✓•		✓		
Mudgeon Vean				✓	✓		✓	✓	✓				✓		
Oldaport Farm Cottages			✓	✓	✓		✓	✓	✓•						
Pollaughan Cottages			✓	✓	✓	✓	✓	✓	✓•	✓•			✓•	✓	✓
Rockford Lodge	✓	✓	✓												
Scoles Manor				✓	✓		✓		✓	✓	✓				✓
Sea Meads Holiday Homes		✓	✓				✓				✓				
St Aubyn Estates Cottages	✓•	✓•	✓•	✓•			✓•	✓•			✓•		✓•		✓•
Stowford Lodge Holiday Cottages				✓	✓		✓		✓			✓	✓		
Trefanny Hill				✓	✓	✓	✓		✓			✓	✓		✓
Tregeath				✓				✓					✓		
Trevarrow Cottage	✓	✓	✓										✓		
Trevorrick Farm Cottages			✓				✓		✓	✓		✓	✓		✓
Treworgey Cottages			✓	✓	✓	✓	✓		✓•		✓•	✓	✓		✓
Wooder Manor				✓			✓	✓	✓•		✓•		✓•		
Wringworthy Cottages	✓		✓	✓		✓	✓		✓		✓	✓	✓		
South and South East															
Ashby Farms Cottages	✓•	✓•		✓•									✓•		
Eastwell Mews		✓			✓	✓	✓		✓•	✓•			✓		✓
Pekes				✓	✓		✓		✓•		✓•	✓	✓•	✓	
Cotswolds/Heart of England															
Docklow Manor							✓		✓			✓	✓•	✓	
Glebe Farm							✓		✓						
Hall Farm	✓				✓	✓	✓								
Heath Farm Cottages				✓			✓						✓		
Hillside Cottage/The Bothy	✓			✓			✓	✓				✓	✓		
Mainoaks Farm				✓									✓		
Oast House, The/Manor Farm	✓					✓	✓		✓						
Old Cottage, The	✓												✓		
Old Dairy, The						✓	✓				✓		✓		
Orangery, The	✓						✓				✓				
Owlpen Manor Cottages				✓	✓		✓	✓	✓		✓		✓•		
Stowford Lodge				✓			✓		✓			✓	✓		✓
Sutton Court Farm Cottages				✓	✓		✓		✓•				✓•		
Swiss Chalet, The		✓		✓		✓	✓		✓						
Ireland															
Delphi Cottages		✓		✓	✓		✓						✓		
Holiday House, Ballina	✓	✓											✓		
Killarney Lakeland Cottages	✓					✓	✓	✓	✓		✓	✓	✓	✓	✓
Village and Country Holiday Homes	✓•	✓•	✓				✓		✓•				✓•		

273

Reader Report

We are as interested in readers' comments about properties featured in *The Good Holiday Cottage Guide* as in our own inspectors' reports. So do tell us about your experiences – the good things, as well as the not so good.

Name of property/properties:

Comments

My name/address/phone number/email is:

Please send to:
Swallow Press, PO Box 21, Hertford SG14 2DD.

East Anglia/
East Midlands/
The Shires

Numbers underlined on maps denote agencies
(which in the main text are marked with an asterisk).
With only a few exceptions the location marked on
the map is the letting agency's headquarters, and
it is normal for the agency to be strongly or
even exclusively represented in that
particular region. In the case of the larger
regional and the main national agencies, no
location reference is given.

Gainsborough   Caistor •   58
                             ▲
                        56   Mablethorpe
        ▲
        61   Lincoln   Skegness
              Lincolnshire
Notts
Nottingham   23
  •   25 37
           • Grantham   Hunstanton   28
                         42 ▲ 46 ▲ ▲ 19   47 38 ▲   • Cromer
                            20 31   40
                         27 ▲
                           41 ▲   Fakenham   34 ▲
              Kings Lynn •   29
Leicestershire/Rutland   21 ▲   32 33
   • Leicester   59 ▲   22   36   35
                  • Peterborough   Norwich   Great
                  49   Norfolk •   Yarmouth
      • Kettering   Cambs   Lowestoft
Northants   Diss   12
   Northampton   Newmarket •▲ 1 18   • Southwold
              Bedford Cambridge •   5
   Milton   • Bury   7 ▲
   Keynes •   Beds   St Edmunds 8 ▲ 9 10
                                 Suffolk
Bucks   Ipswich   • Aldeburgh
           4 ▲   Herts   ▲ 3
              St. Albans Essex   ▲ 6
   • Oxford   Colchester   2 ▲
Oxfordshire High   • Harwich
             Wycombe   Chelmsford
             •   Clacton-on-Sea
Map 1   Greater London

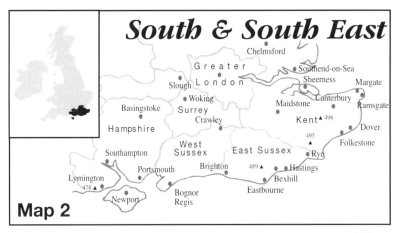

South & South East

Chelmsford
              Greater
Slough   London   • Southend-on-Sea
                     Sheerness   Margate
       • Woking   Canterbury Ramsgate
Basingstoke Surrey   Maidstone •
       •   Crawley   Kent▲ 496
Hampshire   495   Dover
                               ▲   Folkestone
Southampton   West   East Sussex   Rye
              Sussex
   Portsmouth   Brighton 489 ▲ • Hastings
Lymington   •   • Bexhill
 478 ▲   Eastbourne
       Newport   Bognor
Map 2   Regis

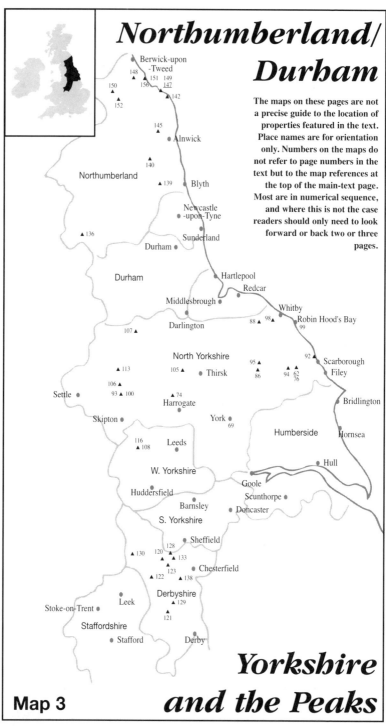

Northumberland/ Durham

The maps on these pages are not a precise guide to the location of properties featured in the text. Place names are for orientation only. Numbers on the maps do not refer to page numbers in the text but to the map references at the top of the main-text page. Most are in numerical sequence, and where this is not the case readers should only need to look forward or back two or three pages.

Berwick-upon-Tweed

148
151 149
156 147
150
152
142

145

● Alnwick

Northumberland
140
▲ 139 ● Blyth

Newcastle-upon-Tyne ●
Sunderland
Durham ●

▲ 136

Durham
● Hartlepool
Redcar
Middlesbrough ●
Whitby
88 ▲ 98 ▲ ● Robin Hood's Bay
107 ▲ Darlington 99

North Yorkshire
92 ▲ Scarborough
95 ▲ Filey
▲ 113 105 ▲ ● Thirsk 86 94 62
106 ▲ 76
Settle ● 93 ▲ 100 ▲ 74 ● Bridlington
Harrogate

Skipton ● York ●
69
Humberside Hornsea
116
▲ 108 Leeds ●
● Hull
W. Yorkshire
Goole
Huddersfield ● Scunthorpe ●
Barnsley ● Doncaster
S. Yorkshire

Sheffield
128
▲ 130 120 ● Sheffield
▲ 133
▲ 122 123 ● Chesterfield
▲ 138

Derbyshire
Leek ● ▲ 129
Stoke-on-Trent ● 121
Staffordshire
● Stafford Derby

Map 3

Yorkshire and the Peaks

Scotland

John o'Groats
Durness
Tongue
Thurso
Wick
Unapool
Kinbrace
Lybster
Lochinver
Highland
Lairg
Brora
Ullapool
Inveran
Dornoch
▲ 204
Gairloch
Invergordon
Lossiemouth
Macduff
203 ▲
Cromarty
Achnasheen
Nairn Elgin Buckie
Banff Fraserburgh
Isle of Skye
189
Rothes
Peterhead
▲ 195
185 ▲
Inverness
Kyle
168 ▲
Huntly
199
Grantown-on-Spey
Invermoriston
Aviemore
Grampian
Aberdeen
Invergarry
Kingussie
Banchory
Mallaig
▲ 196
Stonehaven
Fort William
Pitlochry▲ 166
Brechin
207
211
▲ 198
202
Montrose
209
Glencoe
Tayside
Tobermory
▲ 197
Aberfeldy
Mull
Dundee
Arbroath
200 ▲
Oban
165
Perth
▲ 218
Argyll
▲
167 ▲
St Andrews
Callander
Fife
Stirling
Central
▲ 206
North Berwick
210 ▲
Dunoon
Dumbarton
Dunbar
Greenock
Glasgow
Lothian
Edinburgh
Islay
Paisley
154 ▲
Eyemouth
215
153
Arran
Irvine
Kilmarnock
Galashiels
▲
219 ▲
Melrose
Kelso
Prestwick
Campbeltown
Ayr
Strathclyde
Borders
▲ 162
Girvan
Dumfries
and
Dumfries
Galloway
Stranraer
Kirkcudbright
Whithorn

Map 4

Wales

Holyhead

Llandudno

Gwynedd

Colwyn Bay

Bangor

Clwyd

▲ 326
Caernarfon 329
331

Wrexham ●

Criccieth Porthmadog
▲ 315

Pwllheli ●

▲ 312
▲ 313

332 ▲ ▲
328

Barmouth

Welshpool ●

Aberdovey

● Newtown

Aberystwyth ●

Aberaeron

Powys

● Cardigan 340
▲ 289 ▲ Lampeter

286
Fishguard Dyfed

342 ▲ ● Brecon

276 ▲ ▲
285

▲ 341
Carmarthen

▲ 279

278

277 ▲
Tenby

W. Glam Merthyr Gwent
Swansea
●

M. Glam

S. Glam Cardiff

Map 5

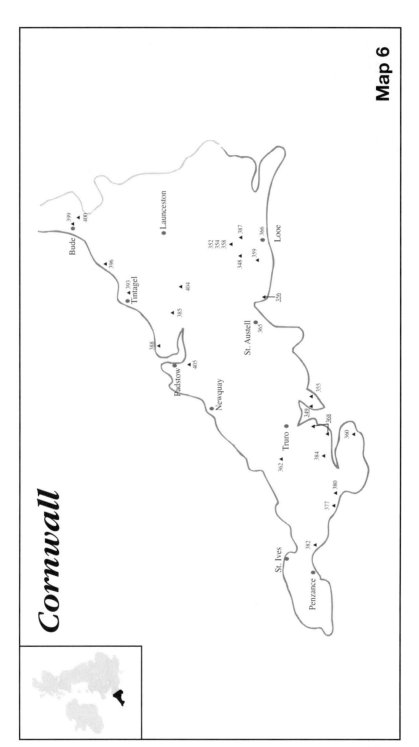

Cornwall

Map 6

Bude 399
400

396

393
Tintagel

388

Padstow 405

Newquay

Launceston

404

385

St. Austell 365

352
354
358

387

348 359

366

Looe

356

355

349
368

362 Truro

384

360

377 380

St. Ives

382

Penzance

West Country (Devon, Dorset, Somerset, Wiltshire, Avon)

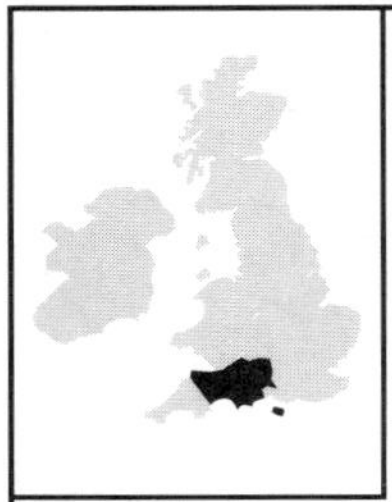

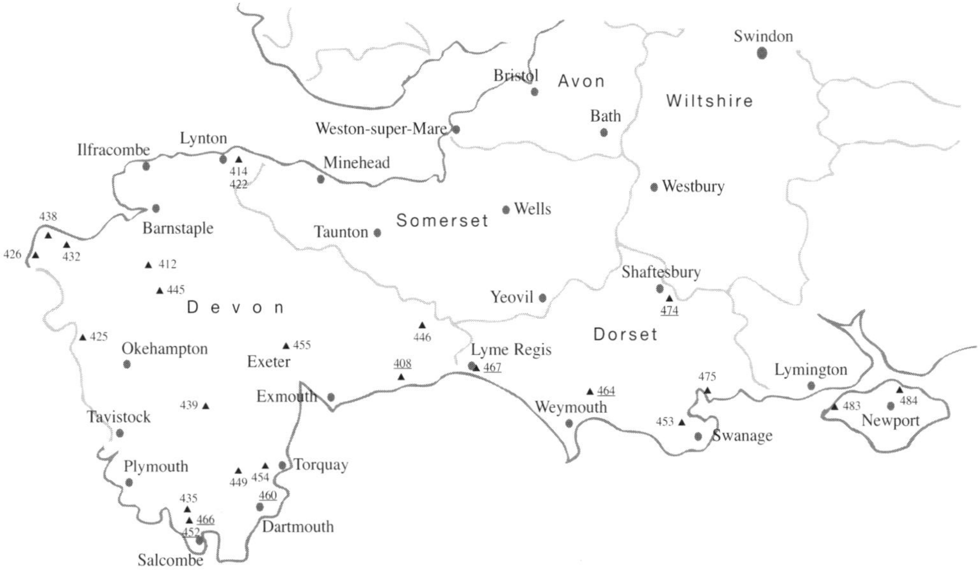
Swindon
Bristol
Avon
Wiltshire
Bath
Weston-super-Mare
Ilfracombe
Lynton
414
422
Minehead
Westbury
438
Barnstaple
Wells
Somerset
Taunton
426
432
412
445
Devon
Shaftesbury
Yeovil
474
446
Dorset
425
455
Okehampton
Exeter
Lyme Regis
408
467
475
Lymington
464
484
483
Exmouth
Weymouth
Newport
439
Tavistock
453
Swanage
Plymouth
449
454
Torquay
435
460
466
452
Dartmouth
Salcombe

Map 7

Cumbria/Lakes/ Lancashire

▲ 222

Carlisle ▲
● 226

▲ 262

C u m b r i a

Penrith ▲ 220
259 ●
▲ 269 ▲ ▲
236
▲ 252
Keswick ●
246 ▲ ▲ 248
259
▲ 265 ▲ 274

243 ▲ 254
● Windermere
▲
250 ● Carnforth
253 273 ▲
▲ ● Kendal

Whitehaven

Barrow-in-
Furness ●

Lancashire

● Blackpool

Map 8

Cotswolds/
Heart of England

Cheshire

Malpas ● ● Nantwich

Shrewsbury
●

Wolverhampton ●
Shropshire   W. Midlands
              Oldbury ●   ● Coventry
    507   Birmingham ●
    ▲   ● Ludlow   Kidderminster   Warwickshire Rugby
                                     ●
Leominster ●   ● Warwick
        ▲ 521
    Worcester ●   ▲ 533
Herefordshire

Hereford ●   ▲   534
        526   ▲
        538 ▲

            546
            ▲

        530 ▲
    ● Gloucester 519
Monmouthshire   Gloucestershire   ● Oxford
    ▲ 506   ▲ 529
510 ▲   ▲ 511 524
                    548
                    ▲
                Oxfordshire

Map 9

Ireland

Letterkenny

Londonderry

Belfast

Donegal

Killyleagh

Enniskillen

Armagh

Sligo

Ballina
563

Dundalk

Navan

Castlebar

Westport
580

Clifden

Athlone

Dublin

Dun Laoghaire

Galway
573

Port Laoise

Wicklow

Carlow

Arklow

Ennis
Limerick

Wexford

Tipperary
581

Waterford

Clonmel

Tralee
Killarney
562

Dingle

Cork

Bantry
572

Map 10

Listed below are brief details of cottages that appear on our associated website, www.goodcottageguide.com, but not in the guide itself.

Enquiries can be directed to info@goodcottageguide.com where an owner does not have their own email.

Walnut Tree Barn, Swanton Abbott, Norfolk. Barn conversion on village outskirts. Well placed for the Norfolk Broads and the coast. Sleeps 4. Telephone (01692) 538888, email: mark@citibuild.co.uk

Bosun's Rest, Blakeney, Norfolk. Fisherman's flint cottage; a stone's throw from the quay, log burning stove, modern appliances, sleeps 4. Telephone (02088) 662683, email: deborah.fitzpatrick1@btinternet.com

Plunketts Cottage in sought after Brancaster. Comfortable and well equipped sleeping up to 8. Close to stunning beaches, golf club and much more. Telephone (01485) 210892. email: roger.raisbury@btinternet.com www.brancasterstaithe.co.uk

Flagstaff House, Burnham Overy Staithe, Norfolk. Several properties with memorable coastal views. Sleep 2-11. Telephone (01278) 638637, email: admin@flagstaff-holidays.co.uk www.flagstaff-holidays.co.uk

Lower Wood Farm Country Cottages, Mautby. Bordering Broads and National Park. Indoor heated pool and facilities ideal for families. Sleep 4-9. Telephone (01493) 722523, email: info@lowerwoodfarm.co.uk www.lowerwoodfarm.co.uk

The Grove Cottages, Cromer, Norfolk. (1/2 mile Cromer). Converted barns in three acre grounds. Heated indoor swimming pool. Sleep 2-6. Telephone (01263) 512412, email: thegrovecromer@btopenworld.com www.thegrovecromer.co.uk

Norfolk House & Courtyard Cottages, Docking (near Burnham Market and Brancaster), North Norfolk. Traditional properties in village. ETC 5 Stars. Telephone (01485) 525341, email: holidays@witleypress.co.uk

Wood Farm Cottages, near Holt, Norfolk. Converted barns and stables in secluded five acres. Children and dogs welcome. Telephone (01263) 587347, email: info@wood-farm.com www.wood-farm.com

Heron Cottage, Horning, Norfolk. Enviable position right on the Broads - rowing dinghy provided! ETC 5 Star. Sleeps 6. Telephone (07788) 853332, email: info@heron-cottage.com www.heron-cottage.com

Wensum View, Great Ryburgh, Norfolk. Spacious cottage for 8+2. Indoor heated pool. Magnificent scenery - a must for artists and anglers. Telephone (01328) 829288, email: wensumview@aol.com www.wensum-view.co.uk

4 The Courtyard, Snettisham. In conservation area 3 miles from Hunstanton and Sandringham. Close to countryside/beaches. Sleeps 4. Telephone (01406) 422569, email: jennifer.overson@ntlworld.com www.cottageguide.co.uk/4.thecourtyard

Anchor Cottage, Blakeney, Norfolk. Charming brick and flint cottage yards from the quay. Sleeps 6. Telephone (01462) 742245, email: anchor_cottage@hotmail.co.uk www.blakeneyhideaways.co.uk

The Old Bakery, a characterful and spacious family cottage in idyllic Blakeney on the North Norfolk coast. Sleeps 6. Telephone (01438) 869334, email: julian@godlee.com www.blakeneycottage.com

The Saltings, Blakeney. Child friendly, traditional cottage, open all year round. Sleeps 6. Telephone (07971) 798802, email: bcarroll@fleetmarsh.co.uk www.thesalting.co.uk

Kingfisher Lure, Wroxham. Ideal for couples or a small family. In quiet backwater with use of dinghy. Sleeps 4. Telephone (01923) 812912, email:info@wroxhamcottage.co.uk www.wroxhamcottage.co.uk

The Old Rectory Cottages, Flixton. Four delightful Victorian properties each sleeping 2. Well behaved dogs welcome. Telephone (01986) 893133, email: enquiries@oldrectorycottagesflixton.co.uk www.oldrectorycottagesflixton.co.uk

Bolding Way Holiday Cottages, Weybourne, North Norfolk Heritage Coastline. Four cottages sleeping 2-14 + cot + 2. Telephone (01263) 588666, freephone UK only 0800 0560996, email GHCG@boldingway.co.uk www.boldingway.co.uk

Bones Cottage, Wiveton, near Blakeney. Charming holiday cottage for two in quiet and peaceful setting, 20 minutes from quayside at Blakeney. Telephone (01263) 740840

Driftway Cottage, Sotherton Corner. 200 year old cottage suitable for up to 4 people, ideally located for walking and cycling. Telephone (01444) 236533, email: jeanhaselip@btinternet.com www.holidaycottagesotherton.co.uk

Cley Windmill. Two well appointed cottages with uninterrupted views over the sea, saltmarshes and Cley Bird Sanctuary. Telephone (01263) 740209, email: info:cleywindmill.co.uk www.cleywindmill.co.uk

Thorpewood Cottages, Thorpe Market, near Cromer. Five holiday cottages converted from old farm buildings in pasture and forest grounds. Telephone (01263) 834493, email: stay@thorpewoodcottages.co.uk, www.thorpewoodcottages.co.uk

Kestrel Holiday Bungalow, Walcott. Idyllic location for water sports a few minutes walk from sandy beach. Sleeps 4+2. Telephone (01375) 360622, email: kestrelholidaybungalow@yahoo.co.uk www.kestrelholidaybungalow.co.uk

Seaview, 6 Hamilton Court, Mundesley. Two bedroom first floor flat on cliff edge with spectacular sea views. Sleeps 4-5. Telephone (01284) 753522, email: suedel_147@hotmail.co.uk www.norfolkcoastallet.moonfruit.com

Anchor and Riverside Cottages, Wroxham, Norfolk Broads. Two well equipped riverside cottages each sleeping up to 8 guests. Short breaks. Telephone (01252) 339022, email: holidays@wroxhamcottages.co.uk, www.wroxhamcottages.co.uk

Mortimers Barn, Preston St. Mary, near historic Lavenham. Converted single storey 15th century thatched threshing barn ideal for disabled access. Telephone (01787) 247786, email: thosegoves@aol.com www.mortimersbarn.co.uk

Cottages at Thatched Farm, Woodbridge, Suffolk. Two countryside cottages just five minutes from A12. VisitBritain 4 stars. Telephone (01473) 811755, email: mailus@thatchedfarm.co.uk www.thatchedfarm.co.uk

Waterside Breaks. Stay in one of many superb riverside cottages and lodges and explore the Norfolk Broads. Telephone (01252) 339020, email: holidays@ukleisurebreaks.com www.watersidebreaks.com

Kett Country Cottages. Over 80 quality, carefully chosen properties from which to explore Norfolk. Accommodation ranging from 2-14. Telephone (01328) 856853, email: info@kettcountrycottages.co.uk www.kettcountrycottages.co.uk

Old School Cottage, Norfolk/Suffolk/Cambs borders. Near Thetford Forest. Ideal for nature lovers, walkers and cyclists. Telephone (01953) 498277, email: oscott@clara.net www.4starcottage.co.uk

Whitensmere Farm Cottages, Ashdon. Cambs/Suffolk/Essex borders. 3 well equipped barn conversions, 1 for disabled. Sleep 4-10. Telephone (01799) 584244, email: gford@lineone.net www.holidaycottagescambridge.co.uk

Thaxted Holiday Cottages, Essex. In beautiful countryside, two cottages, each sleeping 4, plus B & B in converted stables. Telephone (01371) 830233, email: enquiries@thaxtedholidaycottages.co.uk www.thaxtedholidaycottages.co.uk

Hill Farm Holiday Cottages, Ashdon, Essex. Two adjacent cottages in quiet location with stunning views. Ideal for family and business groups. Telephone (01799) 584881, email: hillfarm-holiday-cottages@hotmail.co.uk www.hillfarm-holiday-cottages.co.uk

Mandelay, Epping Green, Essex. Modern 3 star bungalow sleeping 2/4. Convenient for M25, M11, M1. 30 minutes to Stansted Airport. Telephone (01992) 571828, email: enquiries@kingswayholidays.com www.ukholidaycottages.biz

Dalmonds Barn Holiday Cottages, Hertford. Four comfortable and inviting cottages in rural conservation area on working farm. Four units sleeping 4(+1). Telephone (01992) 479151

Wednesday Cottage, Cold Christmas. 4 star cottage close to Ware and Hertford. Less than one hour to London and Cambridge. Telephone (01920) 465696, email: annie@dsl.pipex.com www.wednesdaycottage.co.uk

The Cottage Collection. Superb selection of properties located in every area of Outstanding Natural Beauty around Great Britain. Telephone (01603) 724809, email: bookings@the-cottage-collection.co.uk www.the-cottage-collection.co.uk

Elms Farm Cottage, Fleckney. Comfortable, fully equipped cottage on working farm in the heart of rural Leicestershire. ETC 3 Star. Telephone (01162) 402238, email info@elms-farm.co.uk www.elms-farm.co.uk

Woodthorpe, Lincolnshire (near Alford). Attractive, well equipped cottages near superb sandy beaches. Sleep 2-6. Telephone (01507) 450294, email: enquiries@woodthorpehall.com www.woodthorpehall.com

Belleau Cottage, near Alford. Situated on the edge of the Lincolnshire Wolds, steeped in history and places of interest. Telephone (07984) 437517, email: dom@thepersuadersltd.co.uk www.belleaucottage.co.uk

Waingrove Farm Country Cottages, Fulstow, Louth. Award winning cottages offering a rural retreat in the heart of Lincolnshire countryside. Telephone (01507) 363704, email: ptinker-tinkernet@virgin.net www.lincolnshirecottages.com

Cliff Farm Cottage, North Carlton, Lincolnshire. Converted 19th century farm building with panoramic views across the Trent Valley. Telephone (01522) 730475, email: rae.marris@farming.co.uk www.cliff-farm-cottage.co.uk

Walnut Lake & Lodges, Algakirk. 4 star lakeside lodges in 10 acres of farmland with on site fishing. Telephone day: (07958) 362538, evening (01205) 460482, email: maria@walnutlakes.co.uk www.walnutlakes.co.uk

Kenwick Woods, Louth. Luxury Scandinavian lodges in mature woodlands with excellent leisure facilities. Telephone (01507) 353003, email: anna@kenwick-park.co.uk www.kenwick-park.co.uk

Langham Barns, Mumby, Alford. Three cottages beautifully renovated from 300 year old barns in stunning area of rural Lincolnshire. Telephone (01507) 490313, email: info@langhambarns.co.uk www.langhambarns.co.uk

Old Barn Cottages, Great Sturton. Three fully equipped, luxury cottages located within grounds with croquet, picnic and barbecue areas. Telephone (01507) 578435, email: info@oldbarncottages.net www.oldbarncottages.net

Keld Head, Pickering. Nine cosy stone farm cottages, by North Yorkshire Moors. Four-poster beds. Sleep 2-8 + cots. Telephone (01751) 473974, email: julian@keldheadcottages.com www.keldheadcottages.com

Burton, Turbine, Greystones, Charlie's Stables, Reeth. Stone-built cottages with views to the Pennines, ideal for the Yorkshire Dales. Sleep 2-5. Telephone (01748) 884273, email: cproctor@aol.com www.uk-cottages.com

Baille Hill House, York. Outstanding and sumptuously comfortable gem of a house, overlooking York's historic walls. Sleeps up to 10. Telephone (01845) 597660, email: enquiries@baillehillhouse.co.uk www.baillehillhouse.co.uk

Mel House Cottages, Pickering. 3 properties in extensive grounds. Perfect for York and Moors. Indoor pool. Suitable for mobility impaired. Telephone (01751) 475396, email: holiday@letsholiday.com www.letsholiday.com

Westwood Lodge, Ilkley - Yorkshire's original spa town. Superbly equipped cottages and apartments. M2 disability access award. Sleep 2-9. Telephone (01943) 433430, email: welcome@westwoodlodge.co.uk www.westwoodlodge.co.uk

Bottoms Farm Holiday Cottages, Oakworth. 3 olde worlde character cottages sleeping 4-6. Set in Bronte Country with spectacular views and walks. Telephone (01535) 607720, email: bottomsfarm@btinternet.com

Lilac Cottage, Aldbrough, East Yorkshire. A small charming cottage close to the coast. Sleeps 4. Telephone (01964) 527645, email: nick@seasideroad.freeserve.com www.dialspace.dial.pipex.com/town/walk/aer96/lilac-cottage

Rudstone Walk Farm Cottages, South Cave. Eleven cottages located close to East Yorkshire sandy beaches. Sleep 2-6. Telephone (01430) 422230, email: office@rudstone-walk.co.uk www.rudstone-walk.co.uk

Orchard Cottage, Goathland, North Yorkshire. Quiet location in popular moorland village. Sleeps up to 6. Telephone (01947) 896391, email: enquiries@theorchardcottages.co.uk www.theorchardcottages.co.uk

Cam Beck Cottage, Kettlewell, North Yorkshire. Idyllic 300 year old stone cottage with trout stream running alongside. Many walks from the door. Sleeps 4. Telephone (01132) 589833.

2 Penfold Yard, Richmond. A delightful stone cottage for 2+2 situated in the conservation area of this historic market town in the North Yorkshire Dales. Telephone (01268) 751036, email: susan.horton@southend.nhs.uk

Dales Holiday Cottages offer cosy cottages for 2 up to a splendid 16th Century building for 19. Telephone (01756) 799821, email: info@dales-holiday-cottages.com www.dales-holiday-cottages.com

Country Hideaways. 40 carefully selected properties in stunning locations in the heart of the Yorkshire Dales. Sleep up to 10. Telephone (01969) 663559, email: cottageguide@countryhideaways.co.uk www.countryhideaways.co.uk

Holiday Cottages in Yorkshire, Lancashire, Derbyshire and Cumbria. Over 200 properties from cosy cottages for 2 to spacious barns for 14. Telephone (01756) 700510, email: info@holidaycotts.co.uk www.holidaycotts.co.uk

Three traditional Dales stone cottages in beautiful Peak District National Park. Sleep 1 x 2 and 2 x 2+2. Telephone (07817) 900841, email: halleyr@aol.com www.thimble-cottage.co.uk

Mile House Farm Country Cottages. Four lovely Wensleydale cottages with spectacular views. Telephone (01969) 667481, email: milehouse-farm@hotmail.com www.wensleydale.uk.com

1 New Leeds Cottage, Kettlewell, Upper Wharfedale. Comfortable one bed-room cottage ideally located for exploring the Yorkshire Dales National Park. Telephone (01132) 747924, email: Hilary_tucker@yahoo.co.uk

The Annexe, Acomb. Well furnished accommodation 10 minutes from York city centre. Double bedroom with cot/child bed available. Telephone (01904) 781985 or (07775) 771186, email: melia@theannexeyork.co.uk www.theannexeyork.co.uk

East End Cottage, Near Beverley. In pretty village of Walkington, East Riding of Yorkshire. Sleeps up to 4. Telephone (01482) 849809, email kay@jobber.karoo.co.uk www.eastendcottage.co.uk

The Haybarn, Langtoft. Luxurious three bedroom, two bathroom, mews style cottage for up to 5 in heart of Yorkshire Wolds. Telephone (01482) 871890, email: info@haybarn-cottage.co.uk www.haybarn-cottage.co.uk

Granary Cottage, Snainton. Well situated for York, beaches of Scarborough, Whitby and Filey, and Heartbeat country. Sleeps 4. Telephone (01723) 850402, email: jane.wheldon@btinternet.com www.granary-cottage.com

Old Oak Cottages, Little Thirkleby. Six cottages in delightful rural location on edge of Moors sleeping 2-6+cot. Excellent facilities. Telephone (01845) 501258, email: Amanda@oldoakcottages.com www.oldoakcottages.com

Holiday Homes in Yorkshire. Over 80 superb properties throughout Yorkshire including the coast, Dales, Vale of York and North York Moors. Email: house-parties@globalnet.co.uk www.holidayhomesgroup.co.uk

Yorkshire Cottage Services. A selection of holiday cottages in and around Whitby, between the sea and North Yorkshire Moors. Telephone (01947) 841114, email: yorkshirecottage@btconnect.com www.yorkshirecottageservices.co.uk/linkstoclientssites.htm

Bradley Hall, near Ashbourne, Derbyshire. Highly individual, converted apartments with original features in rural surroundings. Sleep 4-9. Telephone (01335) 370222, email: michelle@pmwproperty.com www.ashbourneselfcatering.com

Badger, Butterfield and Bluebell Cottages, nr Buxton. Comfortable stone cot-tages in the Peak District National Park. Sleep 6-8. Children & pets welcome. Telephone (01298) 872927, email: jan@cosycotts.com www.cosycotts.com

Holestone Moor Barns, Ashover. Two converted barns, one with wheelchair access, sleeping 4+baby and 12+baby, ideal family accommodation. Telephone (01246) 591263, email: HMbarns@aol.com www.hmbarns.co.uk

Tom's Barn & Douglas's Barn, Parwich, nr Ashbourne. Five Star 18th centu-ry limestone barns ideal for couples of any age. Telephone (01335) 390519, email: tom@orchardfarm.demon.co.uk www.tomsbarn.co.uk

Byanna Hall, Eccleshall, Staffordshire. 17th century manor house and butler's annexe. Sleeps 20. Telephone (01785) 850518, email: byannanivas@aol.com www.holiday-rentals.com/index.cfm/property/6416.cfm

Rushop Hall, Castleton. Three historic cottages sleeping 2, 4 and 6 in the Peak District National Park on the Pennine Bridleway. Telephone (01298) 813323, email: neil@rushophall.com www.rushophall.com

Ollerbrook Cottages, Edale Valley. Two 17th century cottages yards from the Pennine Way. Sleep 3 or 5. Telephone (01433) 670083, email: green-lees@ollerbookcottages.fsnet.co.uk www.ollerbrook-cottages.co.uk

Paddock House Farm Holiday Cottages. Five cottages in the beautiful southern 'Peaks' near the famously pretty village of Ashbourne. Telephone (01335) 310282, email: info@paddockhousefarm.co.uk www.paddockhousefarm.co.uk

Swainsley Farm, Manifold Valley, near Dovedale. Former 18th century farm buildings converted into superb accommodation, sleep 2-6. Telephone (01298) 84530, email: info@swainsleyfarm.co.uk www.swainsleyfarm.co.uk

Standlow Farm, Kniveton, near Ashbourne. Five traditional Derbyshire stone cottages sleeping 4-6 plus seven bedroom Farmhouse sleeping 14/16. Telephone (01335) 370222, email: michelle@pmwproperty.com www.ashbourneselfcatering.com

Cotterill Farm, Biggin-by-Hartington. Five 4 star stone cottages in superb central National Park location sleeping 2, 3 and 4 persons. Telephone (01298) 84447, email: enquiries@cotterillfarm.co.uk www.cotterillfarm.co.uk

Lilac Cottage, Chelmorton. Beautifully renovated Derbyshire stone cottage in heart of the Peak District National Park, sleeps 5/6. Telephone (07871) 095262, email: lilaccottage@chelmorton.com www.chelmorton.com

The Holmes Barn, Tideswell Moor. In the heart of the Peak District National Park and ideal for large groups. Telephone (01298) 873098, email: katestrong1@onetel.net www.theholmesbarn.com

Hulmes Vale House, Tideswell Moor. High standard holiday accommodation for large groups, situated in 10 acre grounds. Telephone (01298) 873098, email: katestrong1@onetel.net www.theholmesbarn.com

Breamish Valley Cottages, Branton. Beautifully situated at foot of Cheviot Hills; half an hour from the Northumberland coast. Telephone (01665) 578253, email: peter@breamishvalley.co.uk www.breamishvalley.co.uk

Burradon Farm Cottages, Cramlington, Northumberland. Cottages sleeping 2-4. Fine views and ample parking. Good area for walking/cycling. Telephone: (01912) 683203, email: judy@burradonfarm.co.uk www.burradonfarm.co.uk

Beacon Hill Farm Holidays, Morpeth. Twelve superbly comfortable cottages on Northumberland farm with gym and other facilities. Telephone (01670) 780900, email: alun@beaconhill.co.uk www.beaconhill.co.uk

Britannia House and Cottage, Lindisfarne. Experience the magic of Holy Island; sandy beaches, castle and abbey. Sleep 6 and 4. Telephone (01289) 309826, email: ktiernan@onetel.net.uk www.lindisfarne-cottages.co.uk

Sandpiper Cottage, Low Newton, Northumberland. Delightful 18th century fisherman's cottage in outstanding coastal location. Sleeps 4+2. Telephone: (01665) 830783, email: sandpiper@nccc.demon.co.uk www.northumbria-cottages.co.uk

The Old Byre, Northumberland (near Hexham). Traditionally built farm-steading in 30 acres with panoramic views. Sleeps 6-9. Telephone (01434) 673259, email: enquiries@consult-courage.co.uk www.ryehillfarm.co.uk

Shilbottle Town Foot Farm & Village Farm, near Alnwick. Impressive cottages sleeping 2-12, free leisure facilities open all year. Telephone (01665) 575591, email: crissy@villagefarmcottages.co.uk www.villagefarmcottages.co.uk.

Wanney Cottage, Ridsdale, near Corbridge. Beautifully renovated 19th century cottage with spectacular views towards the Cheviot Hills and Scottish Borders. Telephone (01434) 270144, email: gaby@wanneycottage.co.uk www.wanneycottage.co.uk

The Mews, Hexham. Three bedroom, excellently renovated, Grade II listed mews house sleeping 2-5 tucked away in quiet lane. Telephone (01434) 601533, email: reservations@northumberlandholidaylets.co.uk www.northumberlandholidaylets.co.uk

Coastal Retreats. Five Star-graded collection of 13 luxury self catering holiday cottages with boutique style contemporary interiors. Telephone (01912) 851272, email: info@coastalretreats.co.uk www.coastalretreats.co.uk

The Plaice, featured in various interior magazines, in enviable location in seaside resort of Seahouses. Sleeps 6. Telephone (01912) 851272, email: info@coastalretreats.co.uk www.coastalretreats.co.uk

Ness Street, Berwick-on-Tweed. Luxury 4 storey, Grade II listed holiday cottage in secluded courtyard in heart of conservation area. Telephone (01289) 318069, email: bookings@ness-street.co.uk www.ness-st.co.uk

Laneside Cottage, Barnard Castle, Durham. A haven of tranquillity; former farmhouse with modern facilities and stunning views. Sleeps 8. Telephone (01833) 640209, email: teesdaleestate@rabycastle.com www.rabycastle.com

Kinlochlaich House, Appin, Argyll. Apartments/cottages within period house and grounds in spectacular Highlands. Telephone (01631) 730342, email: enquiries@kinlochlaich-house.co.uk www.kinlochlaich-house.co.uk

Achaglachgach Estate, South Knapsdale. Baronial mansion/cottages in secluded farm estate on shores of West Loch Tarbert. Sleep 4-14. Telephone (07770) 530249, email: Macleanh71@aol.com www.achahouse.com

Harrietfield Cottage, Roxburghshire. Two miles north of picturesque Kelso. Sleeps 2-5. Floors and Mellerstain Castles within easy reach. Telephone (01896) 831052, email: ncunnin640@aol.com

Crailloch Croft Cottages,Wigtownshire. 3 cosy cottages in peaceful countryside. Ideal base for local amenities and day trips to Ireland. Telephone (01776) 703092, email: viv@craillochcroft.freeserve.co.uk www.craillochcroftcottages.co.uk

Alvie Holiday Cottages, Kincraig. Traditional cottages with superb views of the Cairngorms combining tranquillity and sports activities. Telephone (01540) 651255, email: info@alvie-estate.co.uk www.alvie-estate.co.uk

Lochinver Holiday Lodges, Sutherland. Seven lodges by the sea, each sleeping 4. Scottish Tourist Board 4 Stars. Telephone (01571) 844282. www.watersidehomes@bushinternet.com

Tigh-a-Chladaich, Sutherland. Split level house on rocky promontory with spectacular coastal views. Sleeps up to 8 people. Telephone (01571) 844282, email: enquire@by-sea.co.uk www.by-sea.co.uk

Armadale Castle, Isle of Skye. Six comfortable log cottages plus suite with sea/mountain views. Sleep 4-6. Telephone (01471) 844305, email: office@cland.demon.co.uk www.clandonald.demon.co.uk

Pirate Gows Chalets, Eday, Orkney. Five self-catering chalets virtually on the seashore. Beautiful surroundings and views. Telephone (01857) 622285, email: jan.crichton@btinternet.com www.takeabreak.com.au/pirategowschalets.htm

Crosswoodhill Farm Cottages, West Calder. Four exceptional homes on West Lothian hill farm. Visit their award-winning website for a wealth of details and photos, email: gchg@crosswoodhill.co.uk www.crosswoodhill.co.uk

Binnilidh Mhor, Glenmoriston. Large and luxurious cottage for 2-6 near shores of Loch Ness. Suitable for guests with mobility disabilities. Telephone (01320) 340258. email: sheila@binmhor.co.uk www.binmhor.co.uk

Duirinish Holiday Lodges, Ross-shire. Nine lodges offering excellent self catering facilities for up to 4 or 6 on north-west coast of Scottish Highlands. Telephone (01599) 544268, email: sales@duirinishlodges.com www.duirinishlodges.com

Strathconon, Isle of Arran. Luxurious villa in sunny, secluded spot on outskirts of beautiful Whiting Bay. Sleeps 2-8. STB 4 stars. Telephone (01586) 830323, email: enquiries@arranselfcatering.com www.arranselfcatering.com

Dalhougal House Apartments, Croftamie. 200 year old refurbished apartments maintaining cosy Scottish atmosphere in Loch Lomond village. Sleep up to 4. Telephone (01360) 660558, email: dalhougal@croftamie.com www.dalhougal.com

Westloch House, Coldingham, Berwickshire. Ten character cottages sleeping 2 to 6. Coldingham Loch, known for its trout, is a stunning feature. Telephone (01890) 771270, email: westloch@hotmail.com

Leckmelm Holiday Cottages, near Loch Broom. Close to Ullapool, a lively fishing village on Scotland's scenic north west coast. Sleep 2 to 10. Dogs welcome. Telephone (01854) 612471.

Holiday Houses in Scotland. Some of the best self-catering houses and cottages in the most beautiful parts of Scotland. Tel. (01556) 504030, email: lettings@scothols.co.uk www.scothols.co.uk and www.discoverscotland.net

Tigh-na-Mara, Dornie. This well equipped and welcoming property offers marvellous walks and wonderful scenery at the junction of three Lochs. email: nickgp@btconnect.com

Big Sky Lodges, Isle of Ord. Four luxurious detached log houses in glorious Scottish Highlands only 10 minutes from Inverness. Telephone (07752) 253376 Freephone 0800 6343524, email: angus@bigskylodges.co.uk www.bigskylodges.co.uk

3 Dalfaber Park, Aviemore. Well appointed house in quiet location ideally based for touring the Highlands. Telephone (01314) 666917, mobile 07748 817649, email: 3dalfaberpark@blueyonder.co.uk www.dalfaberpark.com

Capercaillie Cottage, Aberfeldy. Modern detached house backing onto woodland comfortable sleeps 6, the perfect centre for exploring Highland Perthshire. Telephone (01363) 877676, email: claire@claireproietti.orangehome.co.uk www.capercaillie-cottage.info

Shallgreen Cottage, Memus. Two bedroom cottage ideally located for those seeking tranquillity and glorious surroundings near Forfar. Telephone (01307) 860303, email: johnagibb@aol.com www.inshewanfishings.co.uk

Dunalistair Holiday Houses, Kinloch Rannoch, Pitlochry. Nine secluded holiday homes amidst magnificent highland scenery sleep 2 to 8. Telephone (0845) 230 1491, email: cottages@dunalistair.com www.dunalastair.com

Steading Cottage, Crieff, Perthshire. Luxury holiday cottage 15 minutes from Gleneagles Hotel. Sleeps 2/4. Dogs welcome. Telephone (07775) 656130, email: steading@selfcatering-cottage.com www.selfcatering-cottage.com

Waterside Breaks. Specialists in high quality waterside self catering Scottish cottage, lodge and log cabin holidays. Telephone (01252) 339020, email: holidays@ukleisurebreaks.com www.watersidebreaks.com

Brook House, near Keswick. Four 17th century stream-side properties in the delightful village of Bassenthwaite. Sleep 2-10. Telephone (01768) 776393, email: a.m.trafford@amserve.net www.holidaycottageslakedistrict.co.uk

Setrah Cottage, near Bassenthwaite. Charming cottage in quiet lane at the heart of Bothel Village. Excellent leisure facilities nearby. Telephone (01697) 320919, email: office@skiddawview.com www.skiddawview.co.uk

Barn House, Braithwaite. Traditional Lakeland Cottage, sleeps 2-6. Superb fells walks from the door and forest mountain bike trails. Telephone (01768) 778411, email: info@braithwaitefarm.wanadoo.co.uk www.barnhouseholidays.co.uk

Bridge End, Eskdale, Cumbria. Award-winning, characterful, Grade II listed cottages in small hamlet in valley beneath Scafell Pike. Telephone (08700) 735328, email: greg@selectcottages.com www.selectcottages.com

The Orchards Apartment and Coach House, Eskdale. Ideal base to explore the Lake District; wonderful views over fells. Sleep 2-4. Telephone (01946) 723374, email: selfcatering@orchards-eskdale.com www.orchards-eskdale.com

Ashness Apartment, Keswick town centre. Beautiful apartment with views of Keswick and Derwent Water. Sleeps 6. Telephone (01768) 780855, email: info@ashness.net www.ashness.net

Acorn Self Catering, Keswick. Three comfortable properties within five minutes of the town centre, sleep 6, 5 and 5. Telephone (01768) 480310, email: info@acornselfcatering.co.uk www.acornselfcatering.co.uk

Richmond Cottage, Orton Hall. Peaceful relaxation in elegant wing of 17th century mansion in unspoilt Cumbrian countryside. Telephone (01539) 624330, email: info@stayinortonhall.com www.stayinortonhall.com

Stonefold Cottages, Penrith. Three cottages within tastefully furnished 18th century stone building next to the Lake District. Telephone (01768) 866383, email: email@stonefold.co.uk www.stonefold.co.uk

Fell View, Cumbria. Cottages/apartments in peaceful grounds close to Lake Ullswater, half a mile from Helvellyn. Pets welcome. Telephone (01768) 482342, email: enquiries@fellviewholidays.com www.fellviewholidays.com

Green View Lodges, Welton. On northern edge of Lake District National Park, close to Scottish Borders, Scandinavian lodges sleeping 4 or 7. Telephone (01697) 476230, email: ghcg@green-view-lodges.com www.green-view-lodges.com

Staffield Hall, Kirkoswald, near Penrith. Seven elegant apartments in a magnificent mansion. Sleep 2 to 5 all with four poster beds. Telephone (01768) 898656, email: goodcotguid@staffieldhall.co.uk www.staffieldhall.co.uk

Cumbrian Cottages. Cottages, apartments and houses in superb locations throughout the Lake District and Cumbria. www.cumbrian-cottages.co.uk

Traditional Lakeland Cottages. An unrivalled selection of self catering holiday retreats within this beautiful corner of England. www.lakelovers.co.uk

Penny Hill Farm Cottage, Eskdale. Once owned by Beatrix Potter and enjoying uninterrupted views of the Lake District fells. Perfect for couples. Telephone (01768) 776836, email: sally@hollinhead.co.uk www.hollinhead.co.uk/pennyhill

Bush Cottage, Tallentire, near Cockermouth. Cosy two bedroom cottage on the edge of the Lake District National Park. Telephone (01946) 812091, email: bushcottage@fsmail.net www.bushcottage.com

Ruby's Cottage, Settlebeck, Sedbergh. Two bedroom Grade II listed cottage with open stream to rear. Sleeps up to 4. Telephone (07982) 458974, email: enquiries@rubyscottage.co.uk www.rubyscottage.co.uk

Apartment 7, Harney Peak, Portinscale. Luxury one bedroom apartment in peaceful setting on edge of Derwentwater. Pets welcome. Telephone (01162) 376453, email: enquiries@yatesestates.co.uk www.yatesestates.co.uk

The Hayloft, Cartmel and Grange-over-Sands. Luxury converted limestone, threshing barn sleeping 7, in stunning South Lakeland Cartmel Peninsula. Telephone (01524) 221390, email: hayloft.info@virgin.net www.hayloftcottageholidays.co.uk

Lakeland Hideaways. Finest selection of cottages in and around Hawkeshead to suit every need. Telephone (01539) 442435, email: bookings@lakeland-hideaways.co.uk www.lakeland-hideaways.co.uk

Langdale View Lodge. Privately owned log cabin within White Cross Bay 5 Star Leisure Park on shores of Windermere. Telephone (01228) 670124, email: rhodes@rhodandjan.orangehome.co.uk www.lakeslogcabin.co.uk

Ashlack Cottages. Five luxury holiday cottages situated close to Coniston Water and between the market towns of Broughton-in-Furness and Ulverston. Telephone (01229) 889888, email: enquiries@ashlackcottages.co.uk www.ashlackcottages.co.uk

Hollens Farmhouse, Grasmere. Sleeping 8 in 4 en-suite bedrooms. Furnished and equipped to a high standard. Panoramic views. VisitBritain 5 Stars. Telephone (01228) 591555, email: info@lakescottageholiday.co.uk, www.lakescottageholiday.co.uk

Cumbria Holidays. Accommodation from country hotels and guest houses to cottages, lodges, caravans, campsites and hostels. Telephone (01228) 564061, email: info@christinemartin.plus.com www.cumbria-holidays.co.uk

Sir Johns Hill Farm Cottages, Laugharne, Carmarthenshire, Wales. Three cottages in secluded location with views. Grazing for visiting horses. Telephone (01994) 427667, email: liz.handford@sirjohnshillfarm.co.uk www.sirjohnshillfarm.co.uk

Penffynnon, Aberporth. Characterful well-equipped properties by sandy beaches. Sea views. Dogs welcome by arrangement. Telephone (01239) 810387, email: tt@lineone.net www.aberporth.com

Melin Llecheiddior, near Criccieth. 2 self catering cottages between the mountains of Snowdonia and the beaches of the Lleyn Peninsula. Telephone (01766) 530635, email: elen@whevans.freeserve.co.uk www.cottages-in-snowdonia.co.uk

Ffynnonofi Farm. Secluded farmhouse in North Pembrokeshire National Park with private beach. Sleeps 7-8 people. Telephone (01179) 268554, email: info@ffynnonofi.co.uk www.ffynnonofi.co.uk

Carno Farmhouse and Little Barn, Libanus. WTB Grade 5/Disabled Access 2, sleeping 4/5 in the heart of the Brecon Beacons National Park. Telephone (01874) 625630, email: june.scarborough@lineone.net www.brecon.co.uk/local/carno

Wales Holidays. Around 550 properties throughout all areas of Wales, many in the Pembrokeshire and Snowdonia National Parks. Telephone (01686) 628200, email: info@wales-holidays.co.uk www.wales-holidays.co.uk

Cefnamwlch, one mile from Tudweiliog, Pwllheli. Three holiday homes on private estate within an area of outstanding natural beauty. Telephone (01758) 770209, email: cefnamwlch@hotmail.com www.cefnamwlch.co.uk

Walnut Tree Cottage, Pantygelli. WTB 5 Stars, pretty cottage with glorious views. Sleeps 4. Telephone (01873) 853468, email: enquiries@walnuttreeholidays.com www.walnuttreeholidays.com

Foxes Reach, Catbrook, near Chepstow. Traditional whitewashed stone character cottage. WTB 5 stars. Dogs/horses accepted. Telephone (01600) 860341, email: fionawilton@btopenworld.com www.foxesreach.com

Broomhill Manor, Cornwall (near Bude). 17 cottages and wing of manor house in beautiful 9-acre gardens. Sleep 2-6. Telephone (01288) 352940, email: chris@broomhillmanor.co.uk www.broomhillmanor.co.uk

Houndapitt, Bude, Cornwall. Traditional farm cottages set in 100 acre estate overlooking Sandymouth Bay. Sleeps 2-9. Telephone (01288) 355455, email: info@houndapitt.co.uk www.houndapitt.co.uk

The Old Farmhouse and Buttermill Cottage. Grade II listed farmhouse and barn conversion sleeping 6/2. Telephone (01288) 341622, email: helebarton@hotmail.com www.helebarton.co.uk

Fresh Breaks, Cornwall. High quality self catering accommodation with extremely comfortable furnishings, all in idyllic locations. Telephone (02089) 932628, email: bookings@freshbreaks.co.uk www.freshbreaks.co.uk

Barclay House, East Looe, Cornwall. Luxury cottages ETC 5 star. Restaurant, lounge/bar, heated swimming pool. Telephone (01503) 262929, email: info@barclayhouse.co.uk www.barclayhouse.co.uk

Kennacott Court, Bude. Overlooking Widemouth Bay a variety of outstanding award winning cottages with excellent leisure centre sleeping 2-10. Telephone (01288) 362000, email: phil@kennacottcourt.co.uk www.kennacottcourt.co.uk

Treworgie Barton Holiday Cottages, St. Genny's. Nine superb character cottages in 36 acres of farmland and woodland setting within North Cornwall Heritage Coast area. Telephone (01840) 230233, email: info@treworgie.co.uk www.treworgie.co.uk

West Tremabe Cottages, Liskeard. Two beautifully converted and well equipped traditional Cornish stone barns, ideal for couples. Telephone (01579) 321863, email: christine.j.foster@btopenworld.com www.west-tremabe-cottages.co.uk

Trenant Park Cottages, near Looe. Four spacious cottages in a country park setting. Sleep 2-5. Five minutes from South Cornwall's superb beaches. Telephone (01503) 263639/262241, email: liz@holiday-cottage.com www.trenantcottages.com

Trevigue Wildlife Conservation, Crackington Haven. Luxurious coastal cottages surrounded by National Trust farmland in North Cornwall. Telephone (01840) 230418. www.wild-trevigue.co.uk

Cant Cove Cottages, Rock. Six exceptional 5 Key Deluxe cottages sleeping 5-8 in private 70 acre setting overlooking the Camel Estuary in North Cornwall. Telephone (01208) 862841, email: info@cantcove.co.uk www.cantcove.co.uk

Penrose Burden, St. Breward. Nine character cottages in peaceful, rural setting, sleeping 2-6 close to Bodmin Moor. Especially suitable for disabled people. Telephone (01208) 850277/850617. www.penroseburden.co.uk

East Rose Farm, St. Breward, Bodmin Moor. Seven beautiful cottages in an Area of Outstanding Natural Beauty and Special Scientific Interest. Sleep 2-6. Telephone (01208) 850674, email: eastrosefarm@btinternet.com www.eastrose.co.uk

Court Farm Holidays, Bude. Excellent cottages, farmhouses and barn conversions with fantastic facilities. Sleep up to 17. Telephone (01288) 361494, email: mary@courtfarm-holidays.co.uk www.courtfarm-holidays.co.uk

Wooldown Farm Hol Cottages, Marhamchurch. Six stylish properties, sleeping 2-8, all with spectacular sea views towards Widemouth Bay and Bude. Telephone (01288) 361216, email: holidays@wooldown.com www.wooldown.com

Classy Cottages. A variety of individual and beautifully equipped properties, sleeping 1-16, in three stunning locations; Polperro, Lanlawren and Lansallos. Telephone: 07000 423000, email: nicolle@classycottages.co.uk

Rooky's Nook, Trewalder, Delabole. Luxury barn conversion for discerning couples. Deep in North Cornish countryside and close to beaches. Telephone (01840) 212874, email: info@rookysnook.co.uk www.rookysnook.co.uk

Trevornick Cottages, Holywell Bay. Three spacious, luxurious cottages in an idyllic setting, perfect for families. Dogs welcome. Telephone (01637) 830531, email: bookings@trevornick.co.uk www.trevornickcottages.co.uk

Looe & Polperro Holidays. Carefully selected cottages, apartments and bungalows in rural and coastal locations. Telephone (01503) 265330, email: info@looeandpolperroholidays.co.uk www.looeandpolperroholidays.co.uk

Apple Cottages.com offers a hand-picked selection of cottages in Cornwall, many in wonderful locations with spectacular views. Telephone (01288) 361216, email: info@applecottages.com www.applecottages.com

Kennall Vale Mills, Ponsanooth. Three granite stone holiday cottages in a peaceful woodland setting next to the river Kennall. Telephone (01209) 861168, email: natasha@austin-uk.co.uk www.kennallvale.co.uk

Cutkive Wood Holiday Lodges, St. Ive, Cornwall. Six well-equipped lodges in idyllic rural setting. Ideally situated for coast and country. Telephone (01579) 362216, email: holidays@cutkivewood.co.uk www.cutkivewood.co.uk

Higher Menadew Farm Cottages, Bodmin. Superb quality cottages in peaceful Cornish countryside. Indoor heated swimming pool and games room. Telephone (01726) 850310, email: mail@stayingincornwall.com www.stayingincornwall.com

Meadowview Cottage, Boscastle. 5 Star luxury accommodation with excellent facilities, sleeping 6+cot. Breathtaking views down the valley towards Bude. Telephone (01840) 261706, email: bolt348@btinternet.com www.meadowviewcottage.co.uk

Tregarthan Barn, near Marazion, Penzance. Two cottages in rural location with panoramic views over St Michael's Mount and the Bay. Telephone (01736) 711078, email: cornishholidays@btinternet.com www.cornishholidayspenzance.com

Coombe Cottage, St Agnes, Cornwall. 16th century thatched cottage sleeping up to four people. Pets welcome by arrangement. Telephone (01335) 345063, email: kaylivesey@yahoo.co.uk

Gulls Nest, St Ives, Cornwall. Smart loft style conversion in the heart of St Ives, yet only five minutes from beaches. Telephone (01335) 345063, email: kaylivesey@yahoo.co.uk

Northleigh Farm Holiday Cottages, near Colyton. Three ETC 4 Star barn conversions in the beautiful rolling countryside of the Coly Valley. Telephone (01404) 871217, email: simon@northleighfarm.co.uk www.northleighfarm.co.uk

Halcyon Cottage, near Honiton. Attractive cottage within easy reach of the East Devon Heritage Coast. Telephone (01404) 549196, email anne_biddle@lineone.net   web.pncl.co.uk/molehayes/

Hill Cottage, Clawton, Devon. Large, private gardens, spectacular countryside views. 20 mins drive from beach. Sleeps 8, children welcome. Telephone (01409) 253093, email: lgsg@supanet.com www.selfcateringcottagesdevon.co.uk

Nature's Watch, Honiton. Two high quality cottages on the edge of the Blackdown Hills in Devon. Panoramic views and wildlife. Telephone (01404) 891949, email: enquiries@natureswatch.com www.natureswatch.com

Kingston Estate, near Totnes. Beautiful cottages in glorious setting; easy reach of Dartmoor, sea and many attractions. Telephone (01803) 762235, email: info@kingston-estate.co.uk www.kingston-estate.co.uk

Beachcomber Cottage, Beer. Period stone cottage close to the beach and South Devon coastal footpath. Sleeps 6+cot. Children and pets welcome. Telephone (01298) 872927, email: jan@cosycotts.com www.cosycotts.com

Chalkway, Cricket St. Thomas. 19th century woodman's cottage sleeping 4 with panoramic valley views. Ideal for exploring Lyme Regis, East Devon and West Dorset. Telephone 0208 444 4296, email: elisa-beth@thebuttonfamily.co.uk www.westcountryhideaway.co.uk

Lancombe Country Cottages, near Dorchester. Five flint and brick cottages with breathtaking views. Indoor heated pool with sauna. Telephone (01300) 320562, email: info@lancombe.co.uk

Dream Cottages, Dorset. Unrivalled selection of 200+ hand-picked cottages, houses and apartments for 2-12 people. Telephone (01305) 789000, email: admin@dream-cottages.co.uk www.dream-cottages.co.uk

The Quarterdeck, Dorset. Spacious family property with sea views close to splendid Swanage beaches. Sleeps 10. Telephone (01929) 553443, email: leanne@purbeckholidays.co.uk www.purbeckholidays.co.uk

Country Ways, High Bickington, North Devon. Beautifully converted stone barns on small farm. Five cottages sleeping up to 21/28. Lovely gardens. Telephone (01769) 560503, email: country-ways@virgin.net www.country-ways.net

Widmouth Farm Cottages, North Devon. Nine cottages (sleeping 2-6) with spectacular views in secluded valley with private beach. Telephone (01271) 863743. email: holiday@widmouthfarmcottages.co.uk www.widmouthfarmcottages.co.uk

West Banbury Farm, Broadwoodwidger. Ten cottages on Devon/Cornwall borders with many leisure facilities. Perfect for families or couples. Sleep 2-8. Telephone (01566) 784946 email: amanda@westbanbury.co.uk www.westbanbury.co.uk

Sweetcombe Cottage Holidays Ltd. Family run booking agency with a vast selection of cottages in East Devon. Telephone (01395) 512130, email: enquiries@sweetcombe-ch.co.uk www.sweetcombe-ch.co.uk

Coast & Country Cottages. Over 300 properties throughout beautiful South Devon. Short Breaks, Special Offers, Couples Discounts, Dog Friendly Properties Telephone (01548) 843773, email: suzanne@coastandcountry.co.uk www.coastandcountry.co.uk

Exmoor Cottage Holidays. Four comfortable and well equipped cottages in Challacombe. Children and pets welcome. Telephone (01598) 763320, email: enquiries@exmoorcottageholidays.co.uk www.exmoorcottageholidays.co.uk

Little Woodford Cottages, Ottery St Mary. Two superb barn conversions sleeping 4-6 on working smallholding in beautiful Otter Valley. Telephone (01404) 811693, email: nickymalden@btinternet.com www.littlewoodford.com

Farm and Cottage Holidays, West Country and Cornwall. Rural and coastal cottages, farmhouses, barn conversions and log cabins. Telephone (01237) 479146, email: enquiries@holidaycottages.co.uk www.holidaycottages.co.uk

Champernhayes, Wootton Fitzpaine. Six luxury cottage conversions from 15th century farm buildings. Heated indoor Jacuzzi and spa bath. Telephone (01297) 560853, email: champernhayes@btinternet.com www.dorset-cottages-lymeregis.co.uk

Steepholme View, Alcombe. Comfortable bungalow sleeping up to 5 with sea views close to Exmoor National Park. Telephone (01643) 831513, email: enquiries@mineheadselfcatering.co.uk www.mineheadselfcatering.co.uk

Lea Hill Cottages, Membury. Six comfortable Devon holiday cottages within eight acres of grounds and gardens with stunning views. Telephone (01404) 881881, email: reception@leahill.co.uk www.leahill.co.uk

Stable/Blackspur Cottages, Norton-sub-Hamdon. Excellent cottages sleeping 2-4 in peaceful Somerset village nestling beside Ham Hill Countryside Park. Telephone (01935) 881789.

The Old Stables and Barley Cottage, Chichester. Cottages on working family farm. Both sleep 4. Telephone (02392) 631382, email: carole.edney@btopenworld.com www.theoldstables.net and www.barleycottage.co.uk

The Thatched Barn, Broadwater, near Andover. Self catering or B & B. Sleeps up to 3 in peaceful village setting. Telephone (01264) 772240, email: carolyn@dmac.co.uk www.dmac.co.uk/carolyn

The Barn at Bombers, Westerham. High quality 16th century barn conversions situated in open countryside. ETC 5 star. Sleep 6. Telephone (01959) 573471, email: roy@bombers-farm-co.uk www.bombers-farm-co.uk

Fairhaven Holiday Cottages. Specialists in Kent and Sussex plus two Wiltshire farm cottages. Almost 100 properties. Sleep from 2-14. Telephone (01208) 821255. www.fairhaven-holidays.co.uk www.scottscastles.com

Windmill Cottage, Milford-on-Sea. Hampshire/Dorset borders. Modern Georgian style house in private, traffic-free close. Sleeps up to 5. Dogs welcome. Telephone (01590) 643516, email: enquiries@windmillcottage.info www.windmillcottage.info

Waterside Breaks. Specialists in high quality self catering on the Isle of Wight, the perfect place for family holidays. Telephone (01252) 239020, email: holidays@ukleisurebreaks.com www.ukleisurebreaks.com

New Forest Living. The New Forest; an ideal cottage holiday destination, whether a forest side home or coastal retreat. Telephone (0845) 680173, email: info@newforestliving.co.uk www.newforestliving.co.uk

Westfield Lodges and Apartments are located in Bonchurch, one of the most scenic areas of the Isle of Wight. Telephone (01983) 852268, email: mail@westfieldlodges.co.uk www.westfieldlodges.co.uk

Westley Farm, Chalford. Five cottages on old-fashioned Cotswold hill farm. Views over the Golden Valley. Cirencester/Stroud 6 miles. Telephone (01285) 760262, email: cottages@westleyfarm.co.uk www.westleyfarm.co.uk

Folly Farm Cottages, Tetbury. Twelve stone cottages nestling on 200 acre estate in the Rural South Cotswolds. Sleep 2 - 8. Telephone (01666) 502475, email info@gtb.co.uk www.gtb.co.uk

Grove House Holidays near Ledbury. Four holiday homes sleeping 2 -5 in country setting within easy reach of the Malvern Hills. Telephone (01531) 650584, email: ross@the-grovehouse.co.uk www.the-grovehouse.com

Combermere Abbey, Whitchurch. 11 cottages in stable block of 12th century Cistercian monastery on 1000 acre estate. Sleep 4-8. Telephone (01948) 662876.email: cottages@combermereabbey.co.uk www.combermereabbey.co.uk

Oatfield Country Cottages, Blakeney. Six cottages converted from Grade II listed 17th century farm buildings overlooking Gloucestershire's Severn Estuary. Ideal touring location. Telephone (01594) 510372. www.oatfieldfarm.co.uk

Wye Lea Country Manor, Ross-on-Wye. 5 Star accommodation with excellent facilities for the whole family in an area of outstanding beauty. Sleep 2-54. Telephone (01989) 562880, email: enquire@wyelea.co.uk www.wyelea.co.uk

Cotswold Property Lettings. Find the perfect holiday home from cosy cottages to large period properties. All personally inspected. Telephone (01386) 858147, email: gill@cotswoldpropertylettings.com www.cotswoldpropertylettings.com

Courtyard Cottages, Upper Court, Tewkesbury. House and cottages in a splendid location with own lake in charming Cotswold village. Sleep 2-11. Telephone (01386) 725351, email: diana@uppercourt.co.uk www.uppercourt.co.uk

Bruern Holiday Cottages, near Chipping Norton, Oxfordshire. Eight award winning ETC 5 star rated cottages with exceptional interiors. Sleep 2-10. www.bruern.co.uk

Pooh Hall Cottages, Woodside, Shropshire. Three beautiful stone cottages sleeping 2 (adults only) with far reaching views over the Clun Valley. Telephone (01588) 640075, email: pooh-hall@realemail.co.uk www.pooh-hallcottages.co.uk

Isis Lakes, near Cirencester: exclusive 3 bedroom lakeside retreat in heart of Cotswolds with stunning views and complimentary fishing. Telephone (0800) 0430697, email: contactus@holidaycottageisis.com www.holidaycottageisis.com

Castle Cliffe, Hereford. Luxuriously renovated 13th century historic holiday home sleeps 6+cot surrounded by beautifully tranquil parkland. Telephone (01432) 272096, email: mail@castlecliffe.net www.castlecliffe.net

Plumtree Cottage, Lechlade-on-Thames, Gloucestershire. Two bedroomed picturesque early 19th century cottage in the south of the Cotswolds. Telephone (01793) 752540, email: janet.p.williams@btinternet.com www.plumtreecottage-cotswolds.co.uk

Discover the Cotswolds. A much admired family run agency with many traditional Cotswold stone cottages on their books. Telephone (01386) 841441, email: info@discoverthecotswolds.net www.discoverthecotswolds.net

Largy Coastal Apartments. Five star accommodation on the beautiful Antrim coast with spectacular views over the Irish Sea. Telephone 0 2828 885635, email: gladyssmith@btopenworld.com www.ireland4you.freeservers.com

Grayling, County Clare, Ireland. Bungalow finished to an impressive standard in an irresistible location close to Galway Bay. Sleeps up to 7. Telephone 00 (353) 65 7071055, email: info@goodcottageguide.com

www.goodcottageguide.com

Share it!

Do tell us about holiday properties you know or have stayed in that you think ought to be included in *The Good Holiday Cottage Guide*.

I recommend the following:

My name/address/phone number/email is:

Please send to:
Swallow Press, PO Box 21, Hertford SG14 2DD.

Index (UK/Ireland)

302

Y